Uncle John's BATHROOM READER. SPORTS SPECTACULAR

By the
Bathroom Readers' Institute

Bathroom Readers' Press
Ashland, Oregon

UNCLE JOHN'S BATHROOM READER
SPORTS SPECTACULAR EXPANDED EDITION®

Articles in this edition have been included from the following books: *The Best of
Uncle John's Bathroom Reader* © 1995; *Uncle John's Ultimate Bathroom Reader* © 1996;
Uncle John's Giant 10th Anniversary Bathroom Reader © 1997; *Uncle John's Great Big
Bathroom Reader* © 1998; *Uncle John's Absolutely Absorbing Bathroom Reader* © 1999;
Uncle John's Legendary Lost Bathroom Reader © 1999; *Uncle John's All-Purpose Extra
Strength Bathroom Reader* © 2000; *Uncle John's Supremely Satisfying Bathroom Reader*
© 2001; *Uncle John's Bathroom Reader Plunges Into History Again* © 2004; *Uncle
John's Ahh-Inspiring Bathroom Reader* © 2002; *Uncle John's Bathroom Reader Plunges
Into the Universe* © 2002; *Uncle John's Bathroom Reader for Kids Only* © 2002; *Uncle
John's Unstoppable Bathroom Reader* © 2003; *Uncle John's Bathroom Reader Plunges
Into Great Lives* © 2003; *Uncle John's Colossal Collection of Quotable Quotes* © 2004;
Uncle John's Slightly Irregular Bathroom Reader © 2004; *Uncle John's Presents Mom's
Bathtub Reader* © 2004; *Uncle John's Bathroom Reader Plunges Into Texas* © 2004;
Uncle John's Fast-Acting Long-Lasting Bathroom Reader © 2005; *Uncle John's Bathroom
Reader Tees Off on Golf* © 2005; *Uncle John's Bathroom Reader Shoots and Scores*
© 2005; *Uncle John's Bathroom Reader Plunges Into Michigan* © 2005; *Uncle John's
Bathroom Reader Plunges Into New Jersey* © 2005; *Uncle John's Curiously Compelling
Bathroom Reader* © 2006; *Uncle John's Bathroom Reader Wonderful World of Odd*
© 2006; *Uncle John's Tales to Inspire* © 2006; *Uncle John's Bathroom Reader Plunges
Into Minnesota* © 2006; *Uncle John's Bathroom Reader Quintessential Collection of
Notable Quotables* © 2006; *Uncle John's Bathroom Reader Takes a Swing at Baseball*
© 2008; *Uncle John's Triumphant 20th Anniversary Bathroom Reader* © 2007.

For information, write:
The Bathroom Readers' Institute, P.O. Box 1117, Ashland, OR 97520
www.bathroomreader.com • 888-488-4642

Cover design by Michael Brunsfeld, San Rafael, CA (*Brunsfeldo@comcast.net*)

ISBN-13: 978-1-60710-034-8 / ISBN-10: 1-60710-034-7

Library of Congress Cataloging-in-Publication Data
Uncle John's bathroom reader sports spectacular. — Expanded ed.
   p. cm.
ISBN 978-1-60710-034-8 (pbk.)
1. Sports—Miscellanea. 2. Sports—Humor.
GV707.U533 2009
796—dc22

2009021956

Printed in the United States of America
First Printing
1 2 3 4 5 6 7 8 9 13 12 11 10 09

THANK YOU!

*The Bathroom Readers' Institute sincerely thanks the people
whose advice and assistance made this book possible.*

Gordon Javna

Amy Miller

Jay Newman

Brian Boone

John Dollison

Thom Little

Julia Papps

Kait Fairchild

Michael Brunsfeld

Angela Kern

Malcolm Hillgartner

Sue Steiner

John Scalzi

J. Carroll

Dan Mansfield

Claire Breen

JoAnn Padgett

Melinda Allman

Sydney Stanley

Monica Maestas

Lisa M. & Amy L.

Lilian Nordland

Ginger Winters

Sarah Rosenberg

David Cully

Mustard Press

Scarab Media

Steven Style Group

John Javna

Karen Malchow

Publishers Group West

Raincoast Books

Porter the Wonder Dog

Thomas Crapper

*...and the many writers,
editors, and other contributors
who have helped make
Uncle John the bathroom
fixture he is today.*

CONTENTS

Because the BRI understands your reading needs, we've divided the contents by length as well as subject.
Short—a quick read
Medium—2 to 3 pages
Long—for those extended visits, when something a little more involved is required
* Extended—for those leg-numbing experiences

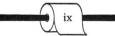

BATTER UP!

O n your mark...get set...go! This is the most action-packed *Bathroom Reader* ever produced! It really packs a punch! It'll bowl you over! It's a hole in one! But *Sports Spectacular* is much more than a bunch of run-of-the-mill sports clichés—it's an engaging study of the human psyche viewed through a very specific lens: What do we do for fun?

To answer that, we plowed through the entire *Bathroom Reader* catalog and found every article we've ever written on sports—from the origins of golf, baseball, football, basketball, hockey, and lacrosse to the science of swimming and Olympic cheaters. Then we added some brand-new articles, including the history of tennis, bowling, and the Tour de France, just to name a few. Then, for this Expanded Edition, we added even *more* new articles: the mayhem of *Lucha Libre* wrestling, the thrill of paintball, and the nail-biting terror of the world's most dangerous races.

But, since this is an *Uncle John's Bathroom Reader*, you know we've got a lot more than just history—we also have the answers to important questions like: Why do baseball players wear two pairs of socks? There's actually a good reason for it. Or perhaps you've always wondered why the Monopoly squares are landmarks from Atlantic City, New Jersey. There's a reason for that, too. What else is in here? Lots.

Flops and blunders: Ever heard of indoor archery or the National Bowling League? Well, you'll read about them here. We also have stories about the golf shot that wiped out an entire country's air force, and the baseball player who managed to bite his own butt.

Pop science: You'll get an in-depth look at a golf swing, what happens when a hockey stick whacks the puck, and how a skateboarder seemingly defies gravity.

Games and toys: Who came up with Bingo? Who made the Game Boy? And just how old is Rock, Paper, Scissors? (Older than you think.)

Quotes: The wise: "You win some, you lose some, and you wreck some." (Dale Earnhardt). The witty: "Managing is getting paid for home runs someone else hits." (Casey Stengel). And then there's this gem from our favorite British motor-sports announcer, Murray Walker: "Either that car is stationary, or it is on the move."

But when all is said and done, it's our competitive spirit that lies at the heart of this book. As they used to say on ABC's *Wide World of Sports*, it's...

The thrill of victory

• The autistic high-school basketball player who came in from the bench and made history

• The female tennis player who conquered male chauvinism

• The horse that never won a race but won the hearts of millions

• Coming up alive at the bottom of Niagara Falls

...and the agony of defeat

• The winning discus throw that the Olympic judges never saw

• The on-court fistfight that overshadowed the careers of two pro basketball players

• The world's greatest chess player who staged a protest by sitting in front of a bathroom door

• *Not* coming up alive at the bottom of Niagara Falls

And if that's all too profound for you, you can simply learn how to rig a coin toss and be done with it.

But before we suit up and hit the showers with a nine-iron, let's give a hip-hip-hooray to the BRI All-Stars: Amy (our offensive coordinator, clutch hitter, and goalie); Jay, Brian, Thom, John D, Malcolm, Sue, Scalzi, and J. Carroll (the all-pro writing squad); Julia and Michael (special teams); and Angie, Dan, and Claire (the referees, umpires, and rules committee).

And finally, thank *you*. Whether you're a new fan or an old friend, we're honored that you're reading this book. To use one last sports cliché—you're the most valuable player of them all!

Keep on reading. And as always...

Keep on going with the Flow!

—Uncle John, the BRI Staff, and Porter the Wonder Dog

SPORTS & MEASURES

Most people never give a second thought to life's most important questions, such as: How many people can you cram into a Cornhuskers game? Or how tall should a bowling pin be? Fortunately for them, Uncle John does.

• A **soccer ball** must measure between 27 and 28 inches in circumference and weigh 14 to 16 ounces.

• During a single **Wimbledon tournament,** 42,000 tennis balls are used.

• A **bowling ball** should be 27 inches in circumference and weigh no more than 16 pounds.

• A **bowling pin** should weigh between 3 pounds 2 ounces and 3 pounds 10 ounces and should be exactly 1 foot 3 inches tall.

• A **dart** cannot be more than 1 foot in length, or weigh more than 50 grams.

• A **dartboard** must be hung so that the bull's-eye is 5 feet 8 inches above the floor. The person throwing the dart must stand 7 feet 9 ¼ inches from the board.

• Points scored by basketball legend **Kareem Abdul-Jabbar** over his 20-year career: 38,387.

• **Ice hockey** is the only team sport that's divided into three time periods. It used to be divided into halves, but the ice got so rutted during the game that they added an extra intermission…to clean off the playing surface.

• A **golf ball** must weigh no more than 1.62 ounces, with a diameter no less than 1.68 inches. (A standard tee is 2 ⅛ inches long.)

• When the **University of Nebraska Cornhuskers** play a home football game, Memorial Stadium becomes the state's third-largest city (it seats 85,500 people).

Nearly all races on tracks are run counterclockwise.

FOUNDING FATHERS

You already know the names—here are the people behind them.

JOHN HEISMAN

Heisman coached football at Auburn, Clemson, and Georgia Tech in the 1890s and early 20th century. In the 1930s, he worked as athletic director at the Downtown Athletic Club in New York City. Since 1935, the club has issued the Heisman Trophy—for the year's best college football player (voted on by sports reporters)—in his honor. Past winners include Reggie Bush, Barry Sanders, Tony Dorsett, Roger Staubach, and O. J. Simpson.

IGNAZ SCHWINN

Born in Germany, Schwinn left school in 1871 at the age of 11 to become a mechanic's apprentice. He soon went to work for himself, traveling the German countryside fixing bicycles by day, working on his own designs at night. When he showed them to Heinrich Kleyer, an established bicycle maker, Kleyer hired him to design and build a new line of bicycles. In 1895 Schwinn formed his own company in the United States. Early bicycles were labor-intensive to build, which made them expensive. But Schwinn found ways to lower the cost, making them available to more people—especially children, who became their biggest consumers and helped establish the classic association between American kids and bikes. His company's most popular model, the Sting-Ray, came out in 1963 and is the best-selling bike ever.

ENZO FERRARI

The man who created one of the world's best-known race cars (and most sought-after sportscars) began his transportation career shoeing mules for the Italian army in World War I. In the 1920s, Ferrari became one of Italy's most famous race-car drivers and a designer for the Alfa Romeo racing team. In 1929 he started his own racing team, building sportscars only to help finance the racing side of the business. When he died in 1988, Ferrari had sold almost 50,000 cars.

John Heisman coined the word "hike" and split football games into four quarters.

OOPS!

Everyone's amused by tales of outrageous blunders—probably because it's comforting to know that someone's screwing up even worse than we are. So go ahead and feel superior for a few minutes.

FUTBOL FAKERS

Their dream was to watch their country's soccer team play in a World Cup game in Germany in 2006, but the admission price was more than the three Argentinians wanted to pay. Determined to see the match, they found a loophole: Discounted seats were being offered to disabled people. So they somehow got themselves three wheelchairs and rolled into the match against Holland, claiming a handicapped viewing spot near the field.

The ruse probably would have worked, too, if one of them hadn't gotten so excited after a play that he jumped out of his chair with his arms raised in the air. "A person near us thought there was a miracle happening," one of the fakers told reporters outside the stadium—which is where the three fans spent the second half of the game after security escorted them out (on foot).

MAJOR-LEAGUE DUSTUP

"A deceased Seattle Mariners fan's last wishes went awry when the bag containing his cremated remains failed to open as a plane attempted to scatter them over Safeco Field, the Mariners' home stadium, which has a retractable roof. Instead, the entire bag of ashes fell onto the closed roof of the stadium in one piece, bursting into a puff of gray smoke as it hit. A startled eyewitness called 911, and officials ordered the stadium to be evacuated.

"It took more than an hour for sheriff's deputies to trace the tail number of the plane and determine that the mysterious substance on the stadium roof was the ashes of a Mariners fan, not anthrax or some other kind of terrorist attack."

—*Seattle Times*

FRIENDS IN LOW PLACES

"As he pulled his car into the Yankee Stadium VIP parking lot, a driver claimed to be a friend of Yankees owner George Steinbrenner.

Average pay for a batboy for the New York Yankees: $3.50 per hour.

He didn't realize the parking-lot attendant *was* Steinbrenner. 'He looked at me, and said, "Guess I've got the wrong lot,"' said Steinbrenner, who had decided to personally investigate traffic problems at the stadium."

—*Parade*

TAPPED OUT

At the 1983 British Open, two-time U.S. Open champ Hale Irwin had an easy, two-inch tap-in putt to make during the third round. He walked up to the ball and made a casual one-handed swat at the ball…and missed it completely. The putter had hit the ground in front of the ball and bounced over it. And that counts as a stroke. "It was an unintended sword fight with the ground," he explained. The next day Irwin lost the Open to Tom Watson—by one stroke.

HITTING THE DUMB-FECTA

"Roger Loughran, a horse-racing jockey, stood tall and proud in the saddle of Central House at the end of the Paddy Power Dial-A-Bet Chase in December 2005, and waved his whip at the packed grandstand. He was celebrating his first win as a professional jockey. Just for good measure, he swung a looping underarm punch into the air. There was just one problem: they still had 80 meters to run. The 26-year-old had mistaken the end of a running rail for the winning post, and as he eased up on Central House, Hi Cloy and Fota Island galloped past, relegating him to third place. It was an extraordinary, humiliating error, which reduced the crowd to near-silence. Some catcalls followed, but as Loughran returned to the paddock to unsaddle, there was more sympathy than anger."

—*Buzzle.com*

MISSED HIM BY THAT MUCH

"In April 1993, just after Steve Morrow scored the goal that gave the Arsenal team England's League Cup soccer championship, his teammates tossed him into the air in ritual celebration of their victory. However, they failed to catch him when he came down and Morrow was carried off the field on a stretcher with an oxygen mask over his face. It was later determined he had a broken arm."

—*News of the Weird*

If a golf course is within four miles of the coast, it is called a *links*.

FOOTBALL NAMES

Every football team has a storied history. So do their names.

PITTSBURGH STEELERS. Originally named the Pirates after Pittsburgh's professional baseball team, in 1940 owner Al Rooney renamed the team for the city's steel industry.

HOUSTON TEXANS. The Dallas Texans were one of the original AFL teams. They moved to Kansas City in 1963, so when Houston got an expansion team in 2002, they revived the name.

KANSAS CITY CHIEFS. Dallas Texans owner Lamar Hunt was reluctant to relocate to Kansas City until Mayor H. Roe "Chief" Bartle promised to enlarge the city's stadium and guarantee high season ticket sales. Hunt showed his appreciation by naming the team after him.

BALTIMORE RAVENS. Selected by fans (via a telephone poll) from a list of 100 NFL-approved names. Baltimore was once the home of poet Edgar Allan Poe, author of "The Raven."

ATLANTA FALCONS. In 1965 the new team held a contest to name the franchise. A teacher from Griffin, Georgia, suggested Falcons: "The falcon is proud and dignified, with great courage and fight. It is deadly and has a great sporting tradition."

MINNESOTA VIKINGS. General manager Bert Rose came up with the name as a nod to the area's large Nordic population.

INDIANAPOLIS COLTS. Originated as the Baltimore Colts in 1947, the name recognizes Baltimore's long tradition of horse breeding and racing.

SAN FRANCISCO 49ERS. The name is a reference to the gold rush prospectors who came west in 1849, the year after gold was discovered at Sutter's Mill in the mountains east of San Francisco.

TENNESSEE TITANS. Formerly the Tennessee Oilers (after a move from Houston), owner Bud Adams picked the name from Greek mythology. He thought it was appropriate because the team played in Nashville, nicknamed "the Athens of the South."

The Dutch game of *korfball* is the only sport played with mixed teams of 4 men and 4 women.

DUMB JOCKS?

Some are dumb, some are clever, and all are funny.

"He treats us like men. He lets us wear earrings."
—Torrin Polk, University of Houston receiver, on his coach, John Jenkins

"Left hand, right hand, it doesn't matter. I'm amphibious."
—Charles Shackleford, N.C. State basketball player

"[He] called me a 'rapist' and a 'recluse.' I'm not a recluse."
—Boxer Mike Tyson, on writer Wallace Matthews

"In terms of European athletes, she is currently second. A Cuban leads the rankings."
—Paul Dickenson, BBC commentator

"We can't win at home. We can't win on the road. I just can't figure out where else to play."
—Pat Williams, Orlando Magic GM, on his team's poor record

"It's almost like we have ESPN."
—Magic Johnson, on how well he and James Worthy play together

"Me and George and Billy are two of a kind."
—N.Y. Yankee Mickey Rivers, on his relationship with George Steinbrenner and Billy Martin

"I told [GM] Roland Hemond to go out and get me a big-name pitcher. He said, 'Dave Wehrmeister's got 11 letters. Is that a big enough name for you?'"
—Eddie Eichorn, White Sox owner

"Men, I want you just thinking of one word all season. One word and one word only: Super Bowl."
—Bill Peterson, football coach

"I want to rush for 1,000 or 1,500 yards, whichever comes first."
—George Rogers, New Orleans Saints running back

"Raise the urinals."
—Darrel Chaney, Atlanta shortstop, on how management could keep the Braves on their toes

In an average day, Canada imports 822 hockey sticks from Russia.

J-MAC

There's a good chance you saw this on TV in 2006—news outlets ran it about a million times—but it's such a great story that we couldn't leave it out. Whenever you need a pick-me-up, read about this amazing young man.

THE SHORT KID

Jason McElwain was a senior at Greece Athena High School in Rochester, New York. The 17-year-old had autism, which kept him from learning to speak until he was five and inhibited his social skills for many years. But over time he learned to make friends, and became popular at his school. But what Jason loved most was basketball.

When he tried out for the school's varsity team, the Trojans, he didn't make it, but not because of his autism; at 5'6" he was too short. But he was so well liked by the players and coach that he was made team manager. "He became so much a part of us and so much a part of our program that we kind of forgot he was autistic," said teammate Steven Kerr. Jason loved the job. He kept stats, ran the clock, handed out water bottles, and kept the players pumped up.

And on February 15, 2006, he was asked to do a little more.

PUT HIM IN

It was the last home game of the season, and with graduation around the corner, it would be Jason's last game as manager. The coach, Jim Johnson, thought Jason deserved something for his dedication to the team, so he called him into his office and told him not to wear his trademark suit and tie that evening—he wanted him in uniform. The coach wasn't making any promises, but if things worked out, Jason might get a chance to play. When students got the news, they rallied behind him. They made posters with his nickname, "J-Mac," on them, fastened cutouts of Jason's face onto popsicle sticks, and showed up for the game en masse.

AND THE CROWD GOES...

Greece Athena easily handled their opponents, Spencerport High. With four minutes left, they were up 59–43, and the crowd, who had been chanting Jason's name the entire game, could feel it coming.

A badminton shuttlecock travels at speeds up to 112 mph.

Coach Johnson stood up and pointed to the bench, directly at number 52, and Jason leapt up and ran onto the court. The place went crazy. J-Mac posters and Jason's cutout face bounced above the screaming fans in the bleachers. Within seconds, Jason got the ball behind the three-point line and took a shot. "I said to myself, 'Please, Lord, let him get a basket,'" Coach Johnson later said. But Jason missed by a mile. Moments later, he went in for a layup…and missed that, too. Jason's father, David McElwain, wasn't worried, though. "The thing about Jason," he said, "he isn't afraid of anything."

…WILD!

With just under three minutes remaining, Jason got the ball and launched another three-pointer…and made it. The crowd exploded in cheers. A few moments later, he took another three-point shot…Swish. Then he took another. Swish. Then another. Swish. Before he was done, he'd tied the school record with six three-pointers, and finished with 20 points in just over four minutes of play. When he sank his last shot with two seconds to play and the buzzer went off, the crowd—even the opposing players and cheerleaders—stormed the court. They hoisted J-Mac over their heads and carried him off in triumph. "There wasn't a dry eye here," said athletic director Randolph Hutto. "I've coached a lot of wonderful kids," said Coach Johnson, "but I've never experienced such a thrill." But the happiest of all: J-Mac. "I felt like a celebrity," he said.

JUST KEEP DREAMING

Experts who study autism called Jason's moment in the sun a victory for all people with the condition. "A lot of us feel like this is a gift to have this receive so much nationwide publicity," Dr. Catherine Lord of the University of Michigan told ESPN. "There are thousands of Jasons out there, carrying the net for the soccer team, keeping statistics for the baseball team, playing the drum for the school band. This serves as a reminder to give these kids a chance whenever possible."

"I look at autism as the Berlin Wall," said Debbie McElwain, Jason's mom. "And he cracked it." Jason has his own message about his condition. "I don't care about this autistic situation, really," he said. "It's just the way I am. The advice I'd give to autistic people is just keep working, just keep dreaming. You'll get your chance and you'll do it."

THE FINE ART OF THROWING YOUR CLUB

*Oh, those stupid stupid STUPID GOLF CLUBS! They
should know better than to make us play so badly.*

THUNDER BOLT

Tommy Bolt won 15 PGA tournaments in his career,
including one major, the 1958 U.S. Open. If that doesn't
sound like a lot of wins, consider that Bolt is 55th on the all-time
wins list, and that he didn't join the PGA until he was 32 years
old. All those wins came in one 11-year period, from 1951 to
1961. He went on to win 12 more times on the Champions Tour
and was inducted into the World Golf Hall of Fame in 2002.

But Bolt was better known for something else: he was one of
the most competitive and explosive men to ever play the game.
His various nicknames—Thunder Bolt, Terrible Tommy, Tempestu-
ous, and Vesuvius—were all well earned. "You could sense the lava
rising, the ash spewing, the top about to come off," *Los Angeles
Times* columnist Jim Murray wrote. "Mt. Bolt was about to erupt."

THROWING THE GAME

When Thunder Bolt's game went awry, his fellow players, his caddie, and the gallery all knew to watch out…a club (or clubs)
would be flying. There's a famous photo of Bolt taken at the 1960
U.S. Open at Cherry Hills, just after he'd hit two consecutive
shots into the water. It shows him in a full, two-handed backswing,
about to launch his driver into the lake. There were numerous
other incidents. Many of his fellow pros thought Bolt's inability to
control his emotions cost him tournaments. "If we could've just
screwed another head on his shoulders," said his friend Ben Hogan,
"Tommy Bolt could have been the greatest who ever played."

Bolt's club-chucking antics were so notorious that he earned a
dubious honor from the PGA. Because of him, a new rule was
instated: any player who throws a club at any time during play
receives a two-stroke penalty. The rule was affectionately known
as the "Tommy Bolt Rule." (The day after the rule took effect,

---

As a boy, Bill Clinton once caddied for golf legend Tommy Bolt.

Bolt became the first golfer to break it—not because he was mad; he just didn't want some other player to be the first to break "his" rule.)

Bolt's other rule: "If you are going to throw a club," he advised, "it is important to throw it ahead of you, down the fairway, so you don't have to waste energy going back to pick it up."

INCOMING!

Tommy Bolt may be the most famous tosser of shafts, but he certainly wasn't the only one.

John Daly. Going into the third round of the 1997 PGA Championship at Winged Foot, Daly was one under par and just three strokes off the lead. Then he tanked. At the 12th hole, his drive sailed onto the fairway—the 17th fairway—and he snapped. He turned around and launched his club over the gallery and into the woods. Two marshals had to jump the chain-link fence to retrieve it.

Tiger Woods. He won the Bay Hill Invitational four years in a row, from 2000 to 2003. One more and he'd have the PGA record for most consecutive wins at one tournament. But it must have been too much pressure. In the final round, he found himself in 46th place. On the 6th hole, he sent a shot into the water. Then, according to witnesses (he wasn't on camera), he threw his club after it—but accidentally hit his caddie, Steve Williams, instead. "Steve was just as hot as I was," Tiger said later, "so it doesn't really matter." (Williams probably disagrees.)

*   *   *

WHAT A CATCH

At a San Francisco Giants game in May 2006, Andrew Morbitzer left his bleacher seat to get peanuts from a concession stand behind the center-field wall. While he was waiting in line, he heard the crowd inside the stadium let out a tremendous roar. What was going on? Barry Bonds had just slammed his 715th home run, passing Babe Ruth on the all-time list, with the second-most home runs ever hit. The record-breaking ball sailed over the wall and landed…right in Morbitzer's hands. He sold the ball for $220,000.

The Druid Hills Country Club in Atlanta staged a club-tossing competition in 1936.

THE WORLD'S MOST DANGEROUS RACES

Any race, whether by foot, car, or dogsled, has its risks. But some are a lot riskier than others.

ISLE OF MAN TOURIST TROPHY RACE

Since 1907 this island in the Irish Sea has hosted what many consider to be the most prestigious motorcycle race in the world—and one of the deadliest. The route, called the Snaefell Mountain Course, takes 200 twists and turns through 37 miles of narrow streets and rural roads lined with stone walls, pushing the limits of the drivers and motorcycles. (The course was originally designed for bicycles.) In 1914 the race claimed one of its first casualties when a rider named Frank Walker, who had been in the lead, blew a tire. He kept riding, in spite of falling twice, and in a desperate attempt to catch the leaders, he shot past the finish line and crashed into a wooden barrier. He was posthumously awarded third place. Since then, the average speed has risen to almost 130 mph, causing more fatalities. To date, 225 racers have lost their lives.

BIG PARDUBICE (*VELKA PARDUBICKA*)

The course of this venerable steeplechase lies in the quiet university town of Pardubice, 65 miles east of Prague in the Czech Republic. Every October since 1874, about a dozen riders and their horses gallop off from the starting line for a 10-minute cross-country race over a 4 1/4-mile course littered with 31 different jumps, ditches, hedges, and other obstacles. Collisions are commonplace, along with spectacular falls. The fourth jump, known as the Taxis, is considered the most treacherous steeplechase jump in the world. Clearing its 5 1/2-foot-high hedge jump is one thing; navigating the 8-foot descent and the 16-foot water ditch that follows is next to impossible. At the 1984 event, two horses crashed into a third as they fell at the Taxis jump, creating a flailing mass of hooves and riders. More horses fell into the quagmire, and by the end of the race, only 4 of the 12 starters crossed the finish line. No riders were killed, but one horse was injured so badly that it was euthanized on the spot. The high frequency of limb-crushing injuries to both horses and riders has made Big Pardubice the object of numerous animal-rights protests—as well as one of the most-watched races in Europe.

BAJA 1000

This sprint across 1,000 miles of treacherous desert is an automotive clash of dune buggies, motorcycles, and ATVs. Drivers battle brutal terrain while navigating blind turns, washouts, and silt-choked gullies. To make it even more interesting, spectators dig potholes and place homemade jumps on the course, a practice so common—and so dangerous—that drivers alert each other to the makeshift hazards via radio. Over the 40-year history of the event, there have been dozens of crashes and hundreds of injuries but relatively few fatalities. Most of those have involved spectators (and one cow) rather than drivers. Indy 500 legend and Baja 1000 competitor Parnelli Jones once called racing the Baja "a 24-hour plane crash."

THE IDITAROD

In the world's most famous dogsled race, 50 mushers and as many as 800 dogs brave 1,150 miles of rugged Alaskan backcountry in temperatures that can reach –50°F. This so-called "Last Great Race on Earth" is extremely difficult to finish—more people have climbed to the top of Mt. Everest than have crossed the Iditarod finish line. Depending on the severity of the weather, the course can take 10 to 17 days to complete. Human fatalities are rare—the most common injuries are bruised ribs, broken wrists, and concussions from falls off the sled. But the dogs aren't so lucky. The average sled dog burns about 11,000 calories per day during the race—roughly eight times as much as a Tour de France cyclist burns. Each year about one dog out of three is unable to finish the race due to injury or fatigue and has to be flown out. And since 1973, at least 142 dogs have died during the Iditarod.

DAKAR RALLY

In 1977 French racecar driver Thierry Sabine got lost in the Sahara desert during a road race from France to the Ivory Coast in West Africa. The experience convinced him that the North African desert was a perfect location for an off-road endurance car race. A year later, the first Paris–Dakar rally took place, a grinding 5,000-mile marathon that usually begins in Paris, winds its way south to the Mediterranean Sea (where the cars are ferried across to Africa), and then zigzags across the Sahara through some of the world's most inhospitable terrain before it ends in Dakar, Senegal. Over the years, 45 drivers and crewmembers have been killed by every conceivable kind of hazard—crashes due to blown engines and tires, sandstorms, flash floods, and even raids by hostile Tuareg nomads. In 2008 the race was canceled due to threats from Mauritanian rebels. The competition has three classes—cars, motorcycles, and trucks—and teams will do almost anything to win, including sabotage. Each year fewer than half of the racers finish the course. The level of personal risk is so high that every vehicle displays a sign listing its riders' blood types. In 1986 founder Sabine became a victim himself when the helicopter he was riding in crashed into a dune in Mali during a sandstorm.

MARATHON DES SABLES

Runners have their choice of grueling events: marathons, biathlons, and triathlons. And then there's the granddaddy of all footraces: the Marathon des Sables (Marathon of the Sands), a weeklong 150-mile race across the scorching desert of southern Morocco. It's the equivalent of running 5 ½ marathons…in 120°F heat. *And* you have to carry all your own food—enough to last you the whole week. Each year about 700 runners start the race; barely half reach the end. Not surprisingly, dehydration is the single biggest reason runners drop out (a medical team following the racers provides intravenous saline drips). And even the failures can be spectacular. The race's most celebrated washout was an Italian runner named Mauro Prosperi, who was about halfway through the race in 1994 when he got lost in a sandstorm. He wandered off course by several hundred miles, ran out of food and water, and was forced to eat bats and drink his own urine to stay alive. In despair, he tried to commit suicide by slashing his wrists…but he was so dehydrated that his blood clotted too quickly for him to bleed to death. Nomads eventually found him in an abandoned mosque, babbling incoherently. Prosperi recovered and came back to compete in three more Marathons des Sables. He never won.

...and Charles "the Affable" hit his head during a game, slipped into a coma, and died (1498).

OLYMPIC BAD LUCK

Winning at sports takes skill, practice…and a little good luck. Here are some Olympians who could have used a rabbit's foot (or some new officials).

WATCH THIS!
At the 1932 Summer Games in Los Angeles, Frenchman Jules Noël's discus throw went farther than anyone else's, but distracted officials were busy watching the pole vault competition. Result: The throw was "unofficial." They apologized and let him throw again, but it fell short of the previous mark. Noël ended up in fourth place—just short of a medal.

A HORSE TOO SHORT
Olympic gymnasts know that the "horse" in the women's vaulting competition is supposed to be set at 125 centimeters (about four feet) off the floor, and that's what they practice on. But the people who installed the horse at the 2000 Games in Sydney, Australia, set it at 120 centimeters—5 centimeters (about 2 inches) too short. Several gymnasts misjudged the height and fell, including the favorite, Russia's Svetlana Khorkina, who missed her landing and was so shaken that later she also fell off the uneven bars.

TOO GOOD FOR HIS OWN GOOD
At the 1928 Winter Games in St. Moritz, Switzerland, Norwegian ski jumper Jacob Tullin Thams had such a strong jump—30 feet farther than the next competitor—that he flew beyond the sloped landing area and onto a flat surface, which made him crash. Penalized for style points, the longest jump of the day only earned him 28th place.

WHO'S COUNTING?
The 1932 Games in Los Angeles featured a 3,000-meter steeplechase for horses. The race was close as the horses entered the final lap…or what was supposed to be the final lap. Somehow, the judges had lost count and let the race run for an additional lap. American Joseph McCluskey would have won a silver medal, but was passed on that second "final" lap and only won the bronze.

The first home run in an All-Star Game was hit by Babe Ruth (1933).

THE MONOPOLY STORY

You may be surprised to see Monopoly in a sports book, but with world records, international championships, and nervous contestants, it can get as competitive as any sport. And it's the best-selling game in history. Here's how it got its start.

OFFICIAL ORIGIN

According to Parker Brothers, Monopoly was invented by a man named Charles Darrow in the 1920s. Darrow—an engineer by trade—created the game after the stock market crash of 1929, when, he found himself unemployed and, like the rest of the country, short of cash. To kill time (and keep his spirits up), he devised a game involving "plenty of money for the player to invest or speculate with." Because he was interested in real estate, he made buying land the primary focus...and because he personally didn't believe in credit or borrowing money, he made the whole thing a cash proposition.

Darrow had visited Atlantic City shortly before the stock market crashed, so he transferred his fond memories of the town to the board. That's why the Boardwalk, railroad lines, and streets of the New Jersey resort are represented there.

PASSING GO

The original version of the game was crudely painted on a piece of linoleum. But that didn't stop family and friends from getting hooked on it—and demanding their own sets. "I hadn't anything better to do, so I began to make more of the games," Darrow explained. "I charged people $4 a copy." Although Darrow didn't advertise, he soon began to receive orders from all over the country. He was shocked but excited. Looking for more distribution, he took the game to Parker Brothers...and was turned down cold. Says one historian: "George and Charles Parker thought Monopoly took much too long to play, the rules were hopelessly complicated, and there were at least 52 other weak points they believed ruled the game out." Darrow was upset by the decision, but decided to distribute Monopoly on his own. He took it to two major retailers—Wanamaker's in Philadelphia, and FAO Schwartz, New York's

---

The oldest continuous trophy in sports is the America's Cup for yachting, since 1851.

most prestigious toy store—and convinced them to stock his game. When both stores quickly sold their entire stock, the Parker brothers reconsidered. They purchased the rights to Monopoly...and watched, astounded, as it sold as fast as they could make it. Ironically, Monopoly actually kept their toy company—which was on the edge of insolvency—from going bankrupt.

By mid-February 1935, Parker Brothers was selling more than 20,000 sets of Monopoly a week. Darrow, as one would imagine, was financially set for life. And the reluctant toy company had its hands on the most lucrative game in the history of the toy industry.

THE REAL STORY?

Did Darrow really invent the game that he sold to Parker Brothers? Possibly not. In recent years, the Monopoly "legend" has been discredited during a long, bitter legal fight between Parker Brothers and Ralph Anspach, maker of a game called "Anti-Monopoly." Take these facts, for example:

• In 1904—roughly 15 years before Darrow "invented" his game— a Chicago woman named Elizabeth Magie-Phillips patented "The Landlord's Game," a board game that included the purchasing of property, utilities, and a "public park" space.

• She wasn't alone—there were at least eight different groups that played Monopoly-like games before Darrow, including one at Harvard Law School and another at a utopian community in Arden, Delaware.

• There's evidence that Darrow may have learned his version of the game from a group of Quakers in Atlantic City, possibly adding only Chance cards and the railroads as original contributions.

• What was the *real* reason Parker Brothers rejected Darrow's game in the 1920s? One theory: There were so many versions of Monopoly floating around that the company knew it could not legally claim ownership of a game that was already in the public domain. But Darrow's game sold so well, the theory goes, that the Parker brothers changed their minds, bought the rights to his version—as well as to all other known versions of the game—and then spread the story of Darrow's "invention" of the game in order to claim exclusive rights to it. It's a great conspiracy story, but we'll probably never know if it's true.

First basketball player to appear on a box of Wheaties: Michael Jordan in 1988.

GOOOOOOOOOOOOOOAL!

Weird tales from the world of football...no, soccer...no...

POT SHOTS. Newspapers reported in 2004 that Portuguese police were turning a blind eye to marijuana smoking among fans at soccer matches—especially if they were English. A police spokesperson said they hoped it would keep the notoriously rowdy fans calm.

PIN-UP GUY. Swiss newspapers featured cut-out voodoo dolls of English soccer star David Beckham before the Switzerland-England match in the Euro 2004 games. "Let's all rip this page out, pin it on the wall and stick in nails, needles and staples," read the caption. "If we believe it will work, then it will." (It didn't.)

TASTES GREAT. LESS WINNING. The Bernard brewery offered Czech Republic football coach Karel Bruckner 60 liters of beer per year for the rest of his life if the team won the Euro 2004 competition. They also promised 160 liters to every player on the team. "While they will earn a lot of money if they win," said a brewery spokesman, "we think the offer of free beer is extra motivation and will inspire the team to go for gold." (They didn't win.)

KILL YOUR TELEVISION. Police in a Romanian town received several phone calls after explosions were heard all over town. Explanation: the Romanian team had just been knocked out of the Euro 2004 and several fans had thrown their TV sets out of their windows.

WARDROBE MALFUNCTION. During a game between two teams in the Belgian Football Association, a man ran onto the field and pulled the referee's pants and shorts down. Ref Jacky Temmerman said, "I looked very nice in front of a few hundred supporters. That man made a fool of me." The fan faces a lifetime ban from Belgian soccer games.

BLACK MAGIC WOMAN. An award-winning Romanian sports photographer was banned from flying with the Romanian soccer team in 2003 because she's female—and women bring bad luck. The Romanian team is notoriously superstitious: Women aren't

---

First woman to play at St. Andrews golf course: Mary, Queen of Scots, in 1522.

allowed on the team bus, players can't whistle on the bus, and the bus isn't allowed to drive in reverse while players are aboard.

DID THEY WEAR TRUNKS? Prison officials in Thailand wanted to avoid gambling and rivalry troubles during the Euro 2004 tournament. So they scheduled an actual game—inmates versus non-inmates. The non-inmates were trained soccer-playing elephants. They played to a 5–5 tie.

BRING IT ON! Turkish soccer commentator Ahmet Cakar is well-known as an outspoken critic of officials, coaches, players, fans, the game, his fellow Turks, and just about everyone in general. When asked in 2004 if he would enrage someone, he said, "Whoever dares can come and try and take my life." In March 2004, an angry fan shot him five times in the stomach and groin. (He survived the attack.)

HE HAD A DREAM. In January 2004, nine-year-old English soccer fan Billy Harris had a dream: Middlesbrough would beat the Bolton Wanderers 2–1 to win the English League Cup...AND Boudewijn Zenden would score the winning goal. So his dad, who had never bet on a game before, put a £15 ($27) wager on the team. On February 29, Middlesbrough, a 60–1 long shot, beat the Bolton Wanderers and won the cup. The score was 2–1...and Boudewijn Zenden scored the winner. Dad won £900 ($1,600). "It was unbelievable," said Billy. "Now my mum's given me a notepad to write down all my dreams."

AIN'T THAT A KICK IN THE HEAD. "The wind tunnel we've developed enabled us to analyze David Beckham's sensational goal against Greece in the World Cup," said physicist Dr. Matt Carré of England's University of Sheffield. "We know that the shot left his foot at 80 mph from 27 meters out, moved laterally over two meters during its flight due to the amount of spin applied, and during the last half of its flight suddenly slowed to 42 mph, dipping into the top corner of the goal. The sudden deceleration happens at the moment when the airflow pattern around the ball changes, increasing drag by more than a hundred percent. This crucial airflow transition is affected both by the velocity and spinning rate of the ball and by its surface seam pattern. Beckham was instinctively applying some very sophisticated physics calculations in scoring the goal."

Biathlon combines two sports: cross-country skiing and rifle shooting.

THE GRAVITY GRAND PRIX

Here's how a neighborhood contest turned into a sport that's become a passion for thousands of kids: the Soap Box Derby.

SERENDIPITY STRIKES

In 1933 *Dayton Daily News* photographer Myron Scott came across three boys racing homemade engineless carts down a brick road in Dayton, Ohio. Sensing a good story, Scott asked the boys if they'd like to participate in an organized race that awarded a trophy to its winner. The kids agreed, and they scheduled a race time for the following week. On the appointed day, 19 boys showed up, hauling their homemade cars behind them. The vehicles were strange conglomerations made from junk-heap scraps: old buggies, orange crates, and spare pieces of sheet metal. A few hundred spectators assembled to watch the race, and the group had so much fun that Scott realized he was on to something big.

He managed to convince his boss at the newspaper to sponsor another—this time, official—event. Scott called it the Soap Box Derby (even though there's no record of anyone ever actually racing in a soap box). On August 19, 1933, about 360 kids showed up on a street in Dayton with their creations. The contestants included one girl, who took second place. Forty *thousand* people came to watch. Scott's Soap Box Derby was a hit.

KID-BUILT, KID-RACED

Word got out about the kids' cart race in Dayton, and Chevrolet signed on as a sponsor. Chevy dealerships around the country held local races, and the next year, 34 of these local champs came to the race in Dayton.

In those early days, the Derby's rules were fairly simple. Cars had to be built by the children themselves (no help from parents or other adults). After the first two years, when girls were allowed to race, participation was restricted to boys aged 9 to 15 years old.

In baseball, a knuckleball pitch can travel at less than half the speed of a fastball.

(Later, the rules were expanded to include boys and girls of a wider range of ages.)

The 1934 race also included a handicap system that Scott implemented in the hopes of giving everyone a fair shot. The racers with the fastest times in the early heats had to begin with delays of several seconds in later heats. But the "fair" system gave the slower cars too much of an advantage, and an especially slow car (made with baby carriage wheels) ended up winning that year. After that, Scott scrapped the handicap system.

FINDING FAME

In 1935 the Soap Box Derby moved to Akron, Ohio, because it had more hills than Dayton. That year, the Derby also garnered attention from national media. Reporters descended on Akron to cover the event.

During one heat, NBC sportscaster Graham McNamee crossed the safety barriers to get closer to the action at the finish line. Officials warned him back, but he said, "I've broadcast from a plane high in the sky, from a submarine on the ocean bottom, from the fastest cars at Indianapolis. I'm not afraid of a little thing like a kiddiecar!" Just then, one of the contestants lost control of his car and crashed into McNamee. The sportscaster escaped serious injury, but the accident was caught on newsreels and shown in theaters across the country. And the Derby just got more popular.

DERBY DOWNS

In 1936 some Soap Box enthusiasts decided that the Derby needed its own racetrack. B. E. "Shorty" Fulton, a member of the Akron city administration, was one of the main lobbyers for the track. He managed the Akron Municipal Airport (adjacent to the proposed track) and would become the track's manager. Even President Franklin D. Roosevelt agreed; he sent Works Progress Administration employees to Ohio to construct the track.

Named Derby Downs, the new cement raceway was 1,600 feet long. It had 200 feet of runoff space below the finish line and room for thousands of spectators. More than 70 years later, the Derby still takes place at Derby Downs.

Today, the All-American Soap Box Derby is sponsored by

---

33 runners at the 2000 Berlin Marathon were disqualified for taking a shortcut (the subway).

Goodyear, and the rules have changed a bit. There are tournaments in three racing divisions, and parents are encouraged to help their children. The race attracts 200 to 300 contestants each year. Racers range in age from 8 to 17, and many famous fans have jumped on the bandwagon over the years: Ronald Reagan, Richard Nixon, heavyweight boxer Jack Dempsey, *Star Trek* cast member George Takei, and Jimmy Stewart (who postponed his honeymoon to catch the 1949 race).

STARS OF THE DERBY

Here are some of the more innovative racers who've won the Derby over the years

1939: Cliff Hardesty. This contestant from White Plains, New York, was the subject of 52 letters of complaint…and that was before he'd even hit the track. Parents of racers he'd beaten in local competitions complained that Cliff's racer was too flawless— the suspension too sophisticated—to have been built by an 11- year-old. Race officials grilled Cliff about how he built his car and then brought him to a garage, where they told him to build the front suspension of his racer from scratch. After only half an hour, Cliff had built one even better, though he apologized that he couldn't get it quite right because the tools were unfamiliar. The stunned officials let him race, and he went on to win.

1967: Kenny Cline. In 1964 several racers showed up with cars that allowed drivers to lie flat on their backs to cut down on wind resistance, resulting in faster times. The designs were the brainchild of a few boys from Texas, but Kenny Cline, originally from Midland, Texas, improved it. His racer, the "Grasshopper," required that he lie on his stomach while steering. Seemingly cumbersome but successful, his needle-nosed car shot to victory in 1967, and the "lie-down" design has been popular ever since.

1975: Karren Stead. Although a girl placed second in the original 1933 Derby, girls were prohibited from competing in the Soap Box Derby for 40 years. They were officially allowed to race again in 1971, but it wasn't until 1975 that a girl, Karren Stead from Pennsylvania, won the crown. (The 11-year-old won the race despite dislocating her thumb in a water balloon fight just before the starting whistle blew.) That year, girls occupied 5 of the top 10 spots.

WHO'S ON FIRST?

*America's national pastime is more than just a game—it's
a tradition. The component parts are traditions, too.
We got curious about where they come from.*

B ASEBALL GLOVES
Introduced by: Charles Waite, first baseman for the
Boston team of the National Association (forerunner of
the National League), in 1875

History: Until Waite started wearing a thin, unpadded, flesh-
color glove, everyone played barehanded. In fact, when he showed
up on the field with it, rivals jeered that he was a softy. One contemporary wrote: "Waite confessed that he was a bit ashamed to
wear it, but had to save his hand. He also admitted he'd chosen a
color as inconspicuous as possible, because he didn't want to
attract attention."

Note: Though a few players copied Waite, it took a superstar to
popularize the use of gloves. In 1883 the shortstop for the Providence, Rhode Island, team broke a finger on his left hand. To protect it, he wore an oversized, padded buckskin glove. One of
baseball's biggest heroes, John Montgomery Ward, decided to wear
one too...which inspired manufacturers to begin mass-producing
them.

SHIN GUARDS

Introduced by: "One of two black second basemen, Binghamton
[New York]'s Bud Fowler or Buffalo's Frank Grant, who played
minor league ball in the 1880s in the International League."
(From *Only the Ball Was White*, by Robert Peterson)

History: In the 1880s, white ballplayers openly tried to injure
black players. Grant and Fowler "knew that about every player
that came down to second base on a steal...would, if possible,
throw their spikes into them." So one of them came up with the
idea of wrapping wooden slats around their shins.

Note: It only worked for a while...and then the bigots got more
vicious. As one player recalled in 1891: "[When] Grant put wood-

en armor on his legs for protection, the opposition just proceeded to file their spikes to a sharp point and split the shin guards." **Gruesome trivia:** According to *Only the Ball Was White*, that's what first made the feet-first slide popular among white players. Grant ultimately moved to the outfield.

The first catcher to wear shin guards was Roger Bresnahan in 1907. He fashioned them after the leg guards used in the English game of cricket.

SEVENTH-INNING STRETCH

Introduced by: No one's sure

History: According to legend, the stretch began in 1910 when President William Howard Taft got up to leave during the seventh inning of a game between Washington and Philadelphia. "His entourage followed," the story goes, "and fans, seeing a crowd of people standing, stood up also."

That may have happened, but according to *Baseball's Book of Firsts*, the seventh-inning stretch was already part of baseball tradition: "In reality, fans had been standing and stretching at about the seventh inning since the early 1870s." The book says it started in Boston, where the local team tended to score most of its runs near the end of the game. Around the seventh inning, fans would stand and "cheer on the hometown boys."

Note: There's one other claimant—Manhattan College. According to one sports historian: "In 1882 during a baseball game at New York's Manhattan College, the athletic director, a man named Brother Jasper, called a time out during the seventh inning so that the fidgeting students in the stands would have a moment to stretch." True? Who knows?

UNIFORM NUMBERS

Introduced by: The New York Yankees

History: Around 1915, teams experimented with small numbers on uniform sleeves, but they made no difference to fans. In 1929, however, the Yankees—realizing they were attracting lots of new fans who didn't know the players by sight—put big numbers on the backs of uniforms. The original numbers followed the batting order. For example: Babe Ruth, who batted third, got number 3; Lou Gehrig, who batted fourth, was number 4. Later, numbers were assigned at random. It took another 31 years before teams started putting names on the uniforms. Why so long? Apparently, clubs were afraid they'd lose the profits they made from selling scorecards.

CATCHER'S MASKS
Introduced by: Fred Thayer, coach of Harvard University, in 1875 or 1877, depending on the source

History: Catchers originally wore no protection—they stood off to one side of the plate so they wouldn't get hit. In 1877, Thayer decided his catcher would have an advantage if he stood right behind the plate. But the student, James Tyng, refused. Thayer explained: "He had been hit by foul tips and had become timid.... I [had] to find a way to bring back his confidence."

Thayer's solution: armor. He took a fencer's mask to a tinsmith, who cut eyeholes in the wire mesh. "Tyng placed the contraption over his head for a game against the Lynn Live Oaks Baseball Club," writes Lloyd Johnson in *Baseball's Book of Firsts*.

Note: Thayer later changed the mesh to wide-spaced iron bars, and added forehead and chin rests. He patented the mask in 1878, and it immediately became popular. Chest protectors were added in 1885.

BATTING HELMETS
Introduced by: Willie Wells, in 1939

History: In 1905 a "pneumatic batting helmet" that looked like a leather football helmet was introduced, but it was too cumbersome and no one used it. Even after Ray Chapman died when he was hit in the head by a pitch in 1920, there was no interest in helmets.

Once again, one player trying to protect himself changed baseball. Wells, a good-hitting shortstop in the Negro Leagues, hung his head over the plate when he batted—which made him especially vulnerable. He finally got sick of being hit in the head, and showed up at a game wearing a miner's helmet. (No word on whether it had the light in front.) In 1942 he switched to a construction hardhat...which eventually led to helmets made especially for the Major Leagues in 1952.

First Formula One Grand Prix winner: Romanian Ferenc Szisz, driving a Renault, in 1906.

RUN FOR YOUR LIFE

The story of the first "marathon" has been taught in high-school history classes for years. One problem: It may never have happened at all.

THE LONG RUN

The marathon—the grueling 26-mile run that takes place on the last day of every modern Olympics—didn't start out as a competition, but as a life-and-death messenger service. It's a story that's familiar to most sports fans: There was a battle at a town called Marathon near Athens, Greece, and one runner had to travel an unthinkable distance to deliver a message. That much, anyway, seems to be true. But what's not so clear is who the runner was, where he was going, and what that crucial message was.

FANTASTIC VOYAGE

Today, Marathon is a small town, but in 490 B.C.E. it was a powerful city-state that, along with other Greek cities, was at war with Persia. That year, an army of Greeks, despite being hopelessly outnumbered, defeated the Persians in a lopsided battle near Marathon. The Persians lost 6,400 men, while the Greeks lost less than 200. How did the Greeks do it? With better weaponry, tactics, and one piece of invaluable military intelligence: When the Greek general, Miltiades, heard that some of the Persian forces were away doing battle nearby, he pounced on the remaining ones—and won.

Once the Persians were routed, the Greek army needed to send word of their victory to Athens, about 26 miles away. According to legend, a great runner named Pheidippides was recruited for the task. Pheidippides had already proven his talents before the battle by running to Sparta to request help from that city, covering roughly 150 miles in two days. (No luck—the Spartans were in the middle of a religious festival and wouldn't send any men until it was over.) When the Greeks won the Battle of Marathon anyway, Pheidippides was sent to Athens at top speed. A few hours later, he reached the city, shouted *"Nenikékamen!"* ("We have won!"), and then collapsed in exhaustion and died on the spot.

FROM LEGEND TO FACT

That's the story, but is it true? No one knows for sure. Apparently there was a runner named Pheidippides, described in Greek historian Herodotus's *Histories* as the man given the task to ask for help from the Spartans. But what's less clear is whether Pheidippides—or anyone—made the more famous run from Marathon to Athens. Herodotus, who was writing a few decades after the Battle of Marathon, didn't mention the Marathon run at all. Plutarch, a biographer writing a few hundred years later, described the Marathon runner but said he may have been a man named Thersippus, or possibly one named Eukles. But 50 years after that, the Greek writer Lucian attributed the Marathon run to Pheidippides...and the story stuck.

Pheidippides's legendary run got a new lease on life in the late 19th century, when Robert Browning made it the subject of his 1879 poem "Pheidippides." The poem was a popular hit, and its publication coincided with the rise of the movement to revive the ancient Olympic Games. One Olympic enthusiast, a French linguist and historian named Michel Bréal, also loved the Pheidippides legend and pushed for the inclusion of a "Marathon" race at the modern Games, scheduled to open in Athens in 1896. Olympic organizers agreed—and so did the Greeks, who liked the idea that the race would be based on a chapter out of their own history.

SETTING THE STANDARD

At the Athens Olympics, the second "first marathon" fittingly started in Marathon and ended in Athens. And, as luck would have it, first prize (gold medals weren't introduced until 1904) went to a Greek runner, Spyridon Louis. Later, at the 1924 games, the marathon length was standardized to 42,195 meters (26 miles, 385 yards)—slightly longer than the distance from Marathon to Athens. Why the change? Because the 1908 Olympics were held in London, and the English wanted it to run between Windsor Castle and the royal box in the stadium at London: a distance of 42,195 meters. So, some 30 years after an English poet popularized the myth of the Marathon run, an English Olympic committee gave it its official length.

THE ORIGIN OF NACHOS

Readers sometimes ask if we'll ever run out of sports stories to write about. No way. Here's a good example: A lowly snack food that became a household word—thanks to Howard Cosell.

SNACK EMERGENCY

In 1943 Ignacio Anaya, or "Nacho," as he was nicknamed, was working as the maitre d' at a restaurant called the Victory Club in Piedras Negras, Mexico, just across the border from Eagle Pass, Texas. According to Anaya's son, Ignacio Jr., one night the restaurant's cook disappeared just as a group of officers' wives from Fort Duncan Air Base arrived for dinner. Thinking fast, Anaya went into the kitchen and improvised a meal by taking some tostadas and topping them with shredded cheddar cheese, then putting them in a broiler and serving them garnished with jalapeño peppers. The women were impressed. One of them, Mamie Finan, named them "Nachos Especiales" in honor of Anaya's nickname.

The recipe soon became a specialty of many local restaurants, but remained unknown outside of southern Texas until a man named Frank Liberto saw the potential of nachos as a concession-stand item. In 1977 he figured out how to process the cheese to keep it soft all the time, and started selling nachos at Arlington Stadium, then home of the Texas Rangers baseball team. He later replaced the tostadas with tortilla chips...and modern-day nachos were born.

CRUNCH TIME

Nachos might have remained a Texas specialty if not for Howard Cosell and *Monday Night Football*. One night, someone gave Cosell nachos before a game. He loved them...and the funny-sounding name. That night, and for weeks after, Cosell and the broadcast team worked references to nachos into the game analysis as often as possible. Cosell began describing great plays by calling them "nachos," giving the food national recognition, making the term an acceptable adjective for spectacular events, and forever securing its spot as one of the sports fan's favorite finger foods.

NASCAR car driver with the most career wins: Richard Petty, with 200.

THE 20th HOLE

*Golfers talk about "dying" on the 14th hole, but few of them
mean it literally. Be careful, though—even out on the
golf course, Death might want to play through.*

DER BINGLE

In 1977 a doctor told 74-year-old Bing Crosby that
because of his ill health, he should restrict his game to
nine holes. That was a tall order for the famous singer, who for
many years kept his handicap in single digits. On October 14,
Crosby and a friend were playing two Spanish pros at La Moraleja
golf course near Madrid. Crosby was shooting a great game—
prancing around the links and singing out loud. There was no way
he was stopping after nine holes.

Somewhere around the 15th, Crosby's partner noticed he was
favoring his left arm, but the crooner said he was okay and played
the last three holes. The good news: Crosby won, shooting an 85
for the day. The bad news: shortly after proclaiming, "That was a
great game of golf, fellas!" he collapsed. His friends thought he'd
slipped and they carried him back to the clubhouse. But Crosby
hadn't slipped; he'd suffered a major heart attack and died right
there on the links. His wife Kathryn issued a statement, saying: "I
can't think of any better way for a golfer who sings for a living to
finish his round."

HOGG HEAVEN

Jimmy Hogg, 77, was on the first hole at his Fife, Scotland, golf
club in 1996 when he suffered a major heart attack and died. Out
of respect, Hogg's partners waited for the ambulance to come and
take their friend away...then they resumed their round. "I'm sure
Jimmy would have wanted us to do that," said one.

WHAT WAS HE DOING THERE?

China has more than a billion people, but very few of them play
golf—it's a game for the superwealthy. When a civil servant
named Li Zhen'e was killed in a golf cart accident in 2003 (the
cart tumbled 30 feet down a slope onto a paved road), it created

an uproar about government corruption in the Hunan province. How could a modestly paid civil servant afford to play golf? In response to the public indignation, an official inquiry determined that Li Zhen'e was on the links only because he was conducting official government business, and not having fun.

DON'T GREVE FOR ME

A 65-year-old man named Donald DeGreve was golfing near his home in Winter Haven, Florida, in 1992. He died of a heart attack on the 16th green. But it was league day at the club, and dozens of golfers were still playing behind him. Solution: Course officials left DeGreve's body on the 16th green, covered with a sheet. The rest of the field continued playing, going straight from the 15th green to the 17th tee to avoid disturbing the body while the club's management tried to contact the dead man's wife so she could make arrangements to "retrieve" her husband. "Life goes on," said one of the other players, "so we had to keep going."

HIGH-RISK SPORT?

Some fascinating facts about hazards on the links:

• A study in 1999 found that people who walked instead of rode in a cart had improved cholesterol levels and better overall health. (Ironically, however, many golfers spend their recreational time the way they spend their daily commute time—driving.)

• According to an insurance company that sells golf liability insurance, in 1999 alone a total of 9,291 British golfers were injured by golf clubs or balls, including 3,530 head injuries and 677 bone fractures.

• The most likely place to suffer an alligator attack in the United States is not in a swamp…but on a golf course. Still, your odds are pretty good. Of 365 reported alligator attacks on humans in recent years, only 3.6% (13 cases) were fatal.

THE FINAL LIE

Many die-hard players have had their ashes scattered on the greens. And if you can afford it, your remains can be placed inside the shaft of a driver, so you can slice balls into the water long after you're gone.

RODEO LINGO

*Wanna be a rodeo cowboy? Here are some
handy phrases you'll be needin'.*

Bad wreck. When a bull rider is bucked off hard and either horned or stomped on by the bull.

Free hand. Just what it sounds like: the one hand that must be free at all times during bronco and bull-riding events.

Crow hopper. A bull or bronco that jumps stiff-legged straight into the air instead of bucking.

Dogie. An orphaned calf.

Freight trained. When a bull bucks off a rider, then heads straight for him and tramples him. (See "barrel man.")

Suck back. When a bull bucks in one direction and then quickly switches to another. (After the rodeo, it also means to drink a beer quickly.)

Cowboy up. Psyche yourself up, preparing mentally, and give it everything you've got. The 2003 Boston Red Sox famously borrowed the phrase.

Barrel man. Known better as a "rodeo clown," the barrel man hides in a barrel during the bull-riding event. If a rider is thrown, the barrel man springs into action to distract the bull from trampling him.

Arm jerker. A bull so strong it feels like it could yank the rider's arm out of its socket.

Bull rope. A flat braided rope that goes around the middle of a bull that riders hang on to during the bull-riding event.

Hooker. A bull that throws the rider and attempts to hook him with his horns.

Spinner. A bull that spins in circles while trying to shake off his rider. It looks like a puppy chasing its tail.

Good bucker. A bronco or bull that gives a particularly feisty performance.

Houlihan. A head-over-hooves somersault that a steer sometimes makes during the steer-wrestling event.

The French Open is the only Grand Slam tennis tournament played on clay courts.

IT'S A RACKET

Sports are part of the fabric of our culture. They're part of our language, too. Here are the origins of a few common sports terms.

ALLEY-OOP

Meaning: In basketball, a high pass caught in midair by a teammate who tries to stuff the ball in the basket before landing

Origin: "Probably coined by American soldiers during World War I. It's from the French *allez* (go) plus *oop*, a French pronunciation of the English *up*. During the 1920's, *allez-oop* became *alley-oop*, commonly said upon lifting something. In the late 1950s, San Francisco 49er quarterback Y. A. Tittle invented a lob pass called the alley-oop that was thrown over the heads of defenders to his very tall receiver, R. C. Owens. By the 1970s, it had been adapted to describe the schoolyard basketball play it is today." (From *Grand Slam, Hat Tricks & Alley-oops*, by Robert Hendrickson)

BOGEY

Meaning: In golf, one stroke over par

Origin: "*Bogey*, 'an imaginary thing that causes fear,' gives us the *bogeyman*, who scares children, and a popular 1890 song called 'Colonel Bogey.' In England, when you were doing exceptionally well it was said that Colonel Bogey was playing with you. When someone did well on a particular hole, they thought the Colonel was lending a hand; a player doing poorly was said to be losing to Bogey. As golf became organized, par became the standard score and a bogey became one more than the duffer's aim." (From *Where in the Word?*, by David Muschell)

BONEHEAD PLAY

Meaning: A very stupid play

Origin: "The original bonehead play was made in 1908 by Fred Merkle, the New York Giants' first baseman. It was the bottom of the ninth inning. There were two outs. Moose McCormick was on third and Merkle was on first. The next man up singled to center, and McCormick scored the winning run. But Merkle ran into the dugout—he never touched second base. Johnny Evers of the Cubs got the ball and stepped on second, forcing Merkle out. The winning run was nullified and the Giants lost. The Cubs and Giants finished the season tied for first place, and the Cubs won the pennant in a play-off game. A sportswriter's reference to Merkle's blunder as a 'bonehead play' introduced the phrase into the lexicon." (From *Grand Slam, Hat Tricks & Alley-oops*, by Robert Hendrickson)

HAT TRICK

Meaning: The scoring of three goals in a game—usually hockey or soccer—by the same player

Origin: "This American phrase comes from the 19th-century tradition of awarding a new hat (or the proceeds of passing a hat) to British cricket bowlers when they bowled down three wickets with three successful balls. Although it's now mainly associated with hockey, *hat trick* has also been used for a jockey who wins three consecutive races, or a soccer player who scores three goals in one game." (From *Southpaws & Sunday Punches*, by Christine Ammer)

RACKET

Meaning: In tennis, a bat with an oval frame, strung with nylon

Origin: "Tennis balls were originally hit with the palm of the hand, called *raquette*, probably from the Arabic *rahat* meaning the same. As tennis evolved, gloves were used, then boards, then paddles, and finally the long-handled racket used today. All were called by the name *raquette*, which became the English word *racket*. The French still call tennis *le jeu de paume* (the palm game)." (From *Word Mysteries & Histories*, by the American Heritage Dictionary)

TEE

Meaning: The small peg with a concave head that is placed in the ground to support a golf ball before it is struck

Origin: "The first tees were just small handfuls of sand or dirt off which golf balls were hit. The Scottish word was first recorded in 1673 as *teaz*, but people thought this was the plural of *tee* and over the years, *tee* became the singular form. The little wooden pegs we call tees today were invented in the 1920s by William Lowell, a dentist from New Jersey." (From *Word and Phrase Origins*, by Robert Hendrickson)

In 2000 a woman paid $8,000 for a pair of Ty Cobb's false teeth.

WEIRD BAR SPORTS

Here's a look at some of the more unusual ways that bar owners have tried to keep customers busy and entertained while they drink.

DWARF TOSSING
How It's Played: A dwarf dresses up in body padding, a crash helmet, and a harness. Then contestants hurl him across the room into a pile of mattresses. The "winner" is the person who throws the dwarf the farthest. In some contests, dwarfs have been thrown as much as 30 feet. Why do the dwarfs do it? They can make as much as $2,000 a night.

History: Invented at a Queensland, Australia, bar in 1985. It later produced an offshoot—dwarf bowling: "A helmeted dwarf is strapped to a skateboard or mechanic's creeper and rolled headfirst into bowling pins, which are made of plastic."

In 1987 a few American bars tried out this "sport," and it was a commercial success. But the bad publicity—combined with lobbying by groups like Little People of America—killed it.

THE HUMAN (BAR)FLY

How It's Played: Wearing a velcro suit, bar patrons sprint down a runway, leap on a small trampoline, and hurl themselves onto a wall covered with velcro hooks. First prize goes to the person whose feet stick highest on the wall. Getting off the wall can be fun, too. "One of our rules is that the men peel off the women, and the women peel off the men," says a bar owner. "Sometimes it takes three women to peel off one guy."

History: Inspired by David Letterman, who performed the stunt on his show in 1984. The Cri Bar and Grill in New Zealand began holding "human fly" contests in 1991, and other New Zealand bars followed suit. *Sports Illustrated* covered it in 1991; it quickly spread to the United States, where it flourished for a few years.

SUMO SUIT WRESTLING

How It's Played: Participants don 43-pound rubberized vinyl and

---

First African-American woman to win an Olympic event: high-jumper Alice Coachman (1948).

nylon suits that make them look like 400-pound sumo wrestlers—complete with the traditional Japanese sumo "diaper" and a crash helmet with a sumo wig glued on the outside. Then they slam into each other on a big padded mat. (Not to be confused with human cockfighting, in which—no kidding—people dress up in padded chicken costumes and peck, bump, and scratch each other.)

History: Englishman Peter Herzig invented the suits after seeing sumo wrestlers in a Miller Beer commercial. Miller then bought hundreds of the suits and began promoting the "sport" in nightclubs in the early 1990s.

HUMAN BOWLING

How It's Played: Like real bowling, you have to knock down as many pins as you can...but in this sport, the pins are five feet tall and made of canvas and styrofoam; the bowler is strapped *inside* a huge metal-frame bowling ball. A partner rolls him or her down the 30-foot lane toward the pins. "Just because you're in the ball doesn't mean you have no obligations to the team," says Lori Fosdick, a regular bowler. "I've seen some pretty maneuvers—but I've also seen people who seemed to be going straight and rolled right around the pin."

History: Creator Thomas Bell got the idea in the early 1990s after watching some gerbils running on an exercise wheel. He figured humans might enjoy doing the same thing. "Bowling has always been a competitive sport," he says straight-faced. "We're just taking it to a more competitive level."

GERBIL RACING

How It's Played: Eight gerbils race in a portable racetrack that's set up on the wall behind the bar. Betting is not allowed, but customers who pick the winning gerbil win free drinks.

History: Invented in 1992 at a bar in Alberta, Canada, with the blessings of the Canadian SPCA. "My gerbils live to the age of two, unlike wild gerbils, which have a lifespan of only eight months," says Morley Amon, owner of the Alberta track. "They aren't running against their will. They run just to see what's on the other side."

I'LL TRADE YOU A...

In the trade-crazy world of professional sports, some trades still stand out as being...unusually unusual.

BEER FOR A PITCHER: Pitcher Nigel Thatch of the Schaumburg Flyers of the Northern League, a professional baseball league in the northern United States and Canada, was traded in May 2006. The Flyers, according to the official league announcement, "assigned the contract of RHP Nigel Thatch (Rookie) to Fullerton of the Golden Baseball League in exchange for one pallet (60 cases) of Budweiser beer."

...ANNOUNCER FOR A CARTOON CHARACTER: In 2006 NBC took over the Sunday night TV broadcasts of NFL games. They wanted Al Michaels, who had been with ABC for 26 years and the announcer for *Monday Night Football* for 10, to host the show. The Walt Disney Company, who owned ABC, wanted something unusual in return for Michaels: 26 *Oswald the Lucky Rabbit* cartoons that Walt Disney made in 1927. He'd done them for Universal Studios, so he never owned the rights to them, which is why he created Mickey Mouse (the two characters look very similar). Disney had always wanted the rights back, and NBC now owned Universal, so they agreed to trade the rights to Michaels...for the rights to Oswald.

...BALLS FOR A BALLPLAYER: In 1989 pitcher Tim Fortugno was traded by the minor-league Reno Silver Sox to the Milwaukee Brewers organization for $2,500...and 144 baseballs.

...CATCHER FOR HIMSELF: Harry Chiti was a journeyman catcher who played for the Chicago Cubs, Kansas City Athletics, Detroit Tigers, and New York Mets in the 1950s and '60s. His career statistics are unimpressive, but he does hold claim to one fascinating piece of baseball history. In 1962 the New York Mets bought the rights to Chiti from the Cleveland Indians for "a player to be named later in the season." The Mets then traded him back to Cleveland. So the player the Indians ended up getting later in the season: Harry Chiti.

About 1,000 people have climbed to the top of Mt. Everest. More than 160 have died trying.

I SCARE NOTHING! EVEN YOU BECOME NAPKINS!

Uncle John loves martial-arts movies (see the Bruce Lee bio on page 303) because of the action…and hilarious dialogue. Here are some actual English subtitles from martial-arts movies made (and translated) in Hong Kong.

"Fat head! Look at you! You're full of cholesterol."

"The tongue is so ugly. Let's imagine it to be Tom Cruise."

"It took my seven digestive pills to dissolve your hairy crab!"

"Dance the lion for others for just some stinking money! It's like razing my brows with the kung-fu I taught you."

"Alternatively, you must follow my advice whenever I say 'maltose.'"

"If you nag on, I'll strangle you with chewing gum."

"A red moon? Why don't you say 'blue buttocks'?"

"Let us not forget to form a team up together and go into the country to inflict the pain of our karate feets on some ass of the giant lizard person."

"Catherine is a nasbian!"

"A poor band player I was, but now I am crocodile king."

"Aha! I forget nothing. Elephant balls!"

"Watch out! The road is very sweaty."

"The wet nurse wants rock candy to decoct papayas."

"Cool! You really can't see the edges of the tea-bag underwear."

"Beauty and charm is yours, to you I run. I'd never leave, even forced by gun. I'd always want you, even if you were a nun."

"I scare nothing! Even you become napkins!"

"Your dad is an iron worker, your mom sells beans!"

"Same old rules: no eyes, no groin."

"I'm Urine Pot the Hero!"

Fans of the Belgian soccer team K.R.C. Genk go to games dressed as Smurfs.

LORD STANLEY'S CUP

The Stanley Cup, awarded annually to the best team in the National Hockey League, is the oldest trophy in North American professional sports. And you don't have to be a hardcore hockey fan to find the cup's history fascinating.

THE FATHER AND SONS OF HOCKEY

Lord Arthur Frederick Stanley of Preston, England, son of the 14th Earl of Derby, was appointed governor-general of the Dominion of Canada in 1888. When he arrived in the country he brought his seven ice-skating sons with him. They fell in love with the rough-and-tumble game of hockey and went on to become some of the best players of their time.

Nineteen-year-old Arthur Stanley and his brother Algy nagged their father for support in organizing the game into teams and leagues, and for a trophy to show as "an outward and visible sign of the ice hockey championship." Dad finally came through. At a dinner for the Ottawa Amateur Athletic Association on March 18, 1892, a member of the governor-general's staff, Lord Kilcoursie (also a hockey player), made this announcement on behalf of Lord Stanley:

> I have for some time been thinking that it would be a good thing if there were a challenge cup which should be held from year to year by the champion hockey team in the Dominion. There does not appear to be any such outward sign of a championship at present, and considering the general interest which matches now elicit, and the importance of having the game played fairly and under rules generally recognized, I am willing to give a cup which shall be held from year to year by the winning team.

THE TROPHY

Lord Stanley instructed an aide in England to order a gold-lined silver bowl to be used as the trophy. The bowl measured 7 ½ inches high and 11 ½ inches in diameter, and cost about $50. Original name: Dominion Hockey Challenge Cup. But everyone called it the Lord Stanley Cup.

Stanley appointed two trustees and outlined some conditions:

• The winners are to return the Cup promptly when required by

The Stanley Cup trophy weighs 32 pounds.

the trustees in order that it may be handed over to any other team which may win it.

• Each winning team is to have the club name and year engraved on a silver ring fitted on the Cup.

• The Cup is to remain a challenge competition and not the property of any one team, even if won more than once.

• The trustees are to maintain absolute authority in all disputes over the winner of the Cup.

• A substitute trustee will be named in the event that one of the existing trustees drops out.

GOING HOME
The boys got their trophy, and the game of hockey grew in popularity. But, ironically, they never got to play for it, and Lord Stanley, the father of organized hockey, never saw a Stanley Cup game. In July 1893, Stanley's brother died and Stanley was called back to England to become the 16th Earl of Derby. He never returned to watch a game for the trophy that bore his name.

Lord Stanley had the trustees present the trophy the first year, 1893, to the Montreal Amateur Athletic Association, which had won an amateur tournament. Then they arranged for an actual championship game between his hometown Ottawa team and Toronto. But the game never took place.

Ottawa was considered the best team, but the trustees insisted they play a "challenge game" since it was a "challenge cup." They also insisted that the game be played in Toronto. Ottawa refused to do it. So the trustees declared the Montreal AAA the first Stanley Cup champions in 1893, without a playoff.

THE PLAYOFFS BEGIN
The first official Stanley Cup playoff game took place on March 22, 1894, when Ottawa challenged Montreal in the Montreal Victoria Arena before 5,000 fans. Montreal got to keep the Cup, winning the game 3–1.

Lord Stanley's announcement and his order of a small silver cup would mark the beginning of what would become Canada's national wintertime sport…and a game still played internationally more than a century later.

THE HISTORY OF FOOTBALL, PART I

*If you're a fan of the NFL, you may not realize that football
was invented by college students long before the pros
came along. Here's Part I. Hut, hut, hike!*

CLASS WARFARE

In 1827 the sophomores of Harvard University challenged the freshman class to a game of "ball," to be played on the first Monday of the new academic year. The freshmen accepted.

That first game was a pretty informal affair; they just kicked around an inflated pig's bladder—a *pigskin*. There were few rules and there was no limit to how many people could play on each team, so the *entire* freshman class played the *entire* sophomore class, minus anyone who chickened out. The young gentlemen— many of whom were very drunk—must have had a good time, because the freshman-sophomore ball game became an annual Harvard tradition.

…A very violent Harvard tradition: "The game consisted of kicking, pushing, slugging, and getting angry," Allison Danzig writes in *The History of American Football.* "Anyone who felt like joining in and getting his shins barked, his eyes blacked or his teeth knocked out, was free to do so." The sophomores had an advantage, because as returning students they could recognize their teammates on the field; the incoming freshmen could not.

Some years the game erupted into a full-blown riot, and even when it didn't it was still pretty rough; game day became known as "Bloody Monday." The 1860 Bloody Monday game was *so* bloody, in fact, that the university banned football altogether.

FOOTBALL IN AMERICA

By the early 1800s, many East Coast universities were starting to invent their homegrown versions of football, with each college making up its own set of rules. As with Harvard, many of these games were blood-sport rituals that allowed students to bond with their own classmates against men of other classes. Princeton

---

1st person to win 6 Olympic gold medals: Russian speed skater Lydia Skoblikova ('60 & '64).

played a game called "ballown" as early as 1820, and Yale began playing a rowdy form of soccer in 1851.

Because each university's game was different, the schools did not play each other until 1869, when Rutgers and nearby Princeton University both adopted the soccer rules of the London Football Association and played what historians consider to be the country's first intercollegiate football game. (Rutgers won, 6–4.)

Columbia and Yale started playing Rutgers and Princeton in 1870; and in 1871, Harvard lifted their ban on football, but they played their own version, known as "the Boston Game." Unlike the soccer played at other universities, the Boston Game was more than just a kicking game. A player could pick up the ball whenever he wanted and pass it to his teammates; he was even allowed to run with it. As such the Boston Game game had a lot in common with rugby, a game that had been invented at England's now-famous Rugby School in 1823. The game is said to have come into being during an ordinary soccer game, when the ringing of the clock tower's bell was about to bring an end to the game at the stroke of five. The player closest to the ball was too far away from the goal to kick the ball there, so he picked up the ball and ran across the goal line, just as the clock struck five.

Carrying the ball was against the rules, but it was also fun. And as the Rugby students quickly realized, so was tackling the ball carrier. "Rugby rules" football soon began to emerge as a separate sport. Rugby even developed its own egg-shaped ball, which was easier to carry under the arm than the traditional round ball.

CANADIAN IMPORT

In 1874 the rugby team at Canada's McGill University challenged Harvard to a series of three games of football. On May 14, the two schools played the Boston Game. Harvard won, 3–0. The next day, they played rugby, which meant that tackling was allowed, and *carrying* the ball across the goal line and touching the ground with it—making a "touchdown"—was scored just like a kicked goal.

Switching from the Boston Game to rugby wasn't easy for the Harvard team, since no one on the team had ever even seen rugby played before. The game ended in a 0–0 tie, but the Harvard team enjoyed rugby so much that when they made a trip to

Montreal later that year to play the third game, they played rugby again. This time they beat McGill 3–0, and were so taken with the new game that they abandoned the Boston Game and switched to rugby.

GETTING THE BALL ROLLING

In 1875 Yale decided to try rugby and challenged Harvard to a game. The game retained much of its rugby character, with a few concessions to Yale's rules thrown in for good measure: Touchdowns, for example, had no value, but gave the scoring team a chance to kick a goal.

A record crowd of 2,000 spectators showed up to watch the game that day, and though Yale lost, 0–4, the Yale players had fun. They switched to rugby in 1876.

Two Princeton students watching in the stands that afternoon enjoyed the Harvard-Yale game so much that they convinced the Princeton student body to change over to rugby and to invite representatives from Harvard, Yale, and Columbia to form the Intercollegiate Football Association to draw up a uniform set of rules.

THE THIRD MAN

Another person watching from the stands at that first Harvard-Yale game was a 16-year-old named Walter Camp, who would enter Yale the following year. Camp was thrilled by what he'd seen on the playing field, and as he left the game that day he made two promises to himself: 1) the next time, Yale would win, and 2) he would be on the team.

Camp got everything he wanted—he made the team and Yale beat Harvard, 1–0. And he got a lot more than that: He went on to play halfback for Yale (1877–82), then coached the team (1888–92), winning 67 games and losing only two. He also served on every collegiate football rules committee from 1878 until his death in 1925, and was so instrumental in guiding and shaping the new game that sports historians consider him the father of American football.

Ready to advance the ball downfield? Turn to page 101 for Part II of the The History of Football.

...were imported from Europe to help farmers control the jackrabbit population.

"HE SLUD INTO THIRD"

*Some of our favorite sports flubs were committed off
the field...and on the air by sports announcers.*

"He dribbles a lot and the opposition don't like it—you can see it all over their faces."

—Ron Atkinson,
soccer announcer

"This is really a lovely horse. I once rode her mother."

—Ted Walsh,
horse racing announcer

"And here's Moses Kiptanui, the 19-year-old Kenyan, who turned 20 a few weeks ago."

—David Coleman,
track and field announcer

"We now have exactly the same situation as we had at the start of the race, only exactly the opposite."

—Murray Walker,
motor sports announcer

"It's a partial sellout."

—Chip Caray,
baseball announcer

"The Phillies beat the Cubs today in a doubleheader. That puts another keg in the Cubs' coffin."

—Jerry Coleman,
baseball announcer

"Anytime Detroit scores more than 100 points and holds the other team below 100 points, they almost always win."

—Doug Collins,
basketball analyst

"There are no opportune times for a penalty, and this is not one of those times."

—Jack Youngblood,
soccer announcer

"Coming on to pitch is Mike Moore, who is six-foot-one and 212 years old."

—Herb Score,
baseball announcer

"That was a complicated play, folks. So let's have a replay for all of you scoring in bed."

—Bob Kelly,
hockey announcer

"He slud into third."

—Dizzy Dean,
baseball announcer

"We'll be back with the recap after this message."

—Ralph Kiner,
baseball announcer

No ump-dump rule: In pro baseball, you can't replace an umpire unless he's injured or sick.

SWIM LIKE A SHARK

How Olympic swimmers are beating the clock with a little help from high-tech science…and low-tech fish.

SWIMMING SECONDS

Competitive swimming may seem like the simplest of sports, but at the world-class level, the clock is king, and shaving seconds (or hundredths of a second) off the prevailing record has become a painstaking science.

The best swimmers in the world have to master several components to win gold medals. Among them:

• Reaction speed: ability to be quick off the blocks at the start

• Acceleration: ability to reach maximum speed in the shortest possible time

• Maximum speed: peak swimming speed

• Speed endurance: speed that swimmers can sustain for long-distance races

IT'S A DRAG

To further complicate the situation, physics dictates that despite superior abilities, a champion swimmer has to overcome the problem of *drag* when he's trying to go faster. Drag is caused by the friction and pressure created by the water, which resists an object's movement through it.

There's *frontal drag* when an athlete swims and has to move water out of his way, and *skin drag* when water flows across the surface of his body (creating a turbulent wake around him that increases drag even more). Since smooth skin is known to create less skin drag than hairy skin, swimmers often shave off their body hair. This helps them gain about an extra second per 100 meters.

For millions of years, humans have been accustomed to moving through air. But water is nearly 800 times denser than air and 55 times more viscous (resistant to flow). The world's best swimmers have to struggle to get to top speed—which may be only four miles per hour.

Q: What two sports take place on a *piste* (French for "racetrack")? A: Skiing and fencing.

BODY OF WATER

Genetics plays a big part in making great swimmers. A swimmer with the right stuff usually has a tall, lean body. Most elite male swimmers are over six feet (Olympic gold medal winner Alex Popov is 6'7"). Long bodies give swimmers a longer reach for a powerful stroke, and being lean helps a swimmer cut through the water in as streamlined a fashion as possible.

Superswimmers also have big hearts—literally. Studies show that the best swimmers have large heart muscles, and some long-distance swimmers have cardiovascular systems that deliver twice as much oxygen to muscle cells as that of an average young person who's reasonably fit.

TECHNIQUE MATTERS

But it takes more than a "genetically correct" and well-conditioned body to bring home gold. Elite swimmers use constantly evolving technology. Videos, computer analysis, stroke digitalization, and physiological testing equipment are as much a part of world-class competitive swimming as practice laps and endurance conditioning.

One high-tech training tool is the *flume*, a type of "water treadmill" that coaches and sports scientists use to zero in on the strengths and weaknesses of competitive swimmers. Put a great swimmer in a flume, and you can videotape his or her winning form with stationary cameras above and below the water level. *Stroke digitalization* uses computers to identify points on the joints of her shoulder, elbow, wrist, and hand, and tracks these points through a stroke cycle so that even the slightest need for adjustment becomes obvious. During the test, monitors are recording the swimmer's heart rate, oxygen levels, and other metabolic functions.

RUN DEEP

Scientists are also helping athletes by studying the biomechanics of some of the world's other great swimmers—dolphins and sharks. The best human swimmers expend tremendous energy to reach four mph, but a dolphin can cruise easily at 20 mph. At those speeds, dolphins try to avoid the surface, where *wave drag* slows them down. When they're migrating, dolphins swim underwater and lift themselves up out of the water when they need to breathe.

A regulation WNBA ball is 28.5" in circumference—1" smaller than an NBA ball.

Some competitive swimmers are making use of dolphin wisdom: When they turn at the end of a lap, they'll glide faster if they dive and push off the pool wall at a deeper level.

SWIM WITH SHARKS...

Some swimmers try to mimic not just the techniques but also the *bodies* of fish. Sharks have *denticles* on their skin (scales like tiny teeth all facing toward the tail) that direct the flow of water over the shark's body, creating a thin film that reduces drag. A British shark expert helped Speedo design a bodysuit for swimmers called the Fastskin, made of a ridged material that mimics sharkskin. The suit is said to reduce drag by three percent. Does the Fastskin work? Michael Klim and Grant Hackett, who wore Fastskin bodysuits at the 2000 Sydney games, both won Olympic gold medals.

...OR SWIM LIKE A FISH

Some fast-swimming fish have fins that can be tucked away in special grooves to make them more streamlined when they need to move fast. Now some swimmers are wearing (and swearing by) special slithery bodysuits that compress their muscles and make their bodies more streamlined.

But in case you're thinking of taking up the sport and winning with some high-tech equipment, the experts will remind you that what you wear will not replace training and preparation. Technology aside, it's still mostly the body of the swimmer—and how well trained it is—that determines how fast you can go.

*   *   *

THE FISH OLYMPICS

The 100-meter Olympic swimming freestyle record is about 48 seconds, but that's a snail's pace compared to many of the ocean's inhabitants. The fastest fish in the sea—a sailfish—can move as fast as 67 mph, so it could finish the 100-meter human race in about 3.5 seconds.

In 1979 actor Paul Newman placed 2nd in the 24 Hours of Le Mans sports car endurance race.

A DAY AT THE (FOOD) RACES

Our favorite sport to watch is baseball. Our second favorite sport to watch is people dressed up like food chasing each other around a ballpark.

DO YOUR WURST

It's moments before the 7th inning at a game in Milwaukee in 2003. The crowd waits as the four contestants enter through the left-field fence. "Sausages, take your marks," says the public address announcer. "Get set…go!" The wieners start running along the foul line toward the infield. Guido the Italian sausage, wearing a chef's hat, takes an early lead. Trailing close behind are Frankie Furter, a hot dog in a baseball uniform, Brett Wurst in lederhosen, and Stosh the Polish Sausage in a rugby shirt. They're running link and link…until Pirates first baseman Randall Simon steps out of his dugout and hits the top-heavy Guido in back of the head with his bat! The Italian sausage goes down and takes the hot dog with him! Frankie gets up and keeps running. Finally, with the aid of Brett Wurst, Guido gets back up and hobbles to the finish line…in last place.

After the melee, Simon apologized profusely, saying, "I wasn't trying to knock her out. I was just trying to get a tap at the costume." *Her* was the costume wearer: 19-year-old Mandy Block, a Brewers employee. Simon was arrested for assault and taken away in handcuffs, but the 5'3" Block (over 7' tall in her costume) didn't press charges. "It's such a silly little thing," she said. "I'm just a sausage, guys. It's not a big deal. I'm fine." Simon was fined $432 and suspended for three games. He autographed the bat and gave it to Block.

MEAT ME AT THE PARK

Milwaukee's Sausage Races have been a Brewers tradition since 1994. They began as animated characters on the videoboard, but in 2000 the real-life wieners started racing at every home game. (In 2006 they added Cinco, a chorizo sausage who wears a sombrero.)

Roger Clemens built a horseshoe pit at George H. W. Bush's Texas home.

Not long after the Sausage Races became a sensation, other big-league parks decided to pit their "fast food" against each other:

• **The Great Pierogi Race:** The Pirates' Pierogies consist of Cheese Chester (yellow hat), Jalapeño Hannah (green hat), Sauerkraut Saul (in red), and Oliver Onion (in purple). A big hit at home games since 1999, the races begin as cartoons on the videoboard, with the pierogies dashing around Pittsburgh. Finally, they bound into the park from right field. (Twice a year, they take on the Brewers' Sausages in home/home relay races.)

• **Hot Dog Derby:** At every Friday home game in Kansas City, three costumed hot dogs chase each other down the right-field line, each wiener wearing a cap that corresponds to its preferred condiment: red for ketchup, yellow for mustard, and green for relish. (Mustard was the season champ in 2007.)

• **Racing Chili Peppers:** Accompanied by the Mexican Hat Dance and Speedy Gonzalez's shouts of "Arriba, arriba! Andele, andele!" red, yellow, and green chili peppers race each other down the right-field line at Toronto's Rogers Centre.

• **Hot Dog Bun, Ketchup Bottle, and Mustard Bottle** race each other around a virtual diamond on the videoboard at Baltimore's Camden Yards. There are actually more virtual races than real races at big-league ballparks, and not all are centered around food: Seattle has boats, New York has subways, Washington, D.C., has the four presidents from Mt. Rushmore (actually, these are real people in costumes), and, perhaps most exciting, Oakland's virtual race features four dots that chase each other around the screen.

*   *   *

HOW TO MAKE A BASEBALL FILM

"There is an unwritten rule in Hollywood that no baseball movie shall be made where the team actually has the fundamentals down at the start. Also, the first 15 minutes must include at least one scene where four fielders converge on a pop-up that falls between them."

—Paul Katcher, ESPN

Hotdoggers: Mark Grace and Hideo Nomo have both run in Milwaukee's Sausage Race.

LET'S PLAY BATHROOM BLACKJACK!

Tired of reading in the bathroom? Can't afford a trip to Las Vegas? Kill two birds with one stone—turn your commode into a casino. (Gives new meaning to the term "ace in the hole.")

WHAT YOU NEED: A 12-cup muffin pan, 10 nickels (which represent your cards), and 10 dimes (which represent the dealer's cards)

SETTING UP: Mark the cups in the muffin pan so that each one represents a different card. You can do this by writing the card names (ace, king, etc.) on strips of paper and putting one in each cup. Arrange them in order or at random; it doesn't matter.

• Since there are 13 cards in a suit but only 12 cups in the pan, the rim of the pan will represent the 13th card.

• Place the pan on the bathroom floor a few feet from the toilet.

HOW TO PLAY: "Deal" two cards to yourself by throwing two nickels into the pan. Where they land is what you get.

• Since in blackjack the dealer gets one face-up card and one face-down card, you're going to throw only one dime for the dealer right now. The dealer's other card will remain hidden.

• Compare your cards to the dealer's one card and decide if you want to hold or want another card. If you want more cards, throw more nickels. (Careful! If you go over 21, you lose.)

• Now throw a dime at the pan to find out what the dealer's second card is. In blackjack, if the dealer gets 17 or more, he must stay. If he gets 16 or less, he must deal himself another card. So if the value of the dealer's cards is 16 or less, throw another dime to get a third card. The person closest to 21 wins; if you both get 21, the dealer wins. If the dealer goes over 21, he loses.

• Use the remaining coins to play additional hands. If you're still playing when your legs go numb from sitting too long on the pot, it's time to admit you have a problem. Get help—join Bathroom Gamblers Anonymous.

Golfer Howard Twitty let Burger King put its logo on his golf bag. His price: 500 Whoppers.

NOT EXACTLY SEABISCUIT

Here's the story of a pokey little horse who won the hearts of Japanese racing fans...by losing every race she entered.

STEED WITHOUT SPEED

In the summer of 2003, the owners of a struggling track in Kochi, Japan, were looking for a way to keep from going under. Someone noticed that one of the horses competing in an upcoming race, an eight-year-old named Haru-urara ("Glorious Spring"), was just a few races away from losing her 100th race in a row—why not try to get some publicity out of it?

They convinced a local newspaper to do a story on Haru-urara, and the national press picked it up. Until then she'd been just another unknown loser, but Haru-urara turned out to be just the right horse at just the right time: Japan had been on a losing streak of its own—the economy had been in bad shape for more than a decade and unemployment was high—and the losing horse that kept on trying was an inspiration to Japanese workers worried about their own economic futures. Attendance at the racetrack soared from an average of 1,600 fans per day to 5,000 on Haru-urara's 100th race. (She lost.) Thirteen thousand showed up on her 106th. Japan's top jockey rode her...and she lost again.

NEVER GIVE UP

Haru-urara quickly became the most famous horse in Japan. Fans expected her to lose but bet on her anyway, just to get a ticket with her name on it—it was considered good luck. So many people placed bets on her, in fact, that she was often favored to win, even though everyone knew she would lose. Like a pro athlete, she endorsed products (she raced with a pink Hello Kitty riding mask), appeared in beer commercials, had her own line of merchandise, and was the subject of both a pop song and a major motion picture.

Best of all, she was saved from the fate of many losing horses—the slaughterhouse. Her trainer, Dai Muneishi, reportedly arranged for her to retire to a farm on the northern island of Hokkaido in 2006. "I don't really know why she's so popular," Muneishi says, "but I guess the biggest reason is that the sight of her running with all her heart gives comfort to people's hearts."

Fastest tennis serve by a woman ever recorded: 127 mph, by Venus Williams.

CARTWHEEL KICKS

These wrestling moves have very colorful names, but boy are
they violent. In fact, they're so violent that you wonder why
wrestlers don't get killed. Oh! It's because THEY'RE
FAKE! But just to be safe, please don't try them
at home—somebody's brain might get busted.

Forward Russian Leg Sweep. Stand next to your opponent, facing in the same direction. Wrap one arm around his (or her) neck, and step in front of his nearest leg, hooking it. Then fall forward, and cause your opponent to fall face-first onto the mat.

Airplane Spin. Lift your opponent over your head and hold him so he is facing up toward the ceiling. Then spin around and around to make him dizzy, and then drop him on the mat.

Brainbuster. Lift your opponent up across your shoulders, hooking one of his legs with one arm, and cradling his neck in your other arm. Then fall to the side that your opponent's head is on, and release his legs, causing him to fall headfirst onto the mat.

Tilt-a-Whirl Pile Driver. Grab your opponent around the waist, lift him, and spin his body until he is upside down, then wrap your arms around his body to hold him in place. Then sit or kneel, dropping your opponent on his head.

Atomic Drop. Stand behind and to the side of your opponent. Grab his midsection with one arm, and hook one of his legs with the other. Lift him up over your shoulder so that he is parallel to the mat, then drop him tailbone first-on your knee.

Gutbuster Drop. Bend your opponent over in a crouch, then grab him by one leg and across his chest. Lift him up so that his body is facing downward, then drop him stomach-first across your knee.

Cartwheel Kick. Do a cartwheel in the direction of your opponent, taking care to kick him in the head with the side of your foot as it contacts his body.

Shooting Star Press. Climb up onto the top rope, then do a backflip, landing on your opponent.

A new baseball World Series trophy is created every year.

"FAN"-ATICS

Most of us merely pledge lifelong devotion to our favorite baseball team. Compared to these folks, we're wimps.

IF YOU BIRTH IT... Paul and Teri Fields are die-hard Cubs fans. How die-hard? When their son was born in 2007, they named him Wrigley. (Get it? Wrigley Fields.) Said Teri: "We thought if we called him 'Wrigley,' the Cubs would surely go to the World Series." Unfortunately for the Fieldses, they didn't.

TAKE THAT! An especially tense moment came in the Chicago stands during a 2005 World Series game between the White Sox and Astros. A Sox fan who'd been loudly teasing Patty Biggio, wife of Houston's Craig Biggio, somehow entered the Astros' family section, slapped Patty, and ran away. An innocent prank? Not to Patty. "She ran after him," said Craig Biggio after the game. "My brother-in-law ended up putting him against the wall. You don't slap a New Jersey girl and get away with it!"

A SHINING EXAMPLE. A 40-year-old Mets fan named Frank Martinez was once evicted from his apartment for his habit of running down the hallway when his team won, yelling "M-E-T-S!" He was also evicted from the Mets' ballpark, Shea Stadium, for *three years*. Why? In 2007 he brought a high-beam flashlight to a game against the Braves and, from his seat behind home plate, shone it into the eyes of the pitcher and infielders. After the Braves complained, security confronted Martinez and found the flashlight in his bag. (It wasn't just mean, but dumb, too: the Mets were down by seven runs...in a game in April.)

A NIGHT TO REMEMBER. In 2004 seven Red Sox fans road-tripped 1,500 miles to the ballpark in Fort Myers, Florida. Still feeling the sting of their team's heartbreaking loss to the Yankees in the 2003 playoffs, they *had* to be there for the first rematch. So they waited outside the stadium all night to get tickets...to a spring training game. "Hopefully, we'll remember this night when we win the World Series this year," said fan Sam King. "We'll look back and say, 'That's where it all began!'" Turns out, he was right.

The term "fan" was first used to insult baseball "fanatics" in the late 1800s.

ANCIENT ORIGINS OF GOLF, PART I

You might not think of golf as being similar to baseball,
hockey, or polo, but many historians think they are. In fact,
all these stick-and-ball games may have a single ancestor.

SCOTLAND'S GAME?

Most sports historians agree that an early form of golf was being played in Scotland by the 15th century. But games that involved the hitting of a small object—a stone or a carved piece of wood or bone—with a bent stick have been played all over the world for thousands of years. So why do the Scots get the credit? Because they added a simple signature ingredient to the already existing games: the hole. Earlier games had targets—a pole, a doorway, a tree—but historians say the Scots added the cup and made golf the unique game it is today.

And that's not all they added. They built the world's first golf courses, developed the basic rules and equipment that are still in use today, and started many of golf's traditions, including the 18-hole course, the yelling of "Fore!", and probably even the tradition of the visit to the "19th hole."

But what were the ancient games that the Scots took for their own when they created "Scotland's game"?

THE CRADLE OF SPORT

Experts say that golf shares its origins with games that developed in Europe and Asia. Some theorize that the games go all the way back to the cradle of civilization—the city-states of the Sumerians in Mesopotamia (present-day Iraq). As far back as 3000 B.C., they say, the Sumerians played a game known as *pukku-mikku*, a ritual, religious-themed game that was representational of their creation myth. It was played with a stick, the *mikku*, and a hoop or ball, the *pukku*. (The pukku and the mikku are mentioned in the *Epic of Gilgamesh*, the world's oldest known written story, from about 2100 B.C.)

Is it going too far to say this game could be the origin of most of the stick-and-ball games that exist today? Consider this: the

---

Birthplace of bungee jumping: the island nation of Vanuatu, where locals jump...

Sumerians invented the wheel. They also created the 12-month calendar and the world's first writing system. As Sumerian technology spread throughout the ancient world, other aspects of their culture—including their games—probably did, too.

PHARAOH'S FIELD HOCKEY

The oldest known depiction of a stick-and-ball game comes from the ancient Egyptians (who were themselves greatly influenced by the Sumerians). Painted scenes in Egyptian tombs depict people engaged in a variety of sports, such as gymnastics, swimming, juggling, and wrestling. In one famous scene carved into a wall in the burial chamber of Prince Kheti in Beni Hassan in the Nile valley, two men are shown facing each other, bent at the waist and poised over a ball (or possibly a small hoop), holding long sticks with curved ends. Put gloves, helmets, and skates on them and it's a picture of a hockey face-off…made more than 4,000 years ago.

ASIAN GAMES

Some games that may trace their roots to the Sumerians:

• **Chogan.** This game was played on horseback and is believed to be polo's precursor. It was developed by Persian tribes around the sixth century B.C. and was probably first played without horses. An inscription on a stone tablet found in the Persian city of Gilgit (in modern-day Iran) describes the importance of chogan:

> Let other people play at other things.
> The king of games is still the game of kings.

• **Sagol kangjei.** Another pololike game, it was played by the Manipuri people in India as early as 30 B.C. *Sagol* means "pony" or "horse," *kang* means "ball" or "round object," and a *jei* is the stick used for hitting the *kang*. (The Manipuri claim that this is the real ancestor of polo.)

• **Dakyu.** Played in Japan for more than a thousand years, dakyu may be a descendant of chogan, brought to Japan through China. It looks like a cross between polo and lacrosse, with players on horseback using pouch-fitted sticks to hurl a ball toward a goal. Dakyu is still played in Japan today.

THE ROMAN ROAD TO ABERDEEN

A marble sculpture from ancient Greece dating to around 514

B.C. shows young men playing field hockey, a game the Greeks called *keritizin*. It is very likely that they inherited the game from the Egyptians, whom they had conquered. The Romans were greatly influenced by the Greeks and many believe that they took keritizin and developed their own game—*paganica*—from it. It was played on streets or in the countryside and involved hitting a feather- or wool-stuffed leather ball with a specially made stick.

The Romans took paganica with them as they conquered nearly all of Europe. Historians believe that paganica would develop into different games all over the continent... including the one (or ones) that eventually made it to Scotland and became golf. There are many different theories as to exactly how that happened, although spotty historical records make it almost impossible to know with certainty. Every modern region of Europe and many parts of Asia have their own distinct versions of the stick-and-ball game and most claim to be the basis for golf. But which one is the true ancestor?

To find out more about the Roman games and the origins of golf, slice on over to page 167.

*   *   *

TWO BASEBALL MYTH-CONCEPTIONS

Myth: *The tie goes to the runner.*

Fact: Actually, the opposite is true, according to major league umpire Tim McClelland. "There is no rule that says the tie goes to the runner. But the rule book does say that the runner must beat the ball to first base, and so if he doesn't *beat* the ball, then he is out."

Myth: *A player must touch the ball to be charged with an error.*

Fact: It's false, although you wouldn't know it by listening to most baseball analysts during game broadcasts. For some reason, this myth begins in Little League and sticks with players all the way up to the bigs. However, it says clearly near the beginning of rule 10.13: "It is not necessary that the fielder touch the ball to be charged with an error."

GRAY'S ANATOMY

*Uncle John loves stories about people who focus on
what they do have—not on what they don't.*

NOW BATTING...
At the beginning of the 1945 baseball season, the most
famous rookie in the Major Leagues was St. Louis Browns
outfielder Pete Gray. Playing for the Class AA Memphis Chicks in
1944, Gray batted .333 with five home runs and 68 stolen bases,
and won the Southern Association Most Valuable Player award.
While this alone would have been enough to draw the attention
of Major League talent scouts, there was something else that made
Gray remarkable: He only had one arm.

At six years old, Pete had fallen from a farm wagon, catching
his right arm between the spokes of a wheel. The arm had to be
amputated. For most people, that would have ruled out a career in
professional sports, but it didn't stop Pete Gray.

THE ONE-ARMED WONDER!
Growing up in the 1920s, playing ball on the sandlots of his
native northeast Pennsylvania, Gray developed a fielding technique that allowed him to compete with his peers. Catching the
ball in a glove on his one hand, he would roll the ball across his
chest, grab his mitt with the stump of his missing arm, pull his
hand out of the glove, grab the ball, and throw it. He performed
this complicated maneuver so quickly that it appeared to happen
in one quick blur of motion. This talent, coupled with his great
speed and strong throwing arm, made him a defensive star in the
outfield.

At the plate, Gray batted from the left side and, using a stan-
dard-weight bat, developed into a solid hitter. As he grew up, he
became a star in a semipro league, traveling a circuit of Pennsylvania coal towns. By the time he was in his mid-20s, he'd made the
jump to professional minor-league baseball.

During World War II, with much of baseball's talent pool serving in the military, Major League ball clubs had to hunt high and

---

First baseball player to be named Rookie of the Year: Jackie Robinson, in 1947.

low for quality players to fill out their rosters. On the strength of his MVP season in Memphis, Pete Gray got to play for the St. Louis Browns. He lasted only one season, with a somewhat disappointing .218 batting average (like a lot of players, he had trouble hitting a curveball). But during those war years, Gray became a hero for his determination and perseverance. He continued to draw crowds in the minor leagues until his retirement in the mid-1950s.

OTHER WONDERS

• Bert Shepard was a promising minor-league pitcher who joined the Army Air Corps when World War II broke out and then lost a leg when his plane was shot down over Germany. While still in a German POW camp, Shepard relearned how to pitch—a difficult accomplishment with an artificial leg. In 1945 he pitched one game for the Washington Senators, and was awarded the Distinguished Flying Cross in a ceremony between games of a doubleheader.

• Pitcher Jim Abbott was born without a right hand. He was lucky to have played during the era of the designated hitter, when pitchers didn't have to bat. Still, he had a career any pitcher would envy: 10 years in the majors. He even threw a no-hitter for the Yankees in 1993.

*   *   *

A SPORTS FIRST

Name: Georgia Thompson, of Henderson, North Carolina
Claim to Fame: The first woman to parachute from a plane
Date: 1913
Background: Thompson joined the Charles Broadwick stunt parachute team as a 15-year-old wife and mother in 1908, and made her first jump from a home-built biplane over Griffith Park, Los Angeles. In San Diego on July 4, 1914, "Tiny" Broadwick, as she was know professionally, made the world's first jump—man or woman—using a manually operated parachute with a ripcord.

Marathon runners lose an average of 0.4 inches in height during a race.

MUHAMMAD ALI: POET

Muhammad Ali had a knack for promoting himself and his causes (and taunting his opponents) with verse. Here are some examples.

There are two things
That are hard to hit and see,
That's a spooky ghost
And Muhammad Ali.

My face is so pretty,
You don't see a scar,
Which proves I'm the king
Of the ring by far.

I'm a baaad man.
Archie Moore fell in four,
Liston wanted me more,
So since he's so great,
I'll make him fall in eight.
I'm a baaad man,
I'm king of the world!

Keep asking me,
no matter how long,
On the war in Vietnam,
I sing this song:
"I ain't got no quarrel
with them Viet Cong."

I float like a butterfly,
Sting like a bee...
His hands can't hit
What his eyes can't see.

If you ever dream of
beating me,
You better wake up
and apologize.

Stay in college,
Get the knowledge;
Stay there till you are through.
If they can make penicillin
Out of moldy bread,
They sure'll make
Something out of you.

Joe's gonna be smokin'
An' I ain't even jokin',
But I'll be peckin' and pokin'
And pour water on that
smokin'.
Now this might
Astound and amaze ya,
But I will destroy Joe Frazier.

My opponents are like postage
stamps—always gettin' licked.

I done wrestled an alligator,
I done tussled with a whale.
Only last week
I murdered a rock,
Injured a stone,
Hospitalized a brick,
I'm so mean
I make medicine sick.

You don't want no pie
In the sky when you die,
You want something
Here on the ground
While you're still around.

Hi, Mom!

I'M GAME

You've played them. You've loved them.
Now here's a look at where they came from.

THE GAME OF LIFE

In 1860 young Milton Bradley's lithography company was in trouble; sales of his best-selling product, pictures of a clean-shaven Abraham Lincoln, had fallen off drastically when Lincoln grew a beard. Desperate, he printed up a board game called "The Checkered Game of Life." Players who landed on "Idleness" were told to "Go to disgrace"; the "Bravery" square led to "Honor"; and so on. It was perfect for the puritanical Victorian era, and sold so well that Bradley became America's first game mogul.

In 1960 the Milton Bradley Company came out with the 100th-anniversary "Game of Life." It became the second best-selling game of all time (after Monopoly).

PARCHEESI

In the late 1800s, a manufacturer approached Sam Loyd, one of America's premier game designers, with a problem: His company had a surplus of cardboard squares. Could Loyd devise some sort of game that would use the squares, so his company could get rid of them?

Borrowing from a centuries-old Indian game called *pachisi*, Loyd created a "new" game he called Parcheesi. It didn't take him very long. In fact, it was so easy that he only charged the manufacturer $10 for his services. Within a few years, the game became one of the most popular in the United States—but that $10 was the only money Loyd ever got for it.

TRIVIAL PURSUIT

In December 1979, Scott Abbott, a sports editor with the *Canadian Press*, and Chris Haney, a photographer with the *Montreal Gazette*, sat down to play Scrabble. Then they realized their game was missing four pieces. Haney went out to buy a new game...and was astonished that he had to cough up $16 for it. Abbott suggested

---

Women make up 39% of beginning golfers.

that they invent their own game. They tossed around some ideas until they came up with the magic word "trivia."

"I was the sports buff," Abbott remembers, "and Chris was the movie and entertainment buff. We sat down...and started doodling a game board. The whole thing was done in about 45 minutes."

They offered $1,000 shares in the game to friends and coworkers, but hardly anyone was interested. "I heard people call them small-time shysters," one colleague remembers. As Haney puts it, "Of course, it was no, no, no, and they all came to us later, and of course we said no, no, no." Abbott and Haney eventually raised the money to produce 20,000 games...and managed to sell them all, mostly in Canada. Still, according to Matthew Costello in *The World's Greatest Games*:

> Trivial Pursuit might have stayed just a moderate success if the daughter of the Canadian distributor for Selchow & Righter (ironically, the maker of Scrabble) hadn't discovered "this terrific new game." She told her father, and Selchow & Righter bought the rights to it. With their marketing push, North America was besieged by Trivial Pursuit.

Since then, more than 60 million sets—over $1 *billion* worth of the games—have been sold in 33 countries and in 19 languages around the world.

* * *

GREAT SECOND ACT

Athlete: Bob Uecker

First Act: Uecker was signed as a catcher with the Milwaukee Braves in 1956 and played for three teams over nine seasons. He retired in 1967 with a career batting average of .200.

Second Act: Since 1971 he's been the play-by-play announcer for the Milwaukee Brewers. On the air, he honed the personality of a self-effacing, lovable loser and made fun of his terrible baseball career. He carried on the persona in commercials, nationally broadcast games, and dozens of appearances on *The Tonight Show.* He even starred on the ABC sitcom *Mr. Belvedere* in the 1980s and had a minor but memorable role ("*just* a bit outside...") in the 1989 film *Major League.* Uecker was inducted into the Radio Hall of Fame in 2001, and the Milwaukee Brewers retired a Bob Uecker jersey in 2005.

Worst rout in NFL playoff history: the Chicago Bears over the Washington Redskins, 73–0 (1940).

DUBIOUS ACHIEVERS

Here are some of the stranger feats listed in Guinness World Records.

Joe Ponder, Love Valley, North Carolina
Achievement: Lifted a 606-pound pumpkin 18 inches off the ground with his teeth in 1985.

Randy Ober, Bentonville, Arkansas
Achievement: Spit a wad of tobacco 47 feet, 7 inches in 1982.

Neil Sullivan, Birmingham, England
Achievement: Carried a large bag of "household coal" 34 miles on May 24, 1986. It took him 12 hours and 45 minutes.

Travis Johnson, Elsberry, Missouri
Achievement: Held nine baseballs in his hand "without any adhesives" in 1989.

David Beattie and Adrian Simons, London, England
Achievement: Rode up and down escalators at the Top Shop in London for 101 hours in 1989. Estimated distance of travel: 133.19 miles.

Remy Bricka, Paris, France
Achievement: In 1988, using 13-foot-long floating "skis," he "walked" across the Atlantic Ocean from Tenerife, Spain, to Trinidad (a distance of 3,502 miles). The trip took 60 days.

N. Ravi, Tamil Nadu, India
Achievement: Stood on one foot for 34 hours in 1982.

Zolilio Diaz, Spain
Achievement: Rolled a hoop from Mieres to Madrid, Spain, and back—a distance of more than 600 miles. It took him 18 days.

Steve Urner, Tehachapi, California
Achievement: Threw a dried, "100% organic" cow chip more than 266 feet on August 4, 1981.

In baseball's early days, one umpire sat in a padded rocking chair behind the catcher.

HALFTIME

*More than 40 years after the first Super Bowl broadcast,
the halftime show is no longer just something to fill TV
airtime while the football players rest—it's now a
spectacle unto itself. Here are some highlights.*

HUT HUT HUT!
1967: Marching bands from the universities of Arizona
and Michigan perform.

1970: The NFL experiments with big-name celebrity halftime
entertainers. Their first big star: Carol Channing.

1972: "A Salute to Louis Armstrong," with Ella Fitzgerald, Al
Hirt, the U.S. Marine Corps Drill Team…and Carol Channing.
Armstrong had died the previous summer. Songs included "High
Society" and "Hello, Dolly."

1976: Up with People, a "clean-cut" troupe of young dancers and
singers, kicks off the yearlong American bicentennial celebration
with a collection of patriotic songs called "200 Years and Just a
Baby." Up with People returned in 1980 ("Salute to the Big Band
Era"), in 1982 ("Salute to the '60s"), and in 1986 ("The Beat of
the Future," ironically, their last Super Bowl appearance).

1988: Chubby Checker sings "The Super Bowl Twist" while the
Rockettes dance on a giant grand piano–shaped stage. The rest of
the field is filled with 88 grand pianos. The occasion: it's 1988.

1990: "A Salute to New Orleans and Snoopy's 40th Birthday,"
combines New Orleans musicians (clarinetist Pete Fountain,
Cajun fiddler Doug Kershaw, and blues singer Irma Thomas) with
400 dancers, a 500-voice choir, marching bands from three
Louisiana colleges, and actors dressed up like characters from the
Peanuts comic strip.

1992: To promote the upcoming Winter Olympics (to be broadcast, like the 1992 Super Bowl, on CBS), Brian Boitano and
Dorothy Hamill figure skate while Gloria Estefan sings a song
called "Pump It Up, Frosty."

Makes sense: NASCAR driver Jeff Gordon's favorite food is rocky road ice cream.

1993: Michael Jackson sings "Heal the World," accompanied by a choir of 3,500 children.

1995: Disney produces the halftime show, which they use to promote a new Indiana Jones–themed ride at Disneyland with an Indiana Jones–themed show featuring Patti LaBelle, Tony Bennett, Arturo Sandoval, Miami Sound Machine, and 1,000 dancers.

1998: "A Salute to Motown's 40th Anniversary" concludes with Boyz II Men, Smokey Robinson, Martha Reeves, the Temptations, and Queen Latifah all singing "Dancing in the Streets" together.

2003: Shania Twain performs "Man! I Feel Like a Woman" but is accused of lip-synching.

2004: Justin Timberlake and Janet Jackson play Timberlake's hit "Rock Your Body." Jackson's "wardrobe malfunction" introduces a new phrase into the lexicon.

2005: Paul McCartney sings "Drive My Car," "Get Back," "Live and Let Die," and "Hey Jude" (without lip-synching or exposing himself).

OTHER HALFTIME PERFORMERS
OVER THE YEARS

- Clint Black
- James Brown
- Woody Herman
- Helen O'Connell
- U.S. Air Force Band
- New Kids on the Block
- Diana Ross
- Aerosmith
- P. Diddy
- Tanya Tucker
- ZZ Top
- Stevie Wonder
- Phil Collins
- Travis Tritt
- The Blues Brothers
- The Judds
- No Doubt
- Enrique Iglesias
- The Rolling Stones
- Christina Aguilera
- U2
- Britney Spears
- 'NSYNC
- Mary J. Blige
- Prince
- U.S. Marine Corps Drill Team
- Tom Petty
- Bruce Springsteen
- Kid Rock

"We didn't lose the game; we just ran out of time." —Vince Lombardi

HOT WHEELS

*Roller skates have had a topsy-turvy history ever since the 1760s, when
an inventor demonstrated the first pair...and crashed through a
wall-length mirror. Since then, many skating pioneers have
tried to improve on the basic design. Here are some of
the more interesting models they've rolled out.*

ALL-TERRAIN SKATES

The wheels on these skates resemble miniature auto tires: lightweight magnesium alloy wheels with five spokes, mounted with a spring suspension system. With their wide wheelbase and low center of gravity, Skorpion Multi Terrain skates, which debuted in 2005, look like tiny dune buggies and are stable and easy to balance on, even while rolling over uneven ground. They've been billed as "Hummers for your feet."

Invented by a New Zealander who wanted skates that his grandchildren could use on the rough terrain around their home, Skorpion skates strap onto the user's shoes. They can traverse steep mountain trails, skateboard ramps, cracked pavement, cobblestones, grass, and even sand. They're reportedly popular with cross-country skiers who need to train in the summertime.

BODY SKATES

Jean Yves Blondeau, a French industrial designer and skating enthusiast, once said that he wanted "to prove that people can roll in any position." In the 1990s, he tested his theory by attaching more than 30 in-line skate wheels to a full-body aerodynamic plastic suit. He mounted the wheels on the hands, toes, upper chest, forearms, knees, back, butt, and feet. With the suit, a skater can roll while sitting, on hands and knees, while lying flat on the stomach or back, or even against walls.

Wearing his body-skate suit, Blondeau has bulleted down freeways in the Swiss Alps at 60 mph, raced—and beat—a motorcycle, and jetted down subways, staircases, and cobblestone paths at 30 mph. He was once featured on the TV show *Ripley's Believe It or Not!* and now sells his "Buggy Rollin' Suits" for about $4,000.

Q: What are **hurley, wicket, ricket,** and **break-shins**? A: Early names for ice hockey.

STILT SKATES

We're not sure why anyone would want to skate on stilts, but an early version of roller stilts appeared in 1868 in St. Louis, Missouri. Alfred Moe was a roller-skating performer who thrilled audiences by performing figure eights and other skating figures… all on stilts with wheels attached to them.

A more modern version of roller stilts appeared in the 1940s, with skates built onto the bottoms of tall braces fastened near the knee with leather straps. One early user was figure skater Earl Van Horn, who co-owned a popular roller rink in Mineola, New York. During its run from 1934 to 1960, Van Horn's rink often hosted the United States Roller Skating Dance Championships as well as an annual Winter Carnival. At several of these winter shows, skater Richard Brumblay performed on stilt skates, amazing everyone with his ability to *not* cripple or kill himself.

POWERED SKATES

By the 1950s, roller skates had already been popular for decades. But in 1956, a pair designed by a Michigan man named Antonio Pirrello made headlines, appearing on TV shows and in magazines like *Popular Mechanics* and *Life*. Why? His skates were powered by gasoline. A brave skater would wear a 19-pound gas engine on his back, complete with fuel tank and ignition system. A cable from the motor attached to the right skate and propelled it at speeds of up to 40 mph. The left skate, an ordinary unpowered one, was held in front of the powered skate to steer and brake as needed. Other cables ran from the motor to a handheld controller that regulated speed and could shut off the engine altogether to avoid runaway trips into buildings, cars, or bodies of water. (Skill not included.)

Motorized skates had appeared on the market before, but with both skates powered, they'd been hard to control. Pirrello's one-powered-skate design was more manageable for the average user, allowing the skater "to carry on the sport of power roller skating in a safe and enjoyable manner, without excessively increasing the hazard of falling." Still, despite the media attention, the skates never caught on with the public. Nowadays, a few pairs can be found in museums.

Former New York governor Mario Cuomo once played a season in minor-league baseball.

FLUSHMATE

The long and storied tradition of the World Chess Championship was nearly brought to a halt by a tiny bathroom and a player who (allegedly) spent too much time in there.

BACKGROUND

Few sporting events are more intense than the FIDE World Chess Championship. (FIDE stands for Fédération Internationale des Échecs, or the World Chess Federation.) Two chess masters face off in a series of 12 games to determine the world's best player. Because games can last for many hours, at various times breaks are allowed between moves, during which players often get up and walk around. To keep them from cheating—such as calling an outside party for assistance or secretly using a computer program to determine the next move—video cameras are placed throughout the facility...except in the players' private bathrooms. In the 2006 championship, held in the town of Elista in Kalmykia, Russia, it turned out that as many eyes were on a private bathroom as there were on the chess table.

THE ACCUSED

The match pitted Russia's Vladimir Kramnik against the reigning FIDE world champion, Bulgaria's Veselin Topalov. After four games, the two men were tied with one win and one draw apiece. That's when things got weird: Topalov's manager filed a formal protest, accusing Kramnik of taking too many bathroom breaks. The complaint described the breaks as "strange, if not suspicious." He requested that the appeals committee change the rules, eliminating the private bathrooms and setting up a single—and monitored—common toilet for both players.

The appeals committee agreed, but Kramnik was appalled and insulted by the allegations. His manager issued a statement, demanding that the original rules be adhered to: "The resting room is small and Mr. Kramnik likes to walk and therefore uses the space of the bathroom as well. It should also be mentioned that Mr. Kramnik has to drink a lot of water during the games. Mr. Kramnik will stop playing this match as long as FIDE is not ready

---

A piece of gum chewed by baseball player Luis Gonzalez sold at auction for $10,000.

to respect his rights," the statement threatened, "in this case to use the toilet of his own restroom whenever he wishes to do so."

Kramnik's team also insisted that the appeals committee members were unqualified and should be changed. In the meantime, they said, Kramnik would not play again until his demands were met.

THE GAME'S AFOOT

When Kramnik showed up the next day for game five, the appeals committee had not been replaced and, even worse, he found a padlock on his bathroom door. Kramnik refused to start the game, and instead sat on the floor in front of the bathroom door waiting for someone to come and remove the padlock. "My dignity does not allow me to stand this situation!" he fumed as he sat. But no one unlocked the door, and Kramnik was charged with a forfeit, giving the lead in the match to Topalov.

LET'S CALL THE WHOLE THING OFF

The situation became so dire that the FIDE president, Kirsan Ilyumzhinov, issued an ultimatum: If the teams could not come to a bathroom agreement within three days, the remainder of the tournament would be canceled. He added that he had full confidence in the appeals committee, and there were no plans to replace it. After a series of tense meetings, Kramnik and Topalov agreed to adhere to the original bathroom rules. The lock was removed. But Kramnik wouldn't back down on his demand that the committee be replaced, and, as one of the top players in the world, he had considerable clout. Result: a new committee was put in place.

So with the original private bathrooms restored, the match continued...albeit under formal protest from Kramnik's team, who believed that game five should have been replayed instead of forfeited to Topalov. Kramnik, using the jargon of the appeals committee, said, "My further participation will be subject to the condition to clarify my rights regarding game five at later stage." If things didn't go his way, he said, he would sue the FIDE and would "not recognize Mr. Topalov as World Champion under these conditions."

In 2008 Nike debuted the Trash Talk Shoe—the first athletic shoe made of 100% recycled goods.

"YOU'RE A CHEATER!" "NO, YOU'RE A CHEATER!"

Meanwhile, Topalov's team kept on questioning Kramnik's frequent pit stops, citing "coincidence statistics" that showed that Kramnik's moves following his bathroom breaks were an 87% match for what a popular chess computer program would advise. Kramnik laughed off the allegation, claiming that Topalov's "coincidence statistics" in another tournament were even higher.

Kramnik then turned the tables and accused Topalov's team of attempting to plant a device in his private bathroom that would falsely implicate him. Topalov fervently denied Kramnik's new charges, but both bathroom entrances were now being monitored. Topalov refused to shake hands with Kramnik, as per tradition, before each game.

ENDGAME

As the match continued, the hostilities between the two men grew even worse, and FIDE officials found themselves talking more to the press about bathrooms than chess. "This is a black eye for the game," said one. But the game continued—tense even for a chess match. After 12 games, the two players were tied. A "speed chess" tiebreaker was held the next day, and Vladimir Kramnik barely won it, making him the chess champion of the world...even though he sat out one of his games in front of a bathroom door.

Postscript: A month later, Kramnik defended his title against a computer...and lost. (It was the same computer program that he'd been accused of cheating with in his match against Topalov.)

*   *   *

SPORTS WORD ORIGIN

Word: Umpire

Meaning: Person appointed to rule on plays, especially in baseball

Origin: "From the French *noumpere*, which meant the same: 'one who decides disputes between parties.' Around the 15th century, people began to transfer the n in the word to the article: 'a noumpere,' becoming 'an oumpere,' and finally 'an umpire.' (It's the same way 'a napron' became 'an apron,' and 'an ewt' became 'a newt')." (From *Grand Slams, Hat Tricks & Alley-oops*, by Robert Hendrickson)

Pop quiz: What was Sam Malone's (*Cheers*) jersey number? A: 16.

NO SWEAT!

Copy this page and tape it to your fridge. It won't help you lose weight, but it might make you feel better.

"I exercise every morning without fail. One eyelid goes up and the other follows."
—**Pete Postlethwaite**

"Joined a health club last year, spent four hundred bucks. Haven't lost a pound. Apparently, you have to show up."
—**Rich Ceisler**

"I believe every human has a finite number of heartbeats. I don't intend to waste any of mine running around doing exercises."
—**Neil Armstrong**

"My problem with most athletic challenges is training. I'm lazy and find that workouts cut into my drinking time."
—**Dave Barry**

"I'm not into working out. My philosophy: no pain, no pain."
—**Carol Leifer**

"They say the best exercise happens in the bedroom. I believe it, because that's where I get the most resistance."
—**Jeff Shaw**

"I've been doing leg lifts faithfully for about fifteen years. The only thing that's gotten thinner is the carpet where I've been doing the leg lifts."
—**Rita Rudner**

"It is unnatural for people to run around city streets unless they are thieves or victims."
—**Mike Royko**

"Another good reducing exercise consists in placing both hands against the table edge and pushing back."
—**Robert Quillen**

"Exercise is bunk. If you are healthy, you don't need it. If you are sick, you shouldn't take it."
—**Henry Ford**

"I take my only exercise acting as pallbearer at the funerals of my friends who exercise regularly."
—**Mark Twain**

"They say exercise and a proper diet are the keys to a longer life. Oh, well."
—**Drew Carey**

Couch Potatoes: 25% of American adults say they never exercise.

THE BIRTH OF BASEBALL, PART I

Compared to other professional sports, baseball has changed very little since the modern era began in 1893. Before that, though, it went through a lot of rough drafts. So where'd it come from in the first place?

REWRITING HISTORY

One spring day in 1839 in Cooperstown, New York, a young man named Abner Doubleday drew up a diagram of a ball field in the dirt with a stick. He wrote down the rules on a piece of paper, declared the new game "Base Ball," and—voilà!—our national pastime was born. Fact? Unfortunately, no. That story is pure fiction.

Doubleday was a real person, a general who fought in the Civil War, but the account of his "invention" was fabricated at the turn of the 20th century by a former pitcher turned sporting-goods magnate named Albert Spalding. His goal: to increase interest in baseball in order to increase sales of sporting equipment. So Spalding attributed the origin to the heroic Doubleday in an attempt to paint baseball as a truly American game—not a knockoff of the English game of cricket. The Doubleday myth became baseball "fact" for much of the 20th century, and Cooperstown became the official "Birthplace of Baseball."

A REALLY BIG, CONFUSING PUZZLE

So why did Spalding make up the Doubleday story? Because tracking the actual history of the game was difficult. It turns out that baseball wasn't so much "invented" as it was gradually modified from many other similar sports over many decades. Most changes came one or two at a time, like pieces of a puzzle, each bringing baseball a little bit closer to today's game. Baseball historians obsess and argue over basic questions: When was the game first played in the United States? When was it first called "base ball"? Which men were responsible for which rules?

What makes the history so difficult to piece together is that early players didn't think the game important enough to document its every incarnation. Later in their lives, these same men (now seeing how important baseball had become) began taking credit for things they didn't do—or, in Spalding's case, giving credit to a man who may never have even *played* the game. "In short," says prominent baseball historian John Thorn, "recent scholarship has revealed the history of baseball's origin to be merely a lie agreed upon." Thorn and his contemporaries have been attempting to separate myth from reality, and, thanks to them, the fuzzy origin of baseball is becoming clearer.

THE OLD BALL GAME

Ancient Egyptian hieroglyphics reveal that people have been playing games with sticks and balls since at least 1500 B.C. Similar games turn up over the next two and a half millennia in many parts of Europe and Asia. The games that directly led to baseball, however, trace their origins to Great Britain, starting in the Middle Ages.

• **Stoolball.** The common ancestor of both cricket and baseball, stoolball is believed to have been first mentioned in 1086 in the *Domesday Book*, an English land ownership survey (kind of like a census). Gaining popularity in the 16th century, stoolball was played by milkmaids: One attempted to throw a ball at a milking stool while another tried to bat it away with her hand. A version of stoolball is still played (though not exclusively by milkmaids) in Sussex, England, where it is said to have originated.

• **Cricket.** A "wicket" replaced the milkmaid's stool, and a bat was used instead of bare hands. Originating sometime around the 1200s, cricket became England's national sport in the 1700s—and the only one considered acceptable for the well-to-do to play. It's a much different game than baseball—for starters, the bat isn't round—it's flat. One similarity: the batsman is called "out" if a hit ball is caught before it hits the ground.

• **Base ball.** In 1744 British author John Newberry wrote a poem about this sport in *A Little Pretty Pocket-Book*: "The ball once struck / Away flies the boy / From each abandoned post / To the next with joy." This is not the same baseball that we know, but the "abandoned post" is a precursor to the base. One other important word shows up: "boy." Base ball was a game for kids.

• **Rounders.** Much closer to baseball than to cricket, rounders originated in Ireland and became a favorite children's game. Like base ball, it featured four abandoned posts that a batter had to run to (whether he hit the ball or not), laid out in a pentagon-shaped field, perhaps the forerunner of the baseball diamond.

• **Town ball.** Based on rounders, town ball was popular in New England in the 1800s. Not only did its rules vary from town to town, it was known by different names, sometimes going by "cat" when there weren't enough players available for town ball. Some versions included baseball-like features such as, most notably, the first instance of "three strikes, you're out." But the bases were still unmanned pegs sticking up out of the grass; the "striker" hit a piece of wood, not a ball; a runner was retired by "plugging," or throwing the piece of wood at him; and as many as 50 players could play on each team.

THE JOY OF RUNNING AROUND

The first stick-and-ball contests crossed the Atlantic with the Pilgrims in 1620. According to Governor William Bradford's journal, the boys were "pitching ye ball, some at stoole ball and shuch-like sport." These games traveled well because they were easy to teach and required few pieces of equipment—just a good stick and something to hit. With the exception of cricket, though, none were taken seriously. The only reason that "base ball" was even mentioned in a 1791 ordinance from Pittsfield, Massachusetts: Playing it was banned within 80 yards of the town's meeting hall.

By the early 1800s, working people were able to enjoy something we take for granted today: leisure time. Up until the 19th century, unless you were rich or a member of the royalty, every day required long hours of work. But at the onset of the Industrial Revolution, urbanization and factories created America's first middle class, which led to shorter workdays and, even better, weekends.

CHIRP CHIRP

In the early 1800s, cricket was the only field sport in America with organized teams, making it the only "respectable" sport. But as strict Puritan values eased and the taboo against grown men running around playing games began to diminish, a new bias against cricket crept in. In addition to originating in England—from which the United States had only recently gained independence—cricket had another drawback, described by an early baseball player from New York City named William Rufus Wheaton:

> Myself and intimates, young merchants, lawyers, and physicians, found cricket too slow and lazy a game. We couldn't get enough exercise out of it. Only the bowler and the batter had anything to do, and the rest of the players might stand around all the afternoon without getting a chance to stretch their legs...We had to have a good outdoor game, and as the games then in vogue didn't suit us we decided to remodel three-cornered cat and make a new game. We first organized what we called the Gotham Base Ball Club. This was the first ball organization in the United States, and it was completed in 1837.

Was Wheaton telling the truth? He shared this story in an interview he gave in his later years. And when it comes to taking credit for the invention of baseball, Wheaton is far from alone.

PROUD PAPAS

"Every good idea has a multitude of fathers and a bad idea none," writes John Thorn. "Baseball has been unusually blessed with claimants to paternity." In 2001 a newspaper account from 1823 was discovered in New York City that mentioned the sport by name (without describing it in detail), making *that* the birthplace of baseball...until the 1791 Pittsfield ordinance was discovered a few years later. As other local historical societies dig through their archives, who knows what new evidence will be revealed?

Historians do agree on one thing: The "modern" version of the game truly took form when the men who played it took the time to write down the rules. That happened in New York when Wheaton's Gothams and their crosstown rivals, the Knickerbockers, first played each other in the 1840s with teams of nine players each. After that, tracking the evolution of the game gets a little easier.

For Part II of the Birth of Baseball, turn to page 266.

The *New York Times* is part owner of the Boston Red Sox.

OLYMPIC CHEATERS

*Some people become famous at the Olympic games because
they win a medal. Others become infamous because
they don't play by the rules. Here's a look at
the BRI's Olympic Hall of Shame.*

ROMAN EMPEROR NERO
Year: A.D. 67
Place: Olympia

What happened: Nero decided to compete in the chariot race. In the middle of the event, however, he fell off his chariot and was left behind in the dirt. He never completed the course.

Reaction: The Olympic judges, "under extreme pressure," declared him the winner anyway.

SPRIDON BELOKAS, Greek marathon runner
Year: 1896
Place: Athens, Greece (the first modern-day Olympics)

What happened: These Olympics were a matter of national pride for Greeks. So Belokas became a national hero when he won the bronze medal. But shortly after the games ended, he admitted to "hitching a ride in a horse-drawn carriage" during the race.

Reaction: He was stripped of his medal and running shirt, and became a national disgrace overnight.

JOHN CARPENTER, American runner, 400-meter finals
Year: 1908
Place: London

What happened: Scottish champ Wyndham Halswelle, the fastest qualifier and the person favored to win, was rounding the final turn neck-and-neck with three U.S. runners when one of them—Carpenter—shoved him sideways. John Taylor, another of the Americans, "won" the race, but not before a British official broke the tape and declared "no race."

Reaction: Carpenter was disqualified; Halswelle and the other

---

Jack Nicklaus and Sean Connery once teamed up to design a golf course in France.

two American finalists were invited to re-run the race two days later, "this time in lanes separated by strings." The Americans refused. Halswelle re-ran the race alone and won the gold medal automatically, the only person ever to win the gold in a "walkover."

MEMBERS OF THE EAST GERMAN LUGE TEAM

Year: 1968

Place: Grenoble, France (Winter Games)

What happened: The East Germans placed first, second, and fourth in the luge competition. Then Olympic officials discovered that they'd "used a chemical to heat the runners of their toboggans to increase speed."

Reaction: They were disqualified and forfeited their medals. But the East German team never admitted guilt, blaming the incident on a "capitalist plot."

FRENCH OLYMPIC AUTHORITIES AND THE FINNISH OLYMPIC COMMITTEE

Year: 1924

Place: Paris

What happened: Finland's Paavo Nurmi was the world champion long-distance runner. But for some reason, French officials didn't want Nurmi to sweep the gold medals in the 1,500, 5,000, and 10,000-meter events. So they scheduled the 5,000-meter final just 55 minutes after the 1,500-meter final, hoping Nurmi would be too tired to win the second race. Then Finnish officials arbitrarily dropped Nurmi from the 10,000-meter race so Ville Ritola, Finland's second-best runner, would have a shot at a gold medal.

Reaction: Nurmi was furious, but there was nothing he could do about it. He ran the 1,500-meter event...and won in record time. Then, less than an hour later, he ran the 5,000 meter...and won that in record time. Finally, according to legend, "as Ritola won the 10,000 meters by half a lap in world record time, Nurmi ran a lone 10,000 meters outside the stadium and beat Ritola's time."

GOLF GUFFAWS

*Golfing necessities: clubs, balls, beer, and some good
jokes to tell while looking for your ball (again).*

The golfer stood over his tee shot for what seemed like an eternity, looking up, looking down, measuring the distance, figuring the wind direction and speed. Generally, he was driving his partner nuts.

Finally his exasperated partner said, "What the heck is taking so long? Hit the ball!"

"My wife is up there watching me from the clubhouse," the guy answered, "and I want to make this a perfect shot."

His partner pondered this for a moment and then replied, "Forget it, man, you'll never hit her from here."

Golfer: Notice any improvement since last year?
Caddie: Polished your clubs, did you?

A retiree is given a set of golf clubs by his coworkers. He goes to the local pro for lessons, explaining that he knows nothing about the game.

So the pro shows him the stance and swing, then says,

"Just hit the ball toward the flag on the first green."

The novice tees up and smacks the ball straight down the fairway and onto the green, where it stops inches from the hole.

"Now what?" the fellow asks the speechless pro.

"Uh...you're supposed to hit it into the cup," the pro finally says.

"Oh great!" says the beginner, disgustedly. "*Now* you tell me!"

A man was stranded alone on a desert island for ten years. One day, he sees a speck on the horizon. He watches and waits as the speck gets closer and closer until out of the surf emerges a gorgeous woman wearing a wet suit and scuba gear. She calmly walks up to the man and asks, "How long has it been since you've had a cigarette?"

"Ten years!" he says.

She unzips a pocket on her left sleeve and pulls out a pack of cigarettes.

He takes one, lights it, takes

Shaquille O'Neal has a putting green in his front yard.

a long drag, and says, "Man, that's good!"

Then she asks, "How long has it been since you've had a beer?"

"Ten years!" he replies.

She unzips a pocket on her right sleeve, pulls out a bottle of beer, and gives it to him. He takes a long swig and says, "Wow, that's fantastic!"

Then she starts unzipping the longer zipper that runs down the front of her wet suit and says to him, "And how long has it been since you've had some *real* fun?"

And the man replies, "Wow! Don't tell me that you've got a set of golf clubs in there!"

Two friends play a round of golf together. One has a little dog with him and on the first green, when he holes out a 20-foot putt, the little dog starts to yip and stands up on its hind legs.

His friend says, "Wow! That dog's really talented! What does he do if you miss a putt?"

"Somersaults," says the man.

"Somersaults?!" says his friend. "That's incredible! How many does he do?"

"That depends on how hard I kick him."

The pope met with the col-lege of cardinals to discuss a proposal from the prime minister of Israel. "Your Holiness," said one of them, "The prime minister wants to determine who's better—Jews or Catholics—by challenging you to a game of golf!" The pope was greatly disturbed, as he had never played golf in his life.

"Don't worry," said the cardinal, "we'll call America and talk to Jack Nicklaus. We'll make him a cardinal, and *he* can play for us. We can't lose!"

Everyone agreed it was a good idea, so the call was made and Nicklaus agreed to play.

The day after the game, Nicklaus reported back to the Vatican.

"Your Holiness," he said sheepishly, "I came in second."

"Second?" shouted the pope. "Jack Nicklaus came in second to the prime minister of Israel?"

"No," said Nicklaus, "second to Rabbi Woods!"

Q: What are the four worst words you can hear on a golf course?

A: "It's still your turn."

LET'S PLAY STREETWARS!

*Adults can do some pretty odd things trying to
recapture the carefree fun of a lost childhood.*

SHOOT 'EM UP

Did you ever play "Assassin" in high school? That's the
game where every player gets a squirt gun and instructions
to kill another participant. Your mission: Kill your target before
the person who has you as a target finds and kills you. When you
kill someone, their intended target becomes your target, and the
game continues until only one person—the winner—is still
standing.

Assassin used to be limited to school yards, but that was until
2004, when a 29-year-old New York securities lawyer named Franz
Aliquo got bored with his daily routine. "I began thinking I had a
hell of a lot more fun when I was a kid," Aliquo told an interviewer in 2005. "And I thought, 'What is stopping me from having fun
like that now?'" That year he and and a friend from high school,
graphic designer Yutai Liao, decided to create a version of Assassin
that adults could play on city streets during lunch breaks, after
work, and on weekends. They called the game StreetWars and
organized their first tournament on the streets of New York City.

BE CAREFUL OUT THERE

Having people run around New York waving (squirt) guns and
blasting each other on city streets is a little bit much, especially
after the 9/11 attacks. To avoid potential problems, Aliquo and
Liao went to the New York Police Department to get permission
to play the game, and also asked for help in drawing up the rules,
to reduce the risk of public disturbances or being mistaken for real
gun-toting thugs. On the advice of the police, Aliquo and Liao
limited the number of participants and required players to use only
brightly colored squirt guns and Super Soakers that look nothing
like real firearms. (Water balloons are allowed, too.) They also
declared subways, buses and bus stops, and other forms of public

transportation off-limits. And to prevent the risk of participants losing their jobs, they also declared the one-block radius around players' workplaces as no-kill zones.

Getting the police department to sign off on the game was one thing; winning the approval of New York mayor Michael Bloomberg was another. "Aliquo could probably use some psychiatric help," Bloomberg said when he learned about the game. "If he calls one of the public hospitals, we'll try to arrange that. It is not funny in this day and age." Aliquo and Liao felt exactly the opposite—people needed games like StreetWars as a temporary escape from the bad news they confront in the headlines day after day. They went ahead with the game.

Seventy-five people signed up to play the first StreetWars, and it went off without a hitch. (Aliquo never did ask for psychiatric help.) Since then, Aliquo and Liao have organized tournaments in Vancouver, San Francisco, Los Angeles, London, Vienna, Paris, and Chicago.

KILL...OR BE KILLED
Here's how the game works:

• Each StreetWars tournament lasts for three weeks and is played 24 hours a day, seven days a week. It costs $50 to sign up and is open to anyone over the age of 18. When you sign up, you are required to submit a photograph of yourself as well as your home address, work address, and other contact information.

• Shortly before the game begins, players receive an e-mail telling them where to pick up their "assassination packet," containing the photo, addresses, and contact information of the player who has been designated their assassination target. Each player has a target and is the target for another player.

• As with Assassin, each player's mission is to "kill" their target and avoid being "killed" by the person who is targeting them. There are no restrictions on how the target can be hunted down. Stalk them on city streets? Ambush? A fake delivery to their front door? Anything goes. One assassin even staged a fake job interview and "killed" the target when they came to apply for the job.

• Players are allowed to defend themselves from assassins by shooting back and by using an umbrella to block the spray from the assassin's squirt gun. (Raincoats are not allowed.) If the assassin's spray does not hit the target, the target survives the attack.

• If you succeed in killing your target, your victim hands over their assassination packet and their target becomes your next target. How do you know when you've won? When you kill your target and the packet they give you has *your* picture and contact information inside.

• If a winner is not determined at the end of three weeks, the game moves into a one-week sudden-death tournament where Aliquo, who calls himself "Supreme Commander," becomes the target, and the prize goes to the first person who can kill him as he and his escort of bodyguards move by limousine from one safe house to another.

WITH A TWIST

• Aliquo and Liao have added a few more twists to the game, too: Players are free to form teams and work together to kill their targets. But then they, too, become a single target of sorts—if the team captain is killed, the entire team is out of the game.

• There's also a group within the game called the League of Rogue Assassins. These assassins are free to kill the players in the game, but since they are not players, they cannot be killed themselves. Don't feel like taking out your next target? You can hire a member of the League of Rogue Assassins to kill them for you.

• Another departure from Assassin: If you successfully defend yourself against an assassination attempt by shooting your assassin, the attack is thwarted…but the assassin doesn't die. They are free to attack you again at any time in the future.

SEE FOR YOURSELF

That's about all Uncle John has been able to piece together about the game; if you want to know more, you're just going to have to sign up and pay the $50. The official rules to StreetWars are a trade secret and are made available only to people who have signed up to play the game.

How many baseball gloves can be made from a single cowhide? Five.

YOU'RE MY INSPIRATION

*It's always interesting to find out how the icons of the
sports world inspire each other…and themselves.*

WE ARE THE GREATEST

Gorgeous George, with his permed blond hair and purple robes, was one of TV wrestling's original superstars. He sold out arenas wherever he played, and was named "Mr. Television" in 1949. But by 1961, his career was almost over. Meanwhile, a young boxer named Cassius Clay (later Muhammad Ali) was working his way up through the ranks and had just turned pro.

In 1961 George made a wrestling appearance in Las Vegas. To promote it, he went on a local radio show, shouting, "I am the greatest!" As it happened, the other guest on the program that day was young Cassius Clay, who was so impressed with George's theatrics that he went to the wrestling match that evening. The place was packed. "That's when I decided I'd never been shy about talking," Ali remembers, "but if I talked even more, there was no telling how much money people would pay to see me."

ALWAYS ON THE BALL

The National Basketball Association's logo is red and blue with the white silhouette of a player dribbling a ball. Who's the player who served as the model for the logo? Jerry West, star of the Los Angeles Lakers in the 1960s and early '70s.

FROSTY THE TOE-MAN

American Rulon Gardner became a star when he won the gold medal in Greco-Roman wrestling in the Sydney Olympics in 2000. In 2002 he was severely frostbitten after a snowmobile accident, and one of his toes had to be amputated. Gardner, who now travels the country as a motivational speaker, still has the toe. "I keep it in my refrigerator," he says. "It reminds me of what I went through and how lucky I am. It reminds me of how life is there to be lived to the fullest."

LET THERE BE LITE

*What's the number-one sponsor of sporting events in North America?
Beer. So no sports book would be complete without an article
about beer...especially the "lite" kind—which, by the
way, launched an entire 1980s food craze.*

AN UNLIKELY BEGINNING

According to beer industry studies, 30% of American beer drinkers—mostly blue-collar males between the ages of 18 and 49—drink 80% of the beer produced in the country. That means that every major U.S. brewery is trying to attract the same customers.

Traditionally, it also meant that "diet beer" was a recipe for losing money. Heavy beer drinkers weren't interested in dieting, and dieters weren't very interested in drinking beer. Why make a beer for people who won't drink it?

Those few breweries gutsy (or stupid) enough to brew a low-calorie beer were sorry they tried. In 1964, for example, the Piels Brewing Co. introduced Trommer's Red Letter, "the world's first diet beer." It lasted about a month and a half. Three years later, Rheingold Brewing Co. of New York introduced a low-cal brew called Gablinger's—described by one critic as "piss with a head." One company exec lamented: "Everyone tried it—once." At about the same time, the Meister Brau Brewing Co. of Chicago came out with Meister Brau Lite. For some reason, they targeted it at calorie-conscious women. "It failed so badly," said one report, "that it practically took the entire Meister Brau Co. down with it."

LUCKY STRIKE

In the early 1970s, Miller Brewing Co. bought the rights to Meister Brau's brands. They got Lite Beer (which was still in limited distribution in the Midwest) as part of the deal, but no one at Miller paid much attention.

In fact, Lite Beer probably would have been quietly dumped right away if company executives hadn't stumbled on something surprising in Meister Brau's sales reports: Lite was actually *popular* in Anderson, Indiana, a steel town dominated by the same blue-

---

NFL's heaviest player: Leonard Davis of the Dallas Cowboys tips the scales at 392 pounds.

collar workers who were supposed to hate "diet beer." Why did they like Lite? Nobody knew. Curious, the company sent representatives to find out. As Miller advertising executive Jeff Palmer recalls:

> The workers drank Lite, they said, because it didn't fill them up as much as regular beers. As a result, they felt they could drink more. And drinking more beer without having to pay more penalty in feeling filled up is beer drinker heaven.

According to Palmer, the company did more research, and found that male beer drinkers were interested in a good tasting "light" beer but were "clear, if not vehement, that the concept of a *low-calorie* beer was definitely feminine and negative."

So if Miller could figure out how to make Lite taste better, and at the same time think of a way to get rid of the beer's "sissy" image, the company just might find a market for the brew.

LITE CHANGES

Miller president John Murphy decided it was worth a try. He ordered his brewmasters to come up with a beer that tasted like other Miller brands, but still cut the calories per can from around 150 to 96. It took them a little over a year.

Meanwhile, ad people went to work on positioning Lite as a "manly" brew that beer-lovers could drink without being ashamed. They decided to build an advertising campaign around "regular guy" celebrities, famous people with whom beer drinkers would be comfortable having a beer in their neighborhood bars. The first guy they picked was Eddie Egan, the detective whose life was portrayed in *The French Connection*. "Unfortunately," one ad exec remembers, "he was under indictment at the time so we couldn't use him." Their next choice: journalist Jimmy Breslin. But he wasn't available either. The executives' third option: a few professional athletes...But Miller had a problem there, too—federal law prohibits using professional athletes in beer ads.

Miller was stuck. Who could they use? Who was left? While riding on a New York City bus, Bob Lenz, the ad executive in charge of Miller's account, came up with the answer. He noticed a poster of former New York Jet star Matt Snell, and it occurred to him that although advertising codes prohibited Miller from using active athletes to sell beer, there was no reason they couldn't employ *retired* ones. He called Snell.

"We taped him," Lenz recalls, "and once we saw the result, we knew we were onto something." Miller ultimately signed up dozens of ex-athletes for their ad campaign—from baseball players like Boog Powell and Mickey Mantle to bruisers like football's Deacon Jones and hockey's "Boom-Boom" Geoffrion.

SELLING THE BEER

As it turned out, using ex-jocks was a master stroke. Because they were a little older (and paunchier) than their contemporaries, they were easier for beer drinkers to relate to. Plus, they had nothing to prove—they were established heroes. If they said it was okay to drink "sissy" beer, no one was going to argue. "When Joe Frazier, Buck Buchanan, or Bubba Smith stroll into the bar and order Lite," wrote *Esquire* magazine in 1978, "you know you can, too."

Every spot ended with the celebrities heatedly arguing about Lite's best quality—was it that it's "less filling" or that it "tastes great"?—followed by the tagline: "Everything you always wanted in a beer. And less."

When test marketing of Lite exceeded sales projections by an unprecedented 40%, it was attributed largely to the advertising campaign. Blue-collar workers not only felt comfortable drinking a "diet" beer, they also understood that "a third fewer calories" meant that drinking three Lites was only as filling as drinking two regular beers. So rather than cut calories, most Lite drinkers *drank more beer*, and the sales figures showed it.

LITE BONANZA

Lite was introduced nationally in 1975, and had an astounding effect on the Miller Brewing Co.

• In 1972 the company was the eighth-largest brewer, selling 5.4 million barrels of beer—compared to number-one Anheuser-Busch's 26.5 million barrels.

• By 1978—three years after the introduction of Lite—Miller was in second place and gaining, selling approximately 32 million barrels to Anheuser-Busch's 41 million. Schlitz, Pabst, Coors, and other brewers were left in the dust.

As *Business Week* put it, Lite became "the most successful new beer introduced in the United States in this century." Its ads became as well known as the most popular television shows. Some of its spokesmen became better known for their work with Lite than for their sports accomplishments.

THE LIGHT REVOLUTION

It was only a matter of time before other beer makers got into the act. In 1977 Anheuser-Busch brought its muscle "to light" when it introduced Natural Light beer.

Miller fought back, suing to keep any brewers from using the words *Lite* or *Light* in their brand names. But the company only won a partial victory. The court's verdict: Miller's competitors couldn't use the term *Lite*, but were free to use *Light*—since it's a standard English word and can't be trademarked.

Enthusiastic brewers started bottling their own light beers, and "light" became the hottest product in the beer business. By 1985, it made up 20% of the overall market. By 1994, it was a $16 billion business and comprised 35% of the market. It's become a fixture at bars, barbecues, and tailgate parties ever since.

* * *

SPORTS SUPERSTITIONS

• Racecar driver **Christian Fittipaldi** loved driving on slick tracks, and liked a little rain during a race. For a good-luck charm, he attached a rubber ducky to the hood of his million-dollar race car.

• "The goalposts are my friends," says hockey goalie **Patrick Roy**, who played with the Canadiens and Avalanche and won four Stanley Cups. His pregame ritual: a "chat" with the posts. When asked if they talk back, he said, "Yes. They say 'ping.'"

• San Francisco 49ers head coach **George Seifert** won two Super Bowls. When he was coaching, he followed some elaborate superstitions: He wore his lucky blue sweater every Monday; ate Chinese food every Tuesday; refused to step on the helmet painted on the practice field; and, before every game, ran a ritual lap around the locker room...shirtless.

MARTIAL ARTS

There are numerous different forms of martial arts, and they come from all over Asia, including Japan, China, and Korea. Some, like karate and jujitsu, are on the martial end of the spectrum; others, like tai chi, are more, well, arty. Here's a look at some of the most popular forms.

JUJITSU. "Yielding or compliant art" in Japanese. Jujitsu emphasizes yielding to your opponent's force and using it against him. Developed at a time when samurai wore body armor, it also incorporates blows to the face and other unprotected parts of the body.

AIKIDO. A martial art with spiritual and even pacifist origins, this "way of harmonious spirit" idealizes defending yourself from attackers without harming them, largely by locking up their joints and tossing them aside.

JUDO. Translates as "gentle way" in Japanese. Gentle? It turns out that in judo, "gentle" means grabbing your opponent and throwing him to the ground...but without kicking or punching him.

KARATE. "Empty hand" emphasizes fierce blows to vulnerable parts of the body (throat, stomach, etc.) using hands, feet, elbows, and knees.

TAE KWON DO. Translates as "kick punch art" in Korean. Like karate, tae kwon do features sharp blows with bare hands and feet.

KUNG FU. A Chinese form of karate, practiced for more than 1,000 years. Kung fu favors flowing, circular movements over the sharp kicks, punches, and jabs found in other popular forms of karate.

JEET KUNE DO. "The way of the intercepting fist." A style of kung fu formulated by Bruce Lee, jeet kune do abandons the rigid stances found in many martial arts in favor of the more fluid movements Lee had observed in boxing and fencing competitions.

TAI CHI CHUAN. Translates as "supreme ultimate boxing," but it's actually a Chinese method of stress relief and relaxation through stretching, correct posture, and slow movements timed with breathing exercises.

The NBA instituted the three-point shot before the 1979–80 season.

DANCING FOR DOLLARS

One of the hottest TV shows these days is Dancing With the Stars. *But competitive dancing is nothing new. In fact, during its heyday in the Great Depression, it was a deadly serious business.*

LONGER, FASTER...STRANGER

Post–World War I America was in a mood to break all records: popular events included endurance kissing, hand-holding contests, and eating marathons. A guy named Shipwreck Kelly became a national celebrity after sitting atop a flagpole for 7 days, 13 hours, and 13 minutes (see page 133). When someone challenged Bill Williams to push a peanut up Colorado's Pike's Peak with his nose, he agreed. It took him 30 days, and he won $500 for the feat. It all had to do with the mood of the day. But nothing caught the public's fancy as much as dance marathons.

A CRAZE IS BORN

The birth of U.S. dance marathons can be traced to early 1923 when, inspired by a record set in Britain a few weeks earlier, a woman named Alma Cummings took to the floor of the first American dance marathon, which was held in New York City's somewhat seedy Audubon Ballroom. Cummings wore out six male partners over the next 27 hours and set a world record. Within a week, a French college student broke that record. A few days later, Cummings retook the title, which was soon broken again, this time by a Cleveland, Ohio, sales clerk. The challenge was on.

A few weeks after Cummings's win, a Texas dance hall owner got the brilliant idea of charging spectators admission (25¢ during the day, $1 at night). He gave his first winner—Magdalene Williams—a prize of $50. On April 16, Cleveland's Madeline Gottschick beat Williams's record with a time of 66 hours. Within days, that record was broken three times. On June 10, Bernie Brand danced for 217 hours (more than 9 days) and went home with $5,000 in prizes.

In just a few months in 1923, the dance marathon craze had swept the nation and the world. And so it continued throughout the 1920s.

In 1912 the Giants and Yankees played a charity game to raise money for *Titanic* survivors.

THE DOWNBEAT

The deaths of a few supposedly healthy young people at dance marathons—including 27-year-old Homer Morehouse from heart failure after 87 hours of dancing—brought some unwelcome attention to the fad. Officials banded together with church groups (who saw the marathons as immoral) and movie theater owners (who saw them as competition) to try to stomp them out. Critics called the contests "dangerous, useless, and disgraceful," and likened them to dancing manias—strange epidemics of dancing that swept 14th-century Europe.

TAKE A LOAD OFF

In an effort to save their golden goose, dance-marathon promoters added rest periods during which the dancers could lie down on cots, take hot showers, or have their injuries seen to. Some even let dancers take a short walk outside, but eating was done while dancing, at chest-high buffet tables set up in the middle of the floor. The length and spacing of rest periods varied from contest to contest: 15 minutes every hour, 11 minutes out of every 90 minutes, and so on.

Another change was that couples competed, rather than individuals. But a dancer wasn't stuck with one partner for the duration. If your partner gave out, you could dance solo for a set amount of time while seeking another, healthier partner in the group. Now, thanks to rest periods and partners who could hold you up while you slept, a marathon could last for weeks. But watching a dance floor full of droopy couples wasn't going to hold the crowd's attention, so vaudeville skits were added. So were professional dancers, who worked the crowd and posed as good guys and bad guys, like modern-day pro wrestlers.

A marathon that started with 100 contestants would dwindle to a few survivors after a week or two. The remaining couples would drag themselves across the floor, but at specific times the emcee would make an announcement, and the dancers would be expected to run a 10-minute footrace or perform an all-out foxtrot or tango—the losers of which would be eliminated.

Marathons were well established by the arrival of the Depression in 1929, and they became the perfect escape. If you could scrape together the admission, you could come in out of the weather and be entertained; if you were young and strong enough, you could enter and try to win a few thousand dollars. Even if you lost, you'd be well taken care of while you lasted: three square meals, snacks, and medical teams to treat your injuries and give you rubdowns.

Of course, you could be mistreated, too, by "grinds"—show employees whose job it was to prod contestants who fell behind, or generally harass the dancers to keep things exciting. Promoters staged weddings and fights and it was hard to differentiate between what was staged or genuine. But there was plenty of real drama: sleep-deprived dancers suffered hallucinations, delusions, hysteria, and bouts of temporary amnesia.

LAST DANCE

By the mid-1930s, the contests had lost their glitter. What had been lighthearted entertainment became a struggle for survival, and it showed. The country was in a depression in more ways than one. The marathoners, once viewed as respectable and plucky, were now seen as being no better than the vagrants who traveled the country looking for food or work. They became a reminder of the failed American dream, a symbol of how low the country had fallen.

One by one, states and cities across the country banned dance marathons. The shows continued on a small scale until the mid-1940s, but their heyday had long passed. Danceathons gave way to walkathons, which gave way to skateathons, which birthed the roller derby. But that's another story (see page 426).

*   *   *

UNBEATABLE?

According to *Guinness World Records*, the longest dance marathon was won by Mike Ritof and Edith Boudreaux at Chicago's Merry Garden Ballroom. The couple "danced" for seven months, from August 29, 1930, to April 1, 1931. The grand prize: $2,000.

The name *hockey* comes from the French word *hocquet*, meaning "shepherd's hook."

FAMOUS FOR 15 MINUTES

Here it is again—our feature based on Andy Warhol's prophetic remark that "in the future, everyone will be famous for 15 minutes." Here's how a few sporting folks have used up their allotted quarter-hour.

THE STAR: Tony Wilson, 29, a British light heavyweight boxer in the late 1980s

THE HEADLINE: *Boxer Wins Bout...With Help From Mom*

WHAT HAPPENED: In September 1989, Wilson fought a bout with Steve McCarthy. Wilson was losing: In the middle of the third round, McCarthy landed a punch that sent Wilson to the canvas for an eight count, and then pinned him against the ropes as soon as he got up.

That was all Wilson's 62-year-old mother could take. Somehow she managed to jump over rows of spectators, get past security guards, and climb into the ring. She removed her high-heeled shoe and began clubbing McCarthy on the head with it, opening a wound in his scalp. The referee stopped the fight for a few minutes, then ordered McCarthy and Wilson to resume fighting. McCarthy, bleeding profusely from his head, refused...and the referee disqualified him. He awarded the match to Wilson.

THE AFTERMATH: Newspapers all over the world ran the story the following day, turning Wilson from a promising fighter into a laughingstock—the first boxer in the history of the sport to win a match with help from his mother. He barred her from attending any more of his fights, but it was too late; his career was already on the ropes.

THE STAR: Jeff Maier, a kid from Old Tappan, New Jersey

THE HEADLINE: *Most Valuable Player? 12-year-old Cinches Playoff Game for Yankees*

WHAT HAPPENED: On October 9, 1996, Jeff Maier was sitting in the front row of Yankee Stadium's right-field stands, watching a critical playoff game between the Yankees and the Baltimore Orioles. In the eighth inning, New York's Derek Jeter hit a long fly to right field. The Orioles' outfielder probably would have caught it,

---

Babe Ruth claimed that he modeled his hitting technique after "Shoeless" Joe Jackson's.

but Maier stuck out his hand…and deflected it into the stands for a game-tying home run. The Yankees went on to win, 5-4, in 11 innings.

THE AFTERMATH: The home run was replayed on TV so many times that by the end of the game Maier was famous. The next day he made appearances on *Good Morning America*, *Live with Regis and Kathie Lee*, and *Hard Copy*. But he turned down a chance to appear on *The Late Show with David Letterman*, *The Larry King Show*, and *Geraldo* so that he could take a limo (provided by the *New York Daily News*) to see the next playoff game from front-row seats behind the Yankee dugout.

THE STAR: Joe "Mule" Sprinz, a professional baseball player from 1922 to 1948

THE HEADLINE: *Ouch! Blimp Ball Takes Bad Bounce*

WHAT HAPPENED: In 1939, Sprinz, a 37-year-old catcher for the San Francisco Seals, caught five baseballs dropped from the Tower of the Sun (450 feet) at the San Francisco World's Fair. The Seals' publicity agent was impressed and asked Sprinz if he'd catch a ball dropped 1,200 feet from a Goodyear Blimp, which would break the world record of 555 feet, 5 $\frac{1}{8}$ inches. "You'll become famous!" the agent promised.

Two teammates stood alongside Sprinz as the first baseball was dropped, but when they saw it break a bleacher seat…and then saw the second ball "bury itself in the ground," they backed off and let him make the third attempt by himself. "So the third one came down and I saw that one all the way. But nobody told me how fast it would be coming down," Sprinz later recalled. Traveling at a speed of 150 miles per hour, the ball bounced off Sprinz's glove and slammed into his face just below the nose, smashing his upper jaw, tearing his lips, and knocking out four teeth.

THE AFTERMATH: Sprinz spent three months in the hospital (and suffered headaches for more than five years), but recovered fully and continued his baseball career, retiring in 1948. He never made it into the Baseball Hall of Fame…but did earn a place in *Guinness World Records* for the highest baseball catch "ever attempted." Sprinz passed away in January 1994 at the age of 91.

THE HISTORY OF FOOTBALL, PART II

Uncle John has always wondered why college football is so popular in the face of the NFL. Answer: tradition. College is where organized football started. (Part I of the story is on page 49.)

LAYING DOWN THE LAW

In 1876 representatives from Harvard, Yale, Columbia, and Princeton met to form the Intercollegiate Football Association and draft a uniform set of rules that all of the colleges would play by.

The game would be essentially rugby, with some modifications. The size of the field was set at 140 yards by 70 yards (a modern football field is 100 yards long and 160 feet wide). And as in rugby, there would be 15 men on each team. The IFA also decided that one kicked goal counted as much as four touchdowns, and that whichever team scored the most touchdowns was the winner. If a game ended in a tie, a kicked goal would count for more than four touchdowns.

FIGHTING WORDS

The length of the game was set at 90 minutes, which was divided into two 45-minute halves separated by a 10-minute break (the clock was only stopped for scoring, injuries, and "arguments," so the games were usually shorter than football games are today). And instead of letting team captains resolve game disputes themselves, the new rules called for one unbiased referee and *two* opposing umpires, one for each team. That's what led to all the arguments.

"The two umpires discharged their duties like an opposing pair of football lawyers," gridiron historian Parke Davis wrote in the *1926 Football Guide*. "In fact, they were frequently selected more for their argumentative abilities than for their knowledge of the game." Arguing with the referee became a common strategy: if an umpire noticed that his team needed a rest, he could pick a fight with the referee and drag it out for 5 or even 10 minutes, until his team was ready to play.

What's the scientific name for any object that's shaped like a football? A *prolate spheroid*.

Some more rules:

- Every member of the team played both offense and defense.

- The ball remained in play until it went out of bounds or someone scored a touchdown or goal.

- Forward passes were illegal—the ball carrier could throw the ball to teammates on either side of him or behind him, but not to players ahead of him.

FROM SCRUMMAGE...

In rugby, at the line of play, the ball went into what was known as the "scrum" or "scrummage." Neither side had possession of the ball; the ball was tossed in between the rushers on both teams, who heaved and butted against each other as they tried to kick it forward toward the goal.

...TO SCRIMMAGE

Football guru Walter Camp thought the game would be more interesting if, instead of having the forwards on both teams fighting for the ball, "possession" of the ball would be awarded to one team at a time. The team in possession of the ball would have the exclusive right to attempt a touchdown or goal. One forward, called the "snapperback," would be the person designated to put the ball in play, "either by kicking the ball or by snapping it back with the foot," Camp's proposed rule explained. "The man who received the ball from the snapback shall be called the *quarterback*."

Camp pushed his proposal through in 1880. That same year, he succeeded in shrinking the field size to 110 yards by 53 yards and reducing the number of players on a team from 15 to 11. Modern football finally began to diverge from rugby.

A WHOLE NEW BALL GAME

The concept of "possession" changed the nature of football considerably. It vastly increased the role of strategy, elevating the importance of the coach in the process. Because the team in possession *knew* that it was getting the ball, the players could arrange themselves on the field in particular ways to execute planned plays.

But at the same time that possession of the ball increased the

Tim Duncan, the 7-foot-tall center for the San Antonio Spurs, is afraid of heights.

sophistication of the offensive strategy, it also weakened it. The defending team knew that every play would begin with the center snapping the ball to the quarterback, so the defensive forwards were now free to move in closer toward the center, ready to move in for the tackle as soon as the ball was snapped.

Football was already a fairly violent sport, but the new rules made it even more so by increasing the concentration of players at the center of the action. "Bodies now bumped together in massed, head-to-head alignments," Stephen Fox writes in *Big Leagues*. "Instead of glancing tackles in the open field, knots of players butted heads, like locomotives colliding, in more dangerous, full-bore contact."

BACK AND FORTH

There was a delicate balance between the strengths of the offense and defense in football, and the rule changes of 1880 upset that balance in ways the rule makers had not foreseen. Within a year, they would enact new rules to restore the balance, establishing a pattern that would continue for years to come: 1) New rules to counteract new tactics; and 2) New tactics to counteract the new rules.

GOING NOWHERE

The next round of changes was largely the result of outrage over the 1881 Princeton-Yale game. In those days, there was no limit to how long a team could retain possession of the ball and no way the opposing team could force them to give the ball up. A team retained possession until it scored a touchdown, made a field goal attempt, or lost the ball in a fumble. Players quickly realized that if they attempted neither a touchdown nor a field goal, they could retain possession of the ball for the entire half—and denying the opposing team possession also denied them the opportunity to score.

In their 1881 game, Princeton and Yale did just that: Princeton, awarded possession of the ball at the start of the first half, scrimmaged back and forth for the entire 45 minutes without attempting to score, and Yale did the same thing in the second half.

The Princeton and Yale players may have felt their do-nothing tactics were fair, but fans were outraged—and so were the newspa-

---

per sportswriters, who whipped the controversy up into a national scandal. Within days of the game, football fans all over the country were writing to newspapers to air their disgust. According to football legend, one such fan, who identified himself only as "an Englishman," wrote a letter to the editor proposing a solution: Instead of letting a team have possession of the ball for an entire half, why not limit possession to four consecutive scrimmages?

USE IT OR LOSE IT

The newspaper printed the letter, and someone sent it to Walter Camp. He was intrigued, but he was opposed to the idea of taking the ball away from a team that was putting it to good use. If the team in possession of the ball wasn't abusing the system, why should they be forced to give it up before they scored?

Camp finally hit upon the idea of giving a team the right to possess the ball beyond three scrimmages, or "downs," but only if they *earned* that right by advancing the ball at least five yards. If they didn't, they'd have to give the ball to the other team. As long as a team continued to gain at least five yards every three downs, they were allowed to retain possession of the ball.

Camp proposed this idea when the Intercollegiate Football Association met in 1882. It passed, as did Camp's proposal that football fields be marked with chalk lines spaced five yards apart, so that it would be easy to tell if a team had gained the yardage in three downs or not. American football moved another giant step away from rugby.

TOUGH GUYS

The introduction of the downs system helped make the game more interesting, and it changed it in another way that perhaps Camp had not intended: Now that teams had to move forward or lose the ball, agility came to be less valued than sheer mass and brawn, as teams sought to find ways to blast through the opposing team's forward line. Or as Parke Davis puts it, "The passing of the light, agile man of the seventies and the coming of the powerful young giant date from this period."

*Second down. Turn to page 141 for Part III
of The History of Football.*

Surfer Picuruta Salazar once rode a wave on the Amazon River for a distance of 7.8 miles.

BASKETBALL NAMES

On pages 15 and 341, we told about the origins of football and baseball names. Here's what we could dig up about pro basketball names.

Los Angeles Lakers. There are no lakes in L.A. The team was originally the Minneapolis Lakers; Minnesota is the "Land of 10,000 Lakes."

Seattle SuperSonics. Named after a supersonic jet proposed by Seattle-based Boeing in the late '60s. (The jet was never built, and as of 2008, the team is slated to move to Oklahoma City.)

Detroit Pistons. It's not named for that city's auto industry. The team's founder, Fred Zollner, owned a piston factory in Fort Wayne, Indiana. In 1957 the Zollner Pistons moved to Detroit.

New Jersey Nets. Originally called the New York Nets to rhyme with N.Y. Mets (baseball) and N.Y. Jets (football).

Houston Rockets. They began as the San Diego Rockets—a name inspired by the theme of a "city in motion" and its "space age industries."

Orlando Magic. Inspired by Disney's Magic Kingdom.

New York Knicks. Short for knickerbockers, the pants that Dutch settlers in New York wore in the 1600s.

Indiana Pacers. Owners wanted to "set the pace" in the NBA.

Los Angeles Clippers. Started out in San Diego, where great sailing boats known as clipper ships used to land 100 years ago.

Sacramento Kings. When the Cincinnati Royals moved to the Kansas City–Omaha area in 1972, they realized both cities already had a Royals baseball team. They became the K.C. Kings, then the Sacramento Kings.

Atlanta Hawks. Started in 1948 as the Tri-Cities Blackhawks (Moline and Rock Island, Illinois, and Davenport, Iowa), they were named after Sauk Indian chief Black Hawk, who fought settlers of the area in the 1831 Black Hawk Wars. In 1951 the team moved to Milwaukee and shortened the name to Hawks.

NHL player Mike Sillinger has played for a record 12 teams, and has been traded a record 9 times.

DUMB JOCKS

The BRI has been quoting dumb jocks since 1988. We're amazed (and a little alarmed) at how many great new quotes keep dribbling out every year.

"The only problem I have in the outfield is with fly balls."
—Carmelo Martinez, San Diego Padres outfielder

"Ball handling and dribbling are my strongest weaknesses."
—David Thompson, Denver Nuggets player

"All I want is for my case to be heard in front of an impractical decision maker."
—Pete Rose

"We'll do it right if we capitalize on our mistakes."
—Mickey Rivers, Texas Rangers outfielder

"We all get heavier as we get older because there's a lot more information in our heads."
—Vlade Divac, L.A. Lakers

"I would like to thank my parents—especially my mother and father."
—Greg Norman, after winning the 1983 World Match Play Championship

"Either you give me what I demand, or I'll take what you're offering!"
—Joe Torre, St. Louis Cardinals, during salary negotiations

"It's permanent, for now."
—Roberto Kelly, San Diego Padres player, announcing he was changing his name to Bobby

"Sure, there have been injuries and deaths in boxing—but none of them serious."
—Alan Minter, boxer

"I can't really remember the names of the clubs that we went to."
—Shaquille O'Neal, on whether he had visited the Parthenon during his visit to Greece

"Ol' Diz knows the king's English. And not only that, I know the queen is English."
—Dizzy Dean, responding to a letter on air that said he "didn't know the king's English"

BONEHEAD PLAYS

There's something oddly satisfying about seeing major leaguers goof up to the point that they look like Little Leaguers. (Our apologies to all you skilled Little Leaguers out there.)

FOUR! Only once has a big-league player committed four errors on a single play: In 1895 New York Giants third baseman Mike Grady tried to field a routine ground ball, but bobbled it (1). He threw the ball to first, but it sailed over the head of the first baseman (2), who retrieved it and threw it back to Grady as the runner rounded second base. Grady missed the catch (3) and the ball went rolling toward the dugout. He ran over and scooped it up, then tried to throw it to home, but it sailed over the catcher (4), allowing the runner to score on what should have been an easy out at first.

NIGHT OF THE LIVING EDS. In the early 1950s, Phillies right fielder Bill Nicholson hit a high pop-up that was destined to come down somewhere near the mound. Pittsburgh pitcher Bill Werle called for one of his fielders to step in. "Eddie's got it! Eddie's got it!" he shouted. Then everyone in the Pirates' infield stood and watched as the ball landed on the grass...including catcher Eddie Fitzgerald, first baseman Eddie Stevens, and third baseman Eddie Bockman.

FREE PASS. In 1976 Phillies catcher Tim McCarver came up to bat with the bases loaded. Not known for his power, McCarver hit a deep fly ball. He watched it as he ran toward first base...and was elated when it sailed over the wall! McCarver put his head down and kept on running. One problem: Gary Maddox, the runner at first, held up to make sure the ball wasn't caught. McCarver ran right by him. By the time he realized his goof, it was too late—he was called out for passing a runner, thus negating his grand slam. Asked how he did it, McCarver replied, "Sheer speed."

THE BALL WAS JOOST. During a game between the Red Sox and the Philadelphia A's in 1948, Boston's Billy Goodman came up to bat with Ted Williams on at third. Goodman hit a sharp

Ty Cobb racked up 271 errors in his career, the most ever by an American League outfielder.

grounder to A's shortstop Eddie Joost. The ball took a strange hop at the edge of the infield grass—it bounced over Joost's glove, rolled up his arm, and came to rest somewhere inside his jersey. He quickly untucked his shirt and started dancing (it looked like he was being stung by bees) until the ball finally fell out. By the time Joost picked it up, it was too late to even try to throw out Goodman at first. Luckily, the error didn't cost the A's a run—Williams was laughing so hard at Joost's dance that he forgot to run home.

HEAD GAMES. In 1993 Rangers center fielder Jose Canseco ran down a deep fly ball all the way to the warning track, but lost it in the lights. The ball bounced off of Canseco's head…and over the wall for a home run. The error has since become legendary. The television show *This Week in Baseball* awarded it the best blooper in its first 21 years of broadcasting. Also impressed by Canseco's heading skills was a professional indoor soccer team called the Harrisburg Heat, who offered Canseco a contract (which he turned down).

PICK ME UP. In the bottom of the ninth inning, in a tie game with first place on the line in August 2005, Angels closer Francisco Rodriguez threw ball one to Eric Chavez of the A's. Jason Kendall, representing the winning run, was standing on third. The catcher tossed the ball back to the mound. Rodriguez put his glove up…but the ball bounced out and fell softly onto the grass. Rodriguez just looked at it; the rest of his teammates later said they thought the ball wasn't even in play. But Kendall was paying attention. "You're never supposed to take your eye off the pitcher," he said after scoring the winning run just as Rodriguez went to pick up the ball. "That is the first time I've ever seen that happen," said Rodriguez. "Unfortunately, it happened to me."

WHAT RECORD? A reporter asked Red Sox catcher Doug Mirabelli, "Had the streak reached the point where no one on the team wanted to break it?" Mirabelli replied, "Streak?" Apparently, Boston had entered that July 2006 game with the all-time major league team record of 17 games without committing an error. "We set a record?" asked Mirabelli. Yes, they did…until Mirabelli made a high throw to second on a stolen-base attempt. "And I ended it?" he asked. "Sweet. Got to be remembered for something."

In golf, a score of 8 on a single hole is called "making a snowman."

RANDOM ORIGINS

At the BRI we're always asking ourselves, "Where does all this stuff come from?" So we searched through our vast sports library and came up with the following answers.

CHEERLEADING

In the late 1870s, the Princeton University football team (the Tigers) had a male pep squad that supported them from the stands with chants of "Ray, ray, ray! Tiger, tiger, sis, sis, sis! Boom, boom, boom! Aaaah! Princeton, Princeton, Princeton!" In 1884 football was introduced to the University of Minnesota, where a student named Johnny Campbell became the world's first cheerleader: he got up in front of a crowd and urged them to chant "Rah, rah, rah" along with him to help motivate the team. Soon Campbell led five other male cheerleaders (the college was all-male). As college football spread in the early 20th century, cheerleading spread, too. The first female cheerleaders hit the sidelines in 1927 at Marquette University. Paper pom-poms were introduced in the 1930s.

GREYHOUND RACING

Greyhounds have been admired for their speed as far back as ancient Egypt and beyond. For centuries it was a common pastime to release a live rabbit in front of two greyhounds and bet on which dog would catch it—a sport known as "coursing." Modern greyhound racing didn't come along until 1912, when a rabbit-loving New Jersey inventor named Owen Patrick Smith invented a mechanical rabbit, or *lure*, that the dogs could chase instead. The lure was connected to a system of pulleys so that, unlike live rabbits, it "ran" along a prescribed course instead of dashing in any direction. That made circular and oval-shaped dog tracks possible for the first time. Dog tracks were small enough that they could be located in urban areas, where the sport became popular with working-class sports fans for whom horse racing was too expensive.

ROLLERBLADES

In-line skates weren't so much invented as *re*invented: When a Belgian instrument maker named Jean Joseph Merlin attached five

People who practice karate are called *karetkas*.

small metal wheels to a pair of his shoes in 1760 and created what are believed to be the world's first roller skates, he arranged the wheels in a single line. It was difficult to turn or maintain balance with them, and in 1863 a New York inventor named James Plimpton invented the classic side-by-side "quad" skates. His design dominated the sport for more than a century. Then in 1979, Scott Olson, a minor-league hockey player, stumbled onto a pair of in-line skates from the 1960s while looking for something that would allow him to train in the off-season. Olson became a distributor of the skates, and when the manufacturer rejected his suggestions for improvements, he bought the patent rights to a similar skate. In 1982 he started selling Rollerblades (it's a trademarked name). By 1994 the company was selling $260 million worth of skates a year.

THE SAN DIEGO CHICKEN

In 1974 San Diego State University journalism major Ted Giannoulas was hired off the street by a local radio station to dress up in a chicken suit and hand out Easter eggs at the San Diego Zoo. He must have done a good job, because a few weeks later the station had him appear at a San Diego Padres game. The chicken was a hit: Giannoulas ran all over the field, jumping and prancing around, entertaining the fans. After that he became a fixture at the ballpark, performing at 2,500 consecutive Padres home games. (In 1979 the chicken suit was replaced with a custom-made chicken-in-a-baseball-uniform outfit.) The San Diego Chicken led to the emergence of fuzzy mascots throughout Major League Baseball, including the Phillie Phanatic, the Baltimore Bird, and the St. Louis Fredbird. In 1999 *The Sporting News* named the Chicken one of the 100 most powerful sports figures of the 20th century.

"LIVE STRONG" BRACELETS

In 2004 cancer survivor and professional cyclist Lance Armstrong teamed up with Nike in a massive fund-raising drive for his Lance Armstrong Foundation. Nike's ad agency came up with the idea of selling inexpensive rubber wristbands for $1.00 each, with the proceeds going entirely to cancer research. They decided to make the bracelets yellow because of the color's importance in professional cycling (the Tour de France leader wears a yellow jersey). By the summer of 2004, numerous celebrities and Olympic athletes were wearing yellow bracelets emblazoned with the foundation's slogan, "Wear Yellow, Live Strong." The results of the drive far exceeded Armstrong's goal. He'd hoped to raise $5 million by selling the bracelets. To date, more than $70 million worth of "Live Strong" bracelets have been sold. They've also inspired other causes to sell bracelets to raise money. There are bracelets for breast cancer (pink), wounded veterans (camouflage), and epilepsy awareness (half blue and half red). It's even a fashion statement—knockoff yellow wristbands can be found in discount and dollar stores all over the country, but the money doesn't go to any charity.

WORLD CUP SOCCER

Soccer was an Olympic event in the early 20th century, but only amateurs could compete. Professional players wanted to participate, but the Olympics said no, so FIFA, soccer's governing body, began holding tournaments for professional players in the 1910s and later organized the Olympic tournaments for amateurs as well. By the late 1920s, FIFA and the International Olympic Committee (IOC) were again in a dispute over whether professionals should be allowed into the Olympics. To make matters worse, the 1932 Olympics were scheduled to be held in Los Angeles, and soccer wasn't popular in the United States. When the IOC announced that it planned to drop soccer from the Olympics, FIFA stepped in and organized its own world championship, open to professionals and amateurs. Dubbed the "World Cup" by FIFA president Jules Rimet, the inaugural 1930 tournament was won by Uruguay, the reigning Olympic champions. The event went on to become the most popular sporting event in the world: more than 1.2 billion people watched the 2006 World Cup final on TV.

*   *   *

SPORTS FLOP: INDOOR ARCHERY

In the early 1960s, bowling was one of America's hottest sports. Hoping to "do for archery what automatic pin-setters have done for bowling," a number of entrepreneurs opened "archery lanes," with automatic arrow-returns. They expected to have thousands around the United States by 1970. The fad never took off.

THE ORIGIN OF BASKETBALL, PART I

Unlike baseball and football, which trace their roots to games that have been played for centuries, basketball was invented by one man—a Canadian named James Naismith—in a couple of days in 1891. It is the only major sport considered native to the USA. Here's its history.

SOMETHING NEW

Today the YMCA is synonymous with sports, but that hasn't always been the case. In the mid-1880s, it was primarily a missionary group. "In fact," Ted Vincent writes in *The Rise and Fall of American Sport*, "the Young Men's Christian Association condemned almost all sports, along with dancing, card playing, and vaudeville shows, on the grounds that these activities were 'distinctly worldly in their associations, and unspiritual in their influence,' and therefore 'utterly inconsistent with our professions as disciples of Christ.'"

GOOD SPORT

Then, at the YMCA's national convention in 1889, 24-year-old Dr. Luther Gulick started a revolution when he suggested that "good bodies and good morals" might actually go together. He insisted that keeping physically fit could make someone a better person, rather than inevitably leading them down the path of sin. He proposed that the YMCA use organized athletics to reach out to youngsters who might otherwise not be interested in the Y's traditional emphasis on religion.

His proposal met with heavy opposition from conservatives, who argued that a "Christian gymnasium teacher" was a contradiction in terms. But when Gulick's idea was put to a vote, he won. Gulick was put in charge of a brand-new athletics teaching program at the YMCA School for Christian Workers in Springfield, Massachusetts.

CHANGING TIMES

Gulick's ideas were actually part of a larger social movement. For

---

During a NASCAR race, the temperature inside a stock car can reach 140°F.

decades, America had been making the transition from a largely rural, farm-based society to an industrialized economy in which much of the population lived and worked in cities. Americans who had once labored in fields from sunup to sundown were now spending much of their working lives cooped up inside a factory, or behind a desk or sales counter.

"Middle-class Americans in particular reacted to the growing bureaucracy and confinement of their work lives, and to the remarkable crowding of their cities, by rushing to the outdoors, on foot and on bicycles," Elliot Gorn writes in *A Brief History of American Sports*. "Hiking, bird-watching, camping, rock-climbing, or simply walking in the new national parks—participation in all of these activities soared in the years around the turn of the century."

MASS APPEAL

Middle-class Americans who embraced physical activity as the answer to their own yearnings also began to see it as an answer to some of society's ills. The repeal of child labor laws and high levels of immigration meant that the tenement districts in America's major cities were full of immigrant youths who had little or nothing to do. Leaders of the "recreation movement," like Dr. Gulick, felt that building public playgrounds and bringing organized play programs into the slums would help the kids stay out of trouble and make it easier for them to assimilate into American life.

"Reformers thought of themselves as being on an exciting new mission, Americanizing children by helping them to have fun," Gorn says. "Playground reformers sought to clean up American streets, confine play to designated recreational spaces, and use their professional expertise to teach 'respectable' athletics." In an era in which public playgrounds were virtually unheard of, the facilities and athletic programs that organizations like the YMCA were beginning to offer often provided the only positive outlet for urban kids' energies.

BACK TO SCHOOL

As Gulick set up his program to train YMCA physical education instructors, he also decided to require men training to be "general secretaries" (the official title for men who ran local YMCA chapters) to take physical education classes.

These students were older and more conservative than other students. They hadn't been sold on Gulick's newfangled sports ideas and, left to their own devices, would avoid physical education classes entirely. Gulick feared that if he didn't bring these future YMCA leaders around to his point of view while they were in Springfield, they wouldn't implement his programs when they got back home...and his efforts would be fruitless.

COLD SHOULDER

Working with the general secretaries was a snap at first: In the early fall they just went outside and played football or soccer. But when the weather turned cold and they were forced indoors, things got difficult. The best recreation Gulick could come up with was a schedule of military drills...followed by German, French, and Swedish gymnastics. Day after day, the routine was the same, and the students became thoroughly bored.

THE INCORRIGIBLES

Within weeks, the class was in open rebellion, and two successive physical education instructors resigned rather than put up with their abuse. They told Gulick that he might as well give up on "the Incorrigibles," as the class had become known.

Gulick wasn't ready to quit yet. For weeks, an instructor named James Naismith had been arguing that the Incorrigibles weren't to blame for the situation. "The trouble is not with the men," he said, "but with the system we are using. The kind of work for this class should be of a recreative nature, something that would appeal to their play instincts." At one faculty meeting, he even proposed inventing a new indoor game. So when Gulick put Naismith in charge of the class, he commented pointedly, "Now would be a good time for you to work on that new game that you said could be invented."

*For Part II of The Origin of Basketball,
dribble on over to page 241.*

BINGO-BANGO-BONGO

Going down to the golf course for some weekend fun? Here are a few popular golf games and side bets. Just set a dollar amount beforehand (make sure it's one you can afford!) and swing away.

NASSAU. The "$2 Nassau" is probably the most common betting game in golf. It can be played between individuals or teams in match or stroke play. The format consists of three separate bets: one bet on the best score on the front nine, one bet on the back nine, and one bet on all 18 holes.

THE PRESS. This is a popular side bet used in Nassau. Say that, after the 6th hole, you're way behind your opponent and in danger of losing the front nine bet. At this point you can "press" the original bet, meaning make another bet that will start at the 7th hole and also finish on the 9th—so it's a new three-hole bet. If you win that one, but lose the other one, at least you break even. Note: you don't have to accept a press if you're the leader, but it's frowned upon not to.

BINGO-BANGO-BONGO. This game has three different bets per hole and gives less-talented players a chance to win. Separate bets are made on *bingo*, the first ball on the green; *bango*, the closest to the pin once everyone is on the green; and *bongo*, the first ball in the hole.

SCRAMBLE. This is a popular tournament format for teams of two, three, or four players. Each player tees off, then everybody moves their ball to where the best ball landed. They all hit again, and they all move to the best location again. That repeats until someone holes out. The team with the lowest score for the round (or rounds) wins.

GRUESOMES. This is for two two-person teams. Both team members tee off, but only one ball will be played to finish the hole. The fun part: the opposing team decides which ball you play. Obviously, it's going to be the more "gruesome" of the two shots. Whoever hit the gruesome tee shot goes second; teammates alternate after that.

Magic Johnson, at 6 feet 9 inches, was the tallest point guard in NBA history.

CHAIRMAN. This is a points game for three or more players. The first player to win a hole becomes the "chairman." If the chairman wins the next hole, he collects one point from the other players. If it's a tie, there are no points, but still the same chairman. If someone else wins, they become chairman, and so on.

WOLF. This is for four players. Set a teeing-off order and rotate through it so that a new player tees off first on every hole. Whoever tees off first on the first hole is the "wolf." After the second player tees off, the wolf must either select or reject that player as a partner before the next player tees off. Same with the third player. After the fourth player tees off, the wolf must either select that player as a partner or play against *all three* players. To win, the wolf and his partner (if one has been chosen) must have a lower "better ball" score than the other team—the "hunters." Bonus: if the wolf plays alone, he wins double; if he loses, he pays double. Variation: the wolf can declare "lone wolf" before teeing off, thereby immediately declaring his intention to play against the other three.

NINES. In this three- or four-player point game, each hole has a total value of 9 points. Best score is 5 points; second best is 3 points; last is 1 point. If two players tie for best, they split the first- and second-place points—they each get 4, and last place gets 1. If the worst two scores tie, the winner gets 5 points and the other two get 2 each. Three-way tie: 3 points each.

JUNK (or GARBAGE) is the name golfers give to a collection of side bets that can be made regardless of what game you're playing. Maybe you'll win a...

• **Barkie.** Also called a "Seve" (after Seve Ballesteros): if you hit a tree with your ball and still finish in par, you've won the barkie.

• **Cousteau (or shark).** Making par after landing in the water.

• **Sandie.** Making par from a greenside bunker.

• **Greenie.** First player on the green.

• **Nasty (or ugly).** Sinking a shot from off the green to make par.

• **Arnie.** Named after Arnold Palmer, for his ability to get out of trouble. This bet is making par on a par-4 or par-5 without driving on the fairway or reaching the green in regulation.

UNCLE JOHN'S PAGE OF SPORTS LISTS

Random bits of information from the BRI files.

6 Stars Who Took Karate Lessons from Chuck Norris
1. Bob Barker
2. Priscilla Presley
3. Steve McQueen
4. Michael Landon
5. Marie Osmond
6. Donny Osmond

The 6 Major Rodeo Contests
1. Saddle bronco
2. Bareback bronco
3. Calf roping
4. Bull riding
5. Steer wrestling
6. Team roping

The 6 Hockey Positions
1. Center
2. Left wing
3. Right wing
4. Left defense
5. Right defense
6. Goalie

3 Events in an Ironman Triathlon
1. 2.4-mile swim
2. 112-mile bike race
3. 26.2-mile run

4 Most Expensive Ad Spots on a Race Car
1. Hood
2. Lower rear quarter panel
3. Behind rear window
4. Behind driver's window

8 Defunct Olympic Sports
1. Tug-of-war
2. Golf
3. Rugby
4. Croquet
5. Polo
6. Lacrosse
7. Power boating
8. Waterskiing

5 Sports Nicknames Made Up by ESPN's Chris Berman
1. René "La Kook" Arocha
2. Rick "See Ya Later" Aguilera
3. Jim "Hey" Abbott
4. Chuck "New Kid On" Knoblauch
5. Mike "Enough" Aldretti

4 Sports You Can Win Only by Going Backwards
1. Rappelling
2. Rowing
3. Tug-of-war
4. High jump

5 Defunct Golf Tournaments
1. Hardscrabble Open
2. Girl Talk Classic
3. Gasparilla Open
4. Rubber City Open
5. Iron Lung Open

9 Illnesses of Baseball Player Luke "Old Aches & Pains" Appling
1. Astigmatism
2. Fallen arches
3. Sore kneecaps
4. Dizzy spells
5. Insomnia
6. Sore throat
7. Seasickness
8. Gout
9. Not sick enough (his explanation for letting his batting average drop below .300 after 9 seasons)

In 2001 the SF Giants' AT&T Park was also home to the XFL's SF Demons football team.

A TOY IS BORN

You've bought them. You've played with them. You've wondered where they came from and who created them. Now the BRI offers these bits of useless information to satisfy your curiosity.

SUPERBALLS

In the early '60s, a chemist named Norman Stingley was experimenting with high-resiliency synthetics for the U.S. government when he discovered a compound he dubbed Zectron. He was intrigued; when the material was fashioned into a ball, he found it retained almost 100% of its bounce...which meant it had six times the bounce of regular rubber balls. And a Zectron ball kept bouncing—about 10 times longer than a tennis ball.

Stingley presented the discovery to his employer, the Bettis Rubber Company, but the firm had no use for it. So, in 1965, Stingley took his Zectron ball to Wham-O, the toy company that had created Hula Hoops and Frisbees. It was a profitable trip. Wham-O snapped up Stingley's invention, called it a "Superball," and sold 7 million of them in the next six months.

TWISTER

In the early 1960s, Reynolds Guyer worked at his family's sales-promotion company designing packages and displays. He also created premiums—the gifts people get for sending in boxtops and proofs-of-purchase. One day in 1965, the 29-year-old Guyer and his crew started work on a premium for a shoe polish company. "One idea," he says, "was to have kids standing on this mat with squares that told them where to put their feet...but I thought, this is bigger than just a premium."

He expanded the mat to 4' x 6' and turned it into a game. "I got the secretaries and the designers and everyone together to play. You know, in 1965 no one ever touched. It really broke all the rules of propriety having people stand so close together."

At first it was a flop. No one knew what to make of a game where people were the main playing pieces. But when Johnny Carson and Eva Gabor played it on *The Tonight Show* in 1966, America got the point. Overnight, it became a runaway hit.

Average lifespan of a major league baseball: 5 pitches.

BINGO

In 1929 a tired, depressed toy salesman named Edwin Lowe set out on a nighttime drive from Atlanta, Georgia, to Jacksonville, Florida. On the way, he noticed the bright lights of a carnival; he decided to stop to investigate. Lowe found only one concession open—a tent full of people seated at tables, each with a hand-stamped, numbered card and a pile of beans. As the emcee called out numbers, players put beans on the corresponding squares on their cards. If they got five beans in a row, they won a Kewpie doll. The concessionaire called his game Beano. Lowe was so impressed that he tried it at his own home, where one young winner became so excited that she stammered out "B-b-bingo!" instead of "Beano." So that's what Lowe called it.

*   *   *

MARKETING MAGIQ

Who Said It: Los Angeles Lakers basketball star Shaquille O'Neal

Slip of the Lip: Asked in June 2002 about Yao Ming, the NBA's first Chinese player, Shaq replied with a mock-Chinese accent, "Tell Yao Ming 'Ching-chong-yang-wah-ah-so.'" He thought it was so funny, he repeated it in December. When columnist Irwin Tang wrote about it for AsianWeek.com, Asian community groups began protesting and reporters peppered O'Neal with questions.

Insincere Apology #1: O'Neal tried to squirm out of it. "To say I'm a racist against Asians is crazy. I said a joke. It was a 70-30 joke. 70% of the people thought it was funny. 30% didn't. If I hurt anybody's feelings, I apologize."

Insincere Apology #2: Protesters refused to let the issue die. A few days later, O'Neal said, "If I was the first one to do it, and the only one to do it, I could see what they're talking about. But if I offended anybody, I apologize." Asian Americans were still angry.

Insincere Apology #3: Protests grew. After a game against Yao's Houston Rockets in January, O'Neal tried again: "Yao Ming is my brother. The Asian people are my brothers. It was unfortunate that one idiot writer tried to start a racial war over that." He added, "But because of what I said, 500 million people saw this game. You ought to thank me for my marketing skills."

BABE

The other *Babe.*

CHAMPION: Babe Zaharias
BACKGROUND: Born Mildred Ella Didrikson in Port Arthur, Texas, on June 26, 1914

HER STORY: She was a true tomboy who, as a young girl, loved sports and quickly found out that she was very good—better than most of the boys. (The neighborhood boys nicknamed her the "Babe," for her Babe Ruth–esque batting.) In the 1932 Olympic Games, Zaharias won gold medals in the javelin toss and the 80-meter hurdles, and a silver medal in the high jump. She set new world records in almost every event. Then she discovered golf.

Many men give a polite nod to women golfers—but don't do it with this one. Bobby Jones said the Babe was one of the top 10 golfers ever to play the game. He meant women *and* men. Her record as a golfer is possibly the best record of any athlete playing any game in the modern era of sports.

CAREER HIGHLIGHTS

• The Babe won 55 amateur and professional golf events in her career, including the U.S. Women's Amateur tournament in 1946.

• Over a 14-month stretch from 1946 to '47, she won 14 consecutive tournaments and 17 overall. Later in 1947, she won another 12 straight tournaments. That run included the 1947 British Women's Amateur, making her the first American to win the event.

• After turning pro in 1948—at the age of 34—she won 41 tournaments, including ten majors.

• If all those achievements aren't impressive enough, add to the list the fact that her pro career lasted only seven years. Zaharias died from cancer at the age of 42.

• In 2000 *Golf Digest* made their own list of the 100 best golfers of all time: Babe was number 17…ahead of Nick Faldo, Larry Nelson, Ben Crenshaw, Hale Irwin, Johnny Miller, and Greg Norman.

Average speed of a golf ball hit by a PGA Tour player: 160 mph.

CARD SHARKS, PART I

Most of us fantasize about beating the odds and winning big. Some play the lottery, others are hypnotized by the ding-ding-dinging of slot machines. But what if you knew a system that gave you an advantage—every time?

THE HOUSE RULES

It's a given among gamblers that over time the "house" always wins. That's partly because most casino games— roulette, dice, slot machines—are singular events. What happened in the previous throw of the dice, turn of the wheel, or pull of the "one-armed bandit" has no impact on the outcome of the next game. With every throw, turn, or pull, a player has the same chance of winning as in any other throw, turn, or pull, unless the casinos set their wheels and slot machines to improve the house's odds (which, in the case of slots, they do).

But the game of blackjack, or "21," is something else again.

• It's a straightforward game, played head to head against the dealer (the house).

• Cards are dealt one at a time. The player's objective is to get as close to 21 points as possible without going over; the first to go over 21 loses.

• The round is over when all the cards have been dealt.

• Traditionally, a single deck was used for each round of play, with the used cards being set aside after each hand.

All this makes blackjack a game where what happened before any hand actually *does* matter in terms of predicting a winning outcome. If a player can keep track of the cards that have been played, and bet only when the odds shift into his favor, he can win big. What's amazing is that no one ever figured that out...until about 40 years ago.

ENTER THE PROFESSOR

In 1962 a young math professor named Edward Thorp published a book called *Beat the Dealer*. He was the first person to prove mathematically that blackjack could be beaten by systematic card

---

In 2002 Martin Strel of Slovenia swam the entire length of the Mississippi River—2,360 miles.

counting—a system he called "the High-Low Count." When he tested his system in Reno, he doubled his stake of $10,000 in one weekend (he later disclosed that he'd been bankrolled by a mysterious investor called "Mr. X"; Thorp suspected his sponsor of being an underworld kingpin, but used the money anyway).

Thorp's book was an immediate best seller, and soon every blackjack table in Nevada was swarming with would-be card counters trying to score with his system.

THE HIGH-LOW COUNT

Thorp's card-counting system was brilliant in its simplicity. Rather than force a player to remember the value of every card dealt (which would be an incredible feat of memory), Thorp's strategy relied on approximations. He divided the deck into three groups, and gave each group a simple value: The 2, 3, 4, 5, and 6 of any suit would have a value of +1; 7, 8, and 9, a value of 0; and the 10, jack, queen, king, and ace would equal –1. During a game, the player simply had to keep a running total of the count, adding or subtracting as each card was dealt (this isn't as easy as it sounds—it still requires tremendous concentration). A negative high-low count gave the advantage to the casino; when it became positive, the player had the edge. That was the moment to strike: bet heavily and win big.

THE PROFESSOR STOPPER

It should be pointed out that there is nothing illegal about card counting. The player is using information available to everyone at the table. But casinos make their own rules, and as soon as they saw their profits dip when card counting caught on, they stepped in quickly to stem their losses. The first tactic was to shuffle the decks more often. Although effective at ruining the count, the time wasted with extra shuffles drove noncounting (and impatient) gamblers away from the tables in droves. So the casinos dropped that gambit and turned instead to the "Professor Stopper"—a huge card shoe designed to hold more than eight decks. The thinking was that having to count up to 400 cards would be too much for most card counters, but that wasn't the case. It just took a player longer to get to a winning position. The casinos kept losing.

Finally, they decided to use Thorp's system against his own

disciples. Casino employees were taught the high-low system and, more importantly, how to spot card counters by their telltale behavior. Since card counting requires intense concentration, for example, card counters tend not to be very conversational or jovial when they play. Anyone suspected of card counting was shown the door and told not to come back. So was that the end of card counting? Hardly. In fact, the battle between counters and casinos had just begun.

GAMING COMPUTERS

Keith Taft was an electronics engineer from California, and an aggressive card counter. He studied the books, learned the strategy, and spent hours at the tables trying to perfect his game. But the casinos loved him. Why? Because he was also a big loser. His problem was that he kept losing count. Then in 1969 he had a brainstorm: Why not invent a machine that would do his counting for him, a computer just for blackjack?

• **GEORGE.** Two years later, Taft and his son, Marty, unveiled one of the first portable computers ever made, which they called "George." Wearing specially modified shoes, the player would use his toes to tap in the value of the card being played. The main computer, which was harnessed to the player's body, used the data to figure out the best way to play the next hand. That information was then flashed to the player through tiny lights embedded in the frame of a modified pair of glasses. George was a good prototype, but it was too bulky to use in a casino.

• **DAVID.** It took them another four years and the invention of the microchip to build the computer they wanted: about the size of a pocket calculator, with a keyboard no larger than a credit card. The device, called "David," was strapped to the player's thigh; he could work the keyboard through a strategically placed hole in his pocket. But David was more than a fine piece of miniaturization. It took Thorp's High-Low system to an exciting new level. What had made Thorp's system so attractive to blackjack players was that it relied on simple mental arithmetic, which made it accessible to almost any player. But that was also its weakness.

Thorp's system worked on approximations, not on the precise value of each card played. The player still had to make an educated guess on how to play a hand. But David could remember the values of every card played, analyze that information, and tell the player exactly how to play their cards. The player didn't have to guess at all. He or she just had to follow David's recommendations and rake in the dough.

BET ON DAVID

The Tafts debuted David in April 1977 and racked up $40,000 in winnings the very first week. They quickly set up a production line and offered the new blackjack computer for sale at $10,000 apiece. But before they could cash in, Marty Taft was caught with David strapped to his leg. Casino security had never seen anything like it before. They were certain it was a cheating device, but they couldn't figure out how it worked (the Tafts' use of microchip technology was far ahead of its time) and had to let Marty go. He had made a narrow escape, and that was the end of the road for David. In 1985 the Nevada legislature passed the Nevada Devices Law, making it against the law to use a card-counting machine. The maximum sentence was 10 years. Once again, the house ruled.

Or did it?

For part II of the story of the Las Vegas card counters, turn to page 445.

*   *   *

SPORTS FLOP: THE NATIONAL BOWLING LEAGUE

If people are willing to pay to watch professional football, baseball, and basketball teams, they'd pay to watch bowling teams like the New York Gladiators and the Detroit Thunderbirds compete against each other, right? That was the thinking behind the 10-team National Bowling League, founded in 1961. The owner of the Dallas Broncos poured millions of dollars into his franchise, building a special 2,500-seat "Bronco Bowl" with six lanes surrounded by 18 rows of seats arranged in a semicircle; space was also set aside for a seven-piece jazz band to provide entertainment between games. But he couldn't even fill the arena on opening night, and things went downhill after that. The league folded in less than a year.

Since 1876, 69 pro baseball players have hit a home run their first time at bat; 11 never hit another.

ODD, ODD WORLD OF BASEBALL INJURIES

Major League ballplayers are big, tough, manly men who cannot be felled by any mere mortal destructive force...except for ice packs, donuts, sunflower seeds, and handshakes.

• Catcher Mickey Tettleton of the Detroit Tigers went on the disabled list for athlete's foot, which he got from habitually tying his shoes too tight.

• Wade Boggs once threw out his back while putting on a pair of cowboy boots.

• In 1993 Rickey Henderson missed several games because of frostbite—in August. He had fallen asleep on an ice pack.

• Ken Griffey Jr. missed one game in 1994 due to a groin injury. (His protective cup had pinched one of his testicles.)

• Atlanta pitcher John Smoltz once burned his chest. He'd ironed a shirt...while still wearing it.

• Sammy Sosa missed a game because he threw out his back while sneezing.

• While playing for Houston, Nolan Ryan couldn't pitch after being bitten by a coyote.

• Marty Cordova of the Baltimore Orioles went on the disabled list after burning his face in a tanning bed.

• Atlanta outfielder Terry Harper once waved a teammate home, then high-fived him. The act separated Harper's shoulder.

• Pitcher Phil Niekro hurt his hand...while shaking hands.

• Milwaukee's Steve Sparks once dislocated his shoulder attempting to tear a phone book in half.

• San Francisco Giants manager Roger Craig cut his hand "undoing a bra strap."

• To look more menacing, Boston pitcher Clarence Blethen took out his false teeth during a game and put them in his back pocket. Later, while he was sliding into second base, the teeth clamped down and bit him on the butt.

Fencing is believed to have originated in ancient Egypt as a training exercise for war.

- When the San Diego Padres won the National League West in 2005, pitcher Jake Peavy jumped on top of the celebration pileup. He fractured a rib and had to sit out the entire playoff series.

- Jose Cardenal missed a game for the Chicago Cubs because he had been kept awake all night by crickets chirping outside his hotel room.

- Kevin Mitchell of the New York Mets hurt a tooth on a donut that had gotten too hot in a microwave. On another occasion, Mitchell pulled a muscle while vomiting.

- Carlos Zambrano of the Chicago Cubs was on the disabled list after being diagnosed with carpal tunnel syndrome. Cause of condition: too many hours spent surfing the Internet.

- Minnesota's Terry Mulholland had to sit out a few games after he scratched his eye on a feather sticking out of a pillow.

- Pitcher Greg Harris was flipping sunflower seeds into his mouth in the Texas Rangers bullpen. It strained his elbow.

- San Diego pitcher Adam Eaton stabbed himself in the stomach with a knife while trying to open a DVD case.

- Florida pitcher Ricky Bones pulled his lower back getting out of a chair while watching TV in the team clubhouse.

- Outfielder Glenallen Hill has an intense fear of spiders. He went on the disabled list after suffering multiple cuts all over his body. Hill had fallen out of bed onto a glass table while having a nightmare in which he was covered with spiders.

- Before the first game of the 1985 World Series, St. Louis outfielder Vince Coleman was fooling around on the field and managed to get rolled up inside the Busch Stadium automatic tarp-rolling machine. Coleman's injuries caused him to miss the entire series.

*　　*　　*

First professional sports organization in the United States: the Maryland Jockey Club, founded in 1743.

In speed skating, the competitors must change lanes after each lap.

THE OLYMPICS EXPOSED

*The ancient Olympics awarded no medals, didn't have a marathon,
and didn't let women compete. But a time traveler to the ancient
Games would find a lot that's familiar: huge crowds, amazing
performances...and juicy Olympic scandals.*

LET THE GAMES BEGIN

The first known Olympic Games were held in 776 B.C. at
the foot of Mt. Olympus in Greece. No one's sure why they
began; their history blends into myth, with the god Zeus supposedly wanting a festival to celebrate his victory as King of the gods.
But whatever their origins, the Games became hugely popular
with the Greek public—so popular that they were held on that
same site every four years for the next 1,000 years.

The very first Games featured only one event: a 200-yard
footrace called the *stadion*. The winner was Koroibos, a local cook.
The earliest Olympics were informal, and any free, male Greek
citizen could compete. At the time, Greece was made up of city-
states such as Athens and Sparta that were often at war with each
other. But after a few more Olympic Games were held, they
became so popular that a truce was declared every four years so
athletes could travel to Olympia and compete.

The truce didn't always hold, but Greece usually united peace-
fully for the Olympic Games, which became a mix of sporting
event and religious festival. Since the Greeks believed that the
sports-loving—and very male—Zeus would want his festivities to
be for men only, married women were forbidden to even watch
the Games; if they did, they risked being thrown off the cliffs of a
nearby mountain. Female athletes also weren't welcome.

TOUGH...AND IN THE BUFF

The ancient athletes competed in the nude, their bodies gleaming
with perfumed oils. It didn't start out that way; for the first 50
years, the athletes wore shorts. But in 720 B.C., according to
Greek writer Pausanias, one athlete stripped off his trunks, thinking he would run faster. He won, and after that, the Olympics
became clothing-free.

The average baseball spectator spends $7.46 on food; the average luxury box holder spends $30.

THE OLYMPIC DIET

Over the years, the Games expanded to include chariot races, wrestling, boxing, the pentathlon, and discus and javelin throws—in all, 23 different sports. And as the Games grew in popularity, they sparked diet fads. Some trainers insisted that their athletes eat a strict meat diet and no beans. Other trainers swore that a diet of beans alone was best. Wrestler Milo of Croton reportedly ate 40 pounds of meat and bread at a single meal and washed it down with eight quarts of wine. The diet worked—Milo became the most famous wrestler in antiquity, winning six Olympic championships.

DANGEROUS GAMES

The athletes trained hard, sometimes 10 months out of the year, to toughen up—a necessity, since the Games could be deadly. Boxing bouts had no rest periods and no rules against hitting a man when he was down. Boxers fought on until one man surrendered—or died. Killing an opponent wasn't a good thing, though; the dead boxer was automatically proclaimed the winner, so at times the Olympic honors were solemnly awarded to a corpse.

Contestants also died in the *pankration*, an especially savage event. A combination of wrestling, boxing, and extreme martial-arts fighting, the pankration allowed arm-twisting, punching, kicking, breaking bones, and even strangling. Breaking an opponent's fingers often led to a quick win, and one pankratiast got so good at it that he was called "Finger Tips."

The races could also be fatal. In the four-horse chariot race, a driver had to manage a speeding team of horses around a crowded track. Forty chariots started each race, but few finished. Sophocles wrote of one disaster: "As the crowd saw the driver somersault, there rose a wail of pity as he was bounced onto the ground, then flung head over heels into the sky."

Even watching the Olympics could be an ordeal. The Games were held in August and September, and more than 40,000 sweltering fans packed the Olympic stadium—which had no seats. Hats weren't allowed for fear they would block someone's view, so sunburn and heatstroke were common. Relief sometimes came from rain, but that only drenched the uncomfortable crowd. Vendors sold sausages, stale bread, and poor-quality cheese, but there

Greek women, excluded from the first Olympic Games...

was never enough food for everyone. The latrines were outside the stadium in dry riverbeds.

But the inconveniences didn't dampen the fans' enthusiasm. Whenever the Games were in full swing, Olympic fever took such a hold that life in the surrounding area came to a standstill. Even when the Persians raided the region in 480 B.C., thousands ignored the invasion to watch the final boxing bouts.

DOING THE HONORS

Winners didn't get gold medals; instead, they were crowned with a *kotinos*, an olive wreath cut from a sacred tree growing nearby. That may not seem like much of a prize, but the bonuses paid by the city-states to their native champions made it worth the effort. Athens, for example, gave its winners bonuses equal to more than $600,000 today. Athenian champions also got front-row seats at the theater and a pension plan of free meals for life. Throughout Greece, Olympians picked up cash for "appearances" at other festivals and became pampered celebrities.

But the Games weren't free of scandal. Greek philosophers Aristotle, Plato, and Socrates all complained about the declining morality that money brought to the Olympics. One boxer, Eupolus, allegedly bribed his opponents to take a dive. Others were paid cash by one city-state to represent it at the Games instead of the one they were born in.

The ancient Olympics came to an end in A.D. 395 when Roman Emperor Theodosius I, a Christian, banned them because of their origins in pagan worship. By then the Olympics had been going for more than 1,170 years. If our modern Games last that long, they'll still be held in 3066.

*   *   *

LUCKY NUMBER

In 1963 the winners of the Most Valuable Player award in pro football (which had two leagues at the time) and baseball (National and American Leagues) all wore the number 32. The winners: Jim Brown (NFL), Cookie Gilchrist (AFL), Sandy Koufax (National League), and Elston Howard (American League).

...created their own competition, called the Games of Hera.

HUT 1...HUT 2...HIKE!

*Football: A mindless game of men with helmets running into each other?
Or a complex ballet of strategy mixed with speed and brute force?*

"Football isn't a game but a religion, a metaphysical island of fundamental truth in a highly verbalized, disguised society, a throwback of 30,000 generations of anthropological time."
—**Arnold Mandell**

"Let's face it, you have to have a slightly recessive gene that has a little something to do with the brain to go out on the football field and beat your head against other human beings on a daily basis."
—**Tim Green**

"The NFL, like life, is full of idiots."
—**Randy Cross**

"Football isn't a contact sport, it's a collision sport. Dancing is a contact sport."
—**Duffy Daugherty**

"Most football teams are temperamental. That's 90% temper and 10% mental."
—**Doug Plank**

"Pro football is like nuclear warfare. There are no winners, only survivors."
—**Frank Gifford**

"I'd catch a punt naked, in the snow, in Buffalo, for a chance to play in the NFL."
—**Steve Henderson**

"Baseball is what we were. Football is what we have become."
—**Mary McGrory**

"If my mother put on a helmet and shoulder pads and a uniform that wasn't the same as the one I was wearing, I'd run over her if she was in my way. And I love my mother."
—**Bo Jackson**

"I like to believe my best hits border on felonious assault."
—**Jack Tatum**

"The pads don't keep you from getting hurt. They just keep you from getting killed."
—**Chad Bratzke**

"You're kind of numb after 50 shots to the head."
—**Jim Harbaugh**

"Football is a game of clichés, and I believe in every one of them."
—**Vince Lombardi**

Only baseball player to get caught stealing to end the World Series: Babe Ruth, in 1926.

MASCOTS GONE WILD

There's an old adage in Hollywood: "Never work with kids or animals."
These sports teams didn't heed this message (well, the animal part), and
found out what happens when a beast decides to act on its own.

THE ATLANTA FALCON

On September 11, 1966, the Atlanta Falcons took the field for the first time as the NFL's newest expansion team. The first game in franchise history was a major event for a city on the rise. In front of a sellout crowd that included a who's who of local politicians and dignitaries, the Atlanta squad was supposed to be led out onto the field by a real, live falcon—who was trained to make two majestic laps of the stadium before settling onto a high-profile perch from which he would then lend moral support to his team.

Right on cue, the bird of prey gracefully winged out over the field…and kept on going, soaring up over the 54,000 screaming fans and out of the stadium, never to be seen again. Undeterred, the team's owners went out and got a new falcon and tried again—three more times, only to watch their prized falcon fly out of the stadium each time. Atlanta's football Falcons may have wanted to do the same after losing their first nine games in a row.

TEXAS A&M'S REVEILLE

Since 1931 Texas A&M University has had seven different dogs named Reveille serve as the college's official mascot. The latest incarnation is a purebred collie that took over mascot duties in 2001. And Reveille VII has been the most troublesome by far. Her nearly nonstop high-pitched yelping has actually been heard over the school band in a stadium full of 82,000 screaming fans. Worse yet, Reveille bites people. On the field before a football game in 2004, she ran around and tore off a piece of a "yell leader's" pants. She's also snipped at a number of students (fortunately, none seriously). But because Reveille is "the most revered dog on campus," the university has repeatedly refused to replace her. Why? She is, quite simply, Top Dog.

The *Titanic* had rowing machines in its gym.

• As the highest-ranking member in the Corps of Cadets, a student military organization, Reveille (she is the Cadet General) wears a ceremonial blanket studded with five diamonds.

• She's the only non-service dog allowed to roam campus buildings.

• Military cadets must address her as "Miss Reveille, ma'am!"

• If she feels like sleeping on a cadet's bed, the cadet must sleep on the floor.

• She even has her own cell phone (which is carried around by the Mascot Corporal, who acts as her caretaker and secretary).

But some students aren't so sure Reveille is the best dog for the job. They've stopped short of asking for her replacement, but do request that she stay in obedience school until she can handle her duties better. (She's been through several stints already.) "Even though Rev is held in high regard," student columnist Jim Foreman wrote in 2004, "she is certainly outranked by A&M President Robert M. Gates, and God knows what would happen if he were to bite one of the yell leaders."

Update: As Reveille VII has matured out of puppyhood, she's calmed down and seems to be performing her mascot duties honorably...and obediently.

THE AUBURN WAR EAGLE

Animal trainers at Auburn University in Alabama have gone through five eagle mascots since 1930. While they've had a nearly perfect track record of not flying away (only one has escaped), one particular War Eagle (IV) seemed to take an opposing team's touchdown rather personally. It happened in a 1976 game against rival University of Florida, when late in the game Florida receiver Wes Chandler caught a pass and ran the ball 80 yards for a touchdown to put the visiting Gators ahead. Apparently unable to stand by and watch his team go down in defeat, the War Eagle flew onto the field and attacked the startled receiver. "The last Auburn defender who had a shot at me dove and missed," recalled Chandler. "Just about that time, I heard a loud squawk and the bird bit me. It probably would have hurt if I didn't have the pads on." Not quite sure what to do, the referees ended up charging War Eagle with a 15-yard personal foul (fowl?) on the ensuing kickoff. Auburn went on to lose the game.

The UPC Soccer Arena in Styria, Austria, was formerly named Arnold Schwarzenegger Stadium.

THE FORGOTTEN HERO OF FLAGPOLE-SITTING, PT. I

Ever heard of flagpole-sitting? At the height of his fame in 1930, the greatest flagpole-sitter of all, "Shipwreck Kelly," claimed he spent 20,613 hours "in cloudland." For 20 years he climbed flagpoles atop tall buildings, enduring 14,000 hours of rain and sleet, 210 hours in temperatures below freezing, and 47 hours in snowstorms. Since Kelly's time, others have sat on flagpoles in search of the publicity that once surrounded the self-described "luckiest fool alive." Here's the story from Bill Severn's A Carnival of Sports.

LIL' ORPHAN ALVIN

L Alvin Anthony Kelly, born in New York's tough Hell's Kitchen district in 1893, ran off to sea at the age of 13. He was supposedly called "Shipwreck" because of his boast that he had survived several ship sinkings during his years as a sailor. But friends admitted his nickname came from his career as a professional boxer, when opponents dropped him to the canvas so often that fans began chanting, "Sailor Kelly's been shipwrecked again!"

In the early 1920s, the five-foot-seven Irishman got a job with a skyscraper construction crew walking steel girders. Discovering that he had no fear of high places, he decided to become a professional stuntman. He balanced on rooftops, climbed walls as a human fly, put on exhibitions as a high diver, and finally drifted to Hollywood.

In 1924 a Los Angeles theater owner hired him to sit on a flagpole atop the theater as a publicity stunt. Kelly stayed on the pole most of a day, drew a big crowd, pocketed a good fee, and at the age of 31 began a new career.

A STAR IS BORN

Americans in the Roaring Twenties turned out by gawking thousands to stare up at what was then something completely new. "Shipwreck Kelly" on his flagpole, like a man pronged on the point of a giant toothpick, was a headline-making curiosity. Pic-

First baseball game on TV: the Brooklyn Dodgers vs. the Cincinnati Reds, August 26, 1939.

tures of him captured such newspaper space for his sponsors that Kelly was soon earning a hefty $100 a day. He was a one-man sporting spectacle.

But not for long. Dozens of others got into the act, swarming up flagpoles from coast to coast. Some of his many imitators borrowed not only the game but also his name, calling themselves "Shipwreck Kelly." He once counted seventeen other "Shipwrecks" in operation at the same time.

POLE POSITION

Kelly took flagpoling seriously. When he sat atop a pole for days, his perch was a small, 13" wooden disk. He slept in five-minute catnaps with his thumbs locked into holes bored in the pole. Any wavering while he dozed would bring a sharp twinge of pain and alert him instantly so he wouldn't fall off.

When he stood, which was harder and more dangerous, it usually was only for hours instead of days, on an even smaller perch, a tiny six- to eight-inch platform. There were stirrups or rope slings to hold his legs, but no other support to keep him standing.

His food and other necessities were hauled up in a basket on a rope pulley, and the same rope was used to haul down a washbasin and pot that were also needed by a man stranded on a flagpole without bathroom facilities. A covering blanket, discreetly used, afforded privacy.

ABOVE THE LAW

By 1927 the craze he started had so many rivals up on poles that police in Boston, Los Angeles, and several other cities moved to arrest them as public nuisances. Kelly himself later had some brushes with the law. New York police, for example, ordered him down from one pole over a midtown hotel because he was attracting crowds that choked Times Square traffic. But his prestige as the nation's number-one flagpoler usually won him tolerance. Mayors and other public officials were happy to pose for pictures with him and bask in his publicity.

For Part II of the "Flagpole Kelly" story,
turn to page 313.

Soccer player David Beckham installed a $40,000 tree house for his kids.

A PUNCH IN THE ARM

Unacceptable: punching your little brother in the arm. Acceptable: doing it under the guise of a "game." Did you play any of these kids' games?

DOORKNOB! When someone farts, he or she must immediately say "Safety!" If a non-farter detects the fart and says "Doorknob!" before the farter says "Safety," the person who says "Doorknob" gets to punch the farter in the arm. The farter can avoid getting punched if he or she touches a doorknob. But what if there are no doorknobs handy? In such situations (camping or swimming, for example), a substitute must be agreed upon before the first fart.

JINX! When two people say the same thing at the same time, the first person who shouts "Jinx!" wins. The loser is not allowed to speak until someone says his or her name. The penalty for violating the jinx rule is a punch in the arm.
Coke variation: The first one to yell "Jinx! You owe me a Coke!" wins. The loser must then buy the winner a soft drink.
Caveat: It is often quite difficult to actually collect the drink.

SHOTGUN! Who gets to ride in the most coveted position in the car—the front passenger seat, commonly known as "riding shotgun"? The person who yells "Shotgun!" first. But there are rules. To be awarded the front seat, everyone who will be riding in the car must be able to see it before someone yells "Shotgun!" If it's yelled at any time before that, the "Shotgun!" is null and void.

SLUG BUG! (a.k.a. "Punch Buggy") Played while riding in a car, the first person who sees a Volkswagen Beetle and yells "Slug Bug!" gets to hit someone in the arm. If it's a convertible, two hits are awarded.
Variation: A "Pediddle" is a car with only one working headlight. Whoever spots one and yells "Pediddle!" gets to hit someone. If the Pediddle is a Slug Bug, he gets two hits. If the Pediddle is a convertible Slug Bug (rare but not unheard of), then he gets to beat the stuffing out of whoever else is riding in the back seat.

Only brothers to win PGA Golf Championships: Lionel (1957) and Jay Herbert (1960).

THE POKER FACE

Ever wonder what the Big Guys of poker know that you don't? They swear it's all in keeping a straight face and watching the table for the players who don't. Here are a few pointers from the experts.

IT'S ALL IN THE GAME

There are well over 400 great professional poker players in the world today. So if poker is truly a game of "chance," then how can so many people be consistently good at winning? It's not the card itself, say the experts, as much as the flip of the card that gives away the game to people who know what to look for. Players, particularly weaker players, give away "tells," or unconscious reflexes during the game that the tried and true poker player can use to get the edge.

One of the poker greats, the self-proclaimed "Mad Poker Genius," Mike Caro, has made a living from poker and a killing from studying the psychology of the game. On his Web site, Mike Caro's World, he talks at length about the various "tells" to watch for in others, and how to avoid them yourself.

WEAK AND STRONG

The first rule of thumb in gauging your fellow players is the "strong when weak" guideline.

• In general, players who have lousy hands subconsciously act more aggressively; players with strong hands act indifferent and passively. Why? "Because," Caro says, "deception is fundamental to poker—otherwise we'd play with our hands fully exposed."

• When a player looks down and has a lousy hand, he doesn't want to give away his emotions because then he's lost the game up front. So unconsciously, he usually acts the opposite of the way he is feeling. An experienced player knows this and watches for the cues. An even better player will play off these psychological indicators.

TELL ME TRUE

"Tells" are far more prevalent in weak and mediocre players than in the pros. But watch out—really good players are good actors, and a top-of-the-line poker player knows how to fake a "tell" to throw off his opponents. The situation can become so complex that it's next to impossible to tell whether a gulp (for example) was a sign of fear...or simply a great acting job. Here, according to Caro, are some of the universal poker tells to watch for.

• **The Heavy Heart:** A sad sigh during the bet usually means a player has a good hand. Be somewhat cautious and don't call unless your hand is also very good.

• **Shifty Eyes:** A glance away from the table once the hand has been dealt. This usually indicates a player who's holding a good hand and he wants to hide his excitement.

• **Stare Down:** A direct stare into another player's eyes after the cards have been dealt or during a bet is usually a sign of a weak hand. Staring into anyone's eyes is considered somewhat aggressive and can therefore be read that a player is bluffing.

• **Pokerclack:** Pokerclack is a soft clucking noise that sounds morose or shameful. It's a term coined by Caro, and he describes it as the noise you'd make after saying something like, "I'm feeling terrible today. My old dog Shep ran into the street and got run over." It's a sad sound and is almost always done by a poker player when he is hiding excitement about his hand.

• **Flair:** An extra flamboyance at the toss of a poker chip during a bet is almost always a sign that a player is trying to hide a bad hand. He's bluffing.

• **The Jitters:** Shaky hands during a bet suggests excitement, nervousness, tension in the player. Even skilled players often mistake this sign and think the shaky player is bluffing and scared he's going to lose. That's almost never the case, however, according to Caro. Players who are bluffing tend to be rock-steady, not jittery. It's the player who's got a monstrously good hand who sometimes can't contain his excitement.

• **The Big Chill:** When a player goes quiet after betting, you can almost guarantee he's got a lousy hand and he's bluffing.

• **The Babbling Brook:** When a talkative player begins babbling somewhat incoherently or absentmindedly during or after a bet, he's usually got a lousy hand. His hand disrupted his normal conversation and he didn't want to go silent for fear he'd give himself away. But this player's almost surely bluffing.

• **Chip Fondling:** The hands have been dealt and the guy on your right is fingering his poker chips. Read it as a sign that he's raring to place his bet; he's got a great hand.

• **The Stiff:** If you see a player suddenly go rigid and hold his breath following a bet, take it as a sign of bluffing. Call him.

TATTLING & TELLING

It's betting time around your Friday night poker table and your buddy flips his chip in the air with flair and a wink. With all of this newfound knowledge, you know you've just spotted a bluff. What should you do when you notice a "tell?" Mike Caro says, "Don't let your pride destroy the profit you could make from tells. Never announce that, 'I knew you were bluffing,' if you successfully call and win with a weak hand. Say instead, 'I don't know why I called. I almost didn't, but at the last second I decided to test you one time. I guess I got lucky.' That kind of talk encourages an opponent to try again."

*   *   *

THE NAME GAME

There are hundreds—maybe thousands—of poker variations...and some of them sound downright funny when said out loud. A few of our favorite goofy-sounding poker games:

Change the Diaper	The Good, the Bad, and the Ugly
Cowpie Poker	Grocery Store Dots
Dirty Schultz	Howdy Doody
Five Card Stud with a Bug	Linoleum
Making Babies	Mexican Sweat
There Can Only Be Juan	Navy Nurse
Three-Legged Race	Pass the Trash
Trash Bin	Screwy Louie
Want It? Want It? Got It!	

THE GOODYEAR BLIMP

No major sporting event is complete without it. In fact, it's probably the best-known lighter-than-air ship ever (except maybe the Hindenburg, *which is famous for blowing up). Here's the story of the Goodyear blimp.*

NON-STICK PLANS

In 1809 Charles Goodyear, a hardware merchant from Connecticut, saw that rubber had tremendous commercial potential—but only if it could be made less sticky and would hold a shape better than it already did.

So he obtained a large quantity of latex and tried mixing it with everything in his desk, cellar, and pantry—including witch hazel, ink, and cream cheese—with no luck. One day he tried mixing rubber with sulfur. Then, while working on something else, he accidentally knocked the sulfurized rubber mixture onto a hot stove. He found that the rubber had changed form: it was no longer sticky and it snapped back to its original shape when stretched. He named the process "Vulcanizing" after Vulcan, the Roman god of fire.

Goodyear didn't get rich from his discovery—he died penniless in 1860. But when Frank A. Seiberling started a rubber company in Akron, Ohio, in 1898, he decided to name it after the inventor. It's likely he hoped to profit from the confusion created by having a name similar to another Akron rubber company, B.F. Goodrich.

Goodyear's first products were bicycle and horse carriage tires, rubber pads for horseshoes, rubber bands, and poker chips. The company produced its first auto tires in 1901, airplane tires in 1909, and, using a Scottish process for rubberized fabric, the skins for airplanes in 1910. (This was back when airplanes were based on kite designs and made mostly of wood and cloth.)

The same rubberized fabric turned out to be useful for lighter-than-air craft, and Goodyear flew its first dirigible in 1922.

THE MILITARY CONNECTION

The military used Goodyear blimps for observation and reconnaissance during World Wars I and II. After World War II, Goodyear bought five of its blimps back from the armed forces, painted

The fishing reel was invented in China in the 3rd century.

them, and began using them for promotional purposes. But the company's executives didn't see the value of having blimps. In 1958 they tried to ground the airships permanently, to save the operating and maintenance expenses.

The plan was stalled at the last minute by a plea from Goodyear's publicity director, Robert Lane. To demonstrate the blimps' worth to the company, he scheduled a six-month marathon tour that sent the airship *Mayflower* barnstorming the eastern seaboard. It generated so much favorable press that the executives were convinced to keep it.

The blimps' first TV coverage was an Orange Bowl game in the mid-1960s. Now they're used in about 90 televised events a year. Goodyear doesn't charge TV networks; the publicity generated makes the free service worthwhile.

BLIMP FACTS

• Each blimp is equipped with a crew of 23, consisting of 5 pilots, 17 support members who work on rotating schedules, and a public-relations representative. The blimps cruise at a speed of 45 to 50 mph (a maximum of 65 mph unless there's a really good wind).

• Each blimp can carry nine passengers along with the crew. The seats have no seat belts.

• The camera operator shoots from the passenger compartment through an open window from about 1,200 feet up, from which you can see everything, read a scoreboard, and hear the roar of a crowd. The hardest sport to film is golf, because the pilots have to be careful not to disturb a golfer's shot with engine noise or by casting a sudden shadow over the green.

• If punctured, the worst that will happen is that the blimp will slowly lose altitude. Good thing, too, since the company reports that a blimp is shot at about 20 times a year.

• Each blimp is 192 feet long, 59 feet high, and holds 202,700 cubic feet of helium. The helium does leak out, like a balloon's air, and has to be "topped off" every four months or so.

• The word *blimp* is credited to Lt. A. D. Cunningham of Britain's Royal Navy Air Service. In 1915 he whimsically flicked his thumb against the inflated wall of an airship and imitated the sound it made: "Blimp!"

Actual rule at a golf course in India: "Balls eaten by cows may be replaced with no penalty."

THE HISTORY OF FOOTBALL, PART III

*In this part of our football saga, we contemplate the mysteries
of safeties, offensive interference, and tackling below
the waist. (Part II is on page 101.)*

MAKING HIS POINT(S)

In the early days of football, games often ended in a tie,
and the referee decided the winner. Yale coach Walter
Camp thought that instituting a *point* system, something more
sophisticated than just counting touchdowns and field goals, would
solve the problem by making tied games less likely. He pushed his
proposal through the Rules Committee in 1883.

Beginning that year, a touchdown counted for two points, a
goal kicked following a touchdown was worth four points, and
a field goal was worth five points. Then there was the "safety."
Whenever the ball came within 25 yards of the offensive team's
own goal line, it was common practice for them to touch the ball
down behind their own goal line "for safety," because this meant
that the ball would be brought back out to the 25-yard line for a
free kick. Henceforth, if a team was forced to resort to a safety, one
point was awarded to the other team.

The new point system lasted only a year—by 1884 it was obvious that touchdowns were harder to score than field goals, so their
value was raised to four points. The goal after touchdown was low-
ered to two points, the safety was raised to two points, and the
field goal remained unchanged at five points.

GETTING IN THE WAY

Technically, "interference," or protecting the ball carrier from
incoming tacklers, was illegal, just as it was in rugby. But because
the introduction of the system of downs was thought to have
weakened the offense, enforcement of the rules against interference began to decline.

As early as 1879, Princeton protected the ball carrier by running two players alongside him, one on either side. These shielders

didn't actually block the incoming tacklers—that was still against the rules—but they were an intimidating presence. Rather than complain, other teams adopted the tactic themselves.

They also began testing the limits of what else they could get away with—and quickly discovered they could get away with a lot. "A few years later," Stephen Fox writes in *Big Leagues*, "the shielders had moved out ahead of the runner, using their arms and hands to shed tacklers. The old offside rule was no longer enforced. Barely a decade old, football had lost this final vestige of rugby."

LOW BLOW

The gradual acceptance of offensive interference served to strengthen the offense, so in 1888 Walter Camp pushed through two new rules that helped strengthen the defense in response: The first banned blocking "with extended arms," a tacit acknowledgment that other forms of blocking had become legal; the second legalized tackling below the waist, as far down as the knees. The new rules shifted the balance so firmly over to the defense that the offense had to completely rethink its game.

The low tackle proved to be much harder to defend against than tackles above the waist, so forwards had little choice but to move in closer around the center, until they were literally standing shoulder to shoulder, as they do today. The backfield (halfbacks and fullbacks) moved farther up to provide additional protection. Now, instead of being spread out all over the field, players were clumped together in the middle. It was also about this time that centers started using their hands instead of their feet to snap the ball back to the quarterback.

THE V-TRICK

With so many players crowded together, it was probably just a matter of time before someone hit upon the offensive tactic of everybody locking arms and slamming into the defense in one single, devastating mass.

One of the earliest examples of such a "mass play," as it came to be known, was the V-trick, which Princeton invented on the spur of the moment in 1884 during the second half of a 0–0 game against the University of Pennsylvania. (Lehigh University claims to have invented a similar version at about the same time.)

Jousting, the official state sport of Maryland, was the first official sport of any American state.

Princeton wasn't having any luck advancing the ball with its usual strategy of having a halfback carry the ball down the field behind seven other players. Then it occurred to quarterback Richard Hodge that the seven interferers might be more effective if they locked arms together and formed a V, with the point of the V pointing downfield and the ball carrier running safely inside the formation. It worked: Princeton scored a touchdown, and went on to win the game, 31–0.

SECOND TRY

It wasn't until 1888 that Princeton used the V-trick again. This time they sprang it on Yale at the start of the second half. But it was not nearly as effective has it had been four years before, because one of the Yale guards instantly figured out a way to counter it. Author Parke Davis described the scene in his 1911 book *Football: The American Intercollegiate Game*:

> The Princeton players formed themselves into a mass of the shape of the letter V.…The ball went into play and away went the wedge of men, legs churning in unison like the wheels of a locomotive.
>
> But on the Yale team was a young giant by the name of Walter "Pudge" Heffelfinger. He rushed at the mighty human engine, leaped high in the air, completely clearing its forward ramparts, and came down on top of the men inside the wedge, whom he flattened to the ground, among them the ball-carrier.

HUMAN CANNONBALLS

Yale won the game, 10–0, and went on to win every game of its 1888 season, racking up 694 points to 0 for its opponents. Nevertheless, the V-trick was so effective that other teams quickly adopted it and began inventing other mass plays. Likewise, they adopted the defensive tactics of Pudge Heffelfinger, perfecting the art of cannonballing knees-first into chest of the lead man in the wedge. The best players were able to vault the wedge entirely to slam full force into the ball carrier.

Tactics like these led to an increase in the number of serious injuries and even deaths in the game, which led to a general rise in brutality and foul play. "We were past masters at tackling around the neck," Georgia Tech's John Heisman recalled of the period. "There was a rule against it, but that rule was broken

---

Babe Ruth wore a cabbage leaf under his baseball cap to keep cool during games.

often…Fact is, you didn't stand much of a chance making the line in those days unless you were a good wrestler and fair boxer."

THE FLYING WEDGE

In 1890 a Boston lawyer and chess expert named Lorin F. Deland happened to see a Harvard football game. He'd never played football, but had become a fan of the sport, in large part because the strategy seemed to have a lot of parallels with battlefield tactics. His interest in the sport prompted him to read books on Napoléon Bonaparte.

One of the Little Emperor's favorite tricks was massing the full strength of his troops at the enemy's weakest points; Deland thought this would also work well in football. He pitched his idea for what became known as the "flying wedge" to Harvard in 1892. The flying wedge applied the principles of speed and momentum to the Princeton V-trick; Deland proposed using it during kickoffs, which would allow the wedge to get a 20-yard running head start before slamming full-speed into the opposing team.

Harvard agreed to try it against Yale in the fall and spent much of the summer secretly practicing the move. On game day, they introduced it at the start of the second half, when Harvard had the kickoff. The beefiest players gathered on the right side of the field 20 yards away from the ball; the smaller players gathered 15 yards farther back on the left side. When the signal was given, both groups converged in front of the ball at full speed and locked arms to form the wedge as the kicker, Bernie Trafford, tapped the ball with his foot (still legal in those days), then picked it up and passed it to teammate Charlie Brewer, who was running alongside him.

FOOT FAULT

Running from inside the safety of the flying wedge as it plowed into Yale's defensive line, Brewer managed to advance as much as 30 yards and might even have gone all the way for a touchdown, had he not tripped over a teammate on Yale's 25-yard line. Harvard never did score a touchdown—Yale won, 6–0, but the effectiveness of the flying wedge was obvious to everyone. By 1893 almost every college football team in the country had adopted "mass momentum" plays. The golden age of football violence had arrived.

Halftime: After the BRI marching band performs, turn to page 219 for Part IV of our History of Football.

FORE!

Next time you're playing golf, watching a match, or even driving past a course, be forewarned! Golf balls go where they're hit, not always where the player wants them to go. For example, a ball could hit...

A MOVING VEHICLE

Sean Hutchins regularly drives past San Geronimo Golf Club in California. His advice to other drivers: Beware— "The number of golf balls hitting vehicles seems to be on the rise." His current tally: two have hit his truck, one ball hit his friend's Chevelle, another hit that same friend's mother's pickup, a fifth hit the friend's girlfriend's car, and a sixth smacked a California Highway Patrol car.

A BIRD

The small African nation of Benin doesn't have a golf course, but that didn't deter Mathieu Boya. He would routinely practice driving balls in a field adjacent to the Benin Air Base—until one day in 1987 when his ball struck a gull, which then fell into the open cockpit of a jet taxiing the runway, which caused the pilot to lose control, which caused the plane to barrel through the other four Mirage fighter jets sitting on the tarmac...which wiped out the entire Benin Air Force.

A FAN'S FOREHEAD

John Yates, 52, realized a dream-come-true when he got to watch the world's most famous golfer, Tiger Woods, in person at the 2003 Buick Open in Grand Blanc, Michigan. But Yates got more than he bargained for. Woods's approach shot on the seventh hole went wild and struck Yates smack-dab on the forehead. After a few dazed minutes on his back, Yates looked up to see Woods leaning over him, apologizing profusely. For his trouble, the fan got three stitches, the errant ball, and an autographed golf glove. Woods got something out of the deal, too. As Yates recalled: "I helped him out because my head knocked the ball back toward the hole. He birdied the hole, I guess. I didn't see it. But it's my most memorable moment in golf."

The salchow figure-skating jump was invented by the Swedish skater Ulrich Salchow in 1909.

THE BOTTOM OF THE CUP

As the sun was setting on the seventh hole of the Roehampton Golf Club in England in 1964, Bill Carey hit a tee shot that landed near the pin, but because it was getting dark, he couldn't see exactly where it rolled to. So Carey and his opponent, Edgar Winter, went to look for it. After an unsuccessful search of the green and the hill below, Carey finally conceded defeat as darkness settled in. But a few minutes later he found the ball in the one place he never thought to look: at the bottom of the cup. Even though Carey had hit a hole-in-one, he never got credit for it...and lost.

QUICKSAND

Bayly MacArthur, playing in a 1931 tournament in Australia, hit a ball into what he thought was a sand trap. It wasn't—it was quicksand. And unfortunately, MacArthur found out the hard way when he stepped into the quicksand to play the ball. It took four other golfers to pull him out.

A SPECTATOR'S BRA

At the 1973 Sea Pines Heritage Classic in South Carolina, Hale Irwin's worst shot of the match (and perhaps his career) hit a woman's chest and lodged in her bra. She was relieved when Irwin decided to forgo the shot, taking a two-stroke penalty instead.

THREE SPECTATORS

In 1971 Vice President Spiro Agnew played in the pro-am portion of the Bob Hope Desert Classic. After his first two shots injured *three* members of the crowd, Agnew made the wise choice and became a spectator himself.

AN OPPONENT'S ARM

Why hit someone with a golf ball when you've got a golf *club*? In 1980 at the final round of the Boone Golf Club Championship in North Carolina, Margaret McNeil and Earlena Adams were tied for the lead after 18 holes. They had to play one sudden-death hole to decide the match. At the tee, McNeil was practicing her stroke when she accidentally smacked Adams on the arm with her backswing. Result for Adams: her arm was broken; she couldn't play the hole. Result for McNeil: she was awarded first place.

A regulation hole in golf is 4.25 inches in diameter, and "no less than 4 inches deep."

WHY *TWO* PAIRS OF SOCKS?

Wearing two socks—a colored "stirrup" sock over a white sock—is a baseball tradition that, on the surface, makes no sense. After all, other sports seem to get by just fine with only a single pair.

COLOR CODED

Identifying baseball teams by the color of their socks or stockings dates back to the earliest days of the sport—the Cincinnati Reds, professional baseball's oldest team, get their name from their socks—they were originally known as the Red Stockings when they were founded in 1868.

Believe it or not, something as simple and seemingly harmless as wearing colorful stockings came with serious health risks in the 1880s, when spiked shoes came into widespread use. "Spiking" another player by deliberately sliding into him with spikes exposed, or by baring your spikes as another player slid into you, became such a common occurrence that in 1895 there were calls for them to be banned. But they never were banned; if anything, the problem grew worse over time. Ty Cobb, who began his career in 1905, was infamous for sharpening his spikes so they would cut even deeper.

DYING FROM DYEING

If being gashed in the legs by mud- and manure-encrusted baseball spikes wasn't harmful enough, the potential danger was even greater if the victim wore colored socks. In those days, most dyes were not colorfast: The colors ran when the socks got wet...or bloody. The chemicals in the dye could seep into wounds, increasing the risk of infection. Infections were no laughing matter in the days before antibiotics—they could be deadly.

The issue came to a head in 1905 when Nap Lajoie, star second baseman for the Cleveland Naps, was spiked during a game and came down with a life-threatening case of blood poisoning

---

First athlete to appear on a Wheaties box: Lou Gehrig, in 1934.

that was attributed to the dye in his socks. The infection kept him sidelined for two months.

DOUBLE PLAY

No macho ballplayer wanted his obituary to read "Killed by his socks." So when sporting-goods companies, capitalizing on the fear of blood poisoning, started offering undyed, "sanitary" white socks that could be worn underneath the team's colored socks, they found ready buyers.

Wearing two pairs of socks created a new problem—baseball shoes didn't fit as well, so players started cutting off the heels and toes of the dyed socks to create an improvised "stirrup" sock that reduced the bulk inside the shoe and let a little bit of the white sanitary sock show through. Soon sporting goods manufacturers began making their colored socks in that style. In those early days, the stirrups were small enough and low enough on the leg that very little of the white sock could be seen. But the stirrup socks stretched a little every time a player put them on, and fashions changed, too. As the years passed, more and more of the white sanitary sock peeked through, until the stirrup "look" became synonymous with baseball uniforms.

IT HAS ITS UPS AND DOWNS

By 1961 stirrups had gotten so long that baseball officials tried to intervene to prevent them from getting even longer, but they failed miserably. As the years passed, stirrups got longer...and longer...and longer, until so much of the stirrup had disappeared beneath the uniform pants that they didn't even look like stirrups anymore, they just looked like two strips of cloth running from the pants down into the shoe. This "whitewall tire" look remained dominant until the early 1990s, when uniform pants lengthened to the point that the stirrups are now almost completely concealed by the players' pant legs.

*　　*　　*

"It isn't hard to be good from time to time. What is tough is being good every day."

—Willie Mays

HOW TO MAKE ICE

*Uncle John's always wondered: How on
Earth can they play hockey in Miami?*

FREEZING IN FLORIDA
It's a common question from hockey fans: How do they
maintain the ice in hockey rinks, especially in warm-weather
places like Florida? To answer these and other questions, we caught
up with Ken Friedenberger, Director of Facility Operations for the
St. Petersburg Times Forum, home of the 2004 Stanley Cup champions Tampa Bay Lightning. He gave us the simple rundown:

• Two layers of sand and gravel mixture form the foundation of
the ice. The two layers and the precise mixture, Friedenberger
said, prevent it from freezing into permafrost (perpetually frozen
soil), which would "eventually crack the piping and turn it into a
big mess, which would took like spaghetti."

• "The piping" he refers to is perhaps the most important part of
the rink. Five to ten miles of it run under and through a massive
concrete slab that sits on the base. A liquid similar to antifreeze is
cooled by massive air conditioning units to below freezing and
pumped through the piping, making the temperature of the concrete slab below freezing, too.

• Water is hosed onto the concrete and allowed to freeze in a
very thin layer. When it's frozen, more water is added and allowed
to freeze, another layer is added...and the process is repeated until
there are 24 layers of ice, each one from ¾ of an inch to a full
inch thick.

• When all of this is finished, the ice surface temperature hovers
between 22°F and 26°F. And because of the constantly cooled
concrete below, the temperature inside the stadium stays in the
60s or 70s even when the air temperature outside is in the 90s.

• The lines, circles, and spots are painted on before each game,
and four to five new layers of ice are frozen over them to protect
them.

• A Zamboni machine smoothes out the ice before a game—and
it's time for the opening faceoff.

First ice dancers to receive a perfect score: Torville and Dean, at the 1984 Olympics.

WIDE WORLD OF ODD SPORTS

Here are some little-known sports that may tickle your fancy.

CANAL JUMPING

Where They Do It: The Netherlands, where it's known as *fierljeppen*

How It's Played: Contestants fling themselves into the middle of a canal on a long aluminum pole, like pole vaulting, shimmy to the top of the pole with the aid of bicycle inner tubes strapped to their feet, and then vault off—hopefully (but not always) landing on the opposite bank....Victors receive no cash, and no lucrative endorsements. "But to be a Dutch champion," says contest organizer Wim Vandermeer, "is always an honor."

TOE WRESTLING

Where They Do It: England. The world championships are held each year in a bar in Derbyshire.

How It's Played: Rules are simple: Sit on the floor with right foot down and left foot suspended in midair. Lock halluces (big toes). The winner must force the top of the other person's foot down, similar to arm-wrestling. Note: Part of each player's bottom must always be touching the ground. A player may, if the agony becomes too great, surrender by calling out the words 'Toe much.'

AND DON'T FORGET...

• **Grenade Throwing.** "In 1976, 36 million Russians participated in flinging de-activated grenades in a competition which resulted in the nationwide finals in Tashkent. Valentina Bykova, a 39-year-old woman, threw her pineapple 132.8 feet."

• **Fireball Soccer.** According to *Stuff* magazine: "In Java, Indonesia, martial artists douse a soccer ball in gasoline, set it on fire, and then kick it around—with bare feet. They embark on this madness to help them overcome their fear of fire."

Flush away: Shaquille O'Neal's 20,000-square-foot mansion has remote-control toilets.

LITTLE BROTHER OF WAR

What's the national sport of Canada? If you said "hockey," you're half right. Hockey is Canada's national winter sport, but Canada's national summer sport is lacrosse. (It's also the oldest known sport in North America.)

BAGGATAWAY

In 1636 French Jesuit missionary Jean de Brebeuf watched Huron Indians of southeastern Canada play an unusual game called *baggataway*, meaning "they bump hips." He wrote in his journal that the players used curved sticks with net pouches on the end to hurl a small ball. The stick reminded him of the cross carried by French bishops, called the crosier, or *la crosse*. That's the first documented mention—and the origin of the modern name— of one of the fastest-growing sports in the world today, lacrosse. Its roots go back at least to the 1400s and possibly much earlier. Today, organized lacrosse is played in more than 20 countries on five continents, with teams in such diverse places as Japan, Germany, Argentina, South Korea, and the Czech Republic.

And it's still an important game to Native Canadians.

THE BIG LEAGUES

At the time Europeans discovered it, baggataway was already a very popular sport in North America. Different versions with different names were being played by tribes throughout southeastern Canada, around the Great Lakes, and all the way into the southeastern United States. The rules and equipment varied from region to region, but in general the game was as follows:

Players used a wooden stick about three to four feet long with a big curve on one end, kind of like a shepherd's staff. A mesh pouch made of strips of boiled bark was attached to the curve and tied back down the handle of the stick. The stick could be used to pick up, carry, bat, throw, or catch a small ball, which was made of wood, baked clay, or deerskin stuffed with hair. (They could also use the stick to whack their opponents.)

Players would move down the field, then organize strategies,

First sport on film: boxing (Thomas Edison filmed it in 1894).

sometimes using all-out attacks, trying to put the ball through a goal. Goal markers could be a pole or two poles, or rocks or trees at either end of the playing field. As for the playing field: there were no sidelines, and the goals could be hundreds of yards—or several miles—apart. The games could last as long as three days, and, in probably the most stunning aspect of the early game, the teams could number from five to a *thousand* players on each side.

SPORTS MEDICINE

Baggataway wasn't just a game to Native Americans, it was an important part of spiritual life as well. Tribal mythology says that the sport was a gift given to them by the creator. Its purpose was healing, and it was (and still is) known as a "medicine game," because it promoted good health, mental toughness, and community teamwork. It was traditionally played by men, but entire villages would take part in the contests, which were often prepared for with elaborate rituals led by spiritual leaders.

Often it was a war ritual, and the games were prepared for by chanting, drumming, and dancing—the same way a tribe prepared for battle. The Cherokee in the Southeast even named the game accordingly: "Little Brother of War." Its grueling nature and violent style of play—which often resulted in serious injuries—was seen as perfect training for warriors. French fur trader Nicholas Peffot wrote in the late 1600s, "Legs and arms are sometimes broken, and it has happened that a player has been killed."

Sometimes it even substituted for battle, with tribes settling disputes with a game—although that strategy didn't always work. One account says that a game was played in 1790 between the Choctaws and the Creeks to settle a territorial dispute. When the Creeks were declared the winners, the unhappy Choctaw players attacked them, and they ended up in a full-scale war anyway.

ALL LACROSSE THE WORLD

But it wasn't until 200 years after Father de Brebeuf first noted the game that Europeans became active players. In 1834 the Canadian Caughnawaga tribe played a demonstration game for European settlers in Montreal, and lacrosse started its worldwide spread. After it was reported in the newspapers, interest grew among settlers, and leagues started to form. Then it got its biggest boost: in 1856 Dr.

George Beers, a dentist from Montreal, founded the Montreal Lacrosse Club. He wrote down the rules, setting field size, team size, etc., and set lacrosse on the path to becoming the highly organized and successful sport it is today. Beers is still called the "Father of Lacrosse." It became so popular that by 1859, an act of the Canadian Parliament named lacrosse Canada's national sport.

In 1867 white Canadian and Native teams did an exhibition tour throughout Great Britain. People loved it, and leagues started to spring up around the British Isles. The Caughnawaga even played for a special audience: Queen Victoria. She gave the game her blessing, and by the end of the century it had spread to Australia, New Zealand, and South Africa. It had also spread to the United States, becoming part of high school and university programs in the Northeast, with the first intercollegiate tournament held at the Westchester Polo Grounds in New York in 1881. In 1904 and 1908, lacrosse was played in the Olympic Games in St. Louis and London.

LACROSSE FACTS

• The official name for the lacrosse stick: the crosse.

• In the 1960s, Czech Boy Scout groups saw pictures of Native Americans playing lacrosse in *National Geographic* magazine. They made their own sticks, wrote their own rules, and began playing "Czech-lacrosse." It was actually closer to baggataway than today's official lacrosse game.

• NFL Hall of Fame running back (and movie star) Jim Brown is considered by many the best football player to ever play the game. Many say the same thing about his lacrosse play: he was an All-American at Syracuse University in the 1950s and is a member of the Lacrosse Hall of Fame.

• In 1763 the Chippewa and Sauk tribes played a game outside Fort Michilimackinac, a British stronghold in Michigan. When the ball was "accidentally" kicked over the fort walls, the players all rushed after it and, as planned, attacked the soldiers inside. When it was over, 20 British soldiers had been killed, 15 taken prisoner, and the fort belonged to the Indians.

• The Iroquois Nationals, a multitribe team from the New York–Ontario area, is the only team from an indigenous nation participating in international sports competition.

SPACED-OUT SPORTS

They give an awful lot of interviews, but sports stars—and even announcers—aren't always the most articulate people.

"Our similarities are different."

—**Dale Berra, on his father**

"Sutton lost 13 games in a row without winning a ball game."

—**Ralph Kiner**

"It's not so much maturity as it is growing up."

—**Jay Miller, hockey player, asked if his improved play was due to maturity**

"Three things are bad for you. I can't remember the first two, but doughnuts are the third."

—**Bill Petersen**

"There comes a time in every man's life, and I've had plenty of them."

—**Casey Stengel**

"Tony Gwynn was named player of the year for April."

—**Ralph Kiner**

"I just talked to the doctor. He told me her contraptions were an hour apart."

—**Mackey Sasser, on his wife's pregnancy**

"Noah."

—**Barry Bonnel, former Seattle Mariner, asked to name his all-time favorite Mariner**

"His reputation preceded him before he got here."

—**Don Mattingly**

"He slides into second with a stand-up double."

—**Jerry Coleman**

"Not true at all. Vaseline is manufactured right here in the U.S.A."

—**Don Sutton, on accusations that he doctored baseballs with a foreign substance**

"You have to be stupid, and this works out well for me."

—**Bubba Baker, on playing in the NFL**

"What would I do that for? It only gets Spanish stations."

—**Jeff Stone, on why he wouldn't bring his TV back to the U.S. after playing in Venezuela**

Duke Ellington's first job was selling peanuts at Washington Senators baseball games.

IT'S THE WRONG SONG

National anthems played at sporting events are a sign of respect by the host country and a source of pride for competitors. But when the wrong anthem is played, it provides a great source of bathroom reading.

COUNTRY HONORED: Ethiopia
SPORTING EVENT: 1964 Olympics in Tokyo
WRONG SONG: Ethiopian Abebe Bikila won the gold medal for the 26-mile marathon in 1960, becoming the first black African to win a gold medal in any event. But his chances didn't look very good for the 1964 Games: he'd had an emergency appendectomy just 40 days before the race. He ran anyway and captured the world's attention when 75,000 screaming fans greeted him as he entered into Tokyo's Olympic Stadium—four minutes ahead of the second-place runner. He set a world record time and became the first person ever to win two marathon golds. As he stood for the medals ceremony, expecting to sing along with his country's song, Bikila got a surprise: the Japanese orchestra didn't know the Ethiopian national anthem (no one ever dreamed Bikila would win)—so it played Japan's anthem instead.

COUNTRY HONORED: Spain
SPORTING EVENT: 2003 Davis Cup (tennis) in Melbourne
WRONG SONG: Before the finals match between Spain and Australia, trumpeter James Morrison was called upon to play the Spanish national anthem. As soon as Morrison started playing, though, the Spaniards reacted with outrage. Why? He was playing "Himno de Riego," the long-defunct anthem of a regime that had deposed King Alfonso XIII in 1931. (One version of the song has a verse about a man wiping his bottom on the king.) And Alfonso was the grandfather of Spain's current monarch, the hugely popular King Juan Carlos I. When the team threatened to pull out of the competition, the organizer quickly apologized.

COUNTRY HONORED: Philippines
SPORTING EVENT: 2003 Southeast Asian Games in Ho Chi Minh City

WRONG SONG: After the Philippine judo team won two gold medals, the winners were confused during the awards ceremony to hear an anthem they didn't recognize. "We didn't know which one it was, but it wasn't ours," said Bong Pedralvez of the Philippine consulate. Response: The entire delegation ignored the music and sang the correct anthem a cappella.

BONUS BLUNDER: That wasn't the only slip-up. During the volleyball competition, the Philippine team noticed that their flag was upside down. The red stripe was on top and the blue was on the bottom. The error had more meaning than most knew: "If we put red on top," Pedralvez explained, "that means we're at war."

COUNTRY HONORED: Italy
SPORTING EVENT: 2002 World Cup in Japan
WRONG SONG: During the 2002 soccer season, the Italian national team was criticized because their players didn't sing along when their national anthem was played. The coach took the criticism to heart and insisted his players learn the song, "Fratelli d'Italia" ("Hymn of Mameli"), and practice singing it. But the players were insulted by the criticism and announced that they would protest at the World Cup...by not singing the anthem. And they didn't. (In reporting the incident, European newspapers pointed out that many Italians admitted to disliking the song, which ends with the words "We are ready for death!")

*　　*　　*

BASEBALL MYTH-CONCEPTION

Myth: *Minor leaguers refer to the majors as "The Show."*
Fact: This term was popularized by the 1988 film *Bull Durham*. But ESPN analyst Bob Halloran says the screenwriter simply made it up. (He doesn't like the rest of the movie, either.) In his experience, Halloran never heard anyone call the big leagues "The Show," and after asking around, found that no one else had heard them called that, either...although Arkansas Travelers owner Bert Parke said that some minor leaguers refer to the majors as "The Big Club."

At the Duffer's Golf Tournament, whiffs are allowed with no penalty.

THE ROMAN GAMES

The Roman Colosseum is one of the most famous structures in the world. What went on there? You've probably seen a gladiator fight or two in films, but chances are it was tame compared to the real-life action. Here's the gruesome story, from the BRI's Ancient History Department.

A NOBLE END

The ancient Romans believed that restless spirits of the dead could be appeased through bloodshed. So it was common that when a Roman noble died, his friends and loved ones would hire gladiators to fight to the death in a battle arranged especially for the funeral.

The first such battle was held in 264 B.C., and over the centuries they became so popular that people began to hold them whether or not there was a funeral, just for the thrill of watching people die.

As these spectacles grew in popularity, larger and larger staging areas were needed. In A.D. 69, the Roman emperor Vespasian ordered the building of the Flavian Amphitheater, Rome's first permanent amphitheater. Today it's better known as the Colosseum.

Building the Colosseum allowed Vespasian to keep the more than one million citizens of Rome under control by quenching their thirst for blood in a way that did not threaten the empire. Just as the earliest gladiator battles had soothed uneasy spirits, the games at the Colosseum soothed the restless population of Rome. And because most emperors were enthusiastic spectators at the games, it established a bond between emperors and the common person.

THE STRUCTURE

• The amphitheater was the largest building of its kind on Earth. More than 150 feet high, it measured 620 by 513 feet and enclosed an oval arena that was 287 feet long by 180 feet wide. It could hold 50,000 people.

• Seating was arranged according to class: the emperor, his vestal virgins, and other important officials sat in ringside boxes; behind them were tiers of marble seats divided into two areas: one for "distinguished private citizens" and another for the members of the middle class. Behind the marble seats was a section for "slaves and foreigners"; behind that was an enclosed gallery set aside for women and the poor, with wooden seats much like bleachers in today's baseball parks.

A TYPICAL DAY AT THE COLOSSEUM

• Festivities began at dawn and often lasted well into the night. "Second-rate" events were scheduled during mealtimes, however, so that spectators could return home for lunch without missing much. The feeding of Christians to the lions is believed by many historians to have been one of the mealtime events.

• On the mornings of the games, the gladiators rode by chariot from their barracks to the amphitheater and marched into the arena up to the emperor's box, where they saluted the emperor.

• The day often began with bloodless duels that mimicked the more violent events to come. Women, or sometimes dwarfs or cripples, battled one another using wooden swords that were made to look like metal.

• After this event ended, an attendant would blow the *tuba*, or war trumpet, to announce the beginning of the main event—most often a battle between gladiators.

The Gladiators

Finding enough gladiators to keep the bloodthirsty spectators happy was difficult. Most were recruited from the ranks of slaves, convicts, or prisoners of war. A handful were bankrupt nobles and freemen who needed money. Recruits signed contracts in which they agreed to be "burned with fire, shackled with chains, whipped with rods, and killed with steel," and were trained in gladiator schools all over the empire.

• Each gladiator was trained to use a particular set of weapons. There were four main categories:

    1. The Samnite, who wore a helmet, a metal shin guard on the left leg, and a leather sleeve on the right arm. He carried a sword and shield.

    2. The Thracian, who wore no armor but carried a small sword and round shield.

    3. The Myrmillo, or fishman, who wore a helmet and carried a small sword, shield, and a stick weighted with lead.

Regulation length of an ancient Roman chariot race: seven laps around the arena.

4. The Retiarii, who wore no armor and carried only a net, trident (three-pronged spear), and dagger.

• Gladiators sometimes fought either one-on-one or two-on-two. Other times, entire squads of gladiators battled it out. As many as 2,000 men might battle in a single day, with half of them getting killed in the process.

Begging for Mercy

Gladiators usually fought to the death, although the loser had a chance of escaping with his life (but not his dignity) intact. When it became clear to a gladiator that he was going to be defeated, he could cast away his shield and raise a finger on his left hand—this was the gesture used to throw oneself upon the mercy of the emperor.

• The emperor would then ask the crowd to help him decide the gladiator's fate. They would shout *Mitte!* ("Let him go free!") and give the emperor a thumbs-up, or *Iugula!* ("Pay the penalty!") and give a thumbs-down. The emperor would then give either a thumbs-up or a thumbs-down, and his orders would be carried out.

ANIMAL GAMES

The Romans also loved to watch professional *bestiarii* ("beast slayers" who weren't considered gladiators) kill fierce animals such as lions, tigers, bulls, or bears—or just about anything that could bleed to death. Many of the events involved the killing of ostriches, deer, and even giraffes.

• The Romans scoured the empire and its provinces looking for things to kill; by the time the animal hunts were abolished in the sixth century A.D., several species of animals, including the elephants of North Africa, the hippopotamuses of Nubia, the lions of Mesopotamia, and the tigers of Hyrcania, had all been driven to extinction.

• Some of the animal events involved audience participation. Spectators were invited to throw spears from their seats or to use bows and arrows; at other events, skilled hunters entered the arena and chased down the animals with hounds. At still other events, it was the wild animals who hunted *people*, when condemned criminals (or regular criminals, if condemned criminals were in short supply) would be thrown to them completely defenseless.

If one team forfeits a baseball game, what's the score? (It's recorded as 9–0.)

WATER SPORTS

For really special occasions, the heavy wooden planks that served as the floor of the arena would be removed and the stadium flooded with water so that mock sea battles could be staged. The Colosseum's opening-day celebrations in A.D. 80 had just such a sea battle; it involved hundreds of boats, more than 3,000 participants, and was watched by an estimated 50,000 spectators. It was just as bloody as the regular gladiator fights; the only difference was that the gladiators were in boats. The sea battle was followed by an animal hunt, in which more than 5,000 animals were killed.

THE END

When Christianity became the official religion of the Roman Empire in 392, pressure began to build for the games to be abandoned. In 404, a Christian monk named Telemachus tried to break up a gladiatorial duel by jumping into the ring and physically separating the combatants...and was stoned to death by the crowd for his efforts. The resulting scandal was so great that Emperor Honorius, who had previously been a fan of the games, abolished them later that year.

• Was it a mistake? As the empire made a transition from paganism to Christianity, critics predicted that abandoning the old religion and ways—under which the Roman Empire had risen to unparalleled greatness—would cause Rome to collapse. The Colosseum closed amid dire predictions of doom. "If the Colosseum falls, Rome falls," the saying went. Sure enough, in 410, the Eternal City was sacked by the Visigoths.

Note: The Colosseum today looks like it's been damaged by an earthquake, but actually most of the destruction has come at the hands of humans, who've plundered it for building materials over the centuries. (A lot of the stones were used to build St. Peter's Basilica.) The structure's pockmarked appearance is due to the fact that during the Middle Ages—when metal was particularly hard to come by—generations of Romans pried loose the metal fittings that held the stones together. Today gravity is the only thing that holds many of the stone blocks together; and thanks to the vibrations from auto traffic, the stones are slowly shifting and putting the entire Colosseum in danger of collapse.

More than 300 styles of martial arts are named for animals.

IT'S A WEIRD, WEIRD WORLD OF SPORTS

Proof that truth really is stranger than fiction.

SPEED-O

In the 1972 Olympics, mustache-wearing Mark Spitz put on one of the greatest swimming performances in history, winning a record seven gold medals and breaking world records in all seven events. Years later he told *Time* magazine that a Russian coach at the Games had asked him about the mustache. Spitz jokingly replied that it "deflects water away from my mouth, allows my rear end to rise, and makes me bullet shaped in the water, and that's what had allowed me to swim so great." The next year, Spitz said, "every Russian male swimmer had a mustache."

CANADIAN ACHIN'

In 1952 Stan Long, 23, of the Victoria Cougars hockey team in British Columbia had his left thigh completely pierced by a hockey stick. The defenseman had collided with another player whose stick had just broken and was saved only by the fact that there was a doctor in the stands. He recovered from the wound and eventually played hockey again.

HOOP SUIT

In 1991 a California lawyer and his family were playing basketball outside their house when a neighbor, also a lawyer, asked them to quiet down. When they didn't, the irate neighbor sprayed the basketball court with a hose. The family sued, claiming emotional distress. The neighbor then countersued, saying they had reduced the value of his home by building a basketball court next to theirs. And to prove it, he introduced "scientific testimony from acoustical engineers, architects, and real-estate appraisers." The verdict? At first the court restricted the family to six hours of basketball a day. But an appeals court ruled that the lawyer should just close his window.

Pole vaulting originated in ancient Greece, when villagers used long poles to leap over bulls.

RUN FOR THE BORDER

In 2003 *Men's Fitness* magazine named Houston "America's Fattest City." In 2005 a local bike club tried to change the city's image by holding a 40-mile bike rally through downtown Houston. To get people to sign up, they offered free beer and tacos at the end of the race.

OUT OF UNIFORM

Police in Brazil arrested a minor league soccer player named William Pereira Farias after he stripped off his uniform and threw it into the crowd to celebrate the scoring of a goal. "He broke the laws of respectful behavior," police officer Alfredo Faria told reporters. "He offended the townspeople and will likely be suspended from the team."

GRUNT-O-METER

The British newspaper *The Sun* claimed to have set up a microphone that measured the loudness of the grunts made by tennis star Monica Seles during play at Wimbledon in the early 1990s. The paper reported that the star had a grunt volume of 82 decibels, somewhere "between a pneumatic drill and a diesel train."

ETHICALLY CHALLENGED

The 2000 International Paralympics were a resounding success for Spain: The country won 107 medals overall, highlighted by the gold medal awarded to its developmentally disabled basketball team. A few months later, one of the players, Carlos Ribagorda, made the shocking admission that "of the 200 Spanish Paralympic athletes, at least 15 had no physical or mental handicap." Ribagorda, a journalist for the Spanish magazine *Capital*, had joined the intellectually disabled basketball team to expose the corruption. In the two years Ribagorda played for the team, no one ever tested his I.Q. Not only that, says Ribagorda, the team was told to slow down their game so they wouldn't attract suspicion.

A subsequent international investigation concluded that only two members of the basketball team were intellectually disabled. In addition, as Ribagorda had discovered, some members of Spain's Paralympic track, tennis, and swimming teams were found to be only...*morally* handicapped.

MR. GAME BOY

You've probably never heard of Gumpei Yokoi, but if you've ever played a Game Boy, a Color Game Boy, Donkey Kong, or just about any other Nintendo product made between 1970 and 1996, you have him to thank for it. Here's his story.

IN THE CARDS

In the mid-1960s, an electronics student named Gumpei Yokoi graduated from Doshisha University in Kyoto, Japan, and got a job as a maintenance engineer with the Nintendo company, a manufacturer of playing cards.

Keeping the playing card printing machines in good working order must have been boring work, because Yokoi started passing the time building toys—with company materials, using company machines and equipment, on company time.

That didn't exactly fit into his job description, so when Nintendo's president, Hiroshi Yamauchi, found out what he was up to and called him into his office, Yokoi figured that he'd soon be looking for a new job.

Not quite—Nintendo was making so much money selling children's playing cards that it had decided to create an entire games division. Yamauchi transferred Yokoi to the new division and told him to come up with a game that Nintendo could manufacture in time to sell for Christmas.

Yokoi went home and got one of the toys he'd already made: an extendable grabbing "hand" that he made out of crisscrossing pieces of wooden latticework. When you squeezed its handles together like a pair of scissors, the latticework extended and the hand closed its grip.

YOU'VE GOT TO HAND IT TO HIM

Yamauchi was impressed, and production on the Ultra Hand, as they named it, began right away. The company ended up selling more than 1.2 million of the hands at a price of about $6 apiece—the games division's first toy was also its first big hit.

Yokoi's team followed with a series of other toys, including the Ultra Machine (an indoor pitching machine), the Ultra Scope (a

---

On May 25, 1935, track star Jesse Owens broke six world records...in less than 45 minutes.

periscope), and a "Love Tester" that supposedly measured how much love existed between a boy and a girl. All the Love Tester really did was give people an excuse to hold hands, but that was enough—it was a huge success too. So was the Beam Gun, a gun that shot beams of light at optical targets.

Nintendo spent a fortune converting old bowling alleys and shooting galleries into Beam Gun shooting galleries…and nearly went bankrupt. But it recovered after Yamauchi noticed how much money Atari, Magnavox, and other companies were making in the video game business. He licensed their technology and came out with Color TV Game 6, the company's first video game.

GAME & WATCH

As video games were becoming more successful, Yamauchi started pressing Yokoi for a competing product. So the design team came up with the Game & Watch, a series of dozens and eventually hundreds of pocket-sized video games that also displayed the time at the top of the screen.

The games used simple calculator technology—LCD screens and tiny buttons that served as game controllers—and they weren't much bigger than credit cards. Kids could play them anywhere: in cars, at school during recess, or in their rooms before bedtime. Nintendo ended up selling more than 40 million of the devices all over the world between 1980 and 1989.

GAME BOY

In 1983 Nintendo introduced the Famicom (short for Family Computer)—its first cartridge-based video-game system—and then released it in the United States as the Nintendo Entertainment System (NES) in 1985. The system established the company as the dominant world player in the video game business. By 1988, however, the NES was getting a little old and Nintendo's rival Sega was preparing to launch a new system called the Mega Drive. Nintendo's new Super NES system was still in the works, so the company needed a product that would generate revenue and keep fans of the company's products occupied until Super NES was ready.

Lucky for Nintendo, Yokoi had one. Called the Game Boy, it sought to combine the best that the Game & Watch series and

---

In baseball, the five-sided home plate is 17" x 8 1/2" x 12" x 12" x 8 1/2".

the NES had to offer. The Game Boy was portable, about the size of a transistor radio, and it was a cartridge-based system like the NES. With the Game & Watch series, anytime you wanted to play a new game, you had to buy a whole new Game & Watch. With a Game Boy, all you had to do was buy a new cartridge. Better yet, Game Boys could be linked together so that two players could compete against each other.

LOW TECH

The Game Boy wasn't exactly state of the art. It didn't have a color screen or a backlight, because those drained the batteries too quickly and added too much to the cost. You couldn't play it in the dark. The screen was so crude, in fact, that when Atari's engineers saw it for the first time, they laughed. Over at Sony, the response was different. "This Game Boy should have been a Sony product," one executive complained.

The Game Boy went on to become hugely successful, thanks in large part to the fact that the game appealed to adults in a way that the NES didn't. The original Game Boy was packaged with Tetris, an adult-friendly, maddeningly addictive game in which the player has to maneuver and interlock blocks that fall from the top of the screen. Game Boys became a fixture on subways, on airplanes, in company lunchrooms, any place adults had a few free moments. When President George H. W. Bush went into the hospital in May 1991, the leader of the free world was photographed playing a Game Boy. Kids liked to play Game Boys too...whenever they could pry them away from their parents.

NEW AND IMPROVED

Yokoi led the effort to keep the Game Boy product line fresh and profitable over the years. In 1994 his design team came up with an accessory that allowed Game Boy cartridges to be played on the Super NES system. That was followed by the Game Boy Pocket and the first Pokémon (short for Pocket Monsters) cartridge in 1996.

Pokémon was the first game that allowed players to exchange items from one linked Game Boy to another, and though Nintendo's expectations for the game weren't particularly high, the game became an enormous industry unto itself, spawning other toys, trading cards, clothing, an animated TV series, a movie, and even

Lowest Super Bowl score ever: 3, by the Miami Dolphins in 1972 (they lost to Dallas).

food. It's estimated that Pokémon merchandise has racked up more than $20 billion worth of sales for Nintendo since 1996, *not including* the video games. As for the Game Boy product line (which saw the addition of the Game Boy Color in 1998), by 2001 it had sold more than 115 million units and 450 million cartridges, making it the most popular game system of all time.

DOWN AND OUT

Needless to say, Yokoi made Nintendo a lot of money over the years. What did he have to show for it? Not much—in 1995 his Virtual Boy, an addition to the Game Boy line that was kind of like a 3-D View-Master—bombed. The red LED display gave so many players headaches and dizziness that when the product was released in the United States it came with a warning label. One reviewer called it a "Virtual Dog."

Nintendo lost a lot of money on the Virtual Boy, and Yamauchi apparently decided to humiliate Yokoi publicly by making him demonstrate the game system at the company's annual Shoshinkai trade show, even though it was all but dead. "This was his punishment, the Japanese corporate version of Dante's Inferno," Steven Kent writes in *The Ultimate History of Video Games*. "When employees make high-profile mistakes in Japan, it is not unusual for their superiors to make an example out of them for a period of time, then return them to their former stature."

EARLY EXIT

Yokoi must have decided not to wait around for his restoration. He left the company in August 1996 after more than 27 years on the job, and founded his own handheld game company called Koto (Japanese for "small town"). It produced a game system similar to the Game Boy, only with a bigger screen and better speakers. We'll never know what kind of gains he might have made against the Game Boy, because on October 4, 1997, he was killed in a car accident. He was 56.

* * *

"When you come to a fork in the road, take it."
—Yogi Berra

ANCIENT ORIGINS OF GOLF, PART II

(Quietly): Uncle John has just sliced terribly and his ball is now deep in the trees. Let's see if we can get a camera in there—Oh! There he is! His ball went straight into an old, abandoned outhouse! But back to our story... (Part I is on page 62.)

CLOSER TO HOME

Golf may be descended from stick-and-ball games of the Greeks, Egyptians, Persians, or even the ancient Sumerians—no one knows for sure. But what is known is that the ancient Romans had a stick-and-ball game, *paganica*, and they brought it with them when they invaded and conquered nearly all of Europe, including the British Isles, which they ruled from the first through fourth centuries A.D. Although they never conquered Scotland (they tried three times), many golf historians believe that the Romans got close enough for their game, in some form, to have made its way to Scotland over the centuries and become transformed into golf.

The following are some of the theories about how one of those games could be the exact and most recent ancestor of Scotland's golf. There are many theories and few real records—but who cares? They're all good stories and any one of them might actually be true.

HURLING: THE IRISH THEORY

Hurling is an ancient Celtic game. It was—and still is—played with a curved wooden stick, the *hurley*, or *caman* in Irish Gaelic, and a small hard ball, the *sliotar*. The object is to hit the ball down a determined field and between a set of goalposts. The age of the game is unknown. Some historians say it is an offshoot of paganica, but the Irish claim it as their own. Irish mythology mentions it numerous times, dating it all the way back to 1272 B.C. and the legendary Battle of Moytura between the native Fir Bolg peoples and the invading Tuatha De Danann. In lieu of the battle, the two sides held a hurling match. The Fir Bolg won a bloody and bone-breaking game—and then killed their opponents.

Is this very ancient hitting-a-ball-with-a-stick game—played right there in the British Isles—golf's true ancestor? Very possibly. A similar game is played by the Scottish Celtic peoples. *Shinty* is very similar to hurling, and it's just as old, although it may have been brought to Scotland by the Irish.

Interesting fact: The Celtic peoples are believed to have come from eastern Europe and northern Greece. Some believe that at one time they intermingled with the ancient Egyptians—and that the game of hurling actually comes from the same or a similar game as the one depicted on the ancient tomb of Prince Kheti.

CAMBUCA: THE ENGLISH THEORY

Cambuca is believed to have been played in England more than a thousand years ago. It is considered a direct descendant of paganica and may have even been the same game with a new name: *cambuca* is medieval Latin—the language spoken in England at the time of the Roman occupation—for "curved stick or staff."

Cambuca became popular in Britain starting around the 12th century A.D., and it does have its similarities to modern golf: the object was to hit a wooden ball with a curved stick toward a mark in the ground. (Not much more is known about it.) In 1363 King Edward III made cambuca (along with several other games) illegal because men were playing the games instead of practicing their archery, endangering the security of the country.

The Great East Window in Gloucester Cathedral, a huge stained-glass window made in 1349, shows a man preparing to strike a ball with a club or mallet in a surprisingly golflike way. The game being played is believed to be cambuca—and the window was made 100 years before the earliest record of golf in Scotland.

COLF AND *HET KOLVEN*: THE DUTCH THEORY

Many historians say golf, and even the word "golf," comes from the Netherlands. Golf historian Steven J. H. Van Hengel says that as early as the 1300s, the Dutch played *spel metten colve*—"game with clubs." He writes that on December 26, 1297, citizens of the town of Loenen aan de Vecht celebrated a military victory by playing *colf* on their "four-hole" course (they weren't holes, but aboveground targets). The fact that colf was chosen, says Hengel, shows that it must have already been around for quite a while.

Others say the game evolved from another Dutch game called *het kolven*, pointing out the similarity in the words *kolven* and "golf." This game involved driving a ball a long distance with a stick toward a goal such as a tree or a post. It was played either on ice or on land as early as the 1300s.

In any case, these historians like to point to the well-established fact that the Scottish game developed on Scotland's east coast—across the North Sea from the coast of the Netherlands. And the well-known trade routes at the time between the Netherlands and Scotland make the transfer of the Dutch games to Scotland and the evolution to golf easily believable.

Interesting fact: Het kolven was played in the American colonies as early as 1657.

For Part III of "Ancient Origins of Golf," blast over to page 411.

* * *

"STATUS QUO"

This ode came to us via the Internet—from a Longfellow of the links named Victor Biggs.

I read the column Nicklaus writes
And bought a book by Floyd,
About the things that I should do
And those I should avoid.
On TV I watch Dave Pelz
The short game noted whiz,
And listen rapt to all he tells
To make my stroke like his.
I also buy the latest gear
From folks like Orlimar,
For the promise there is clear
For drives both straight and far.
And all the while I'm thinking hard
About the mental game,
But here I am to tell you pard
My score remains the same.

...Kareem Abdul-Jabbar, Wilt Chamberlain, Karl Malone, and Charles Barkley.

TAKE ME OUT TO THE BORU GAME

This is a page for baseball—and language—fans.

The Japanese have adopted baseball as their national game. They've also taken a number of American baseball terms and made them Japanese. Here are some of the words, written phonetically. Some are easy, some confusing. See if you can tell what they mean. Answers are at the bottom of the page.

1. Batta
2. Boru
3. Kochi
4. Besuboru
5. Besu-ryne
6. Chenji appu
7. De gemu
8. Era
9. Herumetto
10. Mitto
11. Maneja
12. Suisaido sukuiizu
13. Homuran

14. Auto
15. Fain puray
16. Kyatcha
17. Pasu boh-ru
18. Sukoa bodo
19. Batta bokkusu
20. Kuriin hitto
21. Foku boru
22. Wairudo pitchi
23. Banto
24. Pitchingu sutaffu
25. Furu kaunto

26. Puray boru!
27. Senta
28. Gurobu
29. Fauru
30. Pinchi ranna
31. Hitto endu ran
32. Battingu sutansu
33. Foa boru
34. Daburu hedda
35. "Gettsu"
36. Katto ofu puray

ANSWERS: 1. Batter; 2. Ball; 3. Coach; 4. Baseball; 5. Baseline; 6. Change-up; 7. Day game; 8. Error; 9. Helmet; 10. Mitt; 11. Manager; 12. Suicide squeeze; 13. Home run; 14. Out; 15. Fine play; 16. Catcher; 17. Passed ball; 18. Scoreboard; 19. Batting box; 20. Clean hit; 21. Fork ball; 22. Wild pitch; 23. Bunt; 24. Pitching staff; 25. Full count; 26. Play ball!; 27. Center field or center fielder; 28. Glove; 29. Foul ball; 30. Pinch runner; 31. Hit-and-run; 32. Batting stance; 33. Four balls (a walk); 34. Doubleheader; 35. "Get two" (double play); 36. Cutoff play

---

Q: What has 18 legs and catches flies? A: A baseball team.

THE REAL ROCKY

*Sylvester Stallone's Rocky movies were based on a real-life person. But
he wasn't from Philadelphia like in the movies; he was from New
Jersey. And he went three rounds...with Stallone's lawyers.*

LEARNING THE ROPES

Chuck Wepner of Bayonne, New Jersey, learned to handle
himself working as a bouncer in the late 1950s. Then, during a stint in the Marine Corps, he learned to box. When he finished his time in the military, he fought in the amateur boxing
circuit on the weekends and evenings. He couldn't make enough
money to quit his day job, so he had to train at night.

One day, at a friend's suggestion, Wepner threw his hat into
the ring for a Golden Gloves match—and won. He made the
jump to professional boxing in 1964, but paying the bills was difficult; he still had to earn a living with a string of jobs: bouncer,
liquor salesman, and security guard. His boxing career was stuck
in a rut; he fought up-and-coming contenders like George Foreman and stars like Sonny Liston, but he couldn't seem to make it
to the next level.

THE BAYONNE BLEEDER

Eventually Wepner earned a reputation not for knocking other
boxers out, but for being able to take a beating. His endurance
became so famous that it earned him the nickname "the Bayonne
Bleeder." He wasn't about finesse; he was about being the last one
standing. He kept on fighting, and in 1975, after he'd racked up a
respectable number of wins, he got a golden opportunity: he was
offered the chance to fight Muhammad Ali for the world heavyweight title. Wepner leapt at it, but the rest of the world was skep-
tical; some experts predicted that the fight would last only three
rounds, if that long.

As predicted, Wepner lost to Ali. But he shocked the boxing
world by lasting 15 rounds—even knocking Ali down with a right
hook in the 9th. But in the 15th round, with Wepner bleeding
from cuts over both eyes and a broken nose, the referee stopped
the fight out of concern for his health. But millions watched the

---

fight on television, and Wepner's gutsy performance earned him features in *Sports Illustrated*, *Time*, and other national magazines.

ENTER ROCKY

Among the millions watching the fight that night was a young New York actor named Sylvester Stallone. A dropout of the University of Miami's drama program, Stallone was acting in off-Broadway plays and the occasional small film, but he also liked boxing. Wepner's underdog performance inspired him to write a screenplay that he ended up calling *Rocky*, the story of a down-on-his-luck tough guy who makes it big in boxing. Stallone sold the screenplay for $150,000 and played the lead role in the 1976 film. The movie was a smash: *Rocky* won the Oscar for Best Picture, and Stallone was nominated for Best Actor. The film became a franchise and spawned five hit sequels.

SEE YOU IN COURT

When Stallone sold the original script, he contacted Wepner to tell him about it. They kept in touch for years, and Stallone even gave him a bit part in *Rocky II*...which wound up on the cutting-room floor. But in 2003 Wepner claimed that Stallone had promised to compensate him for using his story, but he never saw a cent of the millions of dollars the movies generated. According to his lawyer in an interview with CBS News, "Stallone has been using Chuck's name—and continues to this day—in promoting the *Rocky* franchise without any permission or compensation." Wepner wound up suing Stallone three times. Twice the case was dismissed, but the last round ended in an out-of-court settlement for an undisclosed amount.

Wepner, who retired in 1978 with a professional record of 35–14–2, was eventually inducted into the New Jersey Boxing Hall of Fame. Today he still lives in Bayonne and makes a living as a liquor salesman and motivational speaker. He's also written an autobiography, *Toe to Toe with Any Foe*.

*   *   *

"Without my story, *Rocky* would have been nothing but a tale. Nobody would believe it."

—Chuck Wepner

Michael Jordan is a registered member of the Golf Nuts Society of America.

BEAT THE CLOCK

In the early 1900s, one athlete drew fans by the millions, endorsed products from cigars to washing machines, and had the country watching his every move. Who was he? A "crippled" racehorse named Dan Patch.

HARNESS RACING'S HEYDAY

In the 1700s, a new American sport grew up around the horses and buggies that, at the time, were the main mode of transportation. The sport of racing horses in harness, with drivers in carts behind them, had died out with the Roman Empire's chariot races. But it came back again on the long, rural roads of the United States, where farmers and landowners held informal carriage races to see whose horse was the fastest.

Gradually these amateur contests became professionally organized. By 1825 tracks had cropped up around the country, running mile-long races with each driver managing his horse from a two-wheeled cart called a *sulky*. Spectators flocked to the new sport, known as harness racing. County fairs held harness races as part of what was called the Grand Circuit, and crowds by the tens of thousands, enticed by the possibility of seeing a horse break the world record, cheered on the high-speed races. By the beginning of the 20th century, harness racing was one of the most popular sports in America.

TROTTERS AND PACERS

Not just any fast horse could be entered in a harness race. The animals were allowed only two gaits, or strides: a *trotter* moved his left hind leg and right foreleg simultaneously, while a *pacer* moved both legs on the same side in unison. Some horses specialized in trotting; some were pacers. Eventually Americans developed a new horse that was perfect for harness racing—a stocky, sturdy breed called the Standardbred.

Slightly smaller in stature than Thoroughbreds, Standardbreds also had longer bodies and were more muscular. They had better endurance and a calmer disposition than their Thoroughbred cousins, and, most important, they could trot or pace a mile in a

---

The Olympic motto—*Citius, Altius, Fortius*—is Latin for "Swifter, Higher, Stronger."

blistering 2 minutes and 30 seconds, which became known as the "standard" time.

MESSNER'S FOLLY

In 1894 Dan Messner Jr. was a department-store businessman in the small town of Oxford, Indiana. He was also a passionate harness racing fan—a passion that his friends thought would ruin him. That year, he decided to buy Zelica, a high-priced Standardbred mare, hoping she'd have a long racing career. But it wasn't to be—a torn tendon ended her racing days before they began. While Messner drowned his disappointment in a few too many drinks, he made an intoxicated decision to spend most of his savings to send Zelica to Illinois and breed her to Joe Patchen, a fast and famous pacer stallion.

Zelica gave birth in 1895 but the colt, Dan Patch (named for his owner and his sire), dashed Messner's dreams again. Although he was a beautiful dark brown with a white star on his forehead, Dan Patch had such crooked legs that he couldn't nurse without someone helping him to stand. Friends urged him to put the colt out of its misery, but Messner couldn't do it. He later admitted that he saved Dan Patch because he was "friendly and cute."

It didn't take long for Oxford townspeople to nickname the crippled, expensive colt "Messner's Folly." By the time he was two, Dan Patch was gaunt and clumsy, with knees considered too knobby for racing. Still, he could walk well enough to pull a grocery wagon, and that could have remained his fate...if a stable owner named John Wattles hadn't seen some potential in him.

FROM FOLLY TO FAME

In 1899 Wattles began to train Dan Patch to race as a pacer, and to Messner's surprise, the three-year-old took to it with intelligence and speed. But Messner didn't want to risk an entry fee to race the horse. Harness races consisted of at least five mile-long contests, or "heats," with the winner taking three out of five. They were so grueling that horse-doping was a constant problem. One trainer, charged with giving a champion cocaine, indignantly protested that he only used whiskey to perk up his horse, and then only when the animal was thoroughly exhausted. If strong horses found racing so brutal, how could a recovered cripple ever win?

First basketball player to enter the NBA directly from high school: Moses Malone, 1974.

In August of 1900, Messner took a chance and entered Dan Patch as a pacer at a county fair in Boswell, Indiana. By this time, Dan Patch was four years old and well muscled; he'd grown out of his awkwardness. Still, everyone was surprised when he won, and few bet on him at his next start in nearby Lafayette because the competition there was much tougher. As expected, the newbie lost the first heat—but he went on to take the next three heats and won the race.

Dan Patch continued to win. In fact, he didn't lose another heat until the following year, when a win was disqualified because of misconduct by his driver. By that time, Dan Patch was racing in the big leagues, the Grand Circuit. Bigger races and tougher competition made no difference—he didn't lose a race. A bet on Dan Patch had become such a sure thing that track owners in Readville, Massachusetts, pulled him from their betting sheets to avoid financial ruin.

In November 1901, Dan Patch returned to Oxford as the hometown horse made good. He'd earned over $13,000 at a time when the country's top baseball player, Ty Cobb, made $12,000 per year. Oxford celebrated Dan Patch Day (an event still held today), and hundreds of newspapers covered the small-town event. Dignitaries sent the horse flowers, and politicians handed out buttons with Dan Patch's picture on them. Messner happily paraded the horse around Oxford, enjoying the crowds.

RACE AGAINST TIME

Messner enjoyed his good fortune until one of his fillies, Lady Patch, died of a suspected poisoning. Frightened that Dan Patch was the intended victim, Messner sold his superstar in 1902 to a man named M. E. Sturgis for the unheard-of sum of $20,000.

Sturgis was known as a New York "sportsman," or wealthy gambler. When no owner would race their horse against Dan Patch, Sturgis found another way to make money: He ran the pacer in exhibition races against the clock. In the 1902 season, huge crowds paid to watch America's fastest pacer race alone. By then, the world record for pacing a mile had fallen to 1 minute, 59 ¼ seconds. In one race, Dan Patch equaled it. Could he beat it?

Marion "Will" Savage, a wealthy businessman, believed he could. Savage was an Iowa farmboy who'd made a fortune as the owner of a giant food company, and he decided to buy Dan Patch—for the

---

The first permanent concession stand in baseball was built at Chicago's Wrigley Field in 1914.

astronomical sum of $60,000. Savage's estate included a mile track, an indoor half-mile track, and a huge, heated stable topped with an onion dome dubbed the "Taj Mahal." Savage bought a plush, private train car to transport the horse to state fairs across the country, where he gave exhibition races. Sometimes, to add excitement, he paced against—and beat—galloping horses.

But the main focus of the races was the world record. Dan Patch soon broke it with a time of 1:59. Then he broke it again, with 1:58. Then 1:57 ¼, and 1:56 flat…in all, he set a new world record 14 different times. Then in 1905 in Lexington, Kentucky, he clocked in at 1:55 ¼—an official record that would be unequaled for 33 years. A year later, Dan Patch unofficially beat *that* record with a time of 1:55 flat in front of 95,000 spectators. And although that time was later disqualified due to a technicality, many racing fans still accepted it as the true world record. It wasn't until 1960 that another horse, Adios Butler, beat it.

UNSPOILED BY FAME
Dan Patch's friendly personality that had saved him as a colt made him a media star. Journalists reported how the horse interacted with people, recognized his human friends, "danced" to band music, knew how to pose for a photograph, and seemed to understand human conversation. The legend of Dan Patch, hyperintelligent superhorse, was only strengthened by the stallion's habit of stopping on the track before a race to give a majestic nod to the fans—as if the horse was shrewdly "counting the house."

Savage used the horse's charisma—and the constant media attention—to get endorsements that fattened his pocketbook. Americans were soon buying Dan Patch playing cards, chewing Dan Patch tobacco, and smoking Dan Patch cigars. Children played with Dan Patch sleds while moms washed clothes in Dan Patch washing machines. After the horse retired to Savage's Minnesota farm in 1909, a steady stream of tourists traveled there to visit him.

Savage's only mistake may have been turning down a deal to endorse the Dan Patch motor car. By 1916, the public had found a new love—the automobile—that eventually displaced harness racing as the new national craze. That year, at the age of 20, Dan Patch died. His owner, Marion Savage, died less than two day later.

COACHES' CORNER

All right, team, listen up! I want you to read this page and read it good. Anyone who doesn't can drop and give me 20!

"I have nothing to say. And I'll say it only once."

—Floyd Smith

"I wouldn't say that Joe has a sore arm, per se, but his arm is kind of sore."

—Weeb Ewbank

"Our strength is that we don't have any weaknesses. Our weakness is that we don't have any real strengths."

—Frank Boyles

"John didn't flunk his physical, he just didn't pass it."

—Steve Ortmayer

"If we hadn't given them those first four touchdowns, it might have been different."

—"Cootie" Reeves, Hokes Bluff, Alabama, high school football coach, after his team lost 53–0

"It's not how good you can play when you play good. It's how good you play when you play bad and we can play as bad as anyone in the country."

—Hugh Durham

"I don't think there's anybody in this organization not focused on the 49ers—I mean Chargers."

—Bill Belichick

"He wants Texas back."

—Tommy Lasorda, on what Mexican-born pitching sensation Fernando Valenzuela might demand in upcoming contract negotiations

"I've only heard what I've read in the papers."

—Frank Burns

"Managing is getting paid for home runs someone else hits."

—Casey Stengel

"I'm as nauseous as I've ever been. I have a terrible headache. My head is pounding. I feel like throwing up and I'm having trouble swallowing. And the beauty of it is, you want to feel like this every day."

—Tony LaRussa, during the 1996 NL Central Division title race

---

Baseball player Richie Ashburn once hit the same fan twice with foul balls—in the same at-bat.

PING PONG TRIVIA

*Ping Pong, formally known as "table tennis," has made its way
from an amusement for bored Victorians all the way to
the Olympics—and is played by millions. Here are
some great little facts to bat around.*

WHY "TABLE TENNIS"?

The first people who played the game actually played it on their dining-room tables. In England in the 1880s, it was fashionable for families to play miniature versions of lawn games indoors as after-dinner entertainment. By 1890, miniature games had become so popular that dedicated tables were being made for tiny versions of soccer, cricket, and lawn tennis—which evolved into the modern Ping Pong table that you probably have folded up in your basement.

WHIFF WHAFF?

Today, almost everyone calls table tennis "Ping Pong." But Ping Pong was a trademark for a particularly elaborate version of the game developed by English gamemakers J. Jaques & Son Ltd. in 1901, based on a previous version known as Gossima. There were other names for table tennis, including Whiff Whaff, Pom Pom, and Pim Pam. The successor company of J. Jaques & Son continues to sell tables and equipment for the game but calls it "table tennis" in its catalog. Meanwhile, the name "Ping Pong" has stuck with the game in much of the world.

PROGRESSION

The popularity of table tennis faded in the early 1900s, but it enjoyed a revival in the 1920s. The fad led to standardized rules in 1922 and the formation of the International Table Tennis Federation (ITTF) in 1926, with the first world championships held that year in London. That year, Hungarian players swept the singles, doubles, mixed, and team titles.

Table tennis historians divide the history of the game into three eras, distinguished by changes in the equipment and the dominance of one country or region in the championships.

Table tennis was first played using wine corks for balls and cigar box lids for paddles.

- The 1920s to the mid-'50s is known as the Hard Bat era (named for the table tennis paddle used at the time, which had a hard rather than padded surface). Europeans dominated the Hard Bat era, particularly Hungarians but also Romanian and British players.

- In the mid-1950s came the Sponge Bat era, when rackets were covered with a thin layer of sponge padding that sped up the game and made it easier to spin the ball. Asian players, especially the Japanese and Chinese, were the preeminent athletes in the sport during this time.

- After 1988, when table tennis officially became an Olympic sport, the game entered the Olympic era. Today, Chinese players are consistently the stars of the game (with 16 golds and 33 medals overall in Olympic competition), with South Korean and Swedish players running a distant second and third. For many years, the diameter of a regulation table tennis ball was 38 millimeters. But after the 2000 Olympics, the diameter was beefed up to 40 millimeters. The reason? So the ball would show up better on television.

NO GO, U.S.A.

How does the United States do in the competitive world of international table tennis? Poorly. Forrest Gump notwithstanding, the U.S. has never won a men's singles World Championship and hasn't won a women's singles championship since 1936. An American team won the mixed-doubles title at the World Championships in 1956, but the U.S. has never won a medal in Olympic table tennis.

PING PONG'S TIGER WOODS

Despite the Chinese dominance in the modern era, perhaps the most famous table tennis player in the world is a Swedish player named Jan-Ove Waldner. In 1992 Waldner became the sport's first "Grand Slam" champion, having won all three of the sport's major events: The World Championship (which he won in 1989, 1992, and 1997), the World Cup, and the Olympics. According to the ITTF, he's the first person to make more than a million dollars playing table tennis, and a YouTube video of his "great hits" has racked up more than 220,000 views.

In a 1936 Ping Pong tournament, the players volleyed for over 2 hours on the opening serve.

ROCK, PAPER, SCISSORS

*Uncle John was thinking about saving this chapter for the next book, but
Mrs. Uncle John insisted that it should go in this one. They settled the
dispute with a good old-fashioned round of Rochambeau. (Uncle John
threw scissors, Mrs. Uncle John threw a rock.) It's in.*

PAPER TRAIL
No one knows much about the history of Rock, Paper, Scissors, or *Rochambeau*, as it is also known. The game is believed
to be more than a century old, and may have originated in Africa,
Portugal, Scandinavia, or Japan, where it is known as *Jan Ken Pon*.
How it came to be associated with the Comte de Rochambeau, a
French general who commanded French troops under George
Washington during the Revolutionary War, is anyone's guess.

If you haven't played it since you were a kid, here's a refresher
on the rules: A round of Rock, Paper, Scissors is similar to a coin
toss. Two players shake or "prime" their fists three times (sometimes calling out "Ro, sham, beau!" as they do), then make a
"throw" by forming one of three symbols with their hand: a fist
(rock), a flat hand extended straight out (paper), or a V-sign made
by extending only the index and middle fingers (scissors). Paper
beats rock (the rock is covered by the paper), rock beats scissors
(it dulls or smashes the scissors), and scissors beats paper (snip-
snip). If you both throw the same symbol, it counts as a tie, and
you repeat the process until someone wins.

ALL GROWN UP
If Rock, Paper, Scissors used to be just for kids, it isn't anymore.
Today it's practically a professional sport, thanks in large part to
two Canadian brothers named Graham and Douglas Walker. One
cold winter night in 1995, they were both too lazy to leave their
cabin to get more wood for the fire, so they played 15 rounds to
decide who would have to go get it.

Graham won, but before it was over Doug noticed that he had
a habit of throwing whichever symbol would have beaten his previous throw—if he threw a rock, his next throw would be paper,
which beats the rock, followed by scissors, which cuts paper. That

got the brothers thinking that there might be a strategic side to the game that they hadn't thought about before.

The brothers also figured that if they still enjoyed playing the game, other adults would, too. They created an organization called the World RPS Society and put up a Web site. By 2002 they were ready to host their first world championship in Toronto. First prize: $800 and an XBox. Today the grand prize has grown to $10,000, and the tournament's success has led to the formation of the rival USA Rock Paper Scissors League, sponsored by Bud Light. It holds its $50,000 annual championship in Las Vegas. Dave McGill, a 30-year-old bartender from Omaha, won the top prize in 2006.

STRATEGIES

The experts differ on the best strategy for winning:

1. Psychology. One school of thought says you should try to read your opponent, guess which symbol they're going to throw, and respond with the symbol that will beat it. Rock is considered the most aggressive symbol, so if you detect signs of aggression, throw paper to beat their rock. Paper is passive, so throw scissors if your opponent appears weak…and hope they aren't just faking you out. If they look neither aggressive nor passive, throw rock to beat their scissors. Playing several rounds? Use your opponent's past throws to predict what their future throws will be, and respond accordingly. If they throw lots of rocks, throw lots of paper, etc.

2. Runs. Another school of thought says that you should ignore psychology entirely by selecting one or more runs, or "gambits," of three throws each (paper, scissors, paper, for example; or scissors, scissors, rock) and stick to them no matter what your opponent does. By choosing throws at random, you thwart your opponent's attempts to read your psychology. Some of the most popular runs even have names: Paper Dolls (paper, scissors, scissors); Avalanche (rock, rock, rock); and Bureaucrat (paper, paper, paper).

ROCHAMBEAU IN THE NEWS

In the Art World. In 2005 a wealthy Japanese businessman named Takashi Hashiyama decided to auction off four of his company's most valuable pieces of art: paintings by Pablo Picasso, Paul Cézanne, Vincent van Gogh, and a fourth artist named Alfred Sisley. But when he couldn't decide between the rival Christie's and Sotheby's auction houses, he invited both firms to play a game of Rochambeau to decide the winner. Sotheby's says it didn't have a strategy and just picked a symbol at random. Christie's turned for advice to Flora and Alice Maclean, the twin 11-year-old daughters of Nicholas Maclean, head of the modern art department. They suggested scissors. "Everybody knows you start with scissors," Alice explained to an interviewer. Sotheby's picked paper…and lost to Christie's scissors.

Christie's auctioned the paintings for $17.8 million and pocketed several million dollars in fees from the sales (no word on whether Flora and Alice got a share of the loot).

The Legal World. When two opposing lawyers couldn't agree on the location for a witness's testimony to be taken, Florida judge Gregory Pressnell issued a court order instructing that the lawyers settle the matter by playing a round of Rock, Paper, Scissors. So who won? Nobody—after Judge Pressnell's order made international headlines, the lawyers gave in and settled the dispute themselves.

The Natural World. In 1996 a California biologist named Barry Sinervo published a study claiming that the mating habits of the side-blotched lizard (*Uta stansburiana*) demonstrate a pattern similar to that seen in Rock, Paper, Scissors, according to whether the male lizard has an orange, blue, or yellow throat:

• Orange-throated males are the largest and most aggressive lizards; they easily dominated the blue-throated lizards when competing for mates. (Orange beats blue.)

• Similarly, blue-throated males are larger than the yellow-throated males and had no trouble fending them off. (Blue beats yellow.)

• The yellow-throated males most closely resemble the females of the species. While the aggressive orange-throated males are fighting each other for mates, the yellow-throated males are able to slip in among the females and mate with them without being noticed. (Yellow beats orange.) They are unable to do this with the mates of the blue-throated males, because the blue-throated males form stronger bonds with their mates than the orange-throated males do, and can spot the yellow-throated males among the females.

Any baseball player named on at least 75% of ballots cast is elected to the Hall of Fame.

BOWL OF ROSES

One day in 1902, the University of Michigan Wolverines football team squared off against the Stanford University Cardinal in the first Rose Bowl game. Was it an instant American classic? Not by a long shot.

TOURIST ATTRACTION

The Tournament of Roses in Pasadena, California, began in 1891 as a way to promote the warm winter climate of southern California and to attract real estate investors from the snowy East. The midwinter festival included sports, a parade, and unusual contests like ostrich racing, bronco-busting, tug-of-war, and medieval-style jousts. But it failed to capture the nation's attention as the city fathers had hoped, and they needed a star attraction to bring in visitors. So in 1901 tournament officials decided to invite two top college football teams, one from the East and one from the West, to face off in a "Rose Bowl" on New Year's Day.

Choosing the teams was easy. The University of Michigan Wolverines dominated college football in the Midwest. The team's defense played the entire 1901 season without allowing a single point. And their offense's average of 50 points per game caused shell-shocked opponents to nickname Michigan the "Point-a-Minute" team. UM halfback Willie Heston was one of the sport's first great stars. In a time dominated by traditional East Coast football powers such as Harvard and Yale, Michigan had put Midwest football on the map. Many experts of the day ranked the Wolverines as the best team in the nation.

To represent the West, Stanford University of Palo Alto, California, was chosen to oppose the Wolverines. The Stanford Cardinal had lost only one game the previous season, and fans expected them to uphold the honor of West Coast football!

EAST VS. WEST

The first Rose Bowl game kicked off at 3:00 on January 1, 1902. About 8,000 fans crowded onto a wooden grandstand erected on a dry and dusty Pasadena field. Those hoping for a Stanford victory were encouraged by their team's first-quarter performance; Stanford held Michigan scoreless. But by halftime, the Wolverines led

---

The punching post used in karate is called a *makiwara*.

17–0. The rout continued in the second half. Finally, with 10 minutes left in the game and Michigan leading 49–0, the exhausted and embarrassed Stanford captain admitted defeat and forfeited the rest of the game.

Tournament organizers were appalled. Even the ostrich races had been more competitive, the West Coast favorites had been beaten, and the fans hadn't even seen an entire game. Thinking that college football was not such a great attraction after all, they decided to replace it the following year with gladiator-style chariot races. For the next 10 years, the chariot races attracted huge crowds and seemed poised to become a new national pastime... until a spectacular accident during a race forced officials to ban them from future festivals.

FULL CIRCLE

Meanwhile, college football had caught on in the rest of country. By 1916 the game had secured its place as one of the nation's most popular sports, and Tournament of Roses organizers decided to give it another try. This time it was a success and football became an annual festival highlight, rivaling even the parade in popular appeal. Other bowl games eventually caught on across the country, but the Rose Bowl is still the granddaddy of them all.

A Michigan team would not return to the Rose Bowl until 1948 when, coincidentally, the Wolverines defeated the University of Southern California by the same score of 49–0.

* * *

VACATION OF DREAMS

Location: Dyersville, Iowa

Background: Every year more than 50,000 people visit the baseball field from the 1989 movie *Field of Dreams*. It actually straddles two farms: Al Ameskamp owns left and center field; Don Lansing owns the infield, right field, and the bleachers. Both have their own access roads and gift shops (they sell the same stuff).

Be sure to see: One Sunday a month, a local minor league baseball team dresses in early 1900s uniforms, hides in the cornfield, and then emerges to play catch with visitors.

First person to clear 20 feet in pole-vaulting: Ukrainian Sergei Bubka, in 1985.

PASTURE GOLF

*Ah, golf. Crowded courses, long waits, exorbitant greens fees, irritating
dress codes. Has your "nice walk spoiled" gotten more spoiled in
recent years? If so, pasture golf may be the perfect antidote.*

COMMON SCENTS

David Jones is a sheep rancher in Lillooet, British Columbia. In the mid-1980s, he was losing too many of his sheep
to the coyotes, mountain lions, and bears that lived in the surrounding wilderness. He had to do something to protect his business. So he thought about the different ways he might keep
predators off his land...until he came up with a good one: intro-
duce the scent of *their* predators—humans—into the area. But
how could he do that?

Jones also happened to be an avid golfer, which was tough in
Lillooet because there were no courses nearby. He figured that
there had to be other golfers in the area, so he got some flags, dug a
few holes...and soon he had a "golf course" right in the middle of
his 50-acre sheep pasture. For a couple of bucks, locals were welcome to come out to the pasture and play a round of golf in and
around the sheep. With any luck, Jones figured, the golfers would
stink the place up enough to keep the predators away.

SWEET SMELL OF SUCCESS

In 1985 Jones estimated that there were maybe 100 golfers living in
the area; today the Sheep Pasture Golf Course attracts more than
15,000 golfers a year, each of whom pays $9 for a round of nine
holes (or $15 for 18 holes). And their scent has driven predators off
the land, just as Jones had hoped. In the nearly 20 years that the
course has been in business, he hasn't lost a single sheep to predators—or to golfers. It's pretty easy to play around the flock, and even
when a sheep does get hit by a stray shot from time to time, there's
no harm done. "Sheep are pretty well padded," Jones says.

If you think about it, golf at the Sheep Pasture Golf Course
probably has a lot in common with what the sport was like hundreds of years ago. The Scots didn't play on overwatered, over-
groomed fairways designed by landscape architects; they played on

---

In the 1870s, women played baseball in skirts, long-sleeved blouses, and high-heeled shoes.

pastures where natural grasses were kept low by sheep, cows, and other animals. Nor did they have to deal with crowds, inconvenient tee times, or any of the other frustrations associated with the modern golf experience. If a Scotsman had a ball, a stick, and a place to swing it, he had everything he needed to enjoy a round of golf.

BACK TO BASICS

Jones probably didn't realize it at the time—he was just trying to protect his sheep—but he was part of a growing movement to take golf out of overpriced, overcrowded golf courses and return it to its simpler roots. Another pioneer in the pasture golf movement is an Oregon golfer named Bruce Manclark. In 2001 he played a round of golf at a neglected course in Alaska called Fishhook Glen. "It was totally raw, totally unmanicured," he says, "but at the same time amazingly beautiful and really fun." The experience prompted Manclark and his wife to launch a Web site to help promote odd, unconventional, and affordable "courses."

The Manclarks started out by listing the courses they knew of and invited visitors to the site to post their own listings. At last count, the site lists more than 60 courses in 23 states and six countries around the world, and the number is growing. Some courses have only nine holes; others have 18. In most places listed, a round of golf will set you back $10 or less.

PASTURE GOLF AROUND THE WORLD

Annie Lake Golf Course, Whitehorse, Yukon Territory
Description: The course has sand for greens instead of grass. $2 for 18 holes. Par 66.
Comments: "Greens must be swept after play. You can play as late as you want in the summer months, but don't forget the mosquito repellent."

Downs Golf Club, Downs, Kansas
Description: A small, no-frills nine-hole community golf course. $3 for nine holes. Par 35.
Comments: "Outside toilets on hole 1 and hole 3. Shake the door before entering to chase out the bull snakes."

Frozen Lake Golf, in the Matanuska Valley near Palmer, Alaska

---

Media mogul Ted Turner won the 1977 America's Cup as captain of the yacht *Courageous*.

Description: A frozen lake. Free. Par varies each winter depending on how the new course is laid out.

Comments: "Rules of lake golf vary depending on course conditions, size of lake, and lake usage (watch out for the ice fishermen). Interestingly, lake golf is best played wearing ice skates."

Bert Lee Park Golf Course, Flagstaff, Arizona

Description: The course is in a privately owned meadow. Free with permission of owner. Nine holes. Par 35.

Comments: "There are no greens on this course so don't worry about bringing your putter. We just have PVC pipes for pins. We had to give up on flags because the elk kept chewing them off."

PASTURE GOLF TOURNAMENTS

Cowpatty Golf Classic, Lytton Springs, Texas

Description: Held each spring in a cow pasture outside of Lytton Springs, Texas. "Entry fee is $15, a 12-pack of beer or soft drinks, one Miller Lite per player, and two bags of ice per team."

Comments: "No tees allowed—must use cowpatties, horse doo, or fire ant mounds."

Cow Pie International Golf Tournament, held each Fourth of July at the Greens at Yanik Manor, Lebanon, Oregon

Description: A three-hole course in a horse and cow pasture. Holes are played three times for a total of nine holes. Par 36.

Comments: Tournament rules: "Watch for livestock. One added stroke for hitting a cow with a golf ball. No pushing your team members or other team members into pond (unless they deserve it). No playing naked until after dusk. Must have a beer in hand at all times. Cheating allowed if everyone on team agrees."

Cowboy Cow Pasture Golf Tournament, Nenzel, Nebraska

Description: Held in a cow pasture every June. The $30 entry fee includes dinner, a barn dance, and the use of a horse if you don't bring your own.

Comments: "Participants must ride horses between holes. On one hole golfers must tee off from a cow chip, on another, a prairie dog village will be a hazard. The exact penalty for losing a ball in a prairie dog hole has not yet been decided."

The penalty flags thrown by NFL referees are weighted down with unpopped popcorn.

THE BIRTH OF BASEBALL CARDS, PART I

People in the U.S. have been collecting baseball cards for more than 100 years. Bubblegum hadn't even been invented yet when Old Judge cigarettes gave birth to this American institution.

BACKGROUND

Baseball cards have grown from a kid's hobby to a $2 billion-a-year industry. Their history goes back to the early days of baseball.

The Duke of Tobacco. Until the 1880s, when "Buck" Duke took over the Duke Tobacco Company (later The American Tobacco Co.) from his father, most tobacco was sold loose, in tins; people would roll their own cigarettes. In 1885 Buck bought the rights to a machine that put out 200 ready-made cigarettes at a time. Now he was able to concentrate on selling cigarettes instead of tobacco. What he needed was more customers. So he began a huge ad campaign. Soon Duke had 40% of the cigarette market.

To cut costs, Duke replaced tobacco tins with paper cigarette packs. As Pete Williams recounts in *Card Sharks*:

> When he discovered that many of the packs were crushed in shipping, Duke came up with the idea of placing a cardboard insert to stiffen the pack. Not only would they prevent damage, but the "cards" would serve as advertising pieces and premiums to boost sales…He included cards of actors and actresses…[and] his idea inspired competitors to place baseball cards in their products.

The first cards were sold with Old Judge Cigarettes in 1886. They were 1 ½" X 2 ½"—much smaller than today—and pictured stoic-looking players wearing neckties with their uniforms. Eventually they started using "action" shots, which were actually staged photographs of players reaching for, or swinging at, balls on a string. Instead of the statistics and trivia found on the back of today's cards, these early cards had advertising.

The Phillie Phanatic holds the record as the most-sued mascot in Major League Baseball.

WHY BASEBALL?

Baseball cards had three advantages for tobacco companies:
1) They capitalized on the growing popularity of the sport, which was just coming into its own; 2) The connection with sports heroes helped combat the notion that store-bought cigarettes were effeminate; and 3) They were collectible. Pete Williams notes:

> With the cards came card collecting, which presented a challenge since the cards came one to a pack. Collecting became something of a family affair, as young boys would obtain the cards from their fathers and urge them to buy more tobacco products. Non-tobacco users who wished to collect had to pick up the tobacco habit—as the companies hoped—or find a user willing to part with the cards.

THE PRECIOUS SET

Duke Tobacco got out of the baseball card business in 1890, when it combined with other tobacco companies to form American Tobacco. With a virtual monopoly on cigarettes, there was no need for promotions.

But from 1909 to 1911, anti-trust laws were used to break American Tobacco up, so the company went back to using baseball cards as a promotion. They came out with a 524-card set called the "T206"—which has turned into the most valuable baseball card series in history. According to *Card Sharks*, here's why:

> Shortly after production began, shortstop Honus Wagner of the Pittsburgh Pirates (now a Hall of Famer) objected to the use of his photo and threatened legal action if his card was not removed from the set. American Tobacco complied, but not before a quantity of Wagners had been printed and shipped with tobacco.

For a long time, baseball historians believed Wagner objected because he disapproved of cigarette-smoking. Then they found out he'd once endorsed a brand of cigars…and realized he just didn't want them using his likeness without paying for it.

Today, the few Wagner cards that slipped out have become the Holy Grail of baseball card collecting.

In 2007 one was sold at auction for $2.3 million!

There's more. For part II of the baseball card story, turn to page 457.

Capoeira is a Brazilian martial art that blends dance, music, singing, and acrobatics.

BIKRAM YOGA IS HOT

How a Beverly Hills yogi put a new twist on the old practice of yoga.

RELAX, MAN
More than 5,000 years ago, the twisting, flowing exercises that we now call *yoga* were developed in India as a way to unite the mind and body in the quest for spiritual enlightenment. The ancient practice found legions of new followers in the 1960s and '70s when yoga classes began popping up all over North America. For stressed-out Westerners, yoga's emphasis on stretching and relaxation provided a mellow change from the fast-paced competition of most sports and gyms. But in the past few years, an extreme style of yoga has been growing in popularity and changing the face of the yoga industry. It's called Bikram yoga, and it's anything but mellow.

THE HEAT IS ON

The type of yoga most Americans are familiar with is called *hatha* yoga, a mix of hundreds of postures, or *asanas*, that strengthen and flex the body. Bikram yoga, on the other hand, is a sequence of 26 specific asanas, repeated twice during a 90-minute session, always in the exact same order. But the real twist is that they're performed in a hot, humid "torture chamber"—a room that's kept at 105°F, with a humidity of at least 40%.

In this sauna-like atmosphere, Bikram practitioners sweat heavily and are pushed at a pace that significantly raises their heart rate. Forget meditation and relaxation—nausea and dizziness are common, especially for novices. And the heat makes bodies more limber, enabling people to contort themselves into pretzel-like poses. The postures are so demanding that when practitioners sink to the floor to do the "seated" asanas, they often find themselves sitting in a pool of their own sweat.

HOLLYWOOD YOGI

What kind of yoga teacher would subject his students to this kind of misery and still make it one of the most popular types of yoga? A very savvy businessman. Bikram's founder, Bikram Choudhury,

---

First time that three women qualified for the Indianapolis 500:...

was born in 1946, in Calcutta, India, and won that country's National Yoga Contest at the age of 13. By 17, he'd switched to competitive weightlifting, but a crippling knee injury ended his career. He returned to yoga, and after six months of intense sessions, he could walk again. He went on to open several yoga studios while developing his own teaching methods, including the "hot room" and sequence of 26 postures.

Choudhury brought his brand of yoga to the U.S. in the early '70s, but how it happened is a matter of some conjecture. According to one story, he met Richard Nixon when the President was traveling and having a bout of phlebitis, or inflammation of the veins. Choudhury helped treat him, and Nixon was so grateful that he invited the young yogi to come to America.

In any case, Choudhury moved to the U.S. and opened a yoga studio in Beverly Hills. The address may have been glamorous, but the studio was a bare-bones operation. In the Indian tradition, Choudhury charged no money for lessons; instead, people were encouraged to leave donations in a box. It didn't add up to much, so Choudhury slept on the studio floor.

Before long, word got around of his teachings, and Hollywood celebrities such as Shirley MacLaine convinced him to charge for his yoga sessions. Choudhury took the advice to heart—some people say too much—and eventually built his company, Bikram's Yoga College of India, into a multimillion-dollar empire.

STAR-STRUCK

Today Choudhury lives a lavish lifestyle. He owns a fleet of Bentleys and Rolls-Royces, makes no apologies for enjoying his material wealth, and is notorious for aggressive self-promotion. Photos often show him wearing only a Speedo and a Rolex watch, and he frequently name-drops his famous students like Quincy Jones, Michael Jackson, and Madonna. He dismisses his competition—American teachers of other yoga styles—as "clowns" who don't understand what they're doing.

Not surprisingly, the traditional yoga community hasn't taken this lightly. Many have spoken out against his Westernization of yoga, his series of exercises that, they claim, can strain muscles and harm practitioners who have blood-pressure problems. Another hot topic is his promotion of competitions—Bikram teachers have lobbied for the inclusion of yoga in the Olympics. All this, they feel, runs contrary to yoga's ancient, gentle traditions.

The controversy reached a new level in 2002, when Choudhury claimed a copyright on the Bikram sequence of asanas, making them his intellectual property. Anyone teaching his sequence without his permission could—and would—be sued. Bikram instructors now had to be certified by Choudhury himself and pay him a licensing fee. Soon he was building a business based on the models of Starbucks and McDonald's: a standardized sequence and script for classes, with trained teachers who followed it exactly. Choudhury then began to sell franchises of the business—a first in the yoga world—creating what's been called the "McYoga" controversy.

Howls of protest went up all over the yoga community. Critics pointed out that Bikram asanas were standard hatha yoga postures that had existed for thousands of years—so he couldn't possibly own them. Choudhury has countered that Bikram yoga works as well as it does because the special sequence of asanas causes a "tourniquet effect" that applies pressure to veins and arteries and then releases the pressure so the blood floods back in, flushing out blockages and promoting healing and rejuvenation. He also asserts that those who teach his style of yoga should teach it properly and should pay him for the knowledge. Choudhury calls it "the American way."

After a lawsuit in 2005, a U.S. federal court upheld Choudhury's copyright. But in response, the Indian government began cataloging over 1,000 yoga poses recorded in ancient texts in the hopes of preventing anyone else from trying to claim ownership of the ancient tradition of yoga.

STILL SWEATING

Meanwhile, franchised Bikram studios have sprung up around the world. But critics still argue that the spiritual nature of yoga is missing from the standardized Bikram sessions and that the teaching is robotic. Still, the practice has earned thousands of enthusiasts, who claim that the extreme effort—and even the pain—improves their bodies and focuses their minds, forcing everyday problems to the background and bringing them closer to inner peace. As Choudhury says, "You've gotta go through hell to get to heaven."

COCKY JOCKS

Are they grossly arrogant or merely confident?

"I'll watch the highlights every now and then but, as far as watching the game, I feel like I am the game."
—**Terrell Owens**

"They say Elvis is dead. I say, no, you're looking at him. Elvis isn't dead; he just changed color."
—**Dennis Rodman**

"I don't listen to the refs. I don't listen to anyone who makes less money than I do."
—**Charles Barkley**

"I'm glad you're doing this story on us and not on the WNBA. We're so much prettier than all the other women in sports."
—**Martina Hingis, tennis star, in *Detour* magazine**

"Unstoppable, baby!"
—**Marc Jackson, NBA rookie, after he made a lay-up during a 29-point loss**

"If there was ever a man born to be a hitter, it was me."
—**Ted Williams**

"I am the most ruthless, brutal champion ever. There is no one who can match me. I want your heart. I want to eat your children."
—**Mike Tyson**

"If I am to be a chauvinist pig, I want to be the number-one pig."
—**Bobby Riggs, before losing a tennis match to Billie Jean King**

"I already believe I am the best linebacker in the game. Now I have to show one more thing—that I am the most dominating, influential person in the game and the best football player to ever put on a pair of cleats."
—**Ray Lewis**

"It's called talent. I just have it. I can't explain it. You either have it or you don't."
—**Barry Bonds**

"Yeah, I'm arrogant. But that doesn't mean I'm not a nice person."
—**Jeremy Roenick**

"Confidence is a very fragile thing." —Joe Montana

AMAZING FEETS

Fame is fleeting. These legendary soccer players rank among the best who ever played the "Beautiful Game," but unless you grew up in a soccer-crazy country, you may never have heard of them.

THE BLACK SPIDER

Before Lev Yashin came along, goalkeepers didn't get much respect. In fact, in the history of European soccer, he was the first (and is still the only) goalie to be named Footballer of the Year. During his 22-year career with Moscow's Dynamo team (1949–71), Yashin revolutionized the goalkeeper's role's by aggressively punching and kicking out opponents' shots, or catching them and throwing them quickly back into play. All of these skills are regarded as commonplace today, but they were radically new when Yashin came on the scene in the 1950s. A former hockey goalie, he led the Soviet soccer team to the gold medal in the 1956 Olympics, giving up only two goals over the course of the tournament. The team also won the 1960 European Championship. His quick defending, coupled with his habit of always wearing black, earned him the nickname "The Black Spider." In 2000 Yashin was voted Goalkeeper of the Century by FIFA, the international soccer association.

THE BLOND ARROW

In European soccer, Spain's Real Madrid is known a powerhouse team that has produced a string of legendary stars and is consistently in the running for the championship. But it wasn't always that way. If Real Madrid is soccer's Yankees, then Alfredo di Stéfano was their Babe Ruth—the player who put them on the map. Born in 1926 in Buenos Aires, di Stéfano, nicknamed *Saeta Rubia* ("The Blond Arrow"), rose to fame with the River Plate team in the Argentine league, leading them to a league championship in his first season, followed by a South American championship in 1948. At age 27, with the peak of his career seemingly behind him, di Stéfano signed with Real Madrid in 1953. His critics scoffed—the team was a perennial also-ran in the European soccer scene, and few thought that the balding veteran would make much of a difference. Di Stéfano changed their minds in his first game with Real, scoring four goals against then-champions Barcelona. Over the next 10 years, Di Stéfano didn't slow down—and he transformed Real Madrid into the greatest club team in history. In the 1950s, he led his teammates to five consecutive European championships—a feat no team has matched to this day.

THE MAGICIAN

Shots on goal may be the most crowd-pleasing part of soccer, but dribbling is what gets the ball there. And perhaps no one was better at it than Stanley Matthews, known as "The Magician." With uncanny ball control and an endless repertoire of body feints and moves, the English midfielder drove defenders crazy over his 33-year career. When he was honored with the European Player of the Year award in 1956, Matthews was 41 and still at the top of his game. A vegetarian who never drank, he was respected not only for his consummate skill but also his sportsmanship (he was proud of the fact that he was never cautioned for rough play during his career). When he retired from regular play in 1965—at the age of 50—most of the world's top players came to honor him. That same year, Matthews was knighted for "services to sport," the first soccer player ever to receive the honor.

LITTLE BIRD

When Manoel Francisco dos Santos was born in Pau Grande, Brazil, in 1933, the last thing the doctors thought when they tried to salvage his twisted legs was that he would become a soccer player. Sometimes called *Anjo de Pernas Tortas* ("Angel with Bent Legs") but better known as *Garrincha* ("Little Bird"), he overcame his disability to develop a free-flowing playing style that became synonymous with Brazil. When he came onto the international scene in the 1958 World Cup, he entered the tournament as a substitute. But soon, in tandem with fellow legend Pelé, Garrincha stunned the opposition to bring Brazil its first World Cup. Four years later, with Pelé out of the final due to injury, Garrincha led the team to another World Cup win. He was admired not only for his ability to win but for the joy and sense of fun he brought to the game. In one legendary exchange, his footwork confused a

---

...is only superseded by the joy of a good penalty save." —Russian goalkeeper Lev Yashin

defender so completely that the man fell down as Garrincha blew by him. Instead of taking advantage of the situation and going for the goal, Garrincha dribbled back, helped the guy up…then blew past him again and scored.

DER BOMBER

Every soccer team needs one—that player with the proverbial "nose" for the goal, the scorer who instinctively puts himself in the right place at the right time. To this day, Gerhard "Gerd" Müller of Germany is regarded as the model striker, with goal-scoring records that still stand even though his career ended in 1982. But "Der Bomber," as his fans dubbed him, was an unlikely superstar. As a chunky teenager (he attributed his stocky build to his mother's potato salad), Müller joined a semi-pro team, where the coach took one look at him and cracked, "What am I supposed to do with a weightlifter?" Müller wasn't fast, but his thick torso and huge thighs—they measured 25 inches around—yielded a powerful shot that was difficult to defend against. Müller's team Bayern Munich won three consecutive European Cups from 1974–76. But he's probably best remembered for his last goal for the West German national team—one that cemented a 2–1 victory over the Netherlands and won Germany the 1974 World Cup.

JUSTO

Although he's remembered mostly for one great World Cup performance, Just "Justo" Fontaine had a stellar 12-year career. From the time he entered the top French league in 1953, the young French Moroccan began racking up goals—a total of 165 in 200 games. A league All-Star, he led his team to national championships in 1958 and '60. In 1958, as a member of the French national team, Justo earned a spot in the record books with an unprecedented performance in the World Cup—an astounding 13 goals in the tournament. To put the feat in context, only the great Brazilian Ronaldo and Germany's Gerd Müller have scored more goals in World Cup competition. But it took Ronaldo four World Cup tournaments, and Müller two, to surpass the record that Justo set in only one. It earned him that year's Golden Boot for top scorer, and a secure place in the history of the Beautiful Game.

COURT CASE

When a knockout blow almost killed one basketball player and nearly destroyed the life of another, the NBA learned that sports violence had gone way out of bounds.

BLINDSIDED

The scene was a Houston Rockets/Los Angeles Lakers basketball game at the L.A. Forum on December 9, 1977. About midway through the game, the two teams were tied at 55–55. So far, it had been a ho-hum game, but suddenly a tussle erupted between Rocket Kevin Kunnert and Laker Kermit Washington. Teammates rushed in to join the fray, and it blew up into a brawl. In the chaos, Washington saw a blurred figure running toward him at high speed, and was afraid he was about to be hit from behind. So the 6'8", 250-pound player instinctively turned and threw a hard right-handed punch—"the hardest punch in the history of mankind," as assistant Lakers coach Jack McLoskey later called it. The haymaker hit the Rockets' captain, Rudy Tomjanovich, just below his nose. Tomjanovich fell unconscious into a pool of his own blood, and the crowd fell silent at the sight.

BLOWOUT

That one moment, which became known as "the Punch," changed the two players' lives. Tomjanovich had been running at top speed to stop the fight when he was hit, and doctors compared the impact to a crash of two speeding locomotives. The near-fatal collision shattered Tomjanovich's facial bones, dislocated his skull, gave him a cerebral concussion, and caused spinal fluid to leak from his brain. He missed the rest of the 1977–78 season while undergoing five surgeries to reconstruct his broken facial bones—a job that the surgeon compared to "gluing a shattered egg back together."

Washington was suspended for 60 days and ordered to pay a $10,000 fine, a punishment that many found far too light. But he couldn't escape angry fans. He and his family were deluged with hate mail and death threats. When he returned to play that season, the Lakers—who'd previously considered him one of their

---

In Formula One racing, a black flag indicates that a driver is disqualified.

most valuable players—traded him off to Boston. Both of the players, their teammates, and the NBA did their best to move on from the brutal, life-altering moment. It was anything but easy.

NICE GUYS FINISH FIRST

Both players had beaten long odds to make it to the pros. Kermit Washington, 26, grew up in inner-city Washington, D.C., while Rudy Tomjanovich, 29, was from Hamtramck, a poverty-stricken suburb of Detroit. Tomjanovich knew the humiliation of living on welfare; Washington had seen school friends die in gang violence. These two underprivileged kids grew into brilliant athletes and family men, superachievers who were living out their dreams as popular NBA players.

Forward "Rudy T" Tomjanovich was a favorite with Houston fans, a four-time All-Star, and captain of his team. For the Lakers, Kermit Washington had become an invaluable rebounder and the unofficial protector of their star, Kareem Abdul-Jabbar. When opposition players elbowed or pushed Abdul-Jabbar to keep him from shooting, Washington was the "enforcer," the player who faced off with anyone who harassed him.

NBA NIGHTMARE

By the time the two players came together that night at the L.A. Forum, the NBA already had plenty to worry about. Basketball in the mid-'70s wasn't selling many tickets or attracting many TV viewers, and a recent rash of on-court brawls weren't helping its reputation. And unlike hockey and football players, basketball players wore no padding or protective masks, so officials had long feared that someone would be seriously injured if the violence continued. But they had no idea that an injury was only one of many problems a brutal, high-profile fight would bring to the NBA.

Within hours of the brawl, footage of it went to every media outlet in the country. And it didn't take long for reporters to label the two main opponents: Rudy Tomjanovich was the victim, and Kermit Washington was the thug.

BAD REPUTATION

Those labels haunted both players for the rest of their careers. Tomjanovich struggled through months of surgeries and lingering pain before rejoining the Rockets the following season. That year he averaged 19 points per game and made the Western Conference All-Star team, but his success didn't bring him much joy. Tomjanovich felt that fans, with their constant well-wishing and applause, pitied him as a victim. And he was still dealing with the effects of his injuries—headaches, dental pain, and nightmares that impacted his training and playing. He sued the Lakers for failing to control their player, winning a $2 million settlement, but it was a tainted victory. After only three more seasons with Houston, Tomjanovich retired early, his playing days over at the age of 33.

Kermit Washington, who wasn't injured in the fight, suffered in an entirely different way. Since his college days, Washington had been a respected, popular player. But now he was plagued by guilt over what had happened to Tomjanovich, and fans wouldn't let him forget it. Even though he felt he'd acted in self-defense, he was vilified by the media and taunted by spectators. As he wrote later: "I had to have FBI agents sit next to me at the games for fear of being attacked. I was warned not to order room service in my hotel for fear of being poisoned."

ANOTHER COMPLICATION

There was another factor at play, one that made this more than a mere squabble between two athletes. Washington, a black player, had squared off against the white Tomjanovich, and the video replays of Washington's black fist smashing into Tomjanovich's white face aired endlessly, fanning the flames of racism. Washington later said that if he hadn't been a black man duking it out with a white one, the public and media would never have turned on him so vehemently. But he continued playing. It took time and trades— first to Boston, then San Diego, and finally Portland—before he reestablished his popularity and made it to the All-Star Game.

The two men couldn't avoid some contact, and Washington would apologize to Tomjanovich in 1987. But resentments lingered on both sides. As for the NBA, commissioner Larry O'Brien had already imposed stricter penalties on players involved in fighting. What had once been a maximum penalty of $500 and a five-game suspension had changed to $10,000 with suspensions that could last indefinitely. Determined to curtail violence in basketball, the NBA

Oldest major U.S. sporting event: the Kentucky Derby, first held in 1875.

stuck with those tougher penalties and added an extra referee to all games.

LIFE AFTERWARD

After his playing career was over, Tomjanovich stayed with the Rockets as a scout, assistant coach, and finally, head coach, leading the Rockets to two NBA championships in the mid-'80s. For a time, it seemed he'd left the problems of the 1977 season far behind. But it wasn't until he finally dealt with a long-term drinking problem that he began to put aside his feelings about the victim label and the resentments he had harbored toward Washington.

For Kermit Washington, the Forum fallout was even harder to take after he retired. He'd dreamed of coaching for the NBA, but no coaching positions opened up for him. He took a job as a sports talk-radio host, but it seemed like every time violence occurred in sports, the video of his flying fist played on TV, and he was told that his violent reputation made it unlikely he'd be hired.

On May 14, 2000, Washington wrote a piece for the *New York Times* about what it was like to be him over the past 25 years. Sportswriter John Feinstein picked up on the story and wrote a 2003 book called *The Punch: One Night, Two Lives, and the Fight That Changed Basketball Forever*. The best-selling book brought publicity to Washington's Project Contact, a charity he developed to bring doctors, nurses, and medicines to poverty-stricken Africans. And publication of *The Punch* brought Tomjanovich and Washington together to talk about that night, and they've since become friends.

*   *   *

LET'S DO A STUDY!

After studying overweight children playing with weighted and unweighted blocks, researchers at Indiana State University concluded that—surprise!—lifting weights burns more calories than *not* lifting weights. The scientists plan to use the findings to help fight obesity by manufacturing teddy bears with three-pound weights inside.

NASCAR Q&A

Stock car racing has a rich history…and a complicated set of rules and guidelines. Here's a quick guide for the uninitiated.

How did stock car racing begin? During Prohibition (1920–33), bootleggers in the southern United States relied on fast cars to stay ahead of the law. To maintain a low profile, they souped up their engines and shock absorbers but kept the *stock*, or factory-made, bodies. After a night on the run, the bootleggers would sometimes meet to boast about their cars and race them against each other on oval dirt tracks. This soon became a Sunday tradition, complete with picnic baskets.

How did NASCAR begin? In 1938 Bill France Sr., a mechanic and amateur race-car driver, began running operations at a track in Daytona Beach, Florida, near a stretch of beach where several early land-speed records had been set. The young sport of racing was in trouble, though: Shady promoters often wouldn't pay the drivers, and the lack of consistent car guidelines led to frequent disagreements. France worked to legitimize the sport. After a series of meetings that culminated in Daytona Beach on February 21, 1948, he convinced the drivers and promoters to form a single entity—the National Association for Stock Car Auto Racing. France ran NASCAR until 1972, when his son, Bill France Jr., took over. The younger France ran the organization until 2000.

What's the difference between stock cars and other race cars? Race cars such as Formula One are built specifically for auto racing, while stock cars are made by auto manufacturers for use on regular roads. In NASCAR's early days, the cars were *strictly* stock. But starting in the 1950s, certain modifications were allowed to the engines and chassis to make the cars faster and safer.

How fast do stock cars go? It depends on the track. On *short tracks*, which are less than a mile long, the average speed is about 82 mph. On *intermediate tracks*, between one and two miles long, the fastest speeds top out at about 150 mph. Tracks over two miles in length are called *superspeedways*, and there are only two: Talladega, in Alabama, and Daytona, Florida, where the season

---

In 1966 soccer's World Cup trophy was misplaced—and later found under a bush by a dog.

begins each year. These two tracks boast an average speed of 188 mph. It used to be higher…until a horrific wreck at Talladega in 1987 when Bobby Allison's car nearly flew into the stands. NASCAR now uses *restrictor plates* at these two tracks—a device placed over the intake valve to reduce the car's power.

Why are the cars covered with ads? In 1972, two years after losing the right to advertise tobacco products on television, the R. J. Reynolds Company tried a new marketing tactic by sponsoring the first Winston Cup series (now called the Sprint Cup). In the mid-'70s, partial races were telecast on ABC's *Wide World of Sports*, giving NASCAR a wider audience. But it its biggest boost came with the 1979 Daytona 500, the first NASCAR race broadcast live on national television. On a day when the northeastern U.S. was paralyzed by a snowstorm, millions of TV viewers watched the race—which ended in a dramatic wreck on the final lap, followed by a fistfight between Cale Yarborough and Donnie Allison. After that, more companies jumped on the sponsorship bandwagon, creating a marriage of convenience: Stock cars make perfect blank slates for ads, and stock car racing is so expensive that teams can't do it week after week without the millions they receive from sponsors.

Just how popular is NASCAR? Behind the NFL, it's the second-most-watched sport in the United States. With 75 million fans, NASCAR sanctions more than 1,500 races each year at over 100 tracks throughout North America. In fact, 17 of the 20 most-watched sporting events in the U.S. each year are NASCAR races.

How does the point system work? In each race, a driver receives points for every lap in which he or she leads (there have been 15 female NASCAR drivers). The winner of the race gets an additional 185 points, second place gets 170, third 165, and so on. Because this system rewards consistency over winning, fans complained that the racing was getting too conservative. After Matt Kenseth won the 2003 NASCAR Championship with only one victory (but 25 top-10 finishes), NASCAR implemented a playoff system. Now after the first 26 races are completed, the top 12 drivers' point totals are reset to 5,000, plus an additional 10 points for each race they've won. This means that for the final 10 races, now called "The Chase for the NASCAR Sprint Cup," the top 12 are far ahead of the pack and battle each other for the championship. Adding to the drama: *All* of the drivers still participate in the final 10 races, so drivers farther down in the rankings can often act as "spoilers."

What's the deal with pole positions? The term comes from horse racing, where a pole on the inside of the track would mark where the race began. In NASCAR, on the day before the race, one driver at a time takes two laps around the track. The driver with the fastest time gets to start the race in the best best position—on the inside of the track in the front row, known as the *pole position*. After that, each driver begins in the spot corresponding to his qualifying time, with the slowest time yielding the outside spot in the last row.

Who works on a NASCAR "team"? The car's owner secures sponsorships and hires the team's members, including the driver. (Some top drivers are also owners, but many are not.) Next comes the crew chief—he's the lead mechanic responsible for the car meeting NASCAR specifications before each race, and he also communicates with the driver during the race. Then there's the pit crew: the *jackman*, who raises the car; the *front* and *rear tire changers*; the *front* and *rear tire carriers*, who take away the used tires; the *gas man*, who fills up the tank; and the *catch can man*, who uses a special can to catch any overflow fuel. During the second half of the race, an extra pit-crew member cleans the windshield. Then the jackman lowers the car and signals to the driver that he's clear to re-enter the race. And all of this happens in 15 seconds or less.

What do the colored flags mean? If the flag is green, that means the race is on. A yellow flag means caution—there's a wreck ahead (no driver may pass any other while the yellow flag is up). A red flag means "stop now"—there's a really *bad* wreck ahead. A red flag with a yellow "X" means pit road is closed, usually due to a wreck in there. A black flag is used to tell a specific driver to return to pit road, which usually means either he's violated a rule, or the officials have spotted a mechanical problem on the car. A white flag means one lap to go. Then the mad dash begins for NASCAR's most sought-after piece of fabric—the checkered flag.

Sport that causes the most injuries among Americans aged 15–24: basketball.

UNCLE JOHN'S
STALL OF FAME

If you're a fan of the regular Bathroom Reader *series, you've seen our "Stall of Fame" articles, in which we salute the creative ways that people get involved with bathrooms, toilets, toilet paper, etc. Here is an all-baseball version.*

Honoree: The Hudson Valley (New York) Renegades, Class A club of the Tampa Bay Devil Rays
Notable Achievement: Creating bathroom-related team memorabilia
True Story: The Renegades are one of the many minor league teams owned by Mike Veeck, son of legendary owner Bill Veeck, who was known for putting on bizarre promotions. In the Renegades' hometown of Fishkill, New York, the younger Veeck held one promotion in 2006 giving away toilet plungers bearing the Renegades logo, and one in 2007 giving away stadium seat cushions shaped like toilet seats. (Too bad Veeck doesn't own a team in Flushing, New York—who knows what that might inspire?)

Honoree: Glenn Davis, a slugger who hit 190 home runs for the Astros and the Orioles from 1984 to '93
Notable Achievement: Using the head to get his head into the game
True Story: While many players have had some odd pregame rituals, Davis's lands him in the Stall of Fame because he spent about 20 minutes before every game meditating alone in the clubhouse bathroom.

Honoree: The Frisco RoughRiders, the Class AA affiliate of the Texas Rangers
Notable Achievement: Turning the stadium restrooms into pleasing places to pass the time
True Story: At Dr Pepper Park in Frisco, Texas, team owners strive to make going out to the ballpark a pleasant experience for the whole family. "Families are a huge part of the RoughRiders

experience," boasts the team's official Web site. "And everybody knows that behind a good family is a good woman. So the RoughRiders became the first team in all of professional sports to hire an interior decorator to design nine unique women's restrooms at Dr Pepper Ballpark. For all you women out there...enjoy. For all you men out there...tough luck."

The RoughRiders aren't the only minor league club to spruce up their loos. At San Jose Municipal Stadium, the San Jose Giants have adorned both the men's and women's restrooms with painted murals. (The women's bathroom features scenes from the 1992 film *A League of Their Own*.) And on the walls of the ladies' rooms at the Brockton Rox ballpark in Massachusetts, soothing scenes of animals provide relief (so to speak) from all the action outside.

Honoree: The Milwaukee Brewers
Notable Achievement: Getting behind the health of their fans
True Story: Before the April 27, 2007, game at Miller Park in Milwaukee, male Brewers fans were invited to take "free, private, confidential rectal screenings in a mobile clinic vehicle next to the T.G.I. Friday's in the northeast corner of the ballpark." And what did the men get in return for bending over? Two free tickets to a future Brewers home game. To explain the promotion, Dr. William See of the Medical College of Wisconsin offered reporters this grim description: "If you picture six guys sitting at a Brewers game at Miller Park, one of them will be diagnosed with prostate cancer during his lifetime."

Honoree: Matt Elliott, reliever for the Mobile (Alabama) BayBears, the Class AA affiliate of the Arizona Diamondbacks
Notable Achievement: Losing a game because of a bathroom break
True Story: A reluctant entrant into the Stall of Fame, Elliot took the mound in the eighth inning of a June 2007 away game against the Devil Rays' Class AA club, the Montgomery Biscuits, with his team leading 4–3. Elliot retired the side, but not before giving up the game-tying run. Fuming mad, he stormed into the clubhouse bathroom and slammed the door shut. Only problem: He slammed it so hard that it broke and locked him inside. After the BayBears batters went down 1-2-3 in the top of the ninth, Elliot was supposed to go back to the mound...but he couldn't get

"I managed good, but boy, did they play bad." —baseball manager Rocky Bridges

out of the bathroom. Elliot's teammates tried to pry open the door. Then his coaches tried. Then the stadium personnel gave it a shot. But the door stayed stuck. Meanwhile, the rest of the Bay-Bears' defensive team was waiting on the field, along with the Biscuits' leadoff batter. After nearly 10 minutes, the umpire told the BayBears to get a pitcher on the mound or forfeit the game. Another reliever hastily warmed up, went in, and promptly gave up a home run in the 10th, losing the game…all while Elliot had to listen to the play-by-play through the broken bathroom door. Forty-five minutes later, with the fire department en route, a stadium worker was able to pry the door open. Asked about his ordeal the next day, Elliot said that it was "a little hot in there '

Honoree: C. J. Wilson, relief pitcher for the Texas Rangers

Notable Achievement: Exposing the steamy underworld of big-league bullpen bathrooms

True Story: Wilson has spent a lot of time in American League ballparks. In 2007 he chronicled his day-to-day experiences in his blog, calling most bullpen bathrooms "terrifying." "Kansas City has a bathroom with no lock, no lights, and a two-foot-tall roll of TP," he says. "Anaheim has a creepy no-flush urinal. Oakland doesn't even have one, so you have to go to the dugout. And in Seattle your teammates barricade you in and slam fastballs (thrown baseball + metal door = explosion noise) into the door to kill your hearing. Toronto is actually decent, although you have to walk about 100 yards on slippery concrete to get there. Boston? Ha."

*　　*　　*

WELCOME TO THE BIGS

In his major league debut in 2002, San Diego Padres pitcher J.J. Trujillo was called to the mound in the 10th inning of a tied game to face Orioles slugger Tony Batista. Trujillo, who had been called up from Double-A earlier that day, threw a slider…and Batista hit it over the fence to win the game, marking the first and only time that a big-league pitcher ever gave up a game-ending home run to the very first hitter he faced. Trujillo's comment to the throng of reporters that awaited him after the game: "Nice debut, huh?"

In pro table tennis, if players use white balls, they can't wear white shirts. They can't see them.

MONDAY NIGHT FOOTBALL

Here's an instant replay of the show that almost single-handedly converted sports broadcasting from a sleepy, weekends-only affair into one of the biggest moneymakers in TV history.

FALSE START

In 1964 a hot young marketing executive with the Ford Motor Company made an unprecedented proposal to the National Football League and the ABC network: if the league and the network would broadcast a pro football game one evening a week during the football season, Ford would sponsor every broadcast by itself.

Until this point, sports had not been prime-time TV fare. "Sports had neither the prestige of news nor the glamour of entertainment," Marc Gunther and Bill Carter explain in *Monday Night Mayhem*, "and besides, sports programs were messy; they could run long and play havoc with the broadcast schedule....The sports establishment [didn't] welcome the networks, either. The conventional wisdom was that television exposure could ruin a sport. The prevailing attitude was summed up by baseball commissioner Ford Frick. 'The view a fan gets at home,' Frick once said, 'should not be any better than that of the fan in the worst seat of the baseball park.'"

Nevertheless, ABC agreed to give it a try. Weekday games were out of the question—they disrupted football training schedules—and Saturday night was too important for ABC to push aside entertainment shows. That left only Friday night—which was fine with Ford. However, Friday night was also traditionally the time high schools played football; when hard-core fans realized that the show would pose a threat to high-school game attendance, they mounted an intense letter-writing campaign opposing it. Neither Ford nor ABC wanted that kind of publicity, so the idea was scrapped. *Friday Night Football* died before a single game had been broadcast.

Trying to save the deal with Ford, NFL commissioner Pete

Kids, stay in school! You must be a high-school graduate to play for a big-league baseball team.

Rozelle suggested scheduling the games on Monday night instead. But ABC rejected the idea—*Ben Casey*, the network's most popular show, aired on Monday night, and the network didn't want to tamper with it. Prime-time football was quietly shelved.

PASS COMPLETED

Four years later, in 1968, billionaire Howard Hughes revived the idea of Monday night football and approached the NFL with an offer to buy the broadcasting rights. He had just purchased a TV production company and wanted to make his mark by selling football programming to local TV stations around the country.

Rather than cut a deal on the spot, Pete Rozelle pitched the idea to the Big Three networks to see if he could get a better offer. CBS said no—its Monday night lineup was too strong. NBC refused after *Tonight Show* host Johnny Carson balked at being preempted by football games. ABC also said no, but changed its mind when Roone Arledge, president of the sports division, warned that as many as 100 affiliates would dump ABC's Monday night programming to air the football games if Hughes got it. A deal was struck, and *Monday Night Football* was born.

THE TEAM

Arledge knew that *Monday Night Football* would have to be more than a run-of-the-mill sports broadcast to compete against sitcoms, dramas, and other popular evening fare. It had to have something extra: controversy. So he hired *Wide World of Sports* announcer Howard Cosell, who was already famous for sticking up for Muhammad Ali when Ali refused to be inducted into the army.

Arledge figured Cosell could just be himself in the broadcasting booth; Don Meredith, a former Dallas Cowboys quarterback, would provide color; and Keith Jackson, another ABC sports announcer, would handle the play-by-play. (Frank Gifford, a former New York Giants halfback, replaced Jackson the following year.) "Roone put that show together like a Hollywood casting director," Gifford recalls in his book *The Whole Ten Yards*. "Howard was the elitist New York know-it-all, the bombastic lawyer that Middle America loved to hate. Don Meredith was the good ole country boy who put Howard in his place. As for me, I was cast as the nice guy, the one who got the numbers down and the names out."

In falconry, the leather strap attached to the bird's ankle is called a *jess*.

A ROUGH START

Monday Night Football set out to be provocative. Unlike most broadcasters, *MNF* announcers—Cosell in particular—actually expressed their opinions, praising some teams and players and attacking others. TV and sports critics were almost unanimously negative toward the show. One newspaper said Cosell's "retching prattle took the fun out of a really good football game"; another said he displayed a "towering ignorance of football."

Even Ford Motor Company chairman and principal sponsor Henry Ford II hated it. After the first game, he called ABC chairman Leonard Goldenson to complain. "I listened to that gab between Don Meredith and Howard Cosell last night, and I couldn't concentrate on the game. Take that guy Cosell off." But the network talked Ford into withholding judgment for four weeks. That was all it took—once people adjusted to Cosell, they began to warm up to him. The reviews improved, the ratings soared, and Ford called back two weeks later to apologize for attacking Cosell.

TOUCHDOWN

Within weeks, *Monday Night Football* became a cult phenomenon: a man in California added a $3,000 den to his house so he could watch the games without being interrupted by his family; restaurants all over the country began investing in TV sets to recapture customers who were staying home on Monday nights; and according to one report, a Seattle hospital tried to ban baby deliveries between 7:00 and 10:00 p.m. on Monday nights. By the end of the first season, 31 percent of TV viewers in the U.S.—many of whom weren't football fans—were watching football on Monday night, making what critics dubbed "The Howard Cosell Show" the third most popular show, after *The Mary Tyler Moore Show* and *The Flip Wilson Show*.

END OF AN ERA

The show had its ups and downs over the next several years: Don Meredith left in 1974 and was replaced by Fred Williamson and then Alex Karras, but returned in 1977 after Karras didn't work out. Cosell left the show after the 1983 season, and Don Meredith left for good a year later, leaving Frank Gifford, who was still working on the show in 1995. *Monday Night Football* filled the lineup

---

Batons used in relay races may be no longer than 12", and must be 5" in circumference.

with a variety of personalities, including Joe Namath, Jim Lampley, O. J. Simpson, Dan Dierdorf, Al Michaels, and Dennis Miller.

Somehow, though, everything was different without Cosell and Meredith. Although the ratings were consistently high, and *MNF* became the second-longest-running show in TV history (second only to *60 Minutes*), the show never reached the heights it had in the early and mid-'70s. As Gunther and Carter put it in *Monday Night Mayhem*, "Same night, same network, same name. But it was not *Monday Night Football* anymore. It was football on Monday nights."

BEHIND THE SCENES

• Early in the first season, Cosell and company went to Philadelphia to broadcast a game between the Eagles and the New York Giants. During the broadcast, Eagles owner Leonard Tose sent up a "generous jug of vodka martinis," which Cosell—who was freezing in the open-air broadcast booth—drank to keep warm. He apparently drank too much—his words began to slur, to the point where he was pronouncing Philadelphia as "Full-a-dull-fa."

Suddenly at the end of the second quarter, Cosell pitched forward and vomited. "Cosell got sick in the booth, all over his mike, his clothes, and my boots," Meredith recalls. The incident may have actually boosted the fledgling show's ratings: "The next day, rumors ran wild," *TV Guide* reported in 1974. Tales of Cosell getting bombed circulated, and the reputation of *Monday Night Football* as a madcap adventure began to spread.

• At a game in Dallas, Cosell dropped a cigarette butt into what he thought was a trash can under the announcer's table. The butt landed on a pile of debris, setting it on fire and igniting play-by-play announcer Keith Jackson's pants. Jackson actually announced an entire series of plays with his pants on fire before he was able to put it out.

• Frank Gifford had a reputation for stumbling over one name or fact every broadcast. For example, during just about every Atlanta Falcons game, he mispronounced coach Leeman Bennet's name as "Leeman Beeman." The problem was so bad that production assistants set up a betting pool to guess the time and the quarter that he would make the mistake. Gifford even began one broadcast by saying, "Hi Frank, I'm everybody."

Official national sport of Sri Lanka: volleyball.

GRANDFATHERED IN

Or what spitballers, hockey players, and Mariano Rivera have in common.

GRANDPA CLAUSE

Most people are familiar with the "grandfather clause"—a clause that exempts some people from a new rule or law because it would revoke rights they had before the law was enacted. In the world of sports, some athletes are "grandfathered in"—allowed to continue doing something that no other player is allowed to do, simply because they're the last ones doing it.

The Last Spitballer. In 1920 Major League Baseball outlawed the spitball, a pitch wherein the pitcher applies spit—or some other substance—to a baseball in order to make it sink...and much harder to hit. But because many of the best pitchers of the day threw little else, the league decided on 17 pitchers who would be exempt from the new rule. The last major leaguer to legally use the spitball: Hall of Famer Burleigh "Ol' Stubblebeard" Grimes, who finished his career with the New York Yankees in 1934.

The Last Guy Without "Helmet Hair." In 1997 Craig MacTavish, center for the St. Louis Blues NHL hockey team, announced his retirement. Hockey fans called it the end of an era because MacTavish was the last player to play without a helmet. He had joined the league in 1978, the year before the NHL made the use of helmets mandatory, so he got to decide for himself whether or not to wear one. He chose not to, calling it "a comfort thing," and for the next 18 years played helmetless (and was never seriously hurt).

The Last Number 42. In 1997 Major League Baseball commissioner Bud Selig announced that the number 42 would be universally retired and no longer available to be used by any player. It was done to honor baseball's first black major leaguer, Jackie Robinson, who'd begun his career 50 years earlier in 1947, when he wore number 42 with the Brooklyn Dodgers. But Mariano Rivera, star relief pitcher for the New York Yankees, had worn 42 since he joined the team in 1995, so he was allowed to keep it, making him the last baseball player with a 42 on his jersey. "As a minority, I feel honored wearing the No. 42 and carrying the legacy that Jackie Robinson left," Rivera told reporters. "I wear it with good pride."

In field hockey, goalies are the only players allowed to wear protective helmets.

THEY TOOK THE PLUNGE

In 1886 a man named Carl Graham rode a barrel through the rapids below Niagara Falls, starting a craze of riding the rapids in barrels. Soon, people started looking for a bigger challenge: riding the falls.

OVER A BARREL

There are three individual falls at Niagara. At American Falls, 300 tons of water drop 180 feet per second and boulders as big as houses litter the base. No one has ever survived a trip over it. Luna Falls, only 90 feet wide, is too small to ride. At Horseshoe Falls, 2,700 tons of water pass over every second. Rocks cannot withstand the constant onslaught of water, and boulders are pulverized. But there is a deep plunge pool at the bottom, making it the only fall that can be ridden.

DAREDEVILS

Here are the people who have dared to go over Niagara Falls in a barrel:

• **Annie Edson Taylor** (1901). The first person ever to go over Niagara in a barrel, this widowed, unemployed schoolteacher was 63 years old when she did it. Taylor used an oak wine barrel padded with cushions. After the plunge, she spent 17 minutes bobbing around before assistants pulled her ashore. Emerging dazed but unhurt, she said, "No one ought ever do that again." She was in-coherent for several days afterward.

• **Bobby Leach** (1911). This circus stuntman went over the falls in a steel barrel and survived. Fifteen years later, while on tour with his famous barrel in New Zealand, Leach slipped on an orange peel and fell. He broke his leg, which later had to be amputated, leading to gangrene, which killed him.

• **Charles Stephens** (1920). A 58-year-old barber, he had a fair reputation as a high-dive and parachute artist, but thought a trip over Niagara Falls would make him really famous. He attached a 100-pound anvil to the bottom of his barrel for ballast and then got in and strapped his feet to the anvil. He surrounded himself with pillows and inserted his arms into two straps bolted inside the barrel. The force of the plunge caused the bottom to drop out of the barrel. The anvil, together with Mr. Stephens, sank to the bottom. The only part of the barrel recovered was a stave with an arm strap attached to it; Stephens' right arm was still threaded through the strap. A tattoo on the arm read "Forget me not, Annie." Annie was his wife and mother of his 11 children.

- **Jean Lussier** (1928). Lussier made the trip not in a barrel but in a six-foot rubber ball lined with rubber tubes. After bobbing about at the bottom of the falls for an hour, he was pulled to shore and emerged unharmed in front of an audience of more than 100,000. Afterward, he sold small souvenir pieces of the inner tubes for 50 cents each. When he ran out of authentic pieces, he peddled rubber purchased from a nearby tire store.

- **George Strathakis** (1930). This 46-year-old Greek chef went over to generate publicity for his book, *The Mysterious Veil of Humanity Through the Ages*. His airtight barrel was trapped behind the falls for over 14 hours before rescuers could retrieve it; by then it was out of air. Only his pet turtle, Sonny Boy, taken along for good luck, survived.

- **William "Red" Hill Jr.** (1951). Hill, 38, should have known better: his father was a boatman who retrieved the bodies of suicide victims from the waters below the falls. Hill didn't use a barrel, he used "the Thing"—made of 13 inner tubes, a fish net, and canvas straps. Thousands of people watched as the Thing became trapped under the falling water. Finally, a few inner tubes emerged from the mist. His mangled body turned up the next day.

- **Nathan Boya** (1961). He made the trip in a steel sphere covered by six layers of rubber, which he called the "Plunge-o-Sphere." He emerged unhurt to find the police waiting for him. He was fined $100—the minimum sentence for violating the Niagara Parks Act.

- **Karel Soucek** (1984). The first Canadian to survive the plunge. His barrel had liquid foam insulation, two eyeholes, and a snorkel. The fall took 3.2 seconds but left Soucek trapped in dangerous waters for 45 minutes before being pulled free. Fortunately, he suffered only minor injuries. Six months later, he re-created the spectacle at the Houston Astrodome in front of 45,000 people. His barrel was hoisted to the top of the dome by a crane and released into a water tank 10 feet in diameter and 10 feet deep. But the barrel missed—it hit the edge of the water tank and killed him.

- **Steven Trotter** (1985). This Rhode Island bartender went over the falls in two plastic pickle barrels wrapped in inner tubes. At the age of 22, he became the youngest person ever to make the trip. He was fined $5,000 for the stunt, but he more than made up for that with his talk show fees. On the 10th anniversary of the stunt, he returned with a woman named Lori Martin and they became the first couple to go over together.

- **Dave Munday** (1985). Munday has dared the falls four times to date. In 1985 a police officer saw him and immediately radioed Hydro-Control to cut the water flow, which stopped the barrel. Later that year he made the trip successfully in an aluminum barrel. In 1990 his barrel got stuck at the very brink of the falls, but in 1993 he succeeded again, this time in a converted diving bell, and at age 56 became the first person to go over the falls twice.

- **Peter DeBernardi and Geoffrey Petkovich** (1989). Residents of Niagara Falls, Ontario, they were the first people to go over the falls as a team, face to face in the same 10-foot steel barrel. Both men survived, suffering only minor injuries. Petkovich, who had been drinking, emerged wearing only a necktie and cowboy boots. They were arrested by the Niagara Parks Police.

- **Jessie Sharp** (1990). The 28-year-old Sharp rode the falls in a kayak. His plan was to gather so much momentum that he would avoid the thundering water and land in the pools at the bottom, then ride the rapids downstream to Lewiston, New York—where he had dinner reservations. He didn't wear a life jacket or a helmet—he wanted his face to show clearly on the videotape his friends were shooting. Minutes after he entered the water above the falls, police ordered the hydroelectric dam to shut the water flow, intending to stop him. It didn't stop him, but it slowed him down. He dropped over the falls like a sack of bricks. His kayak was recovered, but his body was never found.

- **Robert Overacker** (1995). The 39-year-old Overacker was attracted to thrill sports. He wanted a career as a stuntman and thought performing the ultimate stunt would provide him with good publicity. He went over the falls on a Jet Ski, wearing a self-inflating life vest, a crash helmet, and a wet suit. A rocket-propelled parachute was supposed to be deployed at the brink of the falls—but it failed to inflate. His body was recovered by the tour boat *Maid of the Mist*.

Pro golfer Ky Laffoon once punished his putters by dragging them behind his car.

RANDOM ORIGINS

*More answers to the burning question, "Where
does all this sports stuff come from?"*

THE FOOTBALL HUDDLE

"In 1924 Herb McCracken, the coach of the Lafayette
College football team, discovered that his hand signals
[flashed to players during the game] had been scouted and decoded by Penn, his upcoming opponent. On game day, McCracken
countered by ordering his players to gather en masse, several
yards behind the line of scrimmage, and talk over the plays in a
whisper. It immediately became a ritual." McCracken later helped
start the Scholastic publishing company, "but told family members that he was most proud of giving birth to the huddle." (*New
York Times*)

BASEBALL'S MVP AWARD

The award started out as an effort to publicize a now-forgotten car
called the Chalmers: "Hugh Chalmers announced in 1910 that he
would give a car to the champion batters of each league. He was
delighted when Ty Cobb, a Detroiter, won the American League
championship. But his elation turned to fury when Cobb promptly
sold his prize." (*Wheels of a Nation*)

THE JOCKSTRAP

"Millions of male athletes can thank bicycling—and the cobblestone streets of Boston—for the truss that protects their masculinity.
In 1897 those bumpy Beantown byways got too rough for the
nether regions of bike racers. To address this unexpected need, the
BIKE manufacturing company invented the 'bicycle jockey
strap'—eventually shortened to 'jock.'" (*Bicycling* magazine)

ADIDAS

"Adolf and Rudolf Dassler were the sons of a poor laundress who
grew up in the tiny German milltown of Herzogenerauch, near
Nuremburg. Before World War II, they started a factory there
called Adidas to make house slippers, then branched out to track

---

In baseball, a line drive or grounder hit up the middle close to 2nd base is called a *honey.*

and soccer shoes. They had a violent falling-out, and after the war went their separate ways. Rudolf left Adidas and started a rival athletic shoe company, Puma. Before long Adidas and Puma— both headquartered in Herzogenerauch—were battling head-to-head all over the world. When Adolf died in 1978, the two brothers hadn't spoken to each other in 29 years." (*Everybody's Business*)

* * *

FAMOUS FOR 15 MINUTES

The Star: "Two-Ton" Tony Galento, a saloon bouncer and professional boxer who lived in Orange, New Jersey, in the late 1930s

The Headline: *Two-Ton Tony Flattens the Champ*

What Happened: Two-Ton Tony wasn't much of a boxer; at 5'9", 240 pounds with a shape like a beer barrel, about all he was good at was throwing clumsy—but powerful—left hooks. His training technique consisted of sitting in the bar of New York's Plaza Hotel with his girlfriend and consuming huge quantities of beer, pasta, and cigars while his sparring partners jogged the footpaths of Central Park without him. "Why should I pay them punks all that money," he explained, "and then go out and run in the rain myself?"

His brush with the big time came in 1939, when he was inexplicably signed to fight Joe Louis in a championship bout at Yankee Stadium. "I'll murder the bum," Two-Ton Tony predicted. Needless to say, Louis was as shocked as everybody else when Two-Ton Tony clocked him with a haymaker early in the fight and laid him out flat on the canvas. The blow turned out to be little more than a wakeup call, however: Louis quickly made it back to his feet and proceeded to beat Two-Ton Tony so savagely that frightened ringsiders begged the referee to stop the fight, which he finally did in the fourth round. It took 23 stitches to close the cuts on Galento's face and healing his wounded pride took even more effort. For years afterward he blamed the referee for ending the fight "just when things was goin' my way."

THE AFTERMATH: Two-Ton Tony fought 114 fights between 1929 and 1944 and won 82 of them. In 1947, by then up to 275 pounds, he turned to professional wrestling. His fans had not forgotten him—he sold out his first wrestling fight, and more than 2,000 people had to be turned away. He died in 1979.

In 1976 gymnast Shun Fujimoto won an Olympic gold medal for Japan...with a broken kneecap.

NAME THAT BASEBALL PLAYER

The stories behind some of baseball's most colorful nicknames.

TOMATO FACE

Nick Cullop got the nickname "Tomato Face" because his face turned bright red whenever he got angry, usually after striking out. His face turned red a lot in 1931—he led the league in strikeouts that season. Bonus: That year, Tomato Face played for the Cincinnati Reds.

THE HUMAN RAIN DELAY

Before *every* pitch of *every* at-bat, Mike Hargrove (the 1974 Rookie of the Year) attempted to psych out pitchers with an annoyingly long ritual: He'd step out of the batter's box, adjust his helmet, adjust his batting glove, pull each of his sleeves up, adjust his gloves again, wipe his hands on his pants, adjust his helmet again, etc., and then finally get back in the batter's box. The process took up so much time that sportscasters started equating Hargrove's at-bats with a rain delay.

LADY

Pro sports is a tough, macho world. Unlike many of his Detroit teammates, Charles Baldwin (who played in the 1880s) didn't drink alcohol or smoke cigarettes, and made it a point never to curse. His teammates thought that made him rather ladylike.

PUTT-PUTT

Richie Ashburn ran around the bases so fast that Ted Williams nicknamed him "Putt-Putt," commenting to a reporter that Ashburn "ran as if he had twin motors in his pants."

THE GROUNDED BLIMP

Ernest Phelps was a heavyset guy, which earned him the nicknames "Babe" (like Babe Ruth) and "the Blimp." In the 1940s, his team,

---

Racing dogs wear colored jackets, with the colors corresponding to the dogs' starting positions.

the Brooklyn Dodgers, began to fly to road games, but Phelps opted to take the train because he was afraid of flying, which made him "the Grounded Blimp."

OIL CAN

Dennis Boyd, who pitched for the Red Sox in the 1980s, grew up playing baseball in the hot summers of Mississippi. Every time he'd drink a beverage to cool down, he supposedly remarked that it was so smooth, it was "just like drinking oil."

OLD ACHES AND PAINS

Luke Appling drove his White Sox teammates crazy during the 1930s and '40s because he constantly complained about minor medical discomforts, like a sore back or a sprained finger.

~~DUCKY WUCKY~~ MUSCLES

Joe Medwick waddled when he walked, so fans in the 1930s nicknamed him "Ducky Wucky," or just "Ducky." But Medwick wasn't chubby—he was actually very muscular, so his St. Louis Cardinals teammates (probably too scared to call the tough Medwick "Ducky Wucky") called him "Muscles."

THE GAY RELIEVER

This nickname would mean something entirely different today, but in the 1940s, "gay" meant "happy," and Joe Page, a top relief pitcher with the Yankees, was well known for his sunny disposition.

CATFISH

In 1965 Kansas City Athletics owner Charlie Finley signed pitcher Jim Hunter and decided Hunter needed a flashy nickname. Off the top of his head, Finley created a story that Hunter had earned the nickname "Catfish" as a little boy after he'd caught a giant catfish. The name stuck, and over his entire major league career, Hunter was rarely referred to as Jim.

*　　*　　*

"Baseball is like church. Many attend; few understand."

—Leo Durocher

THE HISTORY OF FOOTBALL, PART IV

Here's the part of our story on the history of football that "red-meat" sports fans have been waiting for: how one of America's most violent sports became even more violent. So violent, in fact, that for a time it looked like some colleges would ban it forever. (For Part III, turn to page 141.)

FOOTBALL IN THE NEWS

The "Hospital Box Score" printed by the *Boston Globe* following the Harvard-Yale game of 1894 (Yale won, 12–4):

> **YALE:** JERREMS, KNEE INJURY; MURPHY, UNCONSCIOUS FROM A KICK IN THE HEAD; BUTTERWORTH, CARRIED FROM THE FIELD.
>
> **HARVARD:** CHARLEY BREWER, BADLY BRUISED FOOT; WORTHINGTON, BROKEN COLLARBONE; HALLOWELL, BROKEN NOSE.

By the mid-1890s, due in large part to the introduction of mass plays like the V-trick and the flying wedge, serious injuries had become such a routine part of football that newspapers began publishing injury reports as part of their sports coverage. How violent had the game become? In the early 1890s, a player was actually allowed to slug another player three times with a closed fist before the referee could throw him out of the game.

THE NAKED TRUTH

The situation was made even worse by the fact that players wore almost no protective padding—not even football helmets, which were not mandatory until 1939. The football players of the late 1880s and early 1890s wore little more than canvas or cotton knickers, a football jersey, high-top shoes with leather spikes, and hard leather shin guards worn underneath wool socks. They topped off the look with a knitted cap with a tassel or pom-pom on top. If a player was worried about getting his ears torn from the grabbing

---

Football has more rules than any other American sport.

style of tackling popular at the time, he could wear earmuffs. "Anyone who wore home-made pads was regarded as a sissy," early football great John Heisman remembered.

One acceptable piece of protective wear: If a player worried about breaking his nose, he could wear a black, banana-shaped rubber nose mask. "Sometimes all 11 players wore them," Robert Leckie writes in *The Story of Football*. "They were indeed a ferocious sight with the ends of their handle-bar mustaches dangling from either side of that long, black, banana-like mask, and their long hair flying in the breeze."

GAME OVER

Thanks to the introduction of mass-momentum plays, the 1893 season was surprisingly brutal, even to hardened football fans. That year's Purdue-Chicago game was so violent that the Tippecanoe County district attorney, who was watching from the stands, ran out onto the field in the middle of the game and threatened to indict every single player on charges of assault and battery. The departments of the Army and Navy were so disturbed by the violent direction that football was taking that they abolished the annual game between their military academies.

Public sentiment was also beginning to turn sharply against mass-momentum plays—not just because people were being hurt and killed, but also because they made the games boring to watch (unless you were there to watch people break bones). So many players crowded around the ball during the mass plays that it was difficult for spectators to see what was going on.

MAKING SOME CHANGES

In 1894 the University Athletic Club of New York invited the "Big Four" football powers—Yale, Princeton, Harvard, and Pennsylvania—to meet in New York to form new rules that would curb the violence in football.

Banning mass-momentum plays outright was out of the question—they were too popular with too many football teams—but the Big Four did agree to a few restrictions. They limited the number of players who could gather behind the line of scrimmage in preparation for a play, and they passed a rule requiring that a ball had to travel at least 10 yards at kickoffs to be considered in play, unless it was touched by a member of the receiving team.

They also made it illegal to touch a member of the opposing team unless the opponent had the ball, and reduced the length of the game from 90 minutes to 70, in the hopes that shorter games would mean less violence.

The new restrictions effectively banned the flying wedge and similar plays during kickoffs, but in the end they were not very effective, because teams kept inventing new mass plays that got around the rules. Injuries continued to mount.

THE BIG TEN IS BORN

The following year, Princeton and Yale proposed banning mass-momentum plays altogether by requiring a minimum of seven players on the line of scrimmage and by allowing only one back to be in forward motion before the snap. Harvard and Penn refused to go along, and rather than sign on to the new rules they broke off from the Big Four and drafted their own set of rules, allowing mass-momentum plays.

When the Big Four split in 1895, the presidents of Chicago, Illinois, Michigan, Minnesota, Northwestern, Purdue, and Wisconsin universities stepped in to fill the breach by forming what grew into the Big Ten Western Conference. (Iowa and Indiana joined in 1899, and the 10th school, Ohio State, signed on in 1912.)

The rise of a competing football conference motivated the students of the Big Four to resolve their differences. In the summer of 1896, Harvard and Pennsylvania returned to the fold, and the Big Four moved a step closer to banning mass-momentum plays with a rule that forbade players from taking more than a single step before the ball was in play, unless they came to a complete stop before taking another step. But it wasn't enough, as Robert Leckie writes in *The Story of Football:*

> As the twentieth century began, football was still a game of mass-momentum….The flying wedge was not completely gone. Hurdling and the flying tackle were common. Slugging was still a familiar tactic up front, and the most acceptable method of getting the ball carrier through the line was to push, pull, or haul him through. Thus the only participant surviving the contest undamaged was apt to be the ball.

The figure at the top of golf's Ryder Cup is Charles Ryder's tutor, Abe Mitchell.

BIG TIME

By the late 1880s, American football was beginning to spread from the original handful of Eastern colleges to schools in other parts of the country. Notre Dame started its football program in 1887, and the University of Southern California followed a year later; Stanford and the University of California both launched programs in 1893. By 1897 teams were popping up all over the country.

Yale University remained the dominant force in American football—it lost only three games in the first 10 years of intercollegiate play. And because coach Walter Camp dominated Yale's program and had been so influential in shaping the modern game, his authority at the center of American football was unchallenged.

A VICTIM OF ITS OWN SUCCESS

But football was too much fun to remain the exclusive preserve of pampered "college boys." As the sport caught on in universities across the nation, athletic clubs in the surrounding communities began to form their own football leagues. So did church parishes, community groups, businesses, and small towns itching to earn big reputations. Regular play between such teams soon led to the same kinds of traditional rivalries and fierce grudge matches that by now were an entrenched part of the college game.

As the violence of these semipro leagues escalated beyond even that of college football, the sport moved ever closer to anarchy. In some areas of the country, Stephen Fox writes in *Big Leagues*, semipro football became little more than "a formalized excuse for beating up men from other communities."

BAD NEWS

Twenty-one people died playing football during the 1904 season; another 23 would die the following year. Only a handful of those killed had been playing on college teams—the majority had been playing on semipro teams. But the college teams were still the organizing force behind football, and in the middle of the 1905 season, President Theodore Roosevelt, himself a football fan, summoned representatives from three of the major football powers—Harvard, Yale, and Princeton—to the White House and ordered them to clean up the sport. "Brutality and foul play," he told them,

---

"should receive the same summary punishment given to a man who cheats at cards."

YALEGATE

Harvard, Yale, and Princeton left the White House meeting promising to do better, but football didn't really change. And football's image was so tattered that some colleges were ready to ban the game with or without presidential support: Columbia abolished its football program in 1905 and did not reinstate it until 1915. Stanford and the University of California replaced their programs with rugby the same year. "The game of football," U.C.'s president Benjamin Wheeler declared, "must be made over or go."

For years, one of the biggest obstacles to cleaning up football had been Walter Camp himself. As chairman of the Intercollegiate Football Rules Committee, he had been able to fend off any fundamental changes to the game. But his iron grip on football loosened considerably beginning in 1905, following the publication of newspaper and magazine articles detailing scandalous financial abuses in the Yale football program. Among the most serious charges were that Camp had a $96,000 slush fund that he used to coddle his star players and had also helped himself to $5,000 a year, at a time when Yale professors earned only $3,500 a year. He hid these items in the budget as "miscellaneous expenses" and "maintenance of the field."

Camp's shady financial practices weren't all that different from any other college coach at the time, but the revelations came just as the pressure to clean up football violence was intensifying, and Camp, with his reputation now seriously in question, was no longer able to block the reformers.

CHANGING OF THE GUARD

When Camp next tried to resist Roosevelt's demand to clean up football, Chancellor Henry MacCracken of New York University decided he'd had enough. He organized a conference of 13 colleges *not* represented on Camp's tightly controlled rules committee, to discuss whether college football should be abolished, or whether one last attempt at cleaning it up should be made.

The original group of 13 schools that met on December 9,

Before lawn mowers, golf greens were often kept trim by grazing sheep.

1905, expanded to 62 schools by the time they met a second time, on December 28. At this meeting the schools voted to form an organization called the Intercollegiate Athletic Association, which in 1910 changed its name to the National Collegiate Athletic Association (NCAA). The group voted to create its own rules committee, headed by Captain Palmer Pierce of West Point, to push through the reforms that Camp had resisted for so long.

CAN'T WE ALL JUST GET ALONG?

Rather than compete against the old Intercollegiate Football Association, when the Intercollegiate Athletic Association met for the third time in January 1906, they agreed to merge, electing a reformer named E. K. Hall to serve as chair of the new joint rules committee. Camp was out as chairman—for good.

Lavatory! Lavatory! Sis, boom, bah! Now turn to page 275 for the final installment of "The History of Football."

*   *   *

IT'S A FAKE...

...Baseball player. In 2006 a Florida chiropractor named Rhonda Schroeder began dating New York Mets pitcher Pedro Martinez. They met through a patient of Schroeder's named Shirley Gordon. When Martinez kept encouraging his new girlfriend to give Gordon gifts of hundreds of thousands of dollars, Schroeder realized that her boyfriend probably wasn't the real Pedro Martinez and called the cops. He wasn't. And Gordon was already wanted by police on identity-theft charges.

...Arm wrestler. In 2007 a professional arm wrestler named Arsen Liliev tried to qualify for a lower (and easier) weight class at a European tournament by sending a look-alike to the pregame weigh-in. Liliev was caught when officials noticed that his look-alike didn't look anything like him.

...Referee. A man named Christopher Norling was arrested in 1996 for running up a huge bill at Milwaukee's Pfister Hotel. Norling told the hotel to bill the National Football League, for whom he worked as a referee. (He was lying.)

June 3, 1988: The Dodgers beat the Reds on the strength of 22 hits—all of them singles.

"HE'S LOST BOTH RIGHT FRONT TIRES"

*British motorsport commentator Murray Walker is
reknowned for his silly—and hilarious—vocal flubs.*

"The young Ralph Schumacher has been upstaged by the
teenager, Jensen Button, who is twenty."

"Only a few more laps to go and then the action will begin,
unless this is the action, which it is."

"There's nothing wrong with the car except that it's on fire."

"Just under ten seconds…call it nine point five in round
figures."

"I imagine the conditions in those cars are totally unimagin-
able."

"Either that car is stationary, or it is on the move."

"With the race half gone, there is still half the race to go."

"And I interrupt myself to bring you this…"

"Mansell is slowing it down, taking it easy. Oh no he isn't!
It's a lap record!"

"He is shedding buckets of adrenaline in that car."

"Mansell can see him in his earphone."

"And he's lost both right front tires!"

"A sad ending, albeit a happy one."

Play a round of golf, then drink 2 cocktails: you've just gained more calories than you burned.

THE HISTORY OF MINIATURE GOLF

We tried to keep this short, but it's such a BIG story...

THE HIMALAYAS

The Ladies' Putting Club in St. Andrews, Scotland, is considered by some to be the world's oldest miniature golf course. The club was founded in 1867 by some members of the Royal and Ancient Golf Club who wanted a place their daughters could play. At the height of the Victorian era, girls and women weren't allowed to lift the club past their shoulder (it was considered vulgar), which meant they couldn't hit the ball very far. So a very hilly and lumpy 18-hole putting green, known as "the Himalayas," was built on the sand dunes next to St. Andrews's famous Old Course. It was an entire 18-hole course designed in miniature size. It became—and remains to this day—hugely popular. (Tom Watson, Craig Stadler, and many other pros have played the Himalayas.)

GOFSTACLE

The earliest mention of a miniature golf game that resembles the one we play today comes from a 1912 article entitled "Bridge, Stick, Tunnel and Box: A Golf Game for Putters." It appeared in the *Illustrated London News* and featured an illustration with the caption "At the Garden Party: An Exciting Moment of Gofstacle." The picture showed a group of young men playing a game that looked like a mix between miniature golf and croquet. Here's how the game was described:

> Gofstacle is played with golf balls and putter. The obstacles to be negotiated include hoops, rings, a tunnel, a bridge, and a box which has to be entered up an incline. It is played like golf croquet, and may also be played as is golf, the obstacles taking the place of holes. It is claimed for it that it is calculated to improve putting. Its popularity is undoubted.

OTHER MINI COURSES

In the early 1900s, small private courses began to be built at the homes of wealthy golfers in North America and Europe. Here are a few examples:

Thistle Dhu: The best known—and possibly the first—miniature course in the United States was built in 1916 at the winter cottage of James Barber in Pinehurst, North Carolina, not far from Pinehurst Golf Club. Barber hired amateur architect Edward H. Wiswell to build an elaborate, tiny course in a garden setting, complete with walkways, benches, flower beds, and a fountain. When it was finished, the story goes, Barber gazed upon his tiny course and exclaimed, "This'll do!" So the course was named "Thistle Dhu," which he thought had a Scottish ring to it. The game didn't catch on with the public, but the concept of a "garden course" did pique the interest of other wealthy golfers.

Astro-Green: In 1922 Scottish-born Thomas McCulloch Fairbairn gave miniature golf an unexpected boost when he constructed a small golf course on his cotton plantation in Mexico. He soon discovered that the dry climate wouldn't allow him to grow decent greens, so he started experimenting with artificial surfaces. He finally came up with a surface made of cottonseed hulls, sand, oil, and green dye. It worked so well that he patented it, and his invention would soon help put miniature golf on the map.

Fairyland: A successful Tennessee businessman named Garnet Carter opened a 700-acre holiday resort on top of Lookout Mountain near the Georgia border in 1924. He called it "Fairyland" because of his wife Frieda's interest in European folklore. One of its promised features: a golf course. But it was taking much longer than expected to be built. As John Wilson writes in *Lookout: The Story of an Amazing Mountain*:

> Before the Fairyland Golf Course was opened, one impatient guest at the Fairyland Inn suggested to Garnet Carter that he construct a putting green in front of the Inn. Carter readily agreed to this idea and, as he was designing the green, he noticed some extra tile and sewer pipe lying nearby. Experimenting, he found that a golf ball could be hit so as to roll through the pipes. So Carter decided to add the pipes as part of the green and thus the worldwide sport of miniature golf was born.

This time, miniature golf caught on. The mini-links soon became

---

"I feel safer on a racetrack than I do on Houston's freeways." —race car driver A. J. Foyt so popular that he had to charge a "greens fee" to keep the huge crowds down.

BOOM!

Carter was an astute businessman—he immediately recognized the potential profits in miniature golf. So he founded the Fairyland Manufacturing Company and began constructing "Tom Thumb" courses all over Tennessee, and eventually the entire South.

By the fall of 1929, the pygmy links invaded California and New York, and soon the rest of the nation. For only $4,500, Carter's company would lay down a course that could be operational in less than a week, and they proved to be so popular (and profitable) that many courses would earn back their initial investment in only a few weeks. The game was the first of many recreational fads of the Great Depression, successful mainly because it was so inexpensive to play.

Within a year, mini-golf courses were everywhere—from highway filling stations to vacant city lots. By the middle of 1930, 20 million Americans were regular players. On any given night, there were close to four million people flooding over 40,000 courses nationwide. People joked that the only industry still hiring during those early years of the Great Depression was miniature golf, which in 1930 employed 200,000 workers and generated profits of more than $225 million. Not only that, the fad helped bolster the flagging cotton and steel industries because of Fairbairn's turf recipe.

THOU SHALT NOT PUTT-PUTT

Even a pastime as harmless as miniature golf was not without controversy. The courses were banned within 50 feet of churches, hospitals, and public schools. The nongolfing element of the population complained that the late-night revelry of reckless young golfers—who would spike their sodas with bootleg liquor—disturbed their sleep. The game also sparked a debate between physicians and pastors. Doctors liked it—miniature golf took young folks out of stuffy movie theaters at night and put them in the fresh outdoor air for some healthy activity. But church officials claimed that playing on the Sabbath—the most popular day for recreation—was a sin. Ironically, a few churches around the coun-

---

Moo: the first golf course in the United States was a cow pasture in Yonkers, New York.

try saw a chance to help pay off their debts and went over to the dark side, encouraging one and all to come and play (but never on the Sabbath).

BUST!

The great mini-golf craze didn't last long. Too many entrepreneurs saw a cheap, profitable Tom Thumb course as their road out of financial hardship. The fatal combination of market saturation and dwindling interest in the game brought about its swift end. In 1931 *Miniature Golf Management*, a year-old publication, noted that every California course was in the red financially. By the mid-1930s, nearly all of the courses were abandoned and many were destroyed. But Garnet Carter survived the fall. In 1929 he had the foresight to sell out to a Pennsylvania pipe manufacturer and settle for royalties from future miniature courses. At the end of the tiny sport's three-year heyday, he emerged unscathed. But that wasn't the end of the craze.

THE RETURN

The postwar boom of the early 1950s saw a rise in wealth, leisure time, cars, and roadside attractions—a perfect recipe for the return of miniature golf. In 1953 an insurance salesman from Fayetteville, North Carolina, named Don Clayton was ordered to take a month off work due to stress. One of the activities he took up was miniature golf. But he hated it—by that time the designs had become even more trick-filled and were less about golf than they were about goofy gadgets. Clayton was more interested in actual golf, so he decided to build his own course...and Putt-Putt miniature golf was born. (They still don't allow windmills.) Other companies, such as Lomma Miniature Golf and Goofy Golf, soon followed and tiny courses started showing up again. And not just in the United States:

• In 1953 Swiss architect Paul Bongni invented his own course and patented the name "Minigolf." Minigolf would become (and still remains) hugely popular all over Europe. Unlike his American counterparts, Bongni saw the game as a true sport and wanted to create standardized courses and rules. His Beton ("concrete" in German) courses had smooth—and very fast—concrete putting surfaces and simple, standardized obstacles.

In darts, hitting the bull's-eye twice in three throws is called a *black dog.*

• In 1958 German designer Albert Hess invented Eternit courses, which were small, transportable courses similar to the Betons, with fiberglass obstacles.

• Swedish Felt courses came next, using wood designs with felt surfaces and obstacles such as ramps and holes to shoot through.

While one-of-a-kind, theme-oriented courses (like Goofy Golf's Easter Island) are the norm in the United States, standardized courses like the Beton, Eternit, and Swedish Felts are more common in Europe.

PROFESSIONAL MINIATURE GOLF?

Yes, you read that correctly. In 1955 a local Putt-Putt tournament event was held in Fayetteville, North Carolina. First prize: a free vacation to Miami Beach. In 1957 the first national putting championship was held. Warren Gaines won the prize—a brand-new Cadillac. Then in 1959, the Putt-Putt Professional Golfers Association was formed. The name was changed a year later to the more businesslike Professional Putters Association (PPA). But if the pro Putt-Putters are embarrassed, they're embarrassed all the way to the bank: the PPA has given out more than $7.6 million in prize money since it began.

The PPA, however, is not to be confused with the USPM-GA—the U.S. Pro Minigolf Association, just one part of the WMF—the World Minigolf Federation, the worldwide governing body of the sport of minigolf. Every year, international competitions are held (several countries even subsidize players so they can take time off work to practice) and one of the biggest events is the Masters—the Minigolf Masters—held every year in Myrtle Beach, South Carolina, the U.S. minigolf capital with more than 100 courses.

WMF players from around the world come to compete for the grand prize of $4,000 (the *other* Masters has a grand prize of more than $1 million). But that doesn't mean that you can't make a living on the Minigolf Tour. David McCaslin, winner of the 2002 Minigolf U.S. Open, has made more than $250,000 as a professional miniature golfer. And mini-golf enthusiasts have petitioned the International Olympic Committee to make it an official sport at future Olympic Games. (No luck yet.)

Charles Barkley entered the NBA with the nickname "Round Mound of Rebound."

TOY FACTS

The BRI takes a look at random info on some
childhood (and adulthood) classics.

WIFFLE BALLS

In 1953 David Mullany noticed that his son and a friend were playing stickball in the small backyard of their Fairfield, Connecticut, home...but they were using one of Mullany's plastic golf balls instead of a rubber ball. It seemed like a good idea; that way the ball couldn't be hit or thrown too far.

Mullany cut holes in some of his plastic golf balls with a razor blade and discovered that, with the right configuration, players using a lightweight plastic ball could even throw curves and sliders. In 1955 he began manufacturing his new creation, marketing it as a Wiffle ball—a name he adapted from the baseball term "to whiff," or strike out.

MAGIC SLATE

In the early 1920s, R. A. Watkins, owner of a small printing plant in Illinois, was approached by a man who wanted to sell him the rights to a homemade device made of waxed cardboard and tissue. You could write on it, but the messages could be erased easily by lifting up the tissue. Watkins couldn't make up his mind; he told the man to come back the next day.

In the middle of the night, Watkins's phone rang; it was the man calling from jail. He said that if Watkins would bail him out, he'd give Watkins the rights to the invention. The printer agreed. He wound up getting a patent for the device—which he called Magic Slate. Since then, tens of millions have been sold.

PICTIONARY

Robert Angel, a Seattle waiter, used to entertain his friends at parties by selecting a word from the dictionary, drawing it, and having them guess what it was. He didn't think about developing it into a game until Trivial Pursuit became popular. Then he spent eight months looking up 6,000 words in the dictionary (2,500 made it into the game) while a friend designed "word

Grades of proficiency in judo are called *dans*. The highest *dan*, the 10th, receives a red belt.

cards" and the board. He borrowed $35,000 to manufacture the game and started selling it to stores in Seattle out of the trunk of his car.

He got his big break when Nordstrom ordered 167 games. They didn't even have a game department. "They let us set up a table in the accessories department," Angel recalls. "If anybody glanced in our direction, we would yell at them to come and watch us play the game." Tom McGuire, a salesman at Selchow & Righter (manufacturer of Trivial Pursuit), played Pictionary at Nordstrom with his family. He was so impressed that he quit his job and began marketing it full-time. By the end of 1987, over $90 million worth of Pictionary games had been sold in the United States alone.

*   *   *

TOY MISCELLANY

• Tonka Toys was originally called the Mound Metalcraft Company. It was renamed *Tonka* after Lake Minnetonka, which dominated the scenery around their Minnesota factory.

• Mattel got its name from its two founders—Harold Matson and Elliot Handler. Handler was in the picture frame business in L.A. In 1946 he had a bunch of extra frame slats, so he and Matson built doll furniture out of them.

• Mattel was the first toy company to advertise on national TV. In 1955 they sold toy burp guns on *The Mickey Mouse Club*.

• Mr. Potato Head used to come with a pipe—which bugged anti-smoking activists. "It's not only dangerous to his health," complained Surgeon General C. Everett Koop, "it also passes on the message to kids that smoking is okay." In 1987 Hasbro gave in; after 35 years of smoking, Mr. Potato Head surrendered his pipe to the surgeon general. Koop was so pleased that he named Mr. Potato Head "Official Spokespud" for the Great American Smokeout.

• World record: A game of Twister was played by 4,160 participants on May 2, 1987, at the University of Massachusetts.

In shooting, "clay pigeons" aren't clay, or pigeons—they're small disks made of lime and pitch.

CRÈME *de la* CRUD: HORSE & BULL STORIES

One of our most popular Bathroom Reader features is "Crème de la Crud," where we bring you "the best of the worst of the worst." In this special sports edition, they happen to revolve around two things: horse racing and bullfighting. Olé!

WORST MATADOR
"El Gallo" (Raphael Gomez Ortega), an early 20th-century bullfighter

El Gallo employed a technique called the *espantada* (sudden flight) that was unique in the history of professional bullfighting—when the bull entered the ring, he panicked, dropped his cape, and ran away. "All of us artists have bad days," he would explain. His fights were so hilarious that he was brought out of retirement seven times; in his last fight in October 1918, he claimed he spared the bull because "it winked at him." (The audience thought it was a big joke, but Ortega's relatives didn't—his brother was so ashamed during that last fight that he entered the ring and killed the bull himself…just to salvage the family's honor.)

WORST JOCKEY
Beltran de Osorio y Diez de Rivera, "Iron" Duke of Albuquerque

The duke developed an obsession with winning England's Grand National Steeplechase horse race when he was only eight years old, after receiving a film of the race as a birthday present. "I said then that I would win that race one day," the amateur rider recounted years later.

• On his first attempt in 1952, he fell from his horse; he woke up later in the hospital with a cracked vertebra.

• He tried again in 1963; bookies placed odds of 66–1 against him finishing the race still on his horse. (The duke fell from the horse.)

• He raced again in 1965, and fell from his horse after it collapsed underneath him, breaking his leg.

- In 1974, having just had 16 screws removed from a leg he'd broken after falling from the horse in another race, he fell while training for the Grand National and broke his collarbone. He recovered in time to compete (in a plaster cast) and actually managed to finish the race while still on his horse—the only time he ever would. He placed eighth.

- In 1976 the duke fell again during a race—this time he was trampled by the other horses and suffered seven broken ribs, several broken vertebrae, a broken wrist, a broken thigh, and a severe concussion, which left him in a coma for two days.

- He eventually recovered, but when he announced at the age of 57 that he was going to try again, race organizers pulled his license "for his own safety."

The Iron Duke never did win the Grand National, as he promised himself he would, but he did break another record—he broke more bones trying to win it than any jockey before or since.

SHORTEST BULLFIGHTING CRAZE

In 1958 the town of Lindsay, Ontario, organized the country's first-ever bullfight. There aren't many bullfighting bulls in Canada, and even fewer matadors, so they had to bring in both from Mexico. But the bulls brought ticks with them, and ticks from other parts of the world aren't allowed into Canada. The bulls had to be quarantined for a week. By the time they got out, the matadors had returned to Mexico. Result: no bullfight.

FOGGIEST IDEA

Horatio Bottomley (great name) was a convicted fraud artist and ex-member of the English parliament. In 1914 he figured out what he thought was a foolproof way to rig a horse race: He bought all six horses in the race, hired his own jockeys to race them, and told them in which order he wanted them to cross the finish line. Then he bet a fortune on the horses he'd picked to win, and also placed bets on the order of finish. Everything went according to plan...until a thick fog rolled in over the track in the middle of the race. It was so thick that the jockeys couldn't see each other well enough to cross the finish line in the proper order. Bottomley lost every bet he placed.

THE PHYSICS
OF HOCKEY

Uncle John is a rabid hockey fan, but he tends to get distracted by questions like "Why is ice so slippery?" and "Exactly how fast can a puck travel?" We've slowed down the fastest game on Earth just long enough to give you a look at the science behind it.

GLIDER RIDE

Ice skating is the fastest way to travel across the surface of the Earth on your feet. When you run, your front foot slows you down every time it hits the ground, but when you're skating, one skate pushes while the other glides, so there's hardly any friction to slow you down. In fact, hockey players can travel at speeds of more than 20 mph in a rink that's just 200 feet long.

ICE VS. ICE

Most hockey players prefer "fast ice." It's hard and cold, and has a smooth surface that makes skating and passing easier. But over the course of a hockey period, fast ice becomes "slow ice"—it warms up and the surface gets rougher. The puck starts to bounce a little, too, so late in the period players become more careful—generally they'll try to make a safe play rather than a finesse play. Then, between periods, the Zamboni machine smoothes the surface again.

You'd think by now that scientists would have nailed down the nature of ice, but there's still some debate. The long-held belief was that pressure or friction melts the ice and creates a water lubricant that helps skates and pucks to slide. But recent research suggests that skates and pucks don't generate enough pressure to instantly liquefy ice. Instead there's a "quasi-fluid," or waterlike, layer on top of ice that makes it slippery. Even ice that's –250°F or colder has this layer. At that way-below-freezing temperature, the slippery layer is only *one molecule* thick. At warmer temperatures, the number of slippery layers increases, so skaters have to slosh through even more molecules, which slows them down.

The world's top table-tennis players can hit the ball at speeds over 100 miles per hour.

The ideal ice temperature for hockey is generally considered to be 16°F. Figure skaters do best at 22°F, because the six-degree difference gives them more control and makes for a softer landing.

THE MAGIC STICK

Players take a highly personal approach to their sticks; some prefer longer, straighter sticks, while some like more curve on the blade. Others like to have a different "lie" in the stick (this determines the amount of blade that comes in contact with the ice). Players can spend hours preparing their sticks for a game.

Stick material is all-important, too. The newer sticks are made of aluminum or carbon-graphite. They're strong and generally lighter in weight than wooden sticks. Rock elm is the ideal wood, but it's become scarce because of Dutch elm disease. Some manufacturers have turned to white ash, which is not as sturdy as elm. Whatever it's made of, a hockey stick has to be just flexible enough to store as much energy as possible, then release it when it's needed.

THE FINER POINTS OF PUCK

Hockey pioneers would make a puck out of anything they found lying around: a knot of wood, a stone, an apple—even a piece of frozen cow dung.

The modern puck made its debut in Montreal in 1875. The first indoor game was played with a rubber ball, but because it bounced around so much it broke the windows, resulting in costly repairs. Legend has it that for the next match, one of the rink owners cut the rounded edges off the ball to reduce the bounce— and inadvertently invented the hockey puck.

The 21st-century puck is made of a rubber compound—sulfur-vulcanized rubber—mixed with other materials to give it more strength and elasticity. It's frozen in a bucket of ice before a game to take some of the bounce out of it, and it's kept frozen between periods for the same reason. When the puck gets warm, it stores more energy and bounces higher, which gives the player less control. Freezing keeps the puck lower to the ground, where the action usually is.

HIT IT!

A slap shot can send the puck across the ice at well over 100 mph. There are three factors involved:

• First, there's the energy produced by the weight that the player transfers to the stick by leaning into the shot.

• Then, there's "stored elastic energy." Like a pole-vaulter's pole or an archer's bow, a hockey stick stores energy during a windup. In hockey, the shaft bends slightly during the swing because the end can't keep up with the velocity of the handle. The stick stores this energy and releases it when it hits the puck. The result is a greater launching speed than you could get from a nonflexible stick. (A stick that's too flexible wouldn't store enough energy.)

• Finally, a slight snap of the wrists at the end of the motion releases the puck from the stick. The snap is crucial: It sets the puck to spinning like a Frisbee, which makes it more stable in flight. If it didn't spin, it would tend to roll side over side, which would make it follow a more erratic path.

A FLICK OF THE WRIST

Wrist shots aren't as powerful as slap shots, but they've been known to send a puck traveling at 80 to 90 mph. Players say they like the wrist shot because of the control and quick release. Without the windup required for a slap shot, the energy comes from the player pressing down on the stick, then releasing it suddenly with a flick of the wrist. The other factor is the amount of time the puck spends in contact with the blade of the stick—in this case, a much longer amount of time than with a slap shot.

WHEN PANTHERS AND PENGUINS COLLIDE

Hockey stick-meets-puck isn't the only source of energy on the floor of a rink. If a 200-pound player is skating across the ice at 20 mph, and he just happens to bump into another player of about the same weight who's traveling at the same rate of speed, physicists have calculated that the collision would generate enough energy to light a 60-watt lightbulb for two minutes. (Or, more likely, sends one 200-pound player to the penalty box for two minutes.)

...another player's tooth embedded in the arm.

CALLING HISTORY

Famous baseball plays…as told by the announcers who witnessed them.

"THE IMPOSSIBLE HAS HAPPENED!"

Situation: With two injured legs and a stomach virus, Dodgers slugger Kirk Gibson wasn't expected to play in the 1988 World Series against the Oakland A's. But in Game 1, down a run in the bottom of the ninth with a man on, manager Tommy Lasorda surprised everyone by calling on Gibson to face the game's best closer, Dennis Eckersley.

Sportscaster: Vin Scully, NBC-TV

The Call: "Look who's coming up!…Sax waiting on deck, but the game right now is at the plate. High fly ball into right field…she is…gone!" *Then Scully goes silent as Gibson limps around the base paths while the Dodger fans cheer. He finally says,* "In a year that has been so improbable, the impossible has happened!"

"GO CRAZY!"

Situation: In the 1985 NLCS, Ozzie Smith and the Cardinals were tied at two games apiece against the Dodgers. Smith, a switch hitter, had never homered from the left side of the plate during his seven-year career. The score was tied in the bottom of the ninth as the "Wizard of Oz" entered the box…batting lefty.

Sportscaster: Jack Buck, CBS Radio

The Call: "Here's the pitch. Smith corks one into right down the line! It may go…Go crazy, folks! Go crazy! It's a home run! And the Cardinals have won the game…by the score of 3 to 2 on a home run by…the Wizard! Go crazy!"

"OH, DOCTOR!"

Situation: In Game 4 of the 1984 NLCS, Steve Garvey of the Padres came up to bat with Tony Gwynn on first and the score tied 5-5 in the bottom of the ninth. San Diego had come back in the game to tie the score, but they were facing elimination against the Chicago Cubs' intimidating closer, Lee Smith.

Sportscaster : Jerry Coleman, Padres radio

The Pros and Cons Golf Invitational is played by touring pros and prison inmates.

The Call: "Pitch on the way to Garvey. Hit high to right field, way back! Going, going, it is…gone! The Padres win it! In a game that absolutely defies description, Steve Garvey, in the ninth inning, hit one over the 370 mark, and the Padres beat the Cubs 7 to 5! Oh, doctor! You can hang a star on that baby!"

"THE GIANTS WON THE PENNANT!"

Situation: The 1951 New York Giants battled back from a 13 ½-game deficit to force a three-game playoff against the Brooklyn Dodgers. After splitting the first two contests, the Giants were down by two runs in the bottom of the ninth at the Polo Grounds when outfielder Bobby Thomson came up to bat.

Sportscaster: Russ Hodges, Giants radio

The Call: "Bobby Thomson up there swinging. He's had two out of three, a single and a double, and Billy Cox is playing him right on the third-base line. One out, last of the ninth. Branca pitches. Bobby Thomson takes a strike called on the inside corner. Bobby hitting at .292. He's had a single and a double, and he drove in the Giants' first run with a long fly to center. Brooklyn leads it, four to two. Hartung down the line at third, not taking any chances. Lockman without too big of a lead at second, but he'll be running like the wind if Thomson hits one. Branca throws. There's a long drive! That's gonna be it, I believe! The Giants won the pennant! The Giants won the pennant! The Giants won the pennant! The Giants won the pennant! Bobby Thompson hits into the lower deck of the left-field stands! The Giants won the pennant, and they're going crazy! They're going crazy! Hey, ho! I don't believe it! I do not believe it! Bobby Thomson hit a line drive into the lower deck of the left-field stands, and the great place is going crazy. The Giants—Horace Stoneham has got a winner. The Giants won it by a score of five to four, and they're picking Bobby Thomson up and carrying him off the field!"

Preserving history: Because this game took place in the days before broadcasts were regularly taped, Hodges's call should have been lost forever. But an overconfident Brooklyn fan taped the broadcast because he wanted to record "Hodges crying" when the Giants lost. Even though his Dodgers got beat, the Brooklyn fan knew he had something special. The next day, he got ahold of Hodges and told him, "You *have* to have this tape."

First to say "He shoots, he scores!": Hockey announcer Foster Hewitt, in 1933.

POKER LINGO

Ever watched rounders and fish splash the pot until they're down to the felt? If so, you've seen some serious poker players. They have their own language, too. Ante up!

- **All in:** Bet all your chips
- **Down to the felt:** So broke all you see in front of you is the green felt of the poker table
- **Tapioca, or Tap City:** Tapped out; out of money
- **Buy the pot:** Make a bet so large that other players are unlikely to match it
- **Tap:** Bet as much as your opponents have on hand, forcing them to bet everything
- **Catching cards:** On a winning streak
- **Railroad bible:** Deck of cards
- **Toke:** The tip you give to the dealer
- **Splash the pot:** Toss your chips into the pot, instead of just placing them there. It's considered bad form because other players can't see how much you're actually betting
- **Rake:** The house's cut
- **Cowboys:** Kings
- **Ladies:** Queens
- **Rock:** A very conservative player, someone who doesn't take big chances
- **Paint:** A face card
- **Trips:** Three of a kind
- **Berry patch:** A very easy game
- **Underdog:** A weak hand that's likely to lose
- **Rag:** An upfacing card so low in value that it can't affect the outcome of the hand
- **Alligator blood:** A player who keeps his cool under pressure has alligator (cold) blood
- **Wheel:** The best hand in lowball poker—6, 4, 3, 2, A
- **Fish:** A very bad poker player. They're only in the game so that you can beat them out of their money
- **George:** A fish
- **Rounder:** A professional poker player. A rounder makes his living parting fishes and georges from their money
- **Base deal:** Dealing from the bottom of the deck
- **In the hole:** In stud poker, the cards dealt facedown, so only you can see them
- **Bullets:** Aces in the hole
- **Big slick:** A king and an ace in the hole
- **Boat:** A full house

First baseball team to fly to a game: the Marysville Merchants (California), in August 1921.

THE ORIGIN OF BASKETBALL, PART II

*Here's more on how the game of basketball
was invented. (Part I starts on page 112.)*

P ROMISES, PROMISES...
As James Naismith admitted years later in his memoirs, the
new game he had in mind was an indoor version of an existing sport, like baseball or rugby. And when Dr. Gulick put him in
charge of the Incorrigibles' physical education classes, he set out
to find one he could adapt.

Naismith spent two weeks experimenting with different games,
but something always seemed to get lost in the translation: Indoor
soccer, for example, was fun—but too many windows were broken.
And rugby turned out to be too dangerous on the gymnasium's
hardwood floors. Other sports were safer...but they were so boring,
the Incorrigibles refused to play them.

Outdoor games were meant to be played outdoors, Naismith
concluded, and that was that.

BACK TO THE DRAWING BOARD

Time was running out. With only 24 hours left until his deadline
for reporting to the faculty on the success of his efforts, Naismith
decided to try a different approach: He would systematically analyze a number of different games, and figure out what made them
challenging and fun. Then he would incorporate many of those
elements into a new game that would be, as he put it, "interesting, easy to learn, and easy to play in the winter and by artificial
light."

DO UNTO OTHERS

Naismith's new game would also have to walk a political
tightrope: it had to be physically challenging enough to sustain
the interest of the Incorrigibles, but not so rough or violent that it
would offend conservatives within the YMCA movement. They

had opposed getting involved with sports in the first place...and Naismith didn't want to give them any excuse to declare the experiment a failure.

HE GOT GAME

Amazingly, Naismith then sat down and, step by step, invented one of the most popular sports of all time.

Step 1. He figured that since nearly all popular sports have balls, his game should have one, too. But should it be small or large? Small balls like baseballs and lacrosse balls required bats, sticks, and racquets. Naismith was afraid players might use them to hit each other. He chose a big ball.

Step 2. Naismith felt that running with a ball would invariably lead to tackling the person carrying it—and tackling was too violent for the YMCA (not to mention too dangerous on a wood floor). So in the new game, the person who had the ball wouldn't be allowed to run with it; they wouldn't even be allowed to move. Instead, the player with the ball would have to stand in one place and pass it to the other players. That was the key to the game. "I can still recall how I snapped my fingers and shouted, 'I've got it!'" Naismith recalled years later.

Step 3. And what about the shape of the ball? It would either have to be round or oblong like a rugby ball. Rugby balls were easier to carry under the arm, but that would encourage tackling. Round balls were easier to throw, which made them perfect for a passing game. Naismith decided to use a soccer ball.

Step 4. Naismith figured that there should be a goal at each end of the gymnasium...but what kind of goal? A huge one, like a soccer goal, would make scoring too easy—so the goal would have to be smaller. But a tiny goal would be easy to block...and blocking the goal would lead to pushing and shoving. So he decided to put the goal high over people's heads, where it would be impossible to block.

Step 5. This led to another consideration: if the goal was vertical, like the goalposts in football, players would throw the ball at it as hard and as fast as they could—which would

At the 1914 Bamberger Trophy golf tournament, 100 caddies went on strike, starting a riot.

be dangerous indoors. It would also reward force over skill, which was the antithesis of what Naismith wanted.

Naismith suddenly remembered a game he'd played as a child, called Duck on the Rock. The object was to knock an object off of a rock by throwing stones at it. The best players always threw their rocks in an arc rather than directly at the duck, so that if they missed, they wouldn't have to run as far to retrieve the rock. That inspired Naismith to use a horizontal goal, parallel to the ground. That way, players wouldn't be able to score just by throwing the ball as hard as they could: they'd have to throw it in an arc to get it in.

SERENDIPITY STRIKES

Naismith figured a wooden box nailed to the balcony that ran around the gym would work pretty well as a goal, and asked the janitor if he had any boxes lying around.

"No," the janitor told him, "but I have two old peach baskets down in the store room, if they will do you any good." "Thus," Robert Peterson writes in *Cages to Jump Shots*, "did the game miss being called box ball."

Naismith nailed one peach basket to the balcony at one end of the gym, and one at the other end. The balcony of the YMCA in Springfield just happened to be 10 feet off the floor—which is why, today, a regulation basket is 10 feet high.

THE FIRST GAME

Naismith typed up a list of 13 rules and posted them on the gym's bulletin board. The following morning, he read the Incorrigibles the rules; then he divided the 18-man class into two teams of nine and taught them to play the game.

He promised to change any rules that didn't work out. "It was the start of the first basketball game," he recounted in his memoirs years later, "and the finish of the trouble with that class."

Basketball still had a long way to go. Turn to page 393 for the last part of our story.

Width of a standard women's balance beam: Four inches (less than the diameter of a CD).

HOOK, LINE, AND SINKER

Here we explore that age-old conflict: man vs. fish.

"Give a man a fish, and you feed him for a day. Teach a man to fish, and you get rid of him on weekends."

—Nancy Gray

"Fishing is the only sport where sitting on your butt under a tree looks like a concentrated activity."

—Jeff MacNelly

"It has always been my private conviction that any man who pits his intelligence against a fish and loses has it coming."

—John Steinbeck

"Some go to church and think about fishing; others go fishing and think about God."

—Tony Blake

"I fish, therefore, I lie."

—Tom Clarke

"The man who coined the phrase 'Money can't buy happiness' never bought himself a good fly rod."

—Reg Baird

"There is no greater fan of fly-fishing than the worm."

—Patrick McManus

"Fly-fishing is the most fun you can have standing up."

—Arnold Gingrich

"There's a fine line between fishing and standing on the shore like an idiot."

—Steven Wright

"I am not against golf, since I cannot but suspect it keeps armies of the unworthy from discovering trout."

—Paul O'Neil

"The best time to go fishing is whenever you can get away."

—Robert Traver

"Men and fish are alike. They both get into trouble when they open their mouths."

—Jimmy Moore

"If people concentrated on the really important things in life, there'd be a shortage of fishing poles."

—Doug Larson

"My biggest worry is that when I'm dead and gone, my wife will sell my fishing gear for what I said I paid for it."

—Koos Brandt

First known essay on sport fishing: Dame Juliana Berners's *A Treatyse of Fysshynge* (1406).

THE EVEREST OF THE SEAS

*Hurricane winds, mountainous waves, bouts of madness…
it's just an average day in the world's toughest yacht race.*

SERIOUS SOLITUDE

Most adventurous sailors dream of sailing around the world. Many have made the voyage—which takes several months and covers at least 24,000 miles—but until 1968, when men were only a year away from walking on the Moon, no one had ever sailed around the globe *alone*, without any stopovers. Most experts didn't even think one person could do it, given the physical demands and isolation.

That year, the publishers of Britain's *Sunday Times* decided to put sailors to the test—they announced the Golden Globe Race, a solo, nonstop, around-the-world sailing contest. Nine sailors began the race; about 10 months later, only one man completed it, British skipper Robin Knox-Johnston. The race proved that one sailor could conquer the globe, but it also highlighted the perils involved: Most of the other boats had been stopped at various points due to bad weather, capsizing, or mechanical failures. One sailor had to be rescued from his sinking vessel, and another had a mental breakdown and apparently committed suicide by jumping overboard. Clearly, it was not a race for the faint of heart. Eighteen years passed before anyone tried it again.

THE KING

By 1986 a Frenchman named Philippe Jeantot, nicknamed "King of the Seven Seas" by *Sports Illustrated*, had already sailed to two victories in the BOC Challenge, a solo round-the-world race with three stopovers. But he had his sights set on besting Knox-Johnston's accomplishment. So on November 26, 1989, Jeantot and 12 other solo yachtsmen set out from the Vendée region on the west coast of France for the first running of the Vendée Globe.

The sailors fared much better this time around. Titouan Lamazou of France came in first with a time of 109 days (a little less

---

Under Mao Tse-Tung's regime (1943–75), grenade-throwing was an official sport in China.

than four months), and six other yachts also made it to the finish line. Even still, the race proved treacherous. Six boats didn't make it; a few capsized or had their masts broken off in violent seas, and several skippers had to be rescued. Jeantot himself was plagued with mechanical breakdowns and came in fourth.

But that race caught the imagination of sailors from all over the world. Since then, the Vendée Globe has been held every four years, with more and more competitors signing up.

TECHNOLOGY VS. THE SEA

Racing yachts have come a long way in the 40 years since Robin Knox-Johnston's teak boat took him around the world in 10 months. Today's contestants sail long, narrow yachts made of carbon fiber, a lightweight material that easily propels through water. Automatic pilots steer the craft when the skipper can't, and yachts are equipped with radar to help them "see" in darkness, fog, and rain. Some sailors employ GPS systems and electronic chart plotters, and satellite communications keep the boat in touch with the mainland, making it easier for rescuers to find them if they get in trouble. Computers and high-speed connections keep sailors in touch with the latest weather forecasts...and with their fans, who can monitor videos and blogs during the race, giving them an inside peek at the ultimate sailing experience.

With sails as high as an 8-story building, the boats can cover 450 miles in 24 hours. Michel Desjoyeaux won the 2008–09 race in less than three months. But all that technology comes with a big price tag: The cost for one boat to complete the race can run as high as $15 million, which far exceeds the winning prize money of 150,000 euros (about $200,000). The pricey innovations have made the Vendée Globe safer, but it is by no means safe.

TREACHEROUS WATERS

The route covered in the first competition remains much the same today. Contestants sail south from France and make a left turn past the Cape of Good Hope at the southern tip of Africa. From there they sail east toward Cape Leeuwin off the south coast of Australia and on through the Southern Ocean to Cape Horn, South America. At that point, the boats turn north to sail up the Atlantic and back to France.

Along the way, the yachts must stay north of certain points of latitude to keep them from straying too close to Antarctica, where icebergs lurk. This also makes it easier to rescue them should they get hit with the hurricane-force winds and 75-foot waves that plague the Southern Ocean—the part of the voyage where most accidents and injuries occur.

That's where the infamous 1996 Vendée Globe ended for four unfortunate sailors. Three had to be rescued after their boats capsized. Canadian Gerry Roufs wasn't so lucky—the rescuers never found him, and his boat washed ashore six months later on the coast of Chile. Roufs is one of three Vendée Globe skippers who met their end in the history of the race. But there are more hazards than death.

THAT WAY MADNESS LIES

All alone, for months on end, the sailors must endure freezing conditions, constant motion, and the deafening noise of waves hitting the hull. And as technologically advanced as these yachts are, they're basically stripped-down, unheated sailboats built for speed rather than comfort. Not afforded the luxury of sleeping for a full night, the contestants must take 20-minute naps several times a day for three or four days, then have to "catch up" on their recuperative sleep, sleeping about an hour and a half, three times a day. Over the course of the voyage, a skipper will sleep about 5 hours out of every 24. After a time, most contestants have admitted they start to "see" things.

So how do the sailors cope with the elements and isolation? Each has his or her own way. For Dee Caffari of England, the first woman to sail around the world alone in both directions, she has music: "I've got about 2,000 tunes on my iPod. It helps, particularly as I sing along, as does talking. I find myself regularly talking to myself, sea mammals, wildlife, and anyone or anything that will listen, really." When Caffari crossed the Vendée Globe finish line in March 2009 (in sixth place), she, like her competitors, was completely worn out from the voyage. But also, like her competitors, Caffari takes great pride in the fact that she belongs to a very exclusive group of athletes. "It's a crazy world," she says, "and I guess it takes a certain type of crazy someone to do this."

One of pitcher Nolan Ryan's jockstraps sold at auction for $25,000.

TRIATHLON Q&A

*Lots of people like to swim, bike, and run. But some people like
to do all three on the same day…while bumping elbows with
hundreds of other athletes. Think you're up for it?
Here are a few facts to get you started.*

WHAT'S A TRIATHLON?

It's an event in which competitors swim, ride a bicycle, and run, one sport right after the other, usually for long distances. The two most popular types are the full-length (or "Ironman") version, which consists of a 2.4-mile swim followed by a 112-mile bike ride and a 26.2-mile marathon run; and the Olympic length, featuring a swim of .9 miles (1,500 meters), a bike ride of 25 miles (40 kilometers), and a run of 6.2 miles (10 kilometers). There are also half-tri's; kids' tri's; and informal, local versions that vary in length.

WHO THOUGHT THIS UP—AND WHY?

• Three-part races are nothing new. In the 1920s, a French race known as *Les Trois Sports* (The Three Sports) had competitors running 3 kilometers, cycling for 12, and then swimming across the Marne River. But the event that's marked as the first modern triathlon took place in San Diego on September 25, 1974, when a few dozen members of the San Diego Track Club inaugurated what became known as the Mission Bay Triathlon. It continues to this day; in 2009 about 1,650 athletes participated.

• The full-length triathlon got its start in 1978, the brainchild of several athletes in Hawaii who'd had a longstanding debate over whether runners or swimmers were more fit. Before the race, one of the competitors joked that whoever won it would be known as the "Ironman"—which became the nickname for its standardized (very long) length. In that first race, 15 men entered. Now more than 80,000 men and women compete each year in local Ironman triathlons to qualify for the World Championship race, still held annually in Hawaii.

• The Olympic-length triathlon began with the formation of the

Most track athletes perform best later in the day, when their body temperature is highest.

International Triathlon Union in 1989, which patterned the distances for each part after existing Olympic races—making it, in effect, three Olympic events in one. Eleven years later, this version of the triathlon became a bona fide Olympic event at the 2000 Games in Sydney.

HOW LONG DOES IT TAKE TO DO AN "IRONMAN"?

While there's no set answer—each athlete is different—Ironman competitions enforce "cutoff times"—times after which athletes are disqualified and not allowed to continue. Competitors must complete the swimming segment within 2 hours and 20 minutes, the biking leg within 8 hours and 10 minutes, and the marathon within 6 hours and 30 minutes, for a total maximum of 17 hours. Top competitors, of course, finish much sooner: The winner of the 2008 Ironman World Championship, Craig Alexander, finished the course in 8 hours, 17 minutes, and 45 seconds.

IS IT ALWAYS SWIM–BIKE–RUN?

To keep things interesting, there are several variations on the formula.

• **Quadrathlon:** The World Quadrathlon Federation takes the full-length triathlon and adds another event to it: kayaking—a grueling 12.4 miles of it—wedged between the swimming and biking portions of a traditional triathlon.

• **Duathlon:** The International Triathlon Union also sanctions duathlons, which substitute another running segment for the swimming portion, so the athlete runs, then bikes, and then runs again. Distances and terrain vary depending on race and venue, and include both on-road and off-road versions, the latter featuring trail running and mountain biking.

• **Extreme Triathlon:** If an Ironman triathlon seems too tame, there's always the Ultraman competition, a three-day, 320-mile competition held in Hawaii. Day one features a 6.2-mile swim followed by a 90-mile mostly *uphill* bike ride. On day two, there's another biking excursion—this time, 174 miles. Day three features a double marathon—a run of 52.4 miles. If you fail to finish each day's events in less than 12 hours, you're disqualified. Good luck!

¡VIVA LA LUCHA LIBRE!

If you thought Jack Black was making up all that wrestler stuff in his movie Nacho Libre, *think again. Here's the story of one of the most popular—and bizarre—spectator sports in the world.*

SPECTACLE OF EXCESS

Like most countries in the world, Mexico is crazy for soccer. But what's the *second* most popular spectator sport in Mexico? It's wrestling—but not the dead-serious grappling you see in the Olympics. This cultural phenomenon is called *lucha libre,* or "free fighting"—a carnival of acrobatic mayhem performed by masked daredevils in tights. Any night of the week, you can find a lucha libre event somewhere in Mexico—the tradition's been going on for more than 75 years. And like professional wrestling in the U.S., it's all about entertainment.

What is lucha libre? At its root, it's no different from other wrestling matches, with rules, referees, winners, and losers. But this "simulated sport" has always been more of a theatrical production than an athletic competition. A lucha libre match transcends mere wrestling to become a spectacle, an epic duel between the symbolic forces of good and evil, lightened with healthy doses of slapstick humor and breathtaking gymnastics. Every bout features a Good Guy vs. a Bad Guy, and every bout has a scripted outcome. Like a good action movie, you usually know who's going to come out on top. And the crowd is encouraged to get into the act—to root for the hero and jeer the villain at every stage of the game. "You really need to witness lucha libre to understand," says journalist Stacy Brandt. "It mixes *The Three Stooges* with Greek mythology, comic books, politics, and plenty of testosterone."

RULES? WHAT RULES?

Like any sport, Mexican wrestling has rules, and athletes can be disqualified for a host of illegal actions. But because in lucha libre no one really "fights" anyone, the bouts are elaborate fantasies, where the Bad Guys (called *rudos,* or "rude ones") always play dirty. They cheat, call their opponents names, and break all the rules—which is why Good Guys (called *técnicos* because they use

---

more skilled, technical moves) are often pushed to the brink of defeat, only to make a gritty, last-minute comeback. The rivalry between a *rudo* and a *técnico* is often played out over a season or more of matches, as promoters spin endless variations on the comic-book storylines. Sometimes allies are introduced to help both wrestlers, expanding the traditional one-on-one duels to tag-team bouts featuring two to eight wrestlers on each team. Good Guys may lose a battle now and then, but they usually win the war.

What really sets Mexican wrestling apart from its northern counterpart is the speed and agility of the wrestlers and their high-flying moves, complete with flips and dives. While most U.S. wrestlers are heavyweights who show off their brute physical strength, the Mexican style favors lighter, quicker fighters who use the ropes to hurl themselves through the air and subdue their opponents with lightning-fast combinations of moves and holds. One popular move involves a dwarf *luchador* (lucha libre prides itself on its political incorrectness—dwarfs and transvestites are popular *rudo* characters). The dwarf is tossed high in the air by his two opponents, then executes a tricky spin as he comes down, grabs each opponent by the wrist, and flips them head over heels onto their backs.

CATCHÁSCAN

The sport didn't begin as the spectacle it is today. Its origins date back to the 19th century, when wrestling matches run by traveling carnivals became popular on both sides of the Atlantic. The style was known as "rough and tumble," and it was literally no-holds-barred—it was legal to bite, scratch, pull hair, eye-gouge, and groin-punch, so long as you won. By the 1840s, a new style of grappling imported from Lancashire, England, known as "catch-as-catch-can" had added a bit of regulation to the sport without sacrificing its freewheeling nature. Some well-known "catch-as-catch-can" enthusiasts included Abe Lincoln and Teddy Roosevelt, and it became the basis for modern professional wrestling. The old name continues to live on in South America as *catch* (Argentina) and *catcháscan* (Peru).

By 1929 the folk tradition of wrestling was well established in Mexico, but matches were still fairly conventional athletic compe-

---

Mt. Everest is 27" taller now than it was when Sir Edmund Hillary climbed it in 1953.

titions. Then a promoter named S. L. Gonzalez caught a wrestling show in Liberty Hall, Texas, and thought the larger-than-life theatrics might go over well south of the border. Gonzalez took a stake he'd won from a bingo game and turned it into the Empresa Mexicana de Lucha Libre—now the oldest professional wrestling production company in the world. From the start, showmanship was the dominant element in Gonzalez's wrestling matches. His first season, featuring a lineup of imported wrestlers with names like Cyclone Mackey and Yaqui Joe, was an immediate success. But it took the arrival of a homegrown fighter to turn lucha libre into the sensation it is today in Mexico.

EL SANTO

It's said that there are two iconic images known by every Mexican: the face of the Virgin of Guadalupe, and the mask of El Santo, the most revered Mexican *luchador* of all time. Born in 1917, Rodolfo Guzmán Huerta got into wrestling as a teenager in the '30s. He struggled along for five years, trying out different personas, until 1942. That's when he stepped into an eight-man free-for-all match in Mexico City wearing a silver mask and a new identity: El Santo ("The Saint"). Fans adored the silver-masked hero, and he quickly rose through the ranks to become the most popular personality in Mexico...and in much of Latin America. It didn't hurt that El Santo was a superb wrestler who constantly improved his craft by introducing stunning new moves into the ring. Some of them are still used today:

• *Topé de Cristo*—a flying somersault ending in a head butt
• *La de a Caballo*—also called a "camel clutch," where the wrestler sits on his opponent's back and applies a chin-lock
• *Plancha*—using the top ring rope as a slingshot to hurl oneself outside the ring onto an opponent (*luchadors* can fight inside *and* outside of the ring). U.S. wrestlers call this a "slingshot crossbody."
• *Running Topé Suicida*—taking a running jump through or over the ropes onto an opponent outside the ring

In 1958 El Santo's fame took another leap forward when he made the first of what would be more than 50 movies. In time he became an action star and folk hero to generations of Mexicans, as his masked character stood up for the little guy against injustice in bout after bout and film after film. His career spanned an amazing five decades, and by his death in 1984, he was considered the most famous Latino entertainer of the 20th century.

MASKED MEN

Not all Mexican wrestlers wear masks—many popular ones fight without them. But masks are so commonplace that they've become a trademark of lucha libre. The practice stems from the ancient Mexican tradition of wearing symbolic masks in festivals, which dates back to before the time of the Aztecs. For Mexicans, when a wrestler puts on his mask, he's no longer a mere human; he becomes the embodiment of an archetypal hero—or villain.

A *luchador* guards his masked identity as zealously as Spider-man or Zorro does. It's his professional persona, one he labors to maintain and develop over his career, and even that drama is played to the hilt in special bouts called "mask vs. mask" wagers, where the loser suffers the ultimate humiliation—to be unmasked by his opponent. Mask vs. mask bouts are far more important than title bouts and are fairly uncommon (most bouts are simple win-or-lose affairs, and everyone comes back to fight another day). The unmasking of the loser by the victor happens after the match, with all the ceremony of an execution. And being unmasked has its consequences: The loser can never wear that mask again; it's the ritual death of that character. But don't worry—wrestlers often return as new characters. Only a select few maintain the same mask for their entire career.

As the ultimate *luchador*, El Santo guarded his masked identity scrupulously. He never showed his own face in public until after he retired—and then it was just for a brief moment. While being interviewed on a TV talk show in 1984, El Santo stunned the audience by abruptly pulling back his mask to partially reveal his face. It caused a national sensation, but he died less than a week later at the age of 66. He was buried, at his own request, in his trademark silver mask.

*　　*　　*

A SIZE TOO SMALL

While bending over to make calls at the 2006 Wimbledon tennis tournament, line judges split 60 pairs of pants.

Most stadium "waves" move at a rate of 20 seats per second.

PIG OUT

According to statistics, Super Bowl Sunday is more than just a sporting event—it trails only Thanksgiving as America's biggest food feast. So what's wrong with a little overindulgence? Read on.

PUTTING ON THE FEED BAG

Every year on a Sunday in February, about a third of the population of the United States gathers in groups around their TV sets to watch the Super Bowl—97 million people did it in 2008. As they watch, they eat. And eat. According to the Snack Food Association of America, during the Super Bowl Americans will snarf down roughly 30 million pounds of snack food—double the nation's average daily consumption—including 11.2 million pounds of potato chips, 8.2 million pounds of tortilla chips, 4.3 million pounds of pretzels, 3.8 million pounds of popcorn, 2.5 million pounds of nuts, and 13.2 million pounds of avocados (for guacamole). Here are some more fascinating Super Bowl food facts:

• Americans spend $50 million on Super Bowl snacks, but that pales next to the $237 million spent on soft drinks.

• What's the most popular item sold in food stores on Super Bowl Sunday—beer? Wrong. It's pizza. In fact, Pizza Hut claims that it sells more pizzas on Super Bowl Sunday than on any other day of the year.

• During the Super Bowl, an average fan might easily pig out on more than 3,000 calories of snack food and beer. (And that's not taking into account calories consumed with pregame snacks and a postgame dinner and dessert.) A plate of nachos contains around 1,400 calories. A dozen chicken wings with blue-cheese dip adds another 1,000. A 180-pound man would have to jog 18 miles in three hours to burn off all those calories.

• Want to hedge your bet on who will win next year's Super Bowl? Each year before the game, the California Avocado Commission whips up guacamole recipes reflecting the competing teams (for instance, the entry for the Seattle Seahawks had shrimp as an ingredient) and holds a "taste-off" to see which is best. The winner of the "C.A.C. AvoBowl" has often won the Super Bowl.

The maneuver used to right a capsized kayak is called an *Eskimo roll.*

BATHROOM TIME KILLERS

This article was originally slated to go in Uncle John's
Top Secret Bathroom Reader for Kids Only, *but
then we thought, why should kids have all the fun?*

TOILET TENPIN

What You Need: Ten golf tees, or other objects that can
serve as bowling pins, and a few rubber bands to serve as
bowling balls. Set the golf tees up in a triangle like bowling pins
as far from the toilet as you can while still having them within
reach—that way you can set them up over and over again and
bowl as long as you want.

How to Play: Have you ever shot a rubber band like a gun?
Make your hand into a pistol—curl your pinkie around the rubber band, then stretch the rubber band around the back of your
thumb and over the tip of your index finger. Hold the pistol
square in the center of your chest, lean back as far as you can,
and when you're ready to shoot, release your pinkie. Aim for the
pins—try to knock them all down.

TRASH CAN FRISBEE

What You Need: A wastepaper basket and some paper plates. If
the wastepaper basket isn't big enough to hold the paper plates,
use a cardboard box or a paper shopping bag. Place the basket on
the bathroom floor as far from the toilet as you can.

How to Play: Fling the paper plates like Frisbees—see if you can
throw them into the wastepaper basket. For a bigger challenge,
try to ricochet them off a wall into the basket.

BATHROOM DARTS

What You Need: A pie tin, a saucer, a small glass, and small
objects you can throw. (Coins or caps from discarded toothpaste
tubes work well.)

How to Play: Put the glass in the center of the saucer, and put
the saucer in the center of the pie tin. Set them all down on

---

the bathroom floor a few feet from the toilet. That's your "dartboard."

Toss the coins ("darts") at your target—if they land in the glass, you get 10 points; if they land in the saucer, you get 5; if they land in the pie tin, you get 1. If you score too well, move the target farther away to make it more challenging.

BATHROOM BLOW GUN

What You Need: A soda straw, some wooden matches, and a hat.

How to Play: Turn the hat upside down and place it on the bathroom floor a good distance away from the toilet. Put a match in the straw, hold the straw up to your mouth, and blow. Try to shoot all the matches into the hat.

FUN WITH A FUNNEL

What You Need: A rubber ball and a funnel. The funnel needs to be big enough to hold the ball.

How to Play: Hold the pointy end of the funnel. Bounce the ball off the wall opposite the toilet and try to catch it in the funnel on the rebound.

BATHROOM BOUNCY BALL

What You Need: An egg carton and some Ping-Pong balls.

How to Play: Write different point values in each of the 12 cups of the egg carton, then place it on the bathroom floor a few feet from the toilet.

Try to bounce the Ping-Pong balls into the egg carton. Start with one bounce, then, as your skills improve, move the carton farther away and bounce the balls twice before they go into the cups. Add up the values for your scores.

BATHROOM BROKEN NECK PREVENTER

What You Need: All the stuff you just spread out all over the bathroom floor to play all these games we just taught you.

How to Play: Pick all that stuff up off the bathroom floor—before somebody gets killed!

The coaching staff for a synchronized swimming team includes a makeup artist.

THE PHYSICS OF GOLF

Get out your calculator—we're going golfing!

S WINGIN'
Golf is a game of calculations and angles. The best golfers in the world have learned not just to pick the right club for the right shot, but how to take into account such factors as wind, temperature, air density, and the unique lie of any given fairway or green. Some have even studied the effects of plaid pants and striped shirts on their bunker play. (Their findings: it only affects *other* people's bunker play.) The mind of a pro golfer acts like a computer, running complicated programs to determine the optimum trajectory for each shot.

Here's what happens when you actually swing a golf club. High school science teaches that force equals mass times acceleration. In golf, this means that the force applied to the ball is equal to the mass of the clubhead multiplied by the speed it is traveling when it hits the ball. In other words, the faster the swing, the longer the drive.

But a really fast swing must also be efficient. The ideal swing is one that moves the clubhead in a perfect circular arc. Energy spent trying to get the club into the proper position to hit the ball is wasted and will slow the clubhead down, decreasing the distance of the shot.

And the shaft of the club affects energy, too. If you've ever seen a slow-motion shot of a golfer's swing, then you've seen how much the shaft bends. That's stored energy. If your timing is right, that stored energy is released in a whip motion as it hits the ball. That's why there are flex ratings on shafts. A golfer with a very fast swing wants a stiff shaft—it stores the energy of the swing better than a very flexible one would. Beginners will have more success with clubs with flexible shafts.

MAKING CONTACT

Now you've got your speeding clubhead—but that's only part of the program. That speeding head has to hit the ball correctly if the ball is going to go where you want it to go. This brings out the

---

"I don't like to watch golf on television. I can't stand whispering." —David Brenner

essential difference between striking the ball with a wood (especially the driver) and an iron.

Think of the golf swing as drawing a U-shape with the clubhead. When you swing a driver correctly, the bottom of the U comes *before* the ball. That means the clubhead makes contact with the ball just after it's reached its lowest point and is on the rise. When you swing an iron correctly, the bottom of the U comes *after* the ball, meaning the clubhead makes contact with the ball before it hits its lowest point and is still descending. That's why when you see a good golfer swing an iron, you see him take a divot—this is the ground in front of the ball. With a driver, there is no divot taken because the ball is generally sitting on a tee. These two different types of contact affect the most important part of what happens next: the spin of the ball.

AERODYNAMICS

The spin of a flying golf ball affects how straight and far it will go. This was first discovered in 1887 by British scientist P. G. Tait. He was taught in his youth that "all spin is detrimental," so he worked very hard at developing a golf swing that would produce very little spin on the ball. Then he started experimenting with golf balls, attaching string to them and having different people hit them. He discovered that a ball spinning quickly on a horizontal axis—with the top of the ball spinning toward the golfer—actually stays in the air longer than a ball with little or no spin. (As for his golf game, he said: "I understand it now, too late by 35 years at least.")

Here's how it works. A spinning golf ball creates the aerodynamic force called *lift*—the same as an airplane. This is because of a law of physics known as the Bernoulli Principle (named after Daniel Bernoulli, who discovered it in 1738), which says that when the speed of a fluid, liquid, or gas increases, its pressure decreases. Simply put: a golf ball with backspin is inducing the air it meets to pass more quickly over its top than its bottom—meaning there will be less air pressure above it and more below it. Result: lift.

Spin also affects the ball when it lands. Getting back to the difference between the driver and the iron: an iron's glancing contact produces more spin than a driver's square contact. In driving, you don't want the backspin—you want the ball to roll when it hits the ground. With irons, especially highly lofted ones, you want a lot of spin to create lift and to keep the ball from rolling when it lands.

HOOKS AND SLICES

Now that we know backspin is good, here's the bad news: if the axis of the spin isn't perfectly (or close to) horizontal, then the spin will not only not help the shot—it can make it worse. That off-horizontal spin is caused by not making square contact with the ball. For right-handers, if your swing comes from too close to your body and across the ball from left to right as it hits it— known as an inside-to-out swing—it will give the ball a counter-clockwise spin. By the Bernoulli Principle, this will create lift on the right side of the ball (lift doesn't necessarily have to be "up"), causing it to curve to the left. That's what causes a hook. If your swing comes from too far from your body, back across the ball from right to left—an outside-to-in swing—it'll make the ball spin clockwise and the lift will curve it to the right. That's a slice.

DIMPLES

In the early days of golf, players realized that scarred balls flew better than smooth ones, and that led to golf balls with dimples. But Here's how the dimples help: By their effect on airflow around the ball, dimpled balls create less drag than smooth balls.

A rough, dimpled surface creates a more turbulent airflow around a ball than a smooth one—that's easily understood, even by nonphysicists. That flow is called a *turbulent boundary layer*. A smooth ball creates a more streamlined flow, called a *laminar boundary layer*. You'd think the smooth flow would create less drag, and it does when it's on the ball, but the flow is also prone to "separation," meaning that it breaks from the surface of the ball quickly. This creates a large and turbulent wake—and *that* creates a lot of drag.

The turbulent flow causes more drag on the ball initially, but it also tends to "hug" the ball as it flies, not separating from the surface until much later than a smooth ball. That creates a much narrower wake and much less drag, so your turbulently flying dimpled golf ball flies a lot farther—as much as twice the distance of a smooth ball.

GOT A WEATHER IRON?

Weather has some obvious effects on the golf ball, too. Raindrops act as resistance on the ball and sap its momentum; hitting a ball into a headwind is more difficult than hitting with a tailwind. But what about less obvious factors like air density or the elevation of a particular golf course?

Dense air offers more resistance to the traveling ball than thinner air would. It slows the ball down, decreasing distance. Air density is determined by pressure and temperature. Higher elevations have less air pressure, which means less air density. Result: golf balls travel farther in the mountains than they do at sea level.

Similarly, warm air is less dense than cold air. With the pressure the same, the ball will go farther on a hot day than on a cold one. Contrary to popular belief, humidity has little effect on driving distances. Humid air is slightly less dense than dry air, but not enough to make much difference.

So now, with the right club for the shot—adjusted according to weather conditions and air density—and with the ideal swing at the proper speed to generate enough force and applying the correct amount of backspin so as to gain lift appropriate to how the wind happens to be blowing at any given moment...all you'll need to work on is your chip shots and putting game.

*　　*　　*

GREAT GOLF GIFTS

• **Poor Putter's Pacifier.** "For the crybaby golfer," a golf ball with a pacifier attached.

• **THE EXPLODER!** This ball explodes into a cloud of talc when struck.

• **Wacky Flat Top Tees.** "Carry these tees for a mooching friend. The angled, flat top makes is impossible to tee up a ball."

• *Everything I Know About Golf*, by <u>Your Friend's Name Here</u>. Give him this hardcover, leatherbound book, with gold-pressed lettering on the cover...and 228 blank pages inside.

• **Camouflaged Golf Ball.** "The ULTIMATE Hard-to-Find Gift!"

A regulation tennis ball must weigh between 2 and 2 1/16 ounces.

SPARE FACTS

Most people know a few things about bowling: strikes, gutter balls, and your bowling shoe size. But here are some great tidbits of bowling trivia to impress your friends next time you're at the lanes.

BOWL LIKE AN EGYPTIAN

In the 1930s, in a child's tomb located just north of Luxor, Egypt, archaeologist Sir Flinders Petrie discovered equipment for a game in which a tiny stone ball was rolled at nine equally small pins. The tomb dated back to 3200 B.C., but Petrie noted the similarity of this ancient Egyptian game to a modern variation of bowling called Norfolk skittles. The twist on both games: The ball first had to be rolled through a gate, similar to the wicket a ball rolls through in croquet. The tiny Egyptian bowling game Petrie found is now on display at the Ashmolean Museum in Oxford, England.

A RELIGIOUS EXPERIENCE

Bowling appeared again in what's now Germany in the third or fourth century A.D. In those days, Germans often carried clubs called *kegels*, a combination of a tool and a weapon. In the region's early Christian churches, a popular game was to stand the kegel at the end of a runway and roll a stone at it. The belief was that if the stone knocked over the kegel, it represented overcoming one's own sins. So early bowlers had a special motivation to aim well.

By the 16th century, bowling was so well established in Germany that Martin Luther, the founder of the Protestant Reformation, built a bowling lane for his kids. Luther was also known to bowl a frame or two himself occasionally, although by then the game had lost its religious overtones.

England's King Henry VIII also enjoyed the game. The International Bowling Museum and Hall of Fame in St. Louis, Missouri, has a diorama of Henry bowling. In his youth, Henry was also an avid tennis player and early proponent of that game (see page 290).

BANNED

Bowling has survived for 5,000 years because it's fun. But at times, it's been too much fun for its own good, leading various governments to ban it. In 1366 English King Edward III outlawed bowling, along with an early form of golf, because he believed they were getting in the way of his soldiers' archery practice, which they needed badly to defeat their enemies, the French.

The state of Connecticut also attempted to ban bowling in 1841. But this time it wasn't interfering with the defense of the nation; it was corrupting the local citizens with gambling. Betting had sprung up wherever bowling flourished (before Connecticut, gambling on bowling had been a problem in England, France, and Germany). To curb the trend, Connecticut expressly prohibited the play of "ninepin," which was the favored form of bowling at the time.

The ban against ninepin, some suggest, was the origin of the tenpin version of the game that's popular today. But that's probably not true; there's evidence that the tenpin version of the game existed in the United States as early as 1810, and the Connecticut law outlawed "Nine-Pins, whether more or less than nine pins are used." But again, the ban didn't last long and bowling soon regained its popularity.

THE 300 CLUB

The first person to officially score a 300—the perfect score in tenpin bowling—was Ernest Fosberg of Rockford, Illinois, in 1902, by rolling a strike on every single turn. Fosberg rolled it in league play sanctioned by the American Bowling Congress, which seven years earlier had codified the rules for tenpin bowling, including setting the top score for ten frames at 300. Although any number of people might have rolled a 300 before then, they weren't recorded for posterity. It would be 28 years before a woman bowled a 300: Jenny Hoverson Kelleher of Madison, Wisconsin.

Here are a few milestones in the history of 300 games:

• Youngest player to bowl a 300: Chaz Dennis of Columbus, Ohio, in 2006, at 10 years, 2 months.

• Oldest player to bowl a 300: Berry Thomas of Nashville, Tennessee, in 2001, at 87 years, 11 months.

• First person to bowl three consecutive 300 games: Jeremy Sonnenfeld of Lincoln, Nebraska, in 1997. (There had been earlier 900s reported, but this one gets the official title.)

"HE SLUD INTO THIRD"

More quips from on-air sportscasters.

"I'm going to make a prediction: it could go either way."
—Ron Atkinson

"From the waist down, Earl Campbell has the biggest legs I've ever seen."
—John Madden

"The batsman's Holding, the bowler's Willey."
—Brian Johnston, reporting a cricket match between Michael Holding and Peter Willey

"It's a hot night at the Garden, folks, and at ringside I see several ladies in gownless evening straps."
—Jimmy Powers

"There've been times when they've had hits from time to time, but they weren't timely hits at the right time."
—Gary Carter

"Azinger is wearing an all-black outfit: black jumper, blue trousers, white shoes, and a pink 'tea-cozy' hat."
—Renton Laidlaw, golf commentator

"If there's a pileup there, they'll have to give some of the players artificial insemination."
—Curt Gowdy

"Juantorena opens wide his legs and shows his class."
—Ron Pickering, commenting on a runner at the 1976 Olympics

"That's a very sad-looking Wattana, but you'd never know it to look at his face."
—Ted Love

"You couldn't really find two more completely different personalities than these two men, Tom Watson and Brian Barnes; one is the complete professional golfer, and the other, the complete professional golfer."
—Peter Alliss

"That's the fastest time ever run—but it's not as fast as the world record."
—David Coleman

"With eight minutes left, the game could be won in the next five or ten minutes."
—Jimmy Armfield

In Olympic archery, the distance to the target is 70 meters. In rifle shooting, it's 50 meters.

THE CAN-DO KID

Don't focus on what this kid doesn't have—because he sure doesn't.

BIG HEART
Kyle Maynard was born different: His arms are both stumps, ending before his elbows. He has no knees, and his deformed feet are useless. Still, Kyle is a star athlete, excelling in swimming and wrestling, without prosthetic limbs. And he's not competing in the Paralympics—this is high school and college sports.

But that's not all. Kyle also excels academically, having graduated high school with a 3.7 GPA. In fact, Kyle can do most things that abled people can do: eat with utensils, use a cell phone, ride a bike. He can even type 50 words a minute. Obviously, none of these skills came easily. How did he do it? He has great parents.

Scott and Anita Maynard knew they were in for a tough time when Kyle was born in 1986 with a rare disorder called *congenital amputation*. They spoon-fed him like any child until he reached the age where kids with hands have to learn to feed themselves. At that point his father said, "If he doesn't figure out how to eat on his own, he's going to starve." So they watched Kyle closely and encouraged him while he learned to pick up objects with his arms and get around on his own. From the start, the toddler was determined to do things himself, and that determination has stayed with him ever since.

IF AT FIRST YOU DON'T SUCCEED...

Kyle joined the wrestling team in high school—and lost the first 35 matches he entered. His ego was bruised, but not enough to make him want to quit. So Kyle's wrestling coach, Cliff Ramos, decided to try a different approach: With his arms inside his shirt-sleeves, Ramos wrestled some of the better members of the team to give him an idea of what Kyle was facing. After working together in the off-season, Kyle and Coach Ramos capitalized on Kyle's strengths: he's just three feet tall, so he has a low center of

---

Nyah! Nyah! An umpire can have you removed from a baseball stadium for heckling.

gravity and great balance; he has speed and agility; he's very strong (he can bench-press 250 pounds); and he has a hard head—which he started using as a battering ram.

The following year was much different for Kyle. He won 35 matches while losing only 16, and finished 12th in his weight division for the entire state of Georgia.

TEACHING OTHERS

Kyle attended the University of Georgia, where he wrestled and majored in public speaking. The busy 22-year-old also travels to high schools around the country to give inspirational speeches about having a positive attitude. Kyle's autobiography, *No Excuses*, has become a motivational tool for thousands. Its message is simple: Reasons why you *can't* do something only exist in your mind...and so does the courage to get past those reasons. One of the most poignant parts is where Kyle speaks of his low spirits after losing those 35 wrestling matches in a row—and how he convinced himself to get back out on the mat.

"I knew it didn't matter how much I was afraid, how much I was in pain, or how impossible the situation appeared to me. I knew the obstacles. This was no different from the rest of my life. We all have challenges to face and to overcome. No obstacle would keep me from accomplishing my dreams."

*   *   *

WORLD CUP MADNESS

"A Beijing soccer fan refused to let the small matter of his house burning down disturb his enjoyment of the 2006 World Cup match between France and Spain. A fire broke out in a *hutong* in the center of the Chinese capital at kick-off time and gutted the traditional courtyard dwelling, the *Beijing Daily Messenger* reported. 'When the neighbors shouted "fire!" I took my little baby and ran out in my nightclothes,' the man's wife said. 'My husband paid no attention to the danger, just grabbed the television and put it under his arm. After getting out of the house, he then set about finding an electric socket to plug in and continue watching his game.'"

—**Reuters**

As a 5'11" sophomore, Michael Jordan was cut from his high school varsity basketball team.

THE BIRTH OF BASEBALL, PART II

On page 79, we told you about the stick-and-ball games that most likely led to baseball. We pick up the story with the first organized teams.

THE CARTWRIGHT MYTH

In the years between 1837 and 1845, while playing games on whatever vacant fields they could find, William Wheaton and his fellow Gothams were busy changing and refining baseball's rules. Their first alteration: eliminating the practice of getting a runner out by throwing the ball directly at him. Instead, at each base they positioned a player whose job was to catch the ball and tag the runner out. In 1845, after Wheaton switched teams to the rival Knickerbockers (based in Lower Manhattan), he took those rules with him—and showed them to a Knickerbockers player named Alexander Cartwright.

Shortly after the Abner Doubleday origin was fully discredited, baseball historians turned their attention to Cartwright—the *new* "Father of Baseball." But they may have been a little too hasty: Recent findings now indicate that Cartwright's role was embellished by him, his son, and subsequent baseball writers. There were many men on the Knickerbockers (including Cartwright) who worked together to improve the game. What is generally agreed upon, however, is that the first prearranged "modern" baseball game took place on June 19, 1846, when Cartwright's Knickerbockers got trounced by the Gothams by a score of 23–1.

THE ADAMS REALITY

Much of what *had* been credited to Cartwright actually came from the Knickerbockers' first team president, Daniel Lucius "Doc" Adams. "It is ironic," says baseball historian Lindsey Williams, "that Cartwright, Spalding, and Doubleday are memorialized at Cooperstown while Adams is not—even though he devised all the modern rules of the game." Here's what Adams contributed.

• Arguing that baseball is a "gentlemen's game" (as opposed to a children's game), Adams moved the bases from 45 feet to 90 feet apart and extended the pitching distance from 37.5 feet to 45 feet.

• Adams also turned baseball into a "fly game" by decreeing that an out would occur when a ball is caught by a fielder *before* it hit the ground, thus negating the "one-bounce" rule.

• Because the baseballs that Adams constructed for the team weighed so little, they couldn't be thrown very far. So he placed an extra player midway between the outfielders and the diamond. His job was to "stop" the "short" throws from the outfielder and relay them to the pitching spot (the mound would come later). Result: the shortstop. As the baseball became heavier, the shortstop moved to its present position between second and third base.

• Another player on that team, an attorney named Louis F. Wadsworth, disagreed with Adams's opinion that a baseball game should be seven innings; he thought it should be nine. Apparently, Wadsworth disagreed a lot, because he was thrown off the team three times. Still, he was able to successfully lobby for nine innings, adding another cornerstone to the foundation of modern baseball.

FINE-TUNING

In all, 20 new "Knickerbocker Rules" were put in place, establishing the "New York Game" as the way baseball would be played (as opposed to the "Massachusetts Game," which still included many features of town ball). Here are three other now-familiar rules that made it onto the Knickerbockers' list.

• Balls hit outside of first or third base are foul.

• On the third strike, the "striker" (batter) may run to first if the catcher does not catch the ball on the fly or on one bounce.

• "All disputes and differences relative to the game are to be decided by the Umpire, from which there is no appeal."

But the modern game wasn't completely set. The Knickerbocker Rules still included some holdovers from town ball, cricket, and other games. For example, foul balls were not yet considered strikes, there were no called strikes, and the game continued until one team scored 21 "aces" (runs), even if the full allotment of innings hadn't been reached. Other changes yet to come: Walks weren't a part of the game until 1863, and the number of balls it took to earn a walk changed from five to seven to nine before being permanently set at four in 1889.

A WALK IN THE PARK

Just as the game was taking shape, so too was the field. As early as the mid-1840s, baseball was already so popular that people began looking for permanent places for their home teams. Because the sport took on its modern form in cities and not in rural areas, people gathered in city parks to play and watch the game—hence the term "park" for a baseball field. The first baseball park was Elysian Fields in Hoboken, New Jersey. Businessmen from New York City took the ferry across the Hudson River to play baseball and cricket there, and it's where the Knickerbockers and Gothams played the first organized game in 1846.

Elysian Fields was also where Henry Chadwick, a reporter who was supposed to be covering a cricket match for the *New York Times*, happened to see his first baseball game in 1856. "I chanced to go through the Elysian Fields during the progress of a contest between the noted Eagle and Gotham Clubs," he later wrote. "The game was being sharply played on both sides, and I watched it with deeper interest than any previous ball match between clubs that I had seen. It was not long before I was struck with the idea that base ball was just the game for a national sport for Americans." Chadwick spent the rest of his life championing the "national pastime," a term coined that same year by the *New York Mercury*.

GETTING ORGANIZED

The sudden popularity of the sport led to new problems: The Knickerbocker Rules were embraced by some ball clubs, but not all of them. Result: Opposing teams often found themselves arguing over how and where to play. Some regulation was needed. So in 1857, the Knickerbockers put out an open invitation to "all of the organized base ball clubs" around the region. To their surprise, 14 teams showed up to baseball's first set of meetings. And more teams were forming in cities such as Boston, Chicago, and even San Francisco, where a club was started by Alexander Cartwright. The consensus was that in order for baseball to thrive, it needed a governing body that presided over *every* club.

Those 15 teams formed baseball's first big league: the National Association of Base Ball Players. In 1858 the association decided to hold a tournament between the "best nines" from each region. This first "all-star game" (between the New York and Brooklyn regions) gave onlookers a look at the future of top-tier baseball: diving catches, pinpoint throws, and perfectly turned double plays. Already popular, baseball became *the* fad among the middle class in the United States. By 1860 the association boasted 60 teams.

That all-star series introduced something else to the game. Up until then, players played for free and crowds watched for free. This time, 4,000 fans showed up and paid 50 cents each to see the game. With that, the spirit of amateurism that had guided the association began to weaken. The business of professional baseball was born, and the game would never be the same again.

For Part III of "The Birth of Baseball," turn to page 358.

Woodcut that appeared in the magazine Porter's Spirit of the Times, 1856. "The Eagles and Gothams playing their great match at the Elysian Fields on Tuesday, September 8th."

The word "sport" comes from the old French *desport*, meaning "leisure."

LAUNCHING AIR JORDAN

If you had to name just one person associated with an athletic shoe, it would be Michael Jordan, right? Here, from the BRI's pop history department, is how Jordan became Air Jordan.

WALKING ON AIR
The air-filled shoe wasn't Nike's idea. The first air sole was patented in 1882, and more than 70 others were registered with the U.S. Patent Office before 1969. They all failed because of technical problems.

In 1969 a designer named Frank Rudy gave it a shot. He left a job at Rockwell International during a downturn in the aerospace industry, and invested his time and money in an effort to develop a running shoe with air soles. After many attempts, he finally succeeded by using a thin polyurethane bag for an air cushion. Then he convinced the Bata shoe company to try it out.

The first prototypes worked great. Unfortunately, it was the middle of the oil embargo of 1974, and Bata's supplier quietly changed its polyurethane formula to use less oil. The new formula wasn't as strong as the old one; when the soles warmed up and air pressure increased, they would explode like a rifle shot. Bata suddenly lost interest.

LAST ATTEMPT

Nearly broke and desperate, Rudy flew to France to show Adidas what he had. He didn't get anywhere with them, but while he was hanging around the Adidas offices, he heard an employee mention a little U.S. company named Nike that was selling running shoes on the West Coast. Rudy made some calls, found out there was a running shoe trade show that weekend in Anaheim, and caught the next flight to Southern California.

He stopped by the Nike booth in Anaheim just as it was closing and got the name of the company's president, Phil Knight. Rudy immediately found a pay phone and called Knight at Nike's

---

Captain Cook, the first Westerner to visit Hawaii, reported seeing native people surfing.

headquarters in Beaverton, Oregon. Knight listened to Rudy's story, then invited him for a visit.

NIKE JUMPS IN

Knight, an amateur runner, personally took Rudy's air-filled shoes for a run. They slowly deflated as he ran, but he saw their potential. "It was a great ride while it lasted," he told Rudy. Then he put Rudy on retainer for six months, to see if he could make the idea work.

After much trial and error, Rudy finally came up with something Nike liked—an inflated midsole that went between the regular sole of a shoe and the runner's foot. Nike called the new creation the *Tailwind* and rushed it into production at $50 retail—the highest price anyone had ever charged for a mass-produced running shoe. But runners bought them anyway. Unfortunately, a last-minute fabric switch resulted in a shoe that fell apart after a short time, infuriating customers. About half of the shoes were returned as defective.

Nike eventually got the bugs out. This time they decided not to release the shoe directly into the marketplace. They were going to wait and try something special.

LUCKY CHOICE

Meanwhile, Nike was reevaluating its marketing strategy. The company had been paying professional athletes anywhere from $8,000 to $100,000 apiece to wear and endorse their shoes. One day in 1983, Nike execs did an analysis and found they "owned" about half of the players in the NBA—at a cost of millions of dollars a year. In fact, they had 2,000 athletes on their endorsement roster. It was getting more expensive all the time and it wasn't necessarily winning them any more business.

So they decided to switch tactics and find one promising rookie...then sign him to a long-term contract before he got too expensive. They considered Charles Barkley and Patrick Ewing, but finally settled on 20-year-old college junior Michael Jordan. Their plan was to design a brand-new shoe for him, push it hard, and tie the product to the man (and vice versa), so when consumers saw the player, they'd think "shoes!"

Only designated hitter to be named World Series MVP: Toronto's Paul Molitor in 1993.

HIS AIRNESS

They had just the right product—the air-cushioned shoe. Nike offered Jordan $2.5 million for a five-year contract, plus royalties on every Air Jordan shoe sold. But Jordan turned them down. He didn't particularly like Nike shoes. In fact, he loved Adidas and was willing to make concessions to sign with them. He told their representatives, "You don't even have to match Nike's deal—just come close." But Adidas wasn't interested. They offered only $100,000 a year, with no special shoe and no royalties. So in August 1984, Jordan signed with Nike.

Nike came up with the distinctive black and red design for the Jordan shoe. In fact, it was so distinctive that the NBA commissioner threatened to fine him $1,000 if he wore Air Jordan shoes during games, because they violated the NBA "uniformity of uniform" clause. Jordan wore them anyway, creating an uproar in the stands and in the press...and Nike gladly paid the fine.

FLYING SOLO

It was the beginning of a brilliant advertising campaign. Air Jordans went on to become the most successful athletic endorsement in history, selling over $100 million worth of merchandise in the first year alone. The dark side: Air Jordans became so popular that it became dangerous to wear them in some cities, as teenagers began killing other teenagers for their $110 sneakers. And the company was embarrassed—or should have been—by the revelation that a worker in its Far East sweatshops would have to work for several weeks to make enough money to buy a pair.

Despite occasional bad publicity and considerable competition over the years, however, Air Jordans became so successful that Nike has sold 23 different versions of the shoe—and it's still on sale today.

*   *   *

SCARY PICTURES

Wrestler Hulk Hogan once allowed his image to be used in a line of cameras for kids. His face was painted on the lens, inserting Hulk into the corner of every photograph.

WIDE WORLD OF ODD SPORTS

Calling all jocks: Tired of baseball, football, etc? Don't fret—
you've got plenty of other options. Here are some
little-known sports that may tickle your fancy.

BOG SNORKELING
Where They Do It: Llanwrtyd Wells, Wales
How It's Played: The idea is to completely immerse your-self in a bog, breathing through a snorkel. One description: "Snorkelers plunge into a smelly ditch near the village of Llanwrtyd Wells and embark on a furious downstream dog paddle. Their aquatic odyssey presents many daunting challenges: the bog's sludgy consistency, the disgusting brown backwash that the swimmers generate, and the determined water scorpions that like to burrow into one's bathing suit."(*Outside* magazine)

If that's not weird enough, there's also bike bog snorkeling, held in Powys, Wales. As *Bizarre* magazine describes it: "The idiots who took part in the inaugural mountain-bike bog snorkeling championship soon realized the error of their ways as they cycled into the slimy abyss. Visibility was down to a few feet, and despite the fact that the bikes had been specially prepared by having every orifice stuffed with lead shot, they did their best to float away....Riders competed against the clock to cycle round a post—with a special prize for anyone who could cycle back out of the bog—this proved to be impossible."

CANINE FREESTYLE DANCING
Where They Do It: Everywhere. There are more than 8,000 enthusiasts around the world.
How It's Played: Dancing with your dog for prizes? Not a sport, exactly, but who can resist? The idea is to move in time with a dog partner, but you're not allowed to hold the dog's paws, the way you would in "at-home dog dancing." In fact, you're not supposed to touch the dog at all. According to the *New York Times*: "Costumed

---

Bossaball, invented in Belgium, is a volleyball-like game with trampolines on the playing field.

owners and their matching-collared pooches exhibit choreography to such tunes as 'The Yellow Rose of Texas' and 'Get Happy' and compete for prizes." "You will discover," says the national Canine Freestyle Federation, "that your dog likes music!...You'll see a new sparkle in his eye, feet stepping higher, and a tail wagging harder."

WADLOPING

Where They Do It: In the Waddenzee, a shallow inlet separating the northern Netherlands mainland from the East Frisian Islands

How It's Played: Entrants leap off a dike on Holland's north coast into the knee-deep sulfurous mud and trudge across the Wadden-zee to Simonzand Island, four hours away by foot (with your feet knee-deep in mud). "Some wadlopers suffer attacks of agoraphobia when they can see no land, just a 360-degree horizon of worm-pocked mud," the *Wall Street Journal* reports. "Veteran wadlopers hike to more distant islands. For the truly obsessed, there's the 'monster walk' to the German island of Borkum, 14 miles away. Borkum, the wadloper's Everest, has been reached by just three men, who waited three years for the lowest possible tide and even then had to walk four miles through neck-high water."

Rules of the Game: "A wrong turn or a change in the wind can put the wadloper in deep water, with no way back to land but to swim. About 15 years ago, a group of wadlopers went astray and had to be rescued by helicopter....The Dutch government has since banned freelance *wadlopen*, requiring wadlopers to travel with trained guides, who carry compasses, maps, two-way radios, and rescue equipment."

AND DON'T FORGET...

• **Finnish Wife-Carrying.** According to *Parade* magazine: "The goal: carry a woman, preferably someone else's wife, over a 780-foot course through water, on sand, grass, and asphalt, and over two fences. Dropping the woman results in a 15-second penalty. The fastest man earns the big prize: The woman's weight in lemonade."

• **Welsh Shin-Kicking.** Also known as "purring." "Two men face each other, each holding the shoulders of his opponent. They kick each other's shins until one man loses his grip on his opponent. To add to the pain, their shoes are reinforced." (Update: The sport has failed to catch on in other nations.)

First female tennis player to wear shorts at Wimbledon: Lili de Alverez, in 1931.

THE HISTORY OF FOOTBALL, PART V

Here's a trivia question: After football was invented in 1880, how much time passed before somebody figured out how to throw a spiral pass? Answer: 25 years. Hard to believe, but true. Here's the story. (For Part IV, turn to page 219.)

CLEANING UP THEIR ACT

When the Intercollegiate Athletic Association met in January 1906, it instituted a number of reforms that they hoped would change the way football was played:

• The reforms cut the length of the game from 70 minutes to 60, dividing the game into two 30-minute halves; and they made it illegal for one player to hurdle over another.

• They required a minimum of six men on the offensive line of scrimmage, which made it difficult to use mass formations like the flying wedge.

• They created a "neutral zone" on the line of scrimmage: Instead of the line of scrimmage being drawn through the *center* of the ball, players now lined up along *either side* of the ball, and were not allowed to step into the neutral zone in between until the ball went into play. This was intended to reduce the bare-knuckled brawling that routinely broke out when opposing players lined up toe-to-toe; sometimes it took as long as 20 minutes to pull fighting players apart and resume the game.

• They raised the number of yards needed for a first down from 5 to 10.

LOOKING FORWARD

But the most important change of all: In 1906 the association legalized the forward pass, largely on the suggestion of Georgia Tech coach John Heisman.

Heisman had witnessed his first forward pass a decade earlier while watching the North Carolina Tar Heels play against the Georgia Tech Yellow Jackets in 1895. The score was tied, 0–0, late in the game, and the Tar Heels were losing ground. On the next down, the Carolina fullback ran behind his scrimmage line hoping to find a place to punt. No luck—there was no room to punt, so he just hurled the ball downfield in desperation; one of his teammates happened to catch it and ran 70 yards for a touchdown, winning the game.

The move was illegal, and the Yellow Jackets' coach demanded that the touchdown be tossed out. But the referee let football's first touchdown pass stand—because he hadn't actually seen it.

I'LL PASS

As concerns over increasing football violence mounted in the decade that followed, Heisman came to see the forward pass as a means of cleaning up the game. He figured that if players could throw the ball over and past mass formations, defending players would have no choice but to spread themselves out across the football field, and mass plays would become obsolete. But he didn't get his way until 1906, when Yale's Walter Camp was finally shoved aside.

At first the forward pass was restricted: If a quarterback wanted to throw a pass, he had to move at least five yards to the left or right of center before throwing. To make officiating easier, football fields were marked with lengthwise stripes five yards apart, changing their appearance from a gridiron to a checkerboard.

If the ball hit the ground or was touched by an interior lineman before it was caught, possession of the ball went to the other team. If the receiver touched the ball but was not able to catch it, it became a free ball. All the defending team had to do to get possession was knock the receiver down or shove him out of the way so that he couldn't catch a forward pass.

TOSS-UP

Making matters worse was the fact that nobody really knew how to throw a football. Some players threw it sidearm; others threw it underhand like a softball or even with both hands, like a medicine ball. Whichever way they were thrown, underhand passes were inaccurate, and the odds of successfully catching them were slim.

Few football coaches thought forward passes were worth the risk, least of all the established football powers in the Northeast.

Bad omen: In 1916 Cumberland College's quarterback was knocked unconscious on the first play...

Mass plays had always worked in the past, and they saw no need to fix something that wasn't broken, no matter what the reformers thought. As a result, it was the less-established football programs in the Midwest and West—with little or nothing to lose—who were the first to become proficient in the use of the forward pass.

FARM TEAM

One of the first such schools was St. Louis University. In the summer of 1906, coach Eddie Cochems took his team out into the countryside near Lake Beulah, Wisconsin, where they experimented with the move for more than two months.

Back then, footballs were nicknamed "blimps"—they were chubbier than they are today—and Cochems had to figure out how best to hold and throw the ball. He instructed his players to grab the ball near the two lacings closest to the end, where it was narrowest, and to throw it overhand with a twist, as if they were pitching a fastball, so that the ball would rotate on its long axis.

Within an hour his players were throwing perfect spirals 40 yards downfield, and in the season that followed, St. Louis won every game it played, scoring a total of 402 points against opponents and yielding only 11. But the Eastern football powers did not take the teams of the West seriously, and continued playing football as they always had.

MORE TO COME

Football was growing rapidly, and so were the number of injuries and deaths. In 1909, 33 people died playing football, and 246 more were seriously injured. The NCAA pushed through another round of reforms in 1910:

• They outlawed aiding the ball carrier by pushing or pulling him down the field, and also banned "interlocked interference"—teammates grabbing onto one another to execute mass plays.

• They increased the number of players on the offensive line of scrimmage from six to seven, further discouraging mass plays.

• Flying tackles were banned, and defensive players were forbidden to interfere with the receiver, other than to catch or block the ball.

• Halves were split into 15-minute quarters, giving tired players a little more time to rest. And for the first time, players who were withdrawn from the game were allowed to return. In the past,

...against Georgia Tech. They went on to lose, 222–0, the worst defeat in football history.

players who were taken out had to stay out; as a result, tired players tended to stay in the game rather than take a break, which
increased the number of injuries.

• Most importantly, the NCAA lifted some of the restrictions on
the forward pass. Now the passer was allowed to throw the ball
anytime he was at least five yards behind the line of scrimmage
(that restriction wasn't removed until 1945), though it was illegal
to throw a pass farther than 20 yards. The requirement that he
move at least five yards left or right of center was removed, and
the checkerboard playing field reverted to the traditional gridiron.

• It was about this time that "head harnesses"—stiff leather caps
with ear flaps—began to come into use, as did the first shoulder pads.

ONE MORE ROUND

Two years later, in 1912, the NCAA made some of the last major
changes to football. They set the field size at 100 yards long by
53 1/3 yards wide, moved the kickoff from midfield to the 40-yard
line, and created the fourth down.

They also lifted most of the remaining restrictions on forward
passes, removing the 20-yard limit and establishing 10-yard "end
zones" at either end of the field. For the first time, catching a pass
thrown over the goal line counted as a touchdown instead of as a
"touchback" that awarded possession of the ball to the defending
team on their 20-yard line.

PASS PERFECT

The major football powers remained suspicious of the forward pass
even with all of the restrictions removed. That changed in 1913
when Notre Dame coach Jesse Harper wrote a letter to the Army
team asking them if they had an opening in their schedule "and if
so, would they give us a game." There was an opening on November 1, 1913, so Army invited Notre Dame to come and play at
West Point.

Notre Dame's quarterback, Charley Dorais, and left end, Knute
Rockne, had spent much of their summer vacation practicing forward passes on the beaches of Lake Erie. "Perfection came to us
only through daily, tedious practice," Rockne wrote in 1930.

Notre Dame played three games before meeting Army, racking
up 169 points—all from forward passing—and giving up only seven

---

Until the 1930s, tenpin bowling balls had only two holes.

to its opponents. But not many people noticed because the school wasn't a major football power at the time.

No one—least of all the Army team—was prepared for the events at West Point that first day of November. "We went out to play Army like crusaders, believing we represented not only our own school but the whole aspiring Middle West," Rockne remembered. "The Cadet body and most of the other spectators seemed to regard the engagement as a quiet, friendly work-out for the Army."

SNEAK ATTACK

Notre Dame began the first quarter playing a fairly conventional game; its defensive line held against Army, forcing them to kick. When Notre Dame got the ball, Dorais's first attempts at throwing short passes failed; then he told his teammates, "Let's open things up."

The next pass was successful; Dorais threw it only 11 yards, but it so startled Army that they held a huddle to discuss it. Following one particularly rough scrimmage, Rockne started limping as if he'd been hurt, and continued limping through the next three plays, as Notre Dame advanced steadily down to the Army 25-yard line. The normally boisterous crowd was silent as it took in the Midwesterners' new kind of game.

"After that third play," he remembered, "the Army halfback covering me figured I wasn't worth watching. Even as a decoy, he figured I was harmless." On the next play, Dorais signaled that he would throw the next pass to Rockne. Football was about to change forever:

> I started limping down the field, and the Army halfback covering me almost yawned in my face, he was that bored. I put on full speed and left him standing there flat-footed. I raced across the Army goal line as Dorais whipped the ball, and the grandstands roared at the completion of a 40-yard pass. Everybody seemed astonished. There had been no hurdling, no tackling, no plunging, no crushing of fiber and sinew. At the moment when I touched the ball, life for me was complete.

A WHOLE NEW BALL GAME

Notre Dame went on to complete 14 out of 17 passes, gaining 243 yards and scoring five touchdowns in the process of beating Army 35–13. The potential of the forward pass was laid out for everyone

"The key to winning baseball games is pitching, fundamentals, and 3-run homers." —Earl Weaver

to see: A team that few people had heard of had come roaring out of the Midwest to humble a major Eastern football power, master of the old-style game, on their own home field.

"Goliath," Tom Perrin writes in *Football: A College History*, "learned again what a missile can do in the hands of David."

With the arrival of the forward pass, all the major elements of modern football were in place. Very little has changed in the game since then, except for the advent of pro football and the NFL...but that's another story (see page 331).

(see page 331)

*   *   *

THE GOOD OLD DAYS

"There was no bad blood between [Yale and Princeton], but...in the very first scrimmage it became apparent that the practice of turning one cheek when the other is smitten is not to be entertained for a moment. As the game progressed, this fact became more potent. The eye of the umpire was the only thing they feared, and when his attention was diverted the surreptitious punches, gouges, and kicks were frequent and damaging....The favorite methods of damaging an opponent were to stamp on his feet, to kick his shins, to give him a dainty upper cut, and to gouge his face in tackling."

—The *New York Times*, describing the national championship game between Yale and Princeton in 1888

LET'S PLAY MAYA BALL

"Among the Maya the ball game was related to fertility, the sun, warfare, and sacrifice by decapitation. A high-ranking captive might be forced to play a game in which he might lose his head. Courts were often built against staircases. In some well-documented instances, the loser in the game was taken to the top, bound up to form a ball, and rolled down the stairs to his death."

—*The Aztecs, Maya, and Their Predecessors,* by Muriel Porter Weaver

THE MYSTERY TOUR

Cycling's Tour de France is a team competition, but only one person can win. And the winner might not be the first to cross the finish line. And not all of it's even in France. What gives? Here's a guide to one of the most complex—and popular—sporting events in the world.

THE PAPER RACE

The world's greatest bicycle race got its start in 1902 as a desperate publicity stunt. *L'Auto* was a Paris-based sports newspaper with money problems. Locked in a deadly circulation war with a rival newspaper, *L'Auto* was losing—badly. One day, over a luncheon at a Paris restaurant, reporter Géo Lefèvre made a proposal to *L'Auto*'s editor, Henri Desgrange. Why not have the newspaper sponsor a bike race across France—the longest one that had ever been held? The exposure might help boost *L'Auto* over its competition. Desgrange presented the idea to the paper's owner, and they decided to call the race the Tour de France.

On July 1 of the following year, 60 racers took off from the Cafe au Réveil-Matin in Paris. Nineteen days later, only 21 finished. The winner, Maurice Garin, took home 20,000 francs, but the other big winner was *L'Auto*. Publicity from the race nearly tripled the paper's sales, and its rival folded.

More than a century later, the Tour de France is as popular as ever. Every July, about 20 teams of 9 cyclists follow a grueling circuit through France and neighboring countries. For weeks they speed over bad roads and steep mountains through high heat, rain, and snow, all while striving to shave precious seconds off their time. Before the race ends on the cobblestoned streets of Paris, they've covered about 2,200 miles—comparable to racing from New York to Arizona—in 23 days.

TEAM SPORT

The Tour puts riders on such a grueling schedule—the equivalent of running a marathon every day for three weeks—that even the greatest cyclists in the world can't do it solo. In every Tour there are 20 or more elite riders who are out to win it, and each one leads a team of eight other people. The eight supporting teammate cyclists, or

---

"Race car" is a palindrome.

domestiques (French for "servants"), help their star make the fastest possible time. *Domestiques* might help their leader maneuver into a good spot in the *peloton* (pack) of nearly 200 riders, or they may speed up the peloton's pace to tire out their leader's opponent. During hot weather, they'll grab drinks from the team car to bring to their star.

One of the most important services that a domestique provides is "drafting." In most races, you expect to see the leader well out in front, but in the Tour a leader will often purposely ride behind a teammate. The domestique in front uses extra cycling energy to move at the same speed because he's facing—and absorbing—wind resistance. He's providing an air pocket behind him where the leader can ride with less wind resistance, saving his energy for the moment to "attack," or speed past, his opponents. Riding in front is difficult work, so leaders need strong teams—if a cyclist who is providing drafting tires is injured, another needs to take his place.

THIS RACE IS STAGED

Tours usually run for 23 days, with only 2 days of rest. The 21 riding days are divided into individual races from one destination to another. These races-within-a-race are called "stages," and the route varies from year to year.

The Prologue: The Tour begins with a short stage—always less than 13 miles long. This is the only stage when everyone starts fresh and rested, so winning the Prologue carries extra prestige. Because the Tour is always changing, the Prologue may be held outside of France. Or, as was the case in 2008, it might not be held at all.

Flat Stages: These usually take place during the first week of the race and cover as many as 155 miles per day. Despite their name, they can include rolling hills and tough climbs. They're also notoriously dangerous, with large packs of cyclists speeding through towns on narrow, twisting lanes.

Mountain Stages: Most Tours are won or lost on these stages, which take place during the second and third weeks of the race. Mountain climbs are categorized by difficulty: Category 4 climbs are the shortest and easiest, while Category 1 are the longest and steepest. Some climbs are so steep and brutal that they're *hors-catégorie*—uncategorized. The uncategorized Col du Tourmalet, a pass in the Pyrenees, has been nicknamed the "Circle of Death."

The total elevation climbed during the Tour de France is equivalent to three Mt. Everests.

Race of Truth: Although the entire Tour is a time trial, when riding in a peloton of 200 riders, many outside factors can affect a cyclist's time—for example, getting stuck behind slower riders or colliding with another cyclist. The Race of Truth stage is a time trial that tries to minimize the effects of the peloton and maximize speed against the clock. Officials stagger the cyclists, with the last-place racer starting first, followed two minutes later by the next-to-last-place rider, and so on—making the race's overall leader the last to start. This stage often occurs near the end of the Tour, and since the best riders can gain precious seconds by finally riding without the traffic of the peloton, it sometimes determines the winner.

Team Time Trials: Each team rides alone, without interference from competing teams. The clock stops on the fifth of the nine team riders to cross the finish line, and the fifth rider's time goes to the entire team. This is a chance for the team leader to help his domestiques win a stage, and the prizes and bonus points help him as well.

Mini Races or Sprints: Within stages, at various places along the route, the first person to speed across a designated spot wins extra bonus points.

AND THE WINNER IS...

A prize of 8,000 euros ($12,657) is awarded to the winner of each stage, along with flowers, a stuffed lion, and a kiss from each of the four beautiful "hostesses" on the winner's podium. But the most prestigious prizes come at the end.

General Classification Winner: This is the big enchilada. The overall time for each rider, calculated over the course of the Tour, is called the General Classification (GC). Win the GC, and you've won the whole Tour de France—along with 450,000 euros ($714,465) and a multitude of endorsement contracts. Lance Armstrong has won the GC a record seven times, from 1999 to 2005. Another American, Greg LeMond, won it in 1990 in an unusual way—without winning a single stage (his overall time was still the best).

Best Young Rider: An award of 20,000 euros ($31,754) goes to the racer under 25 years of age with the best GC. These are usually up-and-coming riders, since Tour winners are generally in their late 20's.

The terms "throw in the towel" and "toss your hat in the ring" both come from boxing.

Points Classification Winner: 25,000 euros ($39,692) go to the rider with the most bonus points overall. Bonus points are units of time that are deducted from a racer's GC when he wins a stage, time trial, or sprint, or when he's the first to crest a mountain or hill.

King of the Mountains: Another 25,000 euros go to the rider with the most bonus points for reaching predesignated points on certain mountains first.

The Winning Domestiques: The winner of the Tour usually divides his prize money among his teammates, since he'll later receive much more money through endorsements.

COLOR-CODED

If you want to know which racers are leading, look at their colors. Colored jerseys are awarded to leaders at the end of each stage and are worn during the following stage.

Yellow: Since 1919, a solid yellow jersey, or *maillot jaune*, has been awarded to the overall leader—the rider with the best GC up to that stage. Yellow was chosen because the pages of *L'Auto* were yellow.

Green: A solid green jersey is worn by the rider with the most bonus points.

Red Polka-Dots: This goes to the leader of the King of the Mountains classification.

White: The leader in the best young rider classification wears white.

Yellow Cap: The team with the best time (combined from the fastest three members) traditionally wear yellow caps, though the practice was suspended for the 2007 and '08 Tours.

UNIQUE TO THE TOUR

Over its 100-plus-year history, the Tour de France has developed some unusual traditions.

The *Lanterne Rouge*: This is the rider ranked last in the GC. (The name means "red lantern," referring to the red light on the caboose of a train.) Since completing a Tour is so difficult, and many cyclists drop out from injury or exhaustion, even a last-place finish is highly respected. And throughout the Tour's history, the

French have shown a special affection for losers—especially the lanterne rouge. In the past, officials sometimes even awarded prize money to the last finisher, so riders who couldn't win slowed down, or even stopped, hoping to finish last. Today the Tour has instituted time limitations to weed out deliberate slackers. But injured and sick cyclists still try for an honorable finish and good press as the lanterne rouge.

The Broom Wagon: This is a vehicle that follows the riders, picking up those who have to abandon the race because they are injured or failed to meet time restrictions. A trip in the broom wagon can be a cyclist's ride of shame.

Un Besoin Naturale: They say everything sounds romantic in French—including this phrase for urinating, which translates as "a natural need." A day of racing can last seven hours, so bathroom breaks are a necessary inconvenience. If you see cyclists riding three or four abreast, supporting each other by holding each other's shoulders, they're probably keeping the balance for a rider who's discreetly performing *un besoin naturale* while still cycling. When a rider has to hurriedly rush to the side of the road—or into the bushes for a more involved break—tradition demands that the riders around him slow down to allow him to catch up again. A rider who ignores this tradition can be punished later, when competitors leave him far behind during his next call of nature. Since there's no provision for traveling Port-a-Potties, and riders can be penalized for urinating in front of spectators, breaks are often planned ahead of time for unoccupied stretches of road.

THE SCANDALS

No other sporting event is as long and grueling as the Tour de France, and from its early years, riders have dulled their pain or improved their performance with banned substances. In 1924 two brothers admitted they'd been aided by chloroform, cocaine, aspirin, and "horse ointment." In 1967 a rider died after using amphetamines to fight exhaustion in the mountains. Recent Tours have been marred by winning cyclists being disqualified after testing positive for anabolic steroids (used to improve muscle strength) and erythropoietin (for endurance). Officials still hold out the hope that constant testing and policing will end the Tour's long string of scandals.

...—only six—that the prize has been called "the kiss of death for college players."

THE COLOR BARRIER

When Tiger Woods won the Masters in 1997, he thanked golfers like Teddy Rhodes, Charlie Sifford, and Lee Elder for opening the doors of professional golf to black Americans. Never heard of them? Here's a look at some of golf's unsung heroes.

CHANGING TIMES

If you ask a person, "Who is Tiger Woods?" how do you think they'd answer the question? They'd probably say something like, "He's the greatest golfer in the world." His African American heritage (Woods also claims Asian, American Indian, and European ancestry), if it was mentioned at all, would probably be a point of pride. But the fact that it doesn't get him thrown off the pro circuit is a measure of just how far professional golf has come in a fairly short period of time. Just 45 years ago, blacks were banned from professional golf.

ON THE JOB

That's not to say that African Americans didn't play golf. Even with discrimination, golf was probably *more* accessible to them than it is now. Before the days of golf carts, courses employed large numbers of caddies—most of them minorities. Caddies spent more time on the golf course than anyone else, observing how experienced golfers played the game and often sneaking in rounds of their own before and after work. One day a week, usually Monday, was "caddie day"—the course was closed to the public and caddies could play as much golf as they wanted. Many caddies developed into some of the finest golfers in the country.

If a caddie was white, he could go as far as his talent could take him—he could give golf lessons, become the club pro, or even play on the PGA Tour. Golf legends such as Lee Trevino, Ben Hogan, and Gene Sarazen, for example, all got their start as caddies.

If a caddie was black, that was a different story. No matter how good they became at golf, blacks rarely got the chance to advance beyond the status of caddies. Playing on the PGA Tour was out of the question: the PGA had discriminated against them since its founding in 1916, and in 1943 it made the policy official by

---

An average pro golfer uses five to eight balls per round.

amending its constitution to restrict membership to "professional golfers of the Caucasian race." The amateur USGA wasn't much better—it didn't have an anti-black clause, but it deferred to golf clubs that discriminated against blacks. Nearly all of them did.

KEEP OUT

Frustrated with not being able to compete and earn money in the growing professional sport, a group of black golfers got together and formed the United States Colored Golfers Association (soon changed to the United Golfers Association)—a black golfing circuit. Their first tournament was in 1925 at the Shady Rest Golf Club in Westfield, New Jersey. In the final round, Harry Jackson defeated John Shippen by three shots. His prize for the victory: $25. The first National Colored Golf Championship, or "the National," was held the following year at the Mapledale in Stow, Massachusetts.

The National became the black golfers' "major," and the UGA grew, expanding to weekly pro tournaments with packed rosters by the 1950s, as well as men's and women's amateur championships. And they were all "open" events—even to whites, who often showed up to play. "We knew what it was like to be excluded," said former UGA president Norris Horton, "and we didn't want to do the same thing to anybody else, so whites, blacks, anybody who qualified and paid the entry fee, could play."

But it wasn't the PGA. First-place money on the UGA tour in the 1950s: about $500...in the PGA: about $20,000. If they wanted to earn a living as pros, black golfers would have to break in.

OPENING THE DOORS

In 1942 seven black golfers tried to enter a USGA-affiliated golf tournament in Chicago and were turned away. When they complained to the USGA, the association refused to do anything about it. That prompted a sympathetic Chicago alderman to write to George S. May, owner of a Chicago country club called the Tam O'Shanter, and ask him to invite black golfers to his upcoming All-American tournament. This was during World War II; May figured that if blacks were fighting in the war just like everyone else, they should be able to play golf like everyone else, too.

By the late 1940s, both the Tam O'Shanter and the Los Angeles

Open were flouting the PGA's caucasians-only clause and allowing blacks to compete in their tournaments. In 1948 two black golfers named Bill Spiller and Teddy Rhodes, both stars of the UGA, scored well enough in the Los Angeles Open to qualify for the upcoming Richmond Open in northern California. Well enough, that is, if they had been white.

Tournament rules stated that the top sixty finishers in the Los Angeles Open were eligible to play in the Richmond Open, but the PGA's rules said that blacks were not allowed to play at all. (Guess which rule the PGA decided to enforce.) Spiller and Rhodes were shooting a practice round of golf at the Richmond Golf Club a few days before the tournament when a PGA official walked up and told them they would not be allowed to play in the tournament. Spiller, Rhodes, and a third golfer named Madison Gunter decided to sue the PGA for discrimination and asked for $315,000 in damages.

One week before it went to trial, the case was settled out of court after the PGA promised not to discriminate against blacks in the future. But then it weaseled out of the deal by switching most of its tournaments from "open" tournaments, for which anyone could qualify, to "invitationals," which were by invitation only.

The caucasians-only clause stayed in place—and the PGA saw to it that no blacks received invitations to its invitationals.

THE BROWN BOMBER

One PGA tournament that kept its open format was the San Diego Open in California, and that's where the next big blowup came, in 1952. That year, the tournament's sponsor, the San Diego County Chevrolet Association, asked retired heavyweight champion Joe Louis, the "Brown Bomber," to play in the tournament. Bill Spiller also qualified for the tournament by scoring well in two qualifying rounds.

Louis still hadn't decided whether or not to go when Horton Smith, the president of the PGA, contacted the organizers of the San Diego tournament and told them that the rules forbade blacks from playing in PGA-sponsored events. That's when the San Diego tournament withdrew its invitation to Joe Louis...and that's when the Brown Bomber decided he was going after all.

Part II of "The Color Barrier" is on page 352.

HULA HOOPS

*The hula hoop was a pioneer, the first major fad created
and fueled by a new power in America—TV ads.*

A **BIG HIT**
The hula hoop originated in Australia, where it was simply a bamboo exercise ring used in gym classes. In 1957 an Australian company began selling the ring in retail stores—which attracted the attention of a small California toy manufacturer named Wham-O.

Wham-O's owners made a few wooden rings for their kids ("They just wouldn't put the hoop down"), took them to cocktail parties ("Folks had to have a couple of drinks in them to take a whack at it")...and then decided they had a hot item on their hands. They began producing a plastic version, naming it the Hula Hoop after the motion it resembled—the Hawaiian hula dance.

Wham-O introduced the hula hoop to the American public in January 1958, and it quickly became the biggest toy craze in history (up to that time). During the year, more than 20 million—$30 million worth—were sold. The hula hoop was *the* quintessential fad, but by November 1958, the *Wall Street Journal* was already announcing, "Hoops Have Had It." A brief comeback occurred in 1965, when Wham-O introduced the "Shoop-Shoop" Hula Hoop, with a ball bearing in it to make noise, but it just wasn't the same.

HOOP FACTS
• According to the *British Medical Journal*, the hula hoop was responsible for an increase in back, neck, and abdominal injuries.
• Indonesia banned hula hoops because they "might stimulate passion." Japan forbade them on public streets.
• The official news agency in China called hula hoops "a nauseating craze." In the Soviet Union, the hoop was seen as a "symbol of the emptiness of American culture."
• Hula hoop endurance records: longest whirl—72 hours, by Kym Coberly in 1984; most hoops twirled simultaneously—105, by Jin Linlin of China, in 2007.

World's fastest ball sport: jai alai, where the ball can reach speeds of 174 mph.

SPHAIRISTIKE, ANYONE?

*From 11th-century monks to the Williams sisters, the
history of tennis has been a long, bouncy road.*

FIRST SET

Humans have been hitting balls back and forth for centuries,
and there are different theories about which ancient culture
first started it. Some historians theorize that the first tennis game
was a variant of handball played in ancient Egypt; others say that
it began in ancient Greece or Rome. But everyone agrees that the
first known players to originate a tennislike game were French.

Sometime during the 11th or 12th century, French monks
improvised a game where they batted a ball across a droopy rope
net in the monastery courtyard. Part of the game was yelling
"Tenez!" (roughly, "Take this!") as they hit the ball, which may
have been the origin of the word "tennis." The name for the
monks' game, though, was *jeu de paume*, or "game of the palm,"
since the monks used the palms of their hands to hit the ball.

OFF THE WALL

Once the French nobility discovered the monks' game, they built
their own narrow, walled courts where the ball could be played off
the walls as well as over the net. Aristocratic players used a glove
to make the game more comfortable, and in time they added web-
bing between the fingers. Later they began using short bats. By
1500 the bat and glove were combined into a wooden frame racket strung with sheep gut. Whether played with a glove or a racket,
from the 13th century on, *jeu de paume* (which came to be called
real tennis, or "royal tennis") was such a popular distraction from
the church that the pope tried—and failed—to ban it.

England's King Henry V brought tennis to Britain in the 1400s,
but the true English king of tennis was Henry VIII. Young King
Henry was a fit, strong athlete. In 1530, on his orders, tennis courts
were added to his Hampton Court palace. According to legend,
Henry loved tennis so much that he didn't attend the beheading of
his second wife, Anne Boleyn, because he was embroiled in an
intense match. Henry VIII is also credited with inventing the mod-

The first tennis balls were stuffed with human hair.

ern practice of tossing the ball in the air to serve it. But as he grew older—and much, much fatter—he had trouble throwing the ball high enough to serve. So his servants threw it for him.

For the next two centuries, *real tennis* was a favorite game of the nobility; at one time, there were as many as 1,800 tennis courts in Paris alone. But social change brought change to tennis as well when, in 1789, French revolutionaries declared their opposition to King Louis XVI at his royal tennis court in Versailles Palace. The declaration became known as the "Tennis Court Oath," and in the minds of the French people, it linked *real tennis* to the decadence and excesses of their rulers. After the revolution, the game practically disappeared from France, and as the aristocracy gave way to the middle class throughout Europe, their aristocratic sport died out with them.

TENNIS GETS A BOUNCE

In England, a few avid tennis players kept the sport going. But they were limited by the fact that the game was still played on a court with walls—a chunk of real estate that few could afford in Victorian Britain. All that changed in 1850 when Charles Goodyear invented vulcanized rubber. Before then, tennis balls had been made with cores of cork, wool, twine, or hair with outer coverings of leather and cloth. Though they could ricochet off walls, *real tennis* balls didn't bounce well off the ground.

But rubber balls, which bounced well on any surface, soon found their way into the game. And with them, two Englishmen, Major T. H. Gem and J. B. Perara, improvised a new game played on a lawn, without walls. The game caught on, and the two formed the world's first tennis club. But it was another Englishman, Walter Clopton Wingfield, who gets credit for inventing tennis as we know it today. In 1873 Wingfield introduced a "portable court," a kit with poles, pegs, netting, four tennis rackets, a bag of balls, and a book of rules.

But it wasn't quite tennis yet. Wingfield called his game *sphairistike*, a Greek word meaning "the art of playing ball." But despite the odd name, the game was essentially *real tennis* without walls. Even the word "love" in Wingfield's rule book was imported from *real tennis*—it's thought to be derived from the French word *oeuf*, or "egg," which the tennis-playing monks used to designate zero.

Youngest person to win a Wimbledon championship: Martina Hingis, in 1996, at age 15.

By 1874 Wingfield's sphairistike kits were hot sellers throughout Britain and its colonies. Just four years later, the All-England Croquet Club at Wimbledon held its first championship for the game, establishing rules that still govern tournaments today. On the other side of the Atlantic, Mary Ewing Outerbridge, who had learned to play tennis on a vacation in Bermuda, brought the game back to New York in 1874. And the craze finally came home to France, with the first national championship held in Paris in 1891. The only part of Wingfield's game that never caught on was the name. At first, people shortened sphairistike to "sticky" and then began calling it "lawn tennis." Eventually it was shortened to just "tennis."

SLAMMING THE PLANET

By the early 1900s, the national tournaments in Wimbledon, France, the United States, and Australia were attracting players from all over the world. These four tournaments, known as the Grand Slam, caught the public's attention and made many tennis players international stars. One early celebrity was 20-year-old Suzanne Lenglen of France. She not only won the Wimbledon title in 1919, she shocked spectators by wearing a short-sleeved dress hemmed at the calves (women's standard tenniswear of the day was an ankle-length, high-necked outfit). Lenglen drank brandy between sets, sobbed with emotion, and served with unladylike power, all of which caused a sensation. In France, she was known as *La Divine*—the Divine One.

Although Lenglen helped tennis lose a few of its Victorian garden-party trappings, the game remained mostly a diversion for the upper crust, where it flourished on large estates and in fancy country clubs. Tennis superstars were expected to be wealthy amateurs who could afford to play for little or no prize money. "Professional" tennis players—those who made a living off the sport—were considered a different class of players, relegated to traveling shows that performed in front of paying audiences. Professionals were banned from the Grand Slam tournaments, which were reserved for amateurs.

OPENING UP

By the late 1960s, the line between amateurs and professionals had blurred. Some amateurs had already been accused of quietly earning money from sponsorships, and sports-equipment manufacturers were eager to pay more players to promote their wares. In addition, many felt a generous prize-money system would help players support themselves and give them time to develop their skills. It also might attract a larger audience. So in 1968 tennis embarked on the Open Era—any player, amateur or pro, could play in the Grand Slam and other major tournaments. This drew better players and larger crowds, and today tennis is one of the most popular sports in the world.

Thanks to rubberized balls and a few diehards who kept the game alive, tennis made the journey from a pastime of the elite to a recreational sport that kids can learn on public courts in nearly every town in the U.S. And with Grand Slam championships now carrying prize money of more than $1 million, some of those kids can—and have—become celebrities and millionaires.

* * *

RANDOM ORIGIN: LASER TAG

A man named George Carter got an inspiration while he was watching *Star Wars* in 1977. It took him years to work out the technology, but in 1984, he opened Photon, a laser tag arcade in Dallas, Texas. Played in a futuristic, cavernous arena, Photon let players shoot light beams at each other while climbing on catwalks surrounded by smoke, lights, and sound effects. Receptors on the players' chests recorded "hits"; three hits eliminated a player from the half-hour match. Laser tag became a local phenomenon, and soon Photon arenas sprang up all over the United States. They were riding high when a home version of their game hit stores in 1985. Then came the competition. Worlds of Wonder—the company responsible for the Teddy Ruxpin doll—released Lazer Tag, a rip-off of the Photon set that sold better than Photon. Nearly 20 other competitors followed…and they all flopped, except for Lazer Tag, which became *the* hot toy for Christmas in 1986. Only problem: Worlds of Wonder couldn't make Lazer Tag sets fast enough to keep up with demand. By the time the company ramped up production, kids had moved on to the next thing. The fad was over, and Worlds of Wonder went bankrupt in 1988. The Photon chain closed in 1989.

PUDGE GOES PRO

Elsewhere in the book, we tell the story of how college football got its start (page 49) and the birth of the NFL (page 331). Here's a story that links the two together: the very first professional football player.

COLLEGE GAME

For more than 50 years, college football was the dominant form of the sport, both in terms of the number of teams and the number of fans. College football *was* football. But what about people who didn't go to college, or grads that wanted to relive their glory days? They wanted to play, too, and they wanted teams they could root for. So in the 1890s local sports clubs and businesses began to organize teams.

These sports clubs, such as the YMCA, had an agenda: their members saw them as stepping-stones to get into even more exclusive clubs and a great way to do that was to belong to a club with a successful sports team. So the pressure was on from the beginning to recruit the best men possible.

One problem: it was against the rules to pay athletes for playing. Amateurism was seen as a noble quality; getting paid to play was seen as crass. So instead of breaking the rules, the clubs bent them. San Francisco's Olympic Athletic Club, for example, promised to find a job for any athlete that joined the club. Even if this didn't technically violate the rules, it certainly violated the spirit of amateurism. But the practice was so widespread that, rather than condemn it, in 1890 the Amateur Athletic Union, which governed amateur clubs, created an entirely new category for that kind of athlete—the "semiprofessional."

LORD OF THE RINGERS

William "Pudge" Heffelfinger was a former All-American for Yale University. One of the best players of his time, Heffelfinger was famous for hurling himself over the heads of interlocked offensive linemen and cannonballing knee-first into the ball carrier's chest.

A popular practice at the time was to cheat by hiring ringers, skilled college players who posed as average Joes and played under assumed names. Heffelfinger was sorely needed by two rival clubs in Pittsburgh, Pennsylvania: the Allegheny Athletic Association and the Pittsburgh Athletic Club. After playing to a 6–6 tie in the citywide championship game in October 1892 (highly contested because Allegheny had stolen some of Pittsburgh's best players), a rematch was set for three weeks later. Both clubs scrambled to field the best teams possible; both clubs secretly met with Heffelfinger.

GAME DAY

More than 3,000 people turned out for the rematch on November 12, even though it was snowing. The Allegheny crowd cheered when Pudge took the field with their team. The Pittsburgh side cried foul—Allegheny was using ringers, after all. They refused to play unless Allegheny agreed that all bets placed on the game were off. (Gambling was another big part of the early game.) After nearly an hour, Allegheny agreed.

For all the hoopla that led up to it, the game itself was pretty uneventful. Pudge scored the only touchdown, and Allegheny won 4–0 (back then, a touchdown only counted for four points—today it counts for six). Even with the low score and the bitterly cold weather, the crowd was entertained by the brutal play and carnage on the field. Several players were injured—three had to be carried off on stretchers.

Today, Pudge Heffelfinger is just a footnote in professional football. He wouldn't even be that, were it not for a single scrap of paper that survived among the Allegheny Athletic Association's financial records for the 1892 season. Today that scrap of paper—an expense sheet for the November 12 game—is on display in the Pro Football Hall of Fame. On it is an entry showing that, in addition to being reimbursed for his expenses, Heffelfinger received a $500 "game performance bonus for playing." And in those days, $500 was about what a schoolteacher made in a year. Although neither Pudge nor Allegheny ever admitted to the transaction, the expense sheet speaks for itself: Heffelfinger was the first documented professional football player in the history of the game.

...and as many as 74,000 people are on the waiting list each year for season tickets.

HOCKEY'S FIRST OLYMPIC MVP

And much more about the high-flying, high-scoring—and violin-playing—Icelandic-Winnipeggian, Frank Fredickson.

ICELAND JONES

The exploits of Frank Fredrickson read like the script for an *Indiana Jones* movie: The charismatic, flamboyant, and handsome Icelander seemed to excel at any endeavor he tried, from hockey to flying airplanes to coaching to music. He was a star in amateur hockey, a star again as a professional in the Pacific Coast Hockey Association (PCHA) and the NHL, an accomplished violinist, a World War I pilot, and a survivor of a torpedoed ship in the Mediterranean Sea. On top of that, he won an Olympic gold medal.

BORN TO GLIDE

Fredrickson's family had moved from Iceland to Winnipeg, Manitoba, in the late 1800s, joining a community of their countrymen in the Canadian city. Born in 1895, Sigurdur Franklin Frederickson spoke no English until he started elementary school at six years of age, and was often teased and bullied by the other "real Canadian" kids. "Luckily for me, I loved sports and played every game as hard as I could to gain acceptance," he said years later. "Because Winnipeg had cold winters, ice surfaces for skating and hockey were plentiful. I was on them every chance I had."

Fredrickson played junior and senior hockey as a teenager in Winnipeg, then was captain of the University of Manitoba team while continuing amateur league play. But his hockey career was put on hold in 1916 when World War I broke out. Frederickson enlisted and shipped off to England with the Canadian Army's 196th Battalion, then to Egypt with the Royal Flying Corps, where he earned his pilot's wings. On a 1918 trip to an active-duty assignment in France, his ship, the *Leasowe Castle*, was torpedoed by a German submarine in the Mediterranean Sea.

Ninety-two men were lost; Frederickson and 2,800 other men made it to the lifeboats. They were rescued a half day later by a Japanese ship.

THE GOLDEN FALCONS

In 1919 Fredrickson returned to Canada, where he helped organize a hockey team called the Winnipeg Falcons. All but one of the team's players were of Icelandic descent. Refused entry by the Manitoba senior amateur league—big mistake—Fredrickson and his friends formed their own three-team league in 1920. After scoring 22 goals in nine league games, and another 22 in six playoff games, Fredrickson challenged the Manitoba league champions to an official "challenge" game. The Falcons won. That got them to the Canadian amateur championship, the still-famous Allen Cup, against the University of Toronto Blues. They won that, too. From there the Falcons went to Antwerp, Belgium, to represent Canada at the 1920 Winter Olympics. Fredrickson lead the team to wins over Czechoslovakia, Sweden, and the United States, and the Falcons—er, the Canadians—won the very first Olympic hockey gold medal. Frederickson—who scored 12 goals in just three games—became the first Olympic hockey MVP.

BORN TO FLY?

Because the newly formed NHL and the PCHA were eagerly seeking players, Fredrickson was a prized commodity. Lester Patrick, one of the PCHA's founders, saw him as a star on the ice—and off, because of his war exploits—and made him a generous offer. Frederickson declined. Instead, he signed a five-year deal to conduct an aerial study of Iceland and make a report on the feasibility of air transport in that country. But the program was canceled after six months, and Frederickson was back in Winnipeg—where he decided to join the Canadian Air Force instead of playing hockey. And in his spare time he played the violin in a hotel orchestra and gave concerts with his pianist wife Bea, a graduate of the Toronto Conservatory of Music. Was hockey ever going to get him back?

The answer came in 1921, when Frederickson signed with the Victoria Cougars for the then-astronomical sum of $2,700 per sea-

---

So much for stereotypes: only 11% of American doctors play golf.

son. Lester Patrick pumped up the publicity for the first meeting of their new 26-year-old star and the league's 37-year-old superstar, Cyclone Taylor of the Vancouver Millionaires. Fredrickson scored two goals in a win over Vancouver, and even Cyclone had words of praise, calling Fredrickson "as fine a player as I've ever seen, with a wonderful quick shot."

Fredrickson spent six years with the Cougars, winning the scoring title in 1922–23 with 39 goals and 55 points in 30 games, a new record. In the 1924–25 season, Fredrickson led the Cougars to the PCHA title. Then they became the last team outside the NHL to make it to the Stanley Cup finals, where they defeated the Montreal Canadiens and their great young star Howie Morenz. (The next year they made it back, but were defeated by the Montreal Maroons.)

When the PCHA was disbanded in 1926, most members of the Victoria team joined the Detroit Cougars of the NHL. Fredrickson became a Cougar along with them, but he'd made his own deal with the new club for $6,500 per season…more than double what the other players were paid. When they discovered his salary, his teammates refused to pass the puck to him, forcing the Cougars to eventually trade him to the Boston Bruins.

MUSIC ON ICE

With the Bruins, Fredrickson's violin was joined by the saxophone of great young defenseman Eddie Shore. But their music sessions on the team's train trips weren't popular with everyone; Bruins boss Art Ross soon banned all musical instruments. Fredrickson later played with the Pittsburgh Pirates (where he was the NHL's first player/coach) and the Detroit Falcons, where a knee injury ended his career in 1931. He stayed in hockey by coaching in the Manitoba Junior Leagues, and for the Royal Canadian Air Force during World War II—where he led the team to another Allen Cup title. In 1958 he was named to the Hockey Hall of Fame.

Extra: One more note about Sigurdur Franklin Fredrickson, one of hockey's historic geniuses: while coaching at Princeton University, according to legendary sportswriter Eric Zweig, he walked to work every day with his neighbor—and fellow violinist—Albert Einstein.

An estimated 70% of the hats sold in the United States are baseball caps.

THE GREAT ONE

When he retired from hockey in 1999, Wayne Gretzky had set more than 50 NHL records and won 10 scoring titles, 9 MVP awards, and 4 Stanley Cups. Here's what it was like to be around that kind of greatness.

"Every time he gets the puck, something exciting happens."
—Islanders G.M. Mike Milbury

"The only way you can check Gretzky is to hit him when he is standing still singing the national anthem."
—Boston G.M. Harry Sinden

"The NHL needs something to hang its hat on, and Gretzky looks like a hat tree.
—Gordie Howe

"Gretzky's got more friends in the media than the guy running the free buffet."
—journalist Dan Bickley

"Wayne's like having your own Fantasy Island. It's so much fun to play with him. I had no goals and no assists before getting on his line, and then I almost made the record book."
—Oilers forward Dave Lumley

"We were just brain-dead. If you're brain-dead against Wayne Gretzky, I mean, he can set my four-year-old son up to score."
—Maple Leafs right wing Tom Fitzgerald

"There should be a league rule where he's passed around from team to team each year."
—Rangers coach Terry O'Reilly

"Gretzky would dominate in any era. It doesn't make any difference. He may well be the smartest hockey player who ever played the game."
—Phil Esposito

"We would have won if we had Wayne Gretzky."
—Paul Reinhart of the Calgary Flames, after losing to Gretzky's Oilers in the 1988 finals

"Some guys play hockey. Gretzky plays 40-mph chess."
—journalist Lowell Cohn

Only member of Rock and Roll *and* Little League Baseball Halls of Fame: Bruce Springsteen.

SKIING—ON WATER?

It's hard enough for a human to skim across water with two sticks tied to his feet. But spins, flips, and 44-person pyramids? How did people ever come up with these water ski stunts? As it turns out, it took a lot of experimenting...and a few accidents.

MELTED SNOW

In 1922 an adventurous Minnesota teenager named Ralph Samuelson had an idea. If skis could carry a person down a snowy slope, why couldn't they carry him across water? So he tied a tow-rope to a motorboat and tried skiing behind it on boards taken from a barrel—which didn't work—and then snow skis, but every kind of ski he tried slipped under the water and caused a fall. So he decided to carve new skis out of 8-foot-long, 9-inch-wide pine boards. After softening the front tips in boiling water, he curved them upward. Then he bound them to his feet with leather straps, got in the water, and tried again. He leaned back, the boat towed him faster and faster and, to everyone's surprise, the wide homemade skis stayed above water—and so did he.

Before long, Samuelson and others were designing better water skis—and stunts to entertain audiences. A 1928 performance in Atlantic City featured a few daring female skiers who slalomed (made wide turns from side to side) on one ski and thrilled the crowd by balancing on each other's shoulders. Ballet moves, costumes, and music were later added, and the waterborne performers sometimes acted out storylines.

A REAL SPORT

Seventeen years after it was invented, water skiing officially became a competitive sport. The first U.S. National Water Ski Championships, held off Long Island in 1939, featured three main events: slalom, ramp jumping, and tricks. The rules were casual and subject to interpretation, and jumps were judged on style, not distance.

One skier at the Nationals who stood out from the rest was Bruce Parker, who became known as "Mr. Water Skiing." While

---

Total prize money awarded at the first tennis U.S. Open in 1968: $100,000....

other contestants did relatively simple tricks, like hopping boat wakes or making snowplow turns by pointing their ski tips together, Parker stole the show by removing one ski and poking his foot through the tow-rope handle, then letting himself be towed by the foot while holding the free ski over his head. Then he put the ski back on—all without crashing. The crowd had never seen anything like it, and Parker won the event and the men's overall title.

Another early skier, Jack Andresen (who was famous for holding the tow rope in his teeth) gave the sport a boost when he invented special trick skis in 1940. The difference: They were slightly shorter than the water skis of the time, *both* ends were turned up, and they had no fins mounted to the bottom, as many early skis did. Though they weren't as stable as finned skis, Andresen's turned more easily, enabling him to complete the first 360° turns, as well as 360° wake turns—rotations in midair while jumping over a boat's wake.

ROUND IT DOWN

Trick skis didn't change much until the early '60s. "Competition" skis were about four feet long, which meant the skier had to make a wide turn unless he was doing a wake turn, and the drag of the water against the long skis slowed him down. Most skis also had sharp, square (rather than rounded) edges. But in the '60s, skier Rick McCormick and his brother Jim noticed that Rick could do better tricks on his *old* skis than on his new ones. The reason: The old skis' rounded edges, ground down from wear and refinishing, made them turn more easily in the water. Competition regulations didn't specify what kind of edge skis had to have, and rules governing ski length had just been relaxed, so the McCormicks experimented by sanding down the edges of Rick's new skis and cutting 8 inches off their length. The new skis were a hit, and Rick McCormick went on to win championships in the 1970s.

The '60s and '70s saw more improvements to skis, such as grooves carved into the bottoms for stability and lighter materials like aluminum and carbon graphite. These innovations led to yet more elaborate tricks such as flips, stepovers (lifting a foot and ski over the rope while turning), side slides (skiing sideways), 720° turns (two full rotations while passing the tow-rope handle from hand to hand twice), and back flips with a 720° twist.

RAMP IT UP

Ski jumping—a mainstay of water skiing contests—also went through its ups and downs over the years. It got off to a rough start in 1925, when a skier named Ralph Samuelson built the first wooden jump ramp. His first attempts ended in spectacular crashes when his skis stuck to the ramp, so he came up with a simple solution: He smeared the ramp with lard. That worked for a time, but the organizers of the 1939 Nationals instead used a complicated ramp with rows of 2-inch wooden rollers to reduce friction. The contraption proved to be dangerous if skiers caught their hands or feet between the rollers—so hazardous that only one contestant, Jack Schiess, was able to make three jumps without crashing. He won.

An accidental discovery in the mid-'50s helped prevent injuries—and also changed the sport of water ski jumping. Until then, jumpers had usually approached the ramp in a straight line. As the skier went up and over the ramp, for a moment he was moving faster than the boat, briefly causing the towline to go slack. This brought a danger that water skiers knew all too well: If the rope managed to wrap itself around the skier's leg, arm, or neck, it could mean a serious injury.

One day during the 1954 Nationals, skier Warren Witherell was approaching a jump with something on his mind: He was competing on *borrowed* skis: The night before, someone had stolen his skis, so he'd been forced to borrow a pair. He decided to approach the jump by skiing wide to one side, then wide to the other side and hitting the ramp at an angle instead of head-on. "I'd never practiced it before," Witherell says. "It was a desperate effort to make up for the handicap of skiing on borrowed skis." The angled approach kept the towline taut, which had two unexpected results: a safer jump, and a much longer one since, without the slack, he was being towed by the boat all through it and hit the ramp with greater momentum—all resulting in an astounding jump of 100 feet. (A week later, he set a world record at 106 feet.)

STILL SKIING

Today's lighter, stronger skis and waxed fiberglass ramps have made much longer jumps possible (the current record is 243 feet). And powerful modern speedboats have ushered in a new era of elaborate stunts—including a record 44-person pyramid in 2003.

THE KING OF KUNG FU

Bruce Lee finished only four films in his lifetime, but many martial arts movie fans still consider them the best kung fu movies ever made. Here's a look at the man behind the myth.

FIGHT CLUB

In 1958 a bunch of Hong Kong teenagers who studied a style of martial arts known as *choy li fut* challenged another group of teens, who studied a style known as *wing chun*, to a fight. Fights like this were fairly common in Hong Kong—the kids would go up on the roof of a local apartment building, pair off, and spar with each other until one fighter forced his opponent over a white line painted on the roof.

But this fight was different—it turned ugly when one of the choy li fut kids punched one of the wing chun kids, Lee Jun Fan, in the face and gave him a black eye. Lee Jun Fan (better known by his English name, Bruce Lee) flew into a rage and gave his opponent quite a beating, even knocking out a tooth or two. When the kid's parents saw what happened, they called the police. Bruce Lee's mom got hauled down to the station and had to sign a paper stating that she would assume full responsibility—and possibly even go to jail—if her son misbehaved again.

COMING TO AMERICA

Fortunately for Bruce's mom, her son had an option that most other Hong Kong teens didn't: he had American citizenship. He'd been born in San Francisco while his parents were touring the United States with a Hong Kong opera company, so he was free to return to America at any time. And as Mrs. Lee saw it, that was probably the best place for him.

Bruce wasn't much of a student—his bad grades and penchant for fighting had gotten him thrown out of more than one school— but even if he had been a good student, Hong Kong was still a British colony and nearly all the best job opportunities were set aside for the British kids. If Bruce stayed in Hong Kong, he'd likely end up on the streets, in jail, or dead. So, Mrs. Lee handed her 17-year-old son $100 and put him on a ship to San Francisco.

At age 18, Bruce Lee won the Crown Colony Cha-Cha Dancing Championship of Hong Kong.

Bruce spent a short time there, then moved to Seattle, where he enrolled in high school and went to work as a waiter in a Chinese restaurant. Bruce was a champion dancer as well as a student of the martial arts, and he gave dancing and kung fu lessons on the side. In time, he dropped the dance lessons and focused on martial arts full-time.

BACK TO BASICS

By 1964 Lee was 24, married, and running two of his own martial arts studios, one in Seattle and a second in Oakland, California. Several months after the Oakland studio opened, a martial arts instructor named Wong Jack Man from nearby San Francisco demanded that Lee stop teaching martial arts to non-Chinese *gweilos*, or "foreign devils." (In those days, many Chinese instructors were opposed to teaching anyone outside their own community.) If Lee refused, Wong Jack Man would challenge him to a fight, and if Lee lost, he would either have to stop teaching martial arts to gweilos or close down his studio altogether.

Lee accepted, and then over the course of the next three minutes gave Wong Jack Man the beating of his life. Other fighters might have been content with such a victory, but Lee wasn't—he figured he should have been able to drop Wong after the first couple of blows. The experience caused Lee to question his entire approach to martial arts. Until then, he had been a devotee of the wing chun school of kung fu (he spelled it *gung fu*), but now he began to study all forms of martial arts, including fencing, Western-style boxing, and Greco-Roman wrestling, incorporating anything he thought was useful and discarding everything else.

NO NONSENSE

Lee had little interest in classical fighting stances, black belts, breaking boards with his fists, and other kung fu clichés. He just wanted to win fights, as quickly and as skillfully as possible. Everything else was fluff—or as he once put it, "ninety percent of Oriental self-defense is baloney." Over the next two years, Lee developed his own stripped-down, back-to-basics style of fighting that he named *jeet kune do,* or "way of the intercepting fist."

Meanwhile, Lee was also beginning to find work in Hollywood. In August 1964, he gave a demonstration at a martial arts exhibi-

The game of marbles dates back to the Stone Age and is found in almost every culture.

tion in Long Beach, California. One person who saw his performance was Jay Sebring, a top Hollywood hairstylist who had a TV
producer named William Dozier as a client. Dozier had produced
The Tammy Grimes Show and *Studio One*, and his new show *Batman*
would soon hit the airwaves. When Dozier mentioned that he was
looking for an Asian actor to play the part of Charlie Chan's "number-one son" in a new project, Sebring told him about Bruce Lee.

BECOMING AN ACTOR

The Charlie Chan project never materialized, but when *Batman*
became a smash hit, Dozier decided to follow up with a similar
show called *The Green Hornet*. Dozier cast Bruce Lee as the Hornet's Asian sidekick, Kato. Lee moved his family to Los Angeles,
and in addition to working on the TV show, he began giving private martial arts lessons to celebrities such as James Coburn, Steve
McQueen, and Kareem Abdul-Jabbar.

The Green Hornet aired for only one season: it premiered in
September 1966 and went off the air in July 1967. Lee earned good
reviews for his performance, but it was difficult for an Asian actor
to land big parts. Three years passed and his career went nowhere.
Lee's celebrity friends helped him land small roles in movies and
TV shows, but they weren't the kinds of jobs that would advance
his career. He helped develop the TV series *Kung Fu* only to learn
in 1971 that he'd lost the lead role to David Carradine, a white
guy who didn't know much about kung fu. *Kung Fu's* producers felt
that Carradine was a better choice for the role because he had the
calm personality that they were looking for in Caine, but Lee's
chances were also hurt by the fear that if an Asian actor were cast
in the lead, fewer people would watch the show.

ON THE OTHER SIDE OF THE WORLD

Lee didn't know it at the time, but while he was struggling in Hollywood, his star was beginning to rise in Hong Kong. By now *The
Green Hornet* had been off the air in the United States for more
than three years, but it was still playing in Hong Kong—where it
had been renamed *The Kato Show*—and it was one of the most
popular shows on the air. Viewers in Hong Kong were thrilled that
one of their own had landed a major role in an American TV
show.

Babe Ruth's favorite radio show was *The Lone Ranger*.

When Lee took a quick trip back to Hong Kong to make arrangements for his mother to come to the United States, he was surprised to learn that he was famous there. Not only that, but two Hong Kong studios wanted to hire him to star in their movies. Lee was still determined to make it in Hollywood, but he decided that when he couldn't find work there, he'd turn to Hong Kong.

UP, UP, AND AWAY

In 1971 and '72, Lee made three films for Hong Kong's Golden Harvest Studios: *The Big Boss* (U.S. title: *Fists of Fury*), *Fist of Fury* (U.S. title: *The Chinese Connection*), and *The Way of the Dragon* (U.S. title: *Return of the Dragon*), which Lee wrote and directed himself. They were all smash hits: *The Big Boss* made $3.5 million in Hong Kong in its first 19 days alone, making it the highest-grossing film in Hong Kong history. *Fist of Fury* smashed that record by making $4 million in about the same amount of time, and *Return of the Dragon* made $5.4 million.

Now that Bruce Lee was Asia's biggest film star, Hollywood finally began to take notice. In late 1972, Warner Bros. agreed to co-produce *Enter the Dragon* with Golden Harvest Studios, the first time that a Hollywood studio had ever partnered with a Hong Kong studio to make a film.

TROUBLE

It took about 10 weeks to shoot *Enter the Dragon*. By May 1973, Lee was back in the Golden Harvest recording studio to dub the sound for the film. It was hot and humid at the studio on May 10—the air conditioners were turned off to keep the noise from interfering with the sound recording. Lee was exhausted from working nonstop on the film. At one point he excused himself and went to use the restroom. When 20 minutes passed and he didn't return, the recording crew went looking for him and found him passed out on the restroom floor. Lee regained consciousness, then passed out again and went into convulsions. The studio rushed him to the hospital, where doctors diagnosed cerebral edema (swelling of the brain). Lee made what was thought to be a full recovery, but in the weeks that followed he continued to complain of headaches.

Bad luck? At the 1978 Masters, golfer Tommy Nakajima shot a 13 on the 13th hole.

EXIT THE DRAGON

Two months later, on July 20, 1973, Lee went to the apartment of an actress named Betty Ting Pei to go over some script changes in an upcoming film called *The Game of Death*. While there, he got a headache, so Ting Pei gave him a tablet of Equagesic (a combination of aspirin and a tranquilizer called meprobamate). The 32-year-old Lee went into the bedroom to lay down and never regained consciousness.

That evening Ting Pei tried to wake him, and when she couldn't, she called for an ambulance. Lee was dead by the time he arrived at the hospital. The cause of death was ruled to be cerebral edema, this time possibly brought on by an extreme allergic reaction to the Equagesic.

Four weeks later, *Enter the Dragon* premiered in Los Angeles. It was one of the highest-grossing films of 1973. Over the years, it has gone on to earn more than $150 million, making it one of the most successful martial arts films in history.

*   *   *

MORE SPACED-OUT SPORTS

"The trouble with officials is they just don't care who wins."
—Tommy Canterbury, basketball coach

"I have a God-given talent. I got it from my dad."
—Julian Winfield, Missouri basketball player

"Ninety percent of putts that are short don't go in."
—Yogi Berra

"It was a once-in-a-lifetime catch that only happens every so often."
—Randy Moss

"I might just fade into bolivian."
—Mike Tyson

"No comment."
—Michael Jordan, on being named one of the NBA's most reporter-friendly players

Title of the movie *Slapshot* in Japan: *Roughhouse Hockey Players Who Curse a Lot and Play Dirty.*

CHILD'S PLAY

What did children do before there were TVs and computers?
These old children's games are taken from the 1920s book
Games for the Playground, Home, School and
Gymnasium, *by Jessie H. Bancroft.*

HUCKLE, BUCKLE, BEAN STALK
Number of Players: 5 to 30
How It's Played: A thimble, cork, ring, or other small object is used for hiding. All of the players leave the room save one, who places the object in plain sight but where it is unlikely to be seen, as on the top of a picture frame, in a corner on the floor, etc. It may be placed behind any other object, as long as it can be seen without moving any object.

Once the object has been placed, the players are called back to the room, and all begin to look for it. When one spies it, he does not disclose this fact, but quietly takes a seat, and says, "Huckle, buckle, bean stalk!" which indicates that he knows where the object is. The game keeps on until all of the players have located the object, or until the leader calls the hunt closed. The first one to find the object hides it for the next game.

THE MINISTER'S CAT
Number of Players: 5 or more
How It's Played: The first player says, "The minister's cat is an avaricious cat," using an adjective that begins with "a" to describe the cat. The next player makes a remark about the cat, using the same initial letter for the adjective; for instance, that it is an "aggressive" cat. This is continued, each player using a different adjective beginning with the letter "a," until the game has gone entirely around the circle. The first player then makes a similar remark about the cat, using an adjective beginning with "b." This goes around, and so on through the alphabet. Any player who fails must drop out. The player who lasts longest wins.

DUMB CRAMBO
Number of Players: 10 to 30

How It's Played: The players are divided into two parties. One party goes outside the room; those remaining choose a verb, which is to be guessed by the other party. The outside party is told a word that rhymes with the chosen verb. They consult among themselves, decide on a verb that they think may be the right one, enter the room, and without speaking, act out the verb they have guessed. The inside party must decide from this pantomime if the correct verb has been guessed. If correct, they clap their hands. If not, they shake their heads. No speaking is allowed on either side. If the outside party is wrong in their guess, they retire and try again, repeating this play until they hit on the right word, when the two sides change places.

ANIMAL BLINDMAN'S BLUFF
Number of Players: 10 to 20
How It's Played: One player is blindfolded and stands in the center of a circle with a stick or cane in his hand. The other players dance around him in a circle until he taps three times on the floor with his cane, when they must stand still. The "blindman" then points his cane at a player, who must take the opposite end of the cane in his hand. The blind man then commands him to make a noise like some animal, such as a cat, dog, cow, sheep, lion, donkey, duck, or parrot. From this the blind man tries to guess the name of the player. If the guess is correct, they change places. If wrong, the game is repeated with the same blind man.

The players should try to disguise their voices as much as possible when imitating the animals, and much sport may be had through the imitation. Players may also disguise their height, to deceive the blind man, by bending their knees to seem shorter or rising on toes to seems taller.

BLIND BANANA FEED
Number of Players: 6 to 20
How It's Played: Blindfold several couples. Give a peeled banana to each person. Have the couples clasp left hands, and at the signal to start they begin trying to feed one another. It may get messy, so it is well to provide bibs for the players by cutting a hole in a sheet of newspaper and dropping it over the head. Whichever team finishes their bananas first is the winner.

Avg. participant in fantasy football: White male, married, age 37. Household income: $78,000.

FOUL BALLS

*Lots of people go to baseball games hoping they'll
catch the next ball that gets hit into the stands.
These fans got lucky...or did they?*

The Fan: Robert Cotter, an 11-year-old boy who went to a Philadelphia Phillies game in 1922

The Catch: One of the players hit a foul ball into the stands, and Cotter managed to catch it. He wanted to keep it, but in those days baseballs were too expensive for teams to give away, so fans who caught fouls were expected to give them back. Cotter refused—even when security guards ordered him to hand the ball over. That evening, he became the first and probably the only kid in professional baseball history to spend the night in jail for refusing to give back a ball.

What Happened: The next day, Cotter was hauled before a judge, who ordered that he be set free. "Such an act on the part of a boy is merely proof that he is following his most natural impulses," the disgusted judge told the court. "It is a thing I would do myself."

Cotter never did get his ball back, but that summer he got something better: A woman in New York who read his story invited him to New York to watch the Yankees play the Philadelphia Athletics. At the game, he got an autographed baseball and even got to meet Babe Ruth.

Aftermath: As home runs became increasingly common in the 1920s, teams realized they'd have problems if they kept jailing fans who kept the balls hit into the stands. So they gave in and decided to allow the practice. Do we have Cotter to thank for it? It's hard to say—even Cotter doesn't remember. "I'm not sure if I caused that," he told *USA Today* in 1998. "I was only eleven."

The Fans: Alex Popov, a health-food restaurant owner from Berkeley, California, and Patrick Hayashi, a college student from San Diego

The Catch: In October 2001, both men were at Pac Bell Park in San Francisco when Giants slugger Barry Bonds hit his record-setting, single-season 73rd home run into the stands. A camera crew recorded the scene: the ball landed in Popov's glove and he man-

---

In golf lingo, a putt on a hilly green is called a "Dolly Parton."

aged to hang on to it for only six-tenths of a second before he was enveloped by a mob of glove-wielding fans who were also trying to catch it. Popov lost the ball. It was at this point that Hayashi says he saw the ball on the ground, grabbed it, and held it up for everyone to see. Security guards escorted him to a room where officials authenticated the ball as genuine and certified him as the owner.

It's not uncommon for home run balls to bounce from one fan to another. But Popov was adamant that the ball landed in his glove first, making him the rightful owner. When Hayashi would not give it back, Popov sued him.

What Happened: The case wasn't tried until 13 months later; then, following a two-week trial, the judge deliberated for an entire month before finally arriving at his decision: *both* claims of ownership were legitimate, so the ball would have to be sold at auction and the proceeds split evenly between them.

Aftermath: Initially, the ball was expected to fetch as much as $2 million, but by the time the lawsuit was resolved, the economy had worsened and public interest in the ball had dropped significantly. In the end it sold for only $450,000, or $225,000 each for Popov and Hayashi. How much money did Popov get for his troubles? Less than zero—in July 2003, his attorney sued him to recover $473,500 in unpaid legal bills relating to the case.

The Fan: Jay Arsenault, a construction worker from Vacaville, California

The Catch: In August 2002, three of Arsenault's buddies gave him a ticket to a Giants game at Pac Bell Park. At the time, Barry Bonds was approaching another record: he was about to become only the fourth player in pro baseball history to hit 600 home runs in his career. The friends all agreed that in exchange for giving Arsenault the ticket, if he caught the 600th ball, he would sell it and they'd all split the proceeds. Amazingly, Arsenault *did* catch the ball—but rather than honor the agreement as promised, he hid from his friends. They filed a lawsuit, claiming breach of an oral contract.

What Happened: In October, Arsenault, claiming he'd been "totally overwhelmed by the situation," backed down and agreed to sell the ball and split the money just like he'd promised. "This is better for both sides," Eric Bergen, one of the friends, told reporters. "This is what we wanted from the beginning."

Baseball Hall of Fame inductees include 227 players, 17 managers, 8 umpires, and 28 "others."

The Fan: Nick O'Brien, a four-year-old boy whose parents took him to a Texas Rangers–St. Louis Cardinals game in June 2004

The Catch: Right fielder Gary Matthews Jr. hit a foul ball into the stands. It landed at Nick's feet, but as he was reaching down to pick it up, a grown man pushed him away and grabbed the ball.

What Happened: Nick's mother, Edie O'Brien, confronted the man. "You trampled a four-year-old boy to get this ball!" she yelled at him, but he refused to give the ball back. The incident, caught on camera, was replayed on the park's giant video screens. Outraged fans started chanting "Give him the ball!" and the mood turned ugly, but still the man that the Rangers announcer called "the biggest jerk in this park" refused to give the ball back. He was literally booed out of the stands. Nick fared a little better: the Rangers invited him and his parents down to the dugout and gave him two autographed bats and four autographed balls, including one signed by Hall of Famer Nolan Ryan.

That might have been the end of it, had the *Dallas Morning News* not identified the Biggest Jerk in the Park as 28-year-old Matt Starr, a married landscaper and former youth minister living in a Dallas suburb. By Wednesday, when Nick and his mom and dad were in New York telling their story on *Good Morning America*, reporters were camped out in front of Starr's house. He was nowhere to be found.

Aftermath: Three days was all it took. On Wednesday night, Starr caved in, called the Rangers, and told them he would give the ball to Nick, along with a letter of apology and tickets to an upcoming game. "He doesn't want any more publicity about this," a Rangers spokesperson told reporters. "He's hoping this will bring some sort of closure."

*　　*　　*

FUZZY LOGIC

Q: Why are tennis balls fuzzy?

A: "The fuzz is to slow the balls down. Tennis balls are made to exacting standards so players have a decent chance of hitting them. The fuzz makes the ball softer and less bouncy and increases wind resistance. In addition, the fuzz adds control to a player's racket because the strings hold onto the surface of the ball longer." (From *Just Curious, Jeeves*, by Jack Mingo and Erin Barrett)

Q: What do basketball and ice hockey have in common? A: Both were invented by Canadians.

THE FORGOTTEN HERO OF FLAGPOLE-SITTING, PART II

Here's part II of the story of "Shipwreck Kelly," the greatest flagpole-sitter of all time who once called himself "the luckiest fool alive"—and created a sensation in the 1930s. (Part I is on page 133.)

CHILD'S PLAY

In 1929 Alvin "Shipwreck" Kelly set a "world's record" for flagpole-sitting by staying aloft 23 days at a Baltimore amusement park. When he came down, the crowd-roaring acclaim made him such a hero to the young that the whole city blossomed with juvenile pole-sitters. Boys and girls as young as eight years old took to the tops of trees and backyard poles at such a rate that in a single week reporters counted 25 young disciples of Shipwreck Kelly at roost.

As the epidemic spread, newspapers and national magazines sounded editorial alarms, and public moralists demanded a mobilization of parents to apply hairbrushes and straps to the posterior of pole-sitting young America. But for the most part, the young pole-perchers were encouraged by adults eager to share their notoriety.

RECORD BREAKER

Kelly accomplished the greatest feat of his own pole-sitting career the next summer at Atlantic City. On June 21, 1930, he climbed atop a 125-foot mast above the New Jersey shore resort's Steel Pier, hoping to stay on his 13-inch perch long enough to beat his previous record of 23 days aloft. When he had smashed the record on July 14, he decided to stay up a little longer.

He kept busy answering hundreds of fan letters basketed up to him, making nightly pole-top radio broadcasts, and sending messages down to the boardwalk crowds below to tell them how much he was enjoying the cool ocean breeze. There was more than a

In 2007 Harlequin introduced romance novels about NASCAR.

breeze at times; storm winds whipped and swayed his flagpole, and he endured thunderstorms and hail.

Finally, on August 9, he decided to come down and prepared to greet his public. A girl the *New York Times* called "one of the prettiest of barberettes" was pulled up the rope to give him a shave, haircut, and manicure.

HERO'S WELCOME

Twenty thousand cheering people were on hand when he made his slow descent that afternoon, and there was a flood of congratulatory telegrams from prominent Americans. Kelly had trouble using his feet when he first touched ground, but was able to shake hands with the official dignitaries who welcomed him back to earth and to pose for newsreel cameramen.

He had been on his flagpole for 1,177 hours, more than 49 days, which was a record nobody broke for nearly another decade. Kelly himself never equaled it again.

A MAN APART

Kelly went on flag-poling through the 1930s and into the '40s, but his fame gradually faded as a new crop of pole-sitters came along. On October 11, 1952, Kelly collapsed on the sidewalk and died of a heart attack not far from Madison Square Garden where his name had once been up in lights. Under his arm was a scrapbook of old news clippings from when he had been a headliner. In the nearby furnished room where he had been living, police found a single duffel bag of personal belongings, mostly flagpole-sitting gear.

Even in the 1970s, there were others still claiming new records, some for perching on high for as long as eight months. But many did their sitting on broad platforms, in tents, huts, and with all the conveniences of home, which Shipwreck Kelly would not have called flagpole-sitting at all.

* * *

"Sports is human life in microcosm."
—Howard Cosell

In China, American football is known as "olive ball."

ANTE UP, MOM

From Mom's Bathtub Reader, *here's a story about the high-stakes world of professional poker…and one working mother who has stood out from the crowd.*

ALL IN A DAY'S WORK

In the never-ending quest of working moms to find the best way to raise a family and earn a living, mothers have moved into such traditionally male-dominated careers as steel working, firefighting, and investment banking. But a card shark? You bet. Just ask Annie Duke, a mother of four and one of the top-rated poker players in the world.

The Bellagio, a luxury hotel in Las Vegas, features an 8.5-acre lake and more than a thousand fountains; it houses upscale stores, botanical gardens…and, of course, poker tables. Up to 40 hours a week, Annie Duke, often dressed comfortably in jeans and a T-shirt, heads off to the Bellagio, where she is one of only a handful of women who are serious contenders in the world of professional poker.

A MAN'S GAME?

The origins of the game of poker are murky. Historians have traced it back to China, Persia, Egypt, and India. Most of the versions played in the United States today are believed to have come from a "bluffing and betting" card game called *poque* that French settlers brought to New Orleans. Poque then evolved into a game that professional gamblers used to fleece travelers on the steamboats of the Mississippi River. By the time of the Civil War, poker had become a popular pastime—for men.

Today the World Poker Tour and the World Series of Poker fascinate tournament crowds and TV fans at home. And if the popularity of poker hasn't faltered since the Civil War, neither has its reputation as a man's game. So in 2000, a thirtysomething soccer mom—who was eight months pregnant—caused a sensation when she won 10th place in the World Series of Poker, the largest tournament in the world. Eight years later, she had earned more than $3.5 million. For Duke, it was just proof that the high-stakes world of poker could be a great career choice for a mother.

THE DUKES OF VEGAS

Good money, job flexibility, time for her kids…playing poker is a dream job for Duke, who came to her unusual profession in the usual way: by having to juggle marriage and kids when she badly needed money. But card playing runs in her family.

Duke grew up on the grounds of a boarding school in New Hampshire where her father taught English. Card games and chess were family obsessions, and poker was one of their favorite games. Annie's older brother, Howard, dropped out of college to play chess, but he eventually became a professional gambler. Now he's also one of the world's leading poker players.

Annie stayed in school and attended Columbia University, where she was a member of its first coed class, and then went on to study psychology at the University of Pennsylvania. She was finishing up her PhD in 1992 when she realized that she didn't want to spend the rest of her life in academia. With a boldness that would eventually serve her well at the poker tables, Annie proposed to her boyfriend, Ben, who said yes. The two married and went to live in Montana.

There, with jobs few and far between, Annie called her brother Howard and asked him to teach her to play poker. She did so well at it that she and her growing family eventually moved to Las Vegas. Her husband, who ran an investment business from home, agreed to take on the child-care chores when she was away at the casino…and the rest, as they say, is poker history.

STRAIGHT FLUSHES, STRAIGHT PRIORITIES

Nowadays, Annie Duke has had so much success that she can afford to skip a few tournaments. For one thing, she refuses to play in women's tournaments, saying, "Poker is one of the few sports where a woman can compete on a totally equal footing with a man, so I don't understand why there's a ladies-only tournament."

Another one she missed was a prestigious tournament with a six-figure prize. Why? It was on the same day as her daughter's sixth birthday party. "I didn't care what kind of money was at stake…I'm not missing that party," she later said. "When she's 25 and in therapy, she's going to be talking about how I missed her birthday party."

Who were the Blondes and the Brunettes? The first paid all-female baseball teams (1875).

FAMOUS FOR 15 MINUTES

Here it is again—our feature based on Andy Warhol's prophetic remark that "in the future, everyone will be famous for 15 minutes." Here's how a few sporting folks have used up their allotted quarter-hour.

THE STAR: Daron Malmborg, a Utah motorist

THE HEADLINE: *Vanity Plate Injures Utah's Vanity*

WHAT HAPPENED: In 1999 it was disclosed that Salt Lake City officials had given cash and other gifts to members of the International Olympic Committee, trying to secure the 2002 Olympics for their city. Outraged, Malmborg ordered commemorative "Olympics" license plates for his car…and customized the tag number to read "SCNDL."

Malmborg had the special plates for 11 months when he received a letter from the Department of Motor Vehicles, ordering him to give them back. Malmborg's lawyer—license plate "ISUE4U"—referred him to the American Civil Liberties Union, which took the case public.

THE AFTERMATH: The Associated Press picked up on the story, and it became fodder for TV and radio talk-show hosts all over the country. Ultimately, the state backed down and let Malmborg keep his plates. According to press reports, "'SCNDL' was Malmborg's second choice for the plate. His first—'BRIBE'—was turned down because someone else already had it."

THE STAR: James Miller, Las Vegas resident and self-proclaimed "fan man"

THE HEADLINE: *Man Floats Like Butterfly into Boxing Ring… Gets Stung Like a Bee*

WHAT HAPPENED: Professional boxers Riddick Bowe and Evander Holyfield were in the middle of their heavyweight title fight on November 6, 1993, when the TV blimp noticed a man with a paraglider (a small parachute-glider) flying about 800 feet over the Caesar's Palace outdoor pavilion. The man circled for about 20 minutes, then suddenly plunged into the ring, stopping the fight.

Ancient Rome's Circus Maximus (for horse and chariot racing) could hold up to 250,000 people.

The fight was delayed for 21 minutes while security officials tackled the man and carried him away on a hospital gurney as he shouted repeatedly, "I'm the fan man, the man with the fan." Reverend Jesse Jackson and Louis Farrakhan of the Nation of Islam were sitting so close to the spot he landed that they became entangled in the parachute lines and might have been injured had they not gotten out of the way in time.

THE AFTERMATH: Miller was arrested again on January 9, 1994, after he circled the Los Angeles Coliseum during a Raiders-Broncos playoff game…and was arrested a third time on February 5, 1994, when he paraglided onto the roof of Buckingham Palace, stripped off his flight suit, and taunted police in the nude as they scrambled to arrest him.

THE STAR: Danny Almonte, 12-year-old pitcher for the Rolando Paulino All-Stars Little League team in the Bronx

THE HEADLINE: *Little League Champ Pitches Perfect Game; Too Bad He's Not as Little as His Parents Say He Is*

WHAT HAPPENED: Almonte became an instant celebrity after he pitched a no-hitter in the opening game of the Little League World Series, the first since 1957. His major league heroes, Randy Johnson and Ken Griffey Jr., called to congratulate him, and New York mayor Rudolph Giuliani gave the entire team the key to the city.

But there was trouble brewing: For months, Almonte had been dogged by rumors that he was actually 14, not 12, which would have made him ineligible to play in Little League. Two rival teams even hired private investigators to look into the rumors, but it wasn't until *Sports Illustrated* obtained a birth certificate that showed Danny was born on April 7, 1987, not April 7, 1989, as his parents claimed, that things started to unravel. Dominican government officials confirmed the authenticity of the certificate, just as investigators in the United States discovered that 14-year-old Danny not only wasn't enrolled in school as his father claimed—a violation of the law—but that he and his father were in the country illegally, on expired tourist visas.

THE AFTERMATH: Danny's father was banned for life from any association with Little League; so was team founder Rolando Paulino. The team was stripped of their third-place title in the

Little League World Series, and all of their records—including Almonte's no-hitter—were expunged from the Little League record book. About the only thing the team didn't lose was its key to the city of New York—Mayor Giuliani said he wouldn't ask for it back, explaining that "it would only add to the hurt and the pain that the innocent children of this team are experiencing." As of 2008, Almonte was pitching and playing right field for Western Oklahoma State University.

THE STAR: Rollin Stewart, a.k.a. Rainbow Man
THE HEADLINE: *Clown-Wigged Crusader Says: John 3:16!*
WHAT HAPPENED: During a 1976 trip to Mardi Gras, Stewart had a vision. It told him to take a sign that read "John 3:16" (a passage in the Bible) to nationally televised sporting events and wave it for the television cameras while wearing a rainbow-colored clown wig.

"I wanted to go into show business," he explained a few years later, "and I got this idea for a character who could be a people pleaser. My ultimate goal was to be an actor and spend an occasional day shooting a commercial, then sit back and collect the residual checks."

Stewart never made much money off of his clown-wig crusade for Christ, but by 1980, the year he gave up the sign, he'd become one of the most recognized figures in the sports world, even if nobody knew who he was.

AFTERMATH: Stewart couldn't bear to be out of the limelight. He blew an air horn on the 16th green of the 1991 Masters Tournament, set off some stink bombs in Robert Schuller's Crystal Cathedral during a service, and then did it again during the title fight between Evander Holyfield and George Foreman. His final "stunt" was in 1992, when, brandishing a .45-caliber assault rifle, he barricaded himself in a hotel room near the L.A. International Airport and threatened to shoot down arriving jumbo jets "if he wasn't given three hours of network television prime time to offer his views of world politics, the weather situation, and the Second Coming of Jesus." The siege ended when a SWAT team broke down the door and took him into custody. Today Stewart is serving three concurrent life sentences in the California prison system.

THE MAN IN THE MASK

*Classical Greco-Roman wrestling can trace its roots all
the way back to the ancient Greeks and Romans. But what
about "professional" wrestling—the kind where costumed
buffoons hit each other with folding chairs? How
old is that? Older than you might think.*

WORLD-CLASS WRESTLING

In 1915 some fight promoters organized an international wrestling tournament at the Opera House in New York. A rising American star named Ed "Strangler" Lewis headlined a roster of other top grapplers from Russia, Germany, Italy, Greece, and other countries. These were some of the biggest matches to be fought in New York City that year.

There was just one problem: almost nobody went to see them.

HO-HUM

Wrestling, at least as it was fought back then, could be pretty boring for the average person to watch. As soon as the bell rang or the whistle was blown, the two wrestlers grabbed onto each other and then might circle round…and round…and round for hours on end, until one wrestler finally gained an advantage and defeated his opponent. Some bouts dragged on for nine hours or more.

Wrestling could also be hard to understand, which made it even more boring. In baseball, an outfielder either caught a fly ball or he didn't. In football, the person with the ball either got tackled or he didn't. Wrestling was different—when two grapplers circled for hours, who could tell at any point in the match who was winning? Did anyone even care?

Even by wrestling standards, 1915 was a particularly boring year because the world's youngest and best wrestlers were all off fighting in World War I. Those that were left were often past their prime and not very entertaining. Not surprisingly, the organizers of the tournament at the Opera House were having trouble filling seats. For the first day or two, it looked like they were going to lose a lot of money.

For the first day or two.

MYSTERY MAN

Things were about to change, thanks to one spectator. He was huge, but he didn't stand out just because of his size—he stood out because he was wearing a black mask that covered his entire head. There was no explanation for what the man was doing there or why he was wearing the mask. He just sat there watching the matches each day, and when they ended, he left as silently as he came.

Then, a few days into the tournament, the masked man and a companion suddenly stood up and loudly accused the promoters of banning the masked man from the tournament. He was the best wrestler of all and the promoters knew it, they claimed. That was why he was being kept out of the tournament, and they demanded that he be let back in. Security guards quickly hustled the pair out of the building, but they came back each day and repeated their demands, generating newspaper headlines in the process. By the end of the week, much of New York City was demanding that the masked man be allowed into the tournament.

OH, ALL RIGHT

Finally, on Saturday, the promoters gave in to the pressure and agreed to let him compete. Just days earlier, some of the world's most famous wrestlers had battled one another in a nearly empty Opera House. Now throngs of New Yorkers ponied up the price of admission to watch the mysterious masked man fight, even though—or more likely *because*—they had no idea who he was or whether he even knew how to fight.

Sure enough, the masked man delivered—although not quite as much as he promised, because he lost one match and only wrestled "Strangler" Lewis to a draw. But he whipped everyone else he wrestled, bringing the packed tournament to a thrilling end. After all the hype leading up to those final bouts, the spectators left satisfied.

MYSTERY REVEALED

The following year, the Masked Marvel was officially *unmasked* after losing a match with a wrestler named Joe Stecher. He turned out to be...Mort Henderson, a railroad detective from Altoona, Pennsylvania, who made his living throwing hobos off trains when

---

"Accordion" to historians, the first song written about baseball was "The Baseball Polka" (1858).

he wasn't in the ring. Henderson had wrestled for years under his own name, but he lost many of his matches and had gone nowhere in the sport. Even when he wasn't wearing a mask, nobody knew who he was.

So how did Henderson do so well at the Opera House? The whole thing was a setup—the promoters planted him in the audience, hoping that he would generate publicity and sell tickets. The other wrestlers were in on the scam, too; that was how he won so many fights.

Many New Yorkers realized that they'd been had, but nobody seemed to mind. The Masked Marvel was *fun*.

FROM SPECTACLE...TO SPORT...TO SPECTACLE

Wrestling had long been full of colorful characters. After all, legitimate professional wrestling traced its roots back to the days when carnival strongmen traveled the country offering cash prizes to any locals who could pin them to the mat.

By 1915 wrestling had matured into a legitimate sport, a test of strength and skill, not quite as exciting as boxing but still a sport that took itself seriously. Mort Henderson could not have realized it at the time, but on the day he donned his mask the first time in 1915, he changed professional wrestling forever. It was "at this point," Keith Greenberg writes in *Pro Wrestling: From Carnivals to Cable TV*, "promoters began copying techniques from vaudeville to keep spectators interested."

PUTTING ON A SHOW

And that vaudeville connection is no coincidence. A lot of the credit for changing pro wrestling into what it is today goes to a former vaudeville promoter named Joseph "Toots" Mondt. He saw wrestlers as theatrical performers, and their matches as just another act to be managed so that profits were maximized.

Rather than let a match run on for hours, he set time limits, which allowed him to book more fights back to back. His traveling troupe of wrestlers fought the same fights—with the same rigged outcomes—in every town they visited. Since the wrestlers didn't have to focus on winning, they were free to thrill audiences with moves like flying drop kicks, airplane spins, and leaps across the ring feet-first to kick opponents in the chest.

At 200 mph, an Indy car driver can cover the length of a football field in less than one second.

Landing fake body blows like these—ones that appeared devastating without actually causing serious physical harm—was elevated to a fine art. "When a grappler threw a punch, he tried to connect using a forearm instead of a fist, softening the blow," Greenberg writes. "A man diving on a foe from the ropes actually grazed the man with a knee or elbow, rather than landing on him directly and causing injury."

ONE-RING CIRCUS

The next big wave of innovation came during the Great Depression of the 1930s, when dwindling ticket sales forced promoters to resort to even greater gimmickry to draw crowds. Wrestlers assumed false ethnic identities so that blue-collar immigrants could root for someone of their own ethnic group, and also to capitalize on whatever geopolitical goings-on might make for an interesting villain. Evil German counts and Japanese generals were popular during World War II; in peacetime, crazy hillbillies and snooty English lords filled the bill, grappling with the noble Indian chiefs and scrappy Irish brawlers that the audiences loved.

Wrestlers fought tag-team matches. They battled it out in cages. They wrestled while chained together. They fought in rings filled with mud (of course) as well as ice cream, berries, molasses, and other gooey substances. Women wrestled. Midgets wrestled. Giants wrestled. Morbidly obese people wrestled, and so did people with disfiguring diseases. Maurice Tillet, the French Angel, suffered from a glandular disease called *acromegaly* that gave him enlarged, distorted facial features. He was such a successful villain that he spawned a host of imitators, including the Swedish Angel, the Golden Angel, the Polish Angel, and the Czech Angel, a number of whom suffered from the same disease.

OLD SCHOOL

What happened to the "genuine" professional wrestlers, the guys who refused to showboat and took their sport seriously? They continued to wrestle one another in honest matches for legitimate championship titles. In 1920, for example, Ed "Strangler" Lewis won a world championship match against Joe Stecher in a three-hour-long bout; he held the title off and on for the next 13 years.

Humphrey Bogart's first line as an actor: "Tennis, anyone?"

After that the title turned over several times before it passed to a wrestler named Lou Thesz, who would win and lose it several times into the 1950s.

Not that anyone cared. Thesz wasn't above a little showmanship—his specialty holds were the "kangaroo" and the "airplane Spin"—but "there was little interest in the championship among the public," Graeme Kent writes in A *Pictorial History of Wrestling.* "This was mainly because Thesz scorned gimmicks, relying on his wrestling ability to carry him through."

STAY TUNED...

Yet it was a gimmick at the end of World War II that would provide the biggest boost to professional wrestling. The emerging medium of TV—and a wrestling innovator called Gorgeous George—helped bring wrestling into American living rooms.

The Masked Marvel was responsible for turning wrestling from a sport into a spectacle, but Gorgeous George deserves the credit for bringing professional wrestling into full bloom. That story is on page 451.

That story is on page 451.

* * *

INSTANT CLIMBER

"Alain Robert, the French 'spider-man' famous for climbing the Eiffel Tower and Empire State Building, walked away from China's 88-story Jinmao Tower—too risky. In February 2001, Han Qizhi, a 31-year-old shoe salesman, just happened to be passing the popular landmark and was 'struck by a rash impulse.' When security guards weren't looking, Han, who had never climbed before, launched himself upon the skyscraper and began to climb. 'He walked around Jinmao a couple of times, told his colleague he was going up, dropped his jacket, and started climbing,' said a police spokesman. Han, bare-handed and dressed in ordinary street clothes, was grabbed by policemen just short of the summit."

—Reuters

Bare fact: *Gymnastics* is from a Greek word meaning "to exercise naked."

NOT-SO-DUMB JOCKS

Okay, okay. They're not all dumb. Here are some genuinely clever remarks from America's sports stars.

"I knew it was going to be a long season when, on opening day during the national anthem, one of my players turns to me and says, 'Every time I hear that song, I have a bad game.'"

—**Baseball manager Jim Leyland**

"I'm the most loyal player money can buy."

—**Don Sutton**

"Once you put it down, you can't pick it up."

—**Pat Williams, NBA executive, on Charles Barkley's autobiography**

"I thought I'd be shot or hung by the time I was 40 anyway, so it's no big deal."

—**Bill Parcels, on his 53rd birthday**

"It's called an eraser."

—**Arnold Palmer, on how to take strokes off your golf game**

"You win some, lose some, and wreck some."

—**NASCAR driver Dale Earnhardt**

"It was a cross between a screwball and a change-up—a screw-up."

—**Cubs reliever Bob Patterson, on one that was hit out of the park**

"In 1962 I was voted Minor League Player of the Year. Unfortunately, that was my second year in the majors."

—**Bob Uecker**

"At first, I said, 'Let's play for taxes.'"

—**Michael Jordan, on playing golf with President Clinton**

"If he was on fire, he couldn't act as if he were burning."

—**Shaquille O'Neal, on Dennis Rodman's acting ability**

"[Tommy] Morrison proved that he is an ambidextrous fighter. He can get knocked out with either hand."

—**Boxing expert Bert Sugar**

"It's been a very good year. Excuse me, it's been a very fine year."

—**Indy car driver Scott Pruett, whose sponsor was Firestone**

Kayaking is a required subject in Greenland's schools.

THE VIDEO GAME HALL OF FAME

Today most video games are played in the home, but in the 1970s and 1980s, if you wanted to play the newest, hottest games, you went to an arcade. Here are the stories of a few of the classics we played back in the golden age of arcade games.

SPACE INVADERS (Taito, 1978)

Object: Using a laser cannon that you scroll back and forth across the bottom of the screen, defend yourself from wave after wave of aliens descending from the top of the screen.

Origin: Space Invaders started out as a test that was used to measure the skill of computer programmers, but someone decided that it might also work well as an arcade game. They were right—the game became a national craze in Japan.

Introduced to the U.S. market by Midway in October 1978, Space Invaders became the biggest hit of the year. It made so much money—a single unit could earn back its $1,700 purchase price in as little as four weeks—that it helped arcade games break out of arcades and smoky bars into nontraditional venues like supermarkets, restaurants, and movie theater lobbies.

TEMPEST (Atari, 1981)

Object: Shoot the moving shapes—red brackets, green spikes, yellow lines, and multicolored balls—before they climb up and out of the geometrically shaped "well" they're in and get you.

Origin: Atari game designer Dave Theurer needed an idea for a new video game, so he went to the company's book of potential themes compiled from brainstorming sessions. The idea he chose to develop was "First Person Space Invaders"—Space Invaders as seen from the perspective of the laser cannon at the bottom of the screen.

Theurer created a game and showed it to his superiors...and they told him to dump it unless he could "do something special with it." Theurer told them about a nightmare he'd had about monsters climbing out of a hole in the ground and coming to get him. "I can put it on a flat surface and wrap that surface around to

---

Karate was invented in India. It was not introduced to Japan until about 1917.

make a cylinder, and rotate the cylinder," Theurer suggested. As he conceived it, the cylinder would move while the player stood still…but he abandoned that idea when the rotating cylinder started giving players motion sickness. "I switched it so the player moved around," Theurer says. "That fixed it."

PAC-MAN (Namco, 1980)

Object: Maneuver Pac-Man through a maze and eat all 240 dots without getting caught by one of the four "ghosts"—Inky, Blinky, Pinky, and Clyde.

Origin: In 1979 a game designer named Toru Iwatani decided to make a game that would appeal to women, who were less interested in violent, shoot-the-alien games like Space Invaders. Iwatani thought that eating things on the computer screen would make a good nonviolent alternative to shooting them. He came up with the idea for the Pac-Man character over lunch. "I was having pizza," he says. "I took one wedge and there it was, the figure of Pac-Man." Well, almost: Pac-Man was originally supposed to be called Puck-Man, because the main character was round like a hockey puck…but the name was changed to Pac-Man because Namco officials "worried about American vandals changing the 'P' to an 'F'."

DONKEY KONG (Nintendo, 1980)

Object: Save the girl from the giant ape.

Origin: One of Nintendo's first video games was a Space Invaders knockoff called Radarscope. It flopped in the United States, nearly bankrupting the distributor—who wanted to stop doing business with Nintendo. What could Nintendo do? They promised to ship new chips to American distributors so the unsold Radarscope games could be turned into new games.

There was just one problem—they didn't have any new game chips. So Nintendo president Hiroshi Yamauchi told the company's staff artist, Shigeru Miyamoto, to come up with something *fast.*

Miyamoto had never made a game before, and he hated tennis games, shooting games, and most games that were popular at the time. So he invented a game about a janitor who has to rescue his girlfriend from his pet ape, who has taken her to the top of a construction site. Miyamoto wanted to name the game after the ape, so he looked up the words for "stubborn" and "ape" in his Japanese/English dictionary... and found the words "donkey" and "Kong." Donkey Kong went on to become one of the most successful video games in history, giving Nintendo the boost it needed to build itself into a multibillion-dollar company and an international video game juggernaut. And it might never have happened if Radarscope hadn't failed.

DEFENDER (Williams Electronics, 1980)

Object: Use your spacecraft to shoot hostile aliens while saving humanoids from being kidnapped and turned into mutants.

Origin: Another game helped along by a dream: Defender was supposed to make its debut at the 1980 Amusement & Music Operators of America (AMOA) convention, but less than two weeks before his deadline, creator Eugene Jarvis had only the rough outlines of a game—the name "Defender" and a spaceship attacking aliens, all against a planetary backdrop dotted with humanoids who didn't really do anything. What was the defender defending?

"The answer came to him in a dream," Nick Montfort writes in *Supercade.* "Those seemingly pointless little men, trapped on the surface below, *they* were the ones to be defended."

Jarvis made his deadline, but the AMOA was afraid the game was too complicated. They were wrong. Defender became one of the most popular games of the year and made so much money that in 1981 the AMOA voted it Video Game of the Year.

LEGENDARY FLOP: LUNAR LANDER (Atari, 1979)

Object: Find a flat spot on the lunar surface and use your booster engines to slow your spaceship (without running out of fuel) and land it safely on the moon.

Origin: The game was adapted from a computer simulation used in college physics courses to teach students about lunar gravity. Atari had high hopes for the game, even designing a special two-handled lever that controlled the booster engines. It flopped. So did the special lever: "Springs on the lever made it snap back in place when it was released," Steven Kent writes in *The Ultimate History of Video Games.* "Unfortunately, some younger players got their faces too close to the lever, resulting in complaints about children being hit in the face."

No clue-ba: Kent Kluba is the only golfer ever to get lost during a tournament.

THE GREAT POZO

Even if the cards are stacked against you,
you have to play the hand you were dealt.

HUMBLE BEGINNINGS

Born May 5, 1977, into an impoverished family in Ghana, Emmanuel Ofusu Yeboah seemed cursed. As soon as his father saw the boy's hopelessly deformed right leg (he was born without a shinbone), he thought it was a punishment from a deity and ran away. Neighbors advised Emmanuel's mother to "see him off," which in Ghanian tradition means to leave the child to die in the forest.

It would have been considered an acceptable choice. Two million people in the West African nation—about 10 percent of the population—are disabled and shunned by society, victims of centuries-old prejudice that considers them mistakes of nature and unfit to live. And if they survive childhood, the disabled in Ghana can look forward only to a life as beggars on the streets.

But Emmanuel's mother, Comfort Yeboah, refused to get rid of her child. Her faith in her firstborn son was so great that she did the unthinkable: she enrolled him in school. In Ghana, as in many developing countries, education is so valuable that it is reserved for those children thought capable of using it to make a better future for their family. To send a disabled child to school was to waste a precious resource. But except for his leg, Emmanuel was perfectly abled—he was smart, strong, and physically fit. So Comfort persisted.

STUBBORN

Following his mother's lead, Emmanuel refused to resign himself to being a beggar. Every day before school, he worked shining shoes for pennies a day. When his mother became sick and could no longer work, Emmanuel left school and worked full-time, becoming the sole breadwinner of his family. It was hard, but he still refused to become a beggar.

In 1991, desperate to find better work, Emmanuel moved to

Polo players are not allowed to play left-handed—it's too dangerous.

Accra, Ghana's capital, 200 miles from his village. Alone and just 14, he witnessed for the first time the harsh reality of being disabled in Ghana. He saw that the disabled could earn as much as $10 a day if they would crawl through the filthy streets, begging for coins. But Emmanuel was determined to work for a living. He found a job making shoes that paid him $2 a day. He kept only what he needed to survive, and sent the rest back to his family.

Meanwhile, his mother grew weaker and weaker. During a phone call in 1997, she reminded him that his life was a gift and that "disability is not inability." She made him promise once again that he would never become a beggar. The next day, Comfort Yeboah died.

A NEW PATH

Strengthened by his mother's dying words, Emmanuel decided to do something for the disabled in Ghana. To raise public awareness, he would ride a bicycle across the country. He needed a special bike, which he got from the Challenged Athletes Foundation in San Diego, California. "I want to ride a bicycle across Ghana," he wrote to them, "to create a brighter future for the disabled."

In July 2002, he made the trip, pedaling a mountain bike with one leg all the way across Ghana. Throughout his journey, he wore a shirt emblazoned with the words "The Pozo," slang for "The Cripple." "I want to send a message to change perceptions," he said. "The only way to do that is by example." His example worked. The Ghanian media covered his ride and dubbed him "the Great Pozo." Soon people all over Ghana were talking about the plight of the disabled and how perceptions had to change. Emmanuel had become a national hero.

Within a year, he become an international advocate for the disabled. He competed in two triathlons in the United States, received a prosthetic limb from Loma Linda University Medical Hospital (they amputated his bad leg below the knee), was the recipient of more than $50,000 in grant money to continue his work, and, in a world where mobility is paramount to success, distributed more than 250 wheelchairs to the disabled back home in Ghana. He continues to be an example, working to help others like him live their lives with dignity.

The 1900 Olympic Games included croquet, fishing, billiards, and checkers.

THE BIRTH OF THE NFL, PART I

On page 294, we tell you about the first professional football player. Here's the story of the NFL—how it went from a ragtag league of misfits to a multibillion-dollar enterprise.

THE FIRST NFL
By the turn of the 20th century, it was clear that professional football was more than a passing fad. Pro teams were popping up in gritty industrial towns in Pennsylvania, New York, Ohio, and Rhode Island. Many were sponsored by steel mills, coal mines, or other businesses to provide a Sunday afternoon diversion on their employees' one day off. These teams usually lost money.

In 1902 David Berry, owner of the Pittsburgh Stars, announced he was forming what he called the "National Football League." It failed miserably, folding within a year.

What went wrong?

• First, only three teams, all from Pennsylvania, joined the new league. Teams from New York and Chicago declined, figuring that fans were more interested in local rivalries.

• Second, pro football's image was at an all-time low. The play was slow, mostly defensive; the players were violent; the games often ended in riots; and the teams were corrupt because big-time gamblers bought out coaches and players.

• The more "refined" games of baseball, golf, and tennis were gaining in stature.

ADDING DIGNITY
In 1915 Jim Thorpe, the nation's most famous athlete, joined the Canton Bulldogs. In addition to being a gold-medal Olympian and champion baseball player, Thorpe conducted himself with a quiet dignity that people looked up to. His addition to pro football gave it some credibility, but it still didn't have much of a following outside of a team's local community.

After World War I, a new attempt was made to form a national

A 1989 PGA study found that touring golf pros make only 54.8% of their 6-foot putts.

league. On September 17, 1920, four team owners met in a Hup-mobile auto dealership in Canton, Ohio, and voted to form what became known as the American Professional Football Association (APFA). Over the next six weeks, they persuaded ten other teams from Ohio, Indiana, Illinois, and New York to join. Jim Thorpe was appointed president, not because he was an experienced man-ager (he wasn't), but because his name generated headlines and gave the new league credibility.

IF AT FIRST...

Like its predecessor, the new league was troubled from the start. They could pay players about $150 per game (not much by today's standards), and the players still had to supply their own protective gear. The game itself was still slow; once a team got a touchdown, they tried to stall for the rest of the game to make it stand. And few fans showed up: the average game that first 1920 season attracted only 3,000 fans—less than a tenth the size of a good col-lege football crowd. Three teams—the Cleveland Tigers, the Detroit Heralds, and the Muncie Flyers—folded after one season; the rest struggled to survive. There was little indication that these working-class teams, who played for money, would one day eclipse the noble college teams, who played for the enjoyment of the sport.

After one year as president of the APFA, Jim Thorpe declined to run for reelection. Joe Carr, manager of the Columbus Panhan-dles, was forced into the job. Although Carr had been involved with football since forming a team in 1904, he had only a fifth-grade education and showed no interest in running the league. But the other APFA members felt that as the manager with the most football experience, Carr was the best candidate, so they waited for him to leave the room and then elected him president without his consent. That turned out to be one of the best things that ever happened to professional football.

TURNING IT AROUND

If he was going to be president, Carr figured he ought to try to improve the game's image, so he made some changes.
• In 1921 his office began releasing official weekly standings of each team in the league so that fans could keep track of how well their teams were doing.

Though only 11 players are allowed on the field at once, a pro football team...

- He assigned each team a geographic territory, then declared it off-limits to all of the other APFA franchises so teams wouldn't drive each other out of business by fighting over the same fans.
- Carr outlawed the practice of hiring college undergraduates to play for pro teams under assumed names. Using ringers was a tempting prospect both for the teams, who needed the talent, and for student athletes, who needed the cash (and had nothing else to do on Sunday afternoons). It drove college coaches crazy.
- In 1922 Carr instituted a standard player's contract (with a reserve clause that gave a player's current team first dibs on him the following season) and capped salaries at $1,200 per game. Both measures helped control costs, which helped strengthen the league.
- The APFA made one other significant change in 1922: they voted to change their name to the National Football League.

RED GRANGE

Thanks to Carr's reforms, this second NFL looked like it might last a little longer than the first one had, but pro football still needed a lot of help. Mostly, it needed more star players to get fans into the stands. It needed Harold "Red" Grange. He'd become famous playing halfback for the University of Illinois. His uncanny ability to dart and weave his way downfield past his opponents made Grange the best player of his day. Fans called him "the Galloping Ghost."

The newly formed Chicago Bears, coached by George Halas, signed Grange in 1925 for the last two games of the season. The first was against the Chicago Cardinals. Bears-Cardinals games usually attracted 10,000 fans, but with Grange on the field they drew 39,000, by far the largest crowd for a pro game to date. That record fell one week later when 70,000 people turned out to watch Grange and the Bears play the New York Giants. (In a sign of things to come, the following day Grange signed an estimated $125,000 worth of commercial endorsement deals.)

A successful 12-day exhibition tour followed, in which Grange and the Bears played eight teams from eight different cities. (They won the first four but were so exhausted that they lost the last four.) But what mattered most was that pro football was finally on the map. The Bears made an estimated $297,000 in 1925, up from $116,500 the year before; and the New York Giants, who were $40,000 in debt and close to collapse when Grange and the Bears rolled into town, ended the season with $18,000 in the bank. By attracting attention to the struggling Giants, Grange is credited with single-handedly saving the franchise.

THE STRUGGLE CONTINUES

But Grange couldn't single-handedly save the NFL, which was still in trouble. Sure, the games he played in drew fans, but others were still sparsely attended. To make matters worse, Grange left the Bears and formed his own team after contract negotiations with the Bears broke down (he wanted a one-third ownership stake in the team). The new team was called the New York Yankees, but the NFL denied admission to them because there already was a football team in New York. So Grange formed a new league, the American Football League, which fared about as poorly as the first NFL and folded after a season. But the NFL also had a tough year without Grange as a draw, so they let the Yankees join in 1927. (The football Yankees folded a year later; Grange played the rest of his Hall of Fame career with the Bears.)

So that saved football, right? Wrong. Teams were still losing money and fans were losing interest. The style of play was more defensive than ever, which resulted in low-scoring games being played in cold, empty stadiums—one bad-weather game in New York drew exactly 83 fans.

And then came the Great Depression, which hit hardest against the working-class fan base that was the backbone of the professional leagues. Hardly anyone could afford the 50 cents it cost to see a game, least of all in the smaller cities, where many teams were located. By 1932 the NFL was down to eight teams.

It was time for yet another man to swoop in and save professional football from itself.

Illegal man downfield—five-yard penalty! Turn to page 431 and read Part II.

*   *   *

"You have to play this game like somebody just hit your mother with a two-by-four."
　　　　　　　　　　　—defensive lineman Dan Birdwell

Cuba has won three Olympic gold medals in baseball, the United States one.

HOW TO BECOME A GOLF PRO

You've got game…so how do you get a "Tour Card"?

GETTING CARDED
The most coveted item for a wannabe professional golfer: an official PGA Tour Card. Tiger has one, Phil has one, Vijay has one, and it allows them to be one of the 150 to 180 golfers who get to compete in the big tournaments on TV. So if you're a very good golfer and think you can play with the big boys, how do you get your first card? There are several ways:

• Special exemptions—an invitation; a free pass

• Open qualifying

• **The Nationwide Tour**—the PGA's minor leagues

• **PGA Tour Qualifying School**—the dreaded "Q School"

Here are some of the details:

SPECIAL EXEMPTIONS

There are 34 different "exemption" categories for playing on the PGA Tour. Most of them apply to established pros. For example, if you finish in the top 125 on the money list, you're automatically "exempt" for all the PGA Tour events the following year—you get to keep your card. But some, such as the sponsor exemptions, make it possible for nonmembers to play with the pros. Here are two "special" categories:

Sponsor Exemptions. Sponsors of PGA Tour events (Buick at the Buick Open, Bell South at the Bell South Classic, etc.) are allowed to hand out four spots to whomever they choose. Just write them a letter and ask for one. The only requirement: you must have a registered USGA handicap index of zero (not just *any* hack can play with the pros). You're allowed to play in up to seven tournaments per season this way, and if in those seven tournaments you win enough prize money to end up in the top 125 on the year's money list, you're officially a member of the Tour for the

---

Arnold Palmer owned over 1,500 putters.

following year. That's a tough challenge, considering that you have to do it in seven tournaments while the average pro is playing in 25. But there's another way to do it: if you happen to win just one of those seven events, you're exempt for the rest of that year and get a PGA Tour card for the next two years. Some people who did it this way:

• Tiger Woods and Phil Mickelson both got their first cards by playing on sponsor exemptions and winning a tournament.

• Up-and-coming stars Matt Kuchar, Charles Howell III, and Hank Kuehne all got their first Tour Cards by playing sponsor exemptions and making the top 125 on the money list.

• The most amazing example: 24-year-old Jim Benepe from Sheridan, Wyoming, got a last-minute sponsor exemption at the 1988 Western Open. He had never played in a PGA tournament before…but he won. The virtual unknown was exempt for the full PGA Tour for the next two years. (It's still the only time anybody has won a PGA event on the first attempt.)

Foreign Exemptions. There are also foreign exemptions for tournaments. The PGA commissioner selects two international golfers per tournament to receive them. But even if you're good enough to get the exemption, that just gets you into the tournaments—you have to do the rest. In 2002 Argentinean Angel Cabrera, already a member of the European PGA, used both foreign and sponsor exemptions to play in as many U.S. tournaments as possible and to make as much money as possible to avoid having to go through Q School. In April he finished ninth at the Masters, bringing his season earnings up to $468,394. That was more than the player at number 125 on the money list in the previous year—another of the 34 exemption categories—and that got him his Tour Card for 2003. He was in.

QUALIFYING

Major Open Qualifying. Two of golf's four major tournaments are restricted—the PGA Championship is for pros only and the Masters is by invitation. The other two majors are not restricted. The "Open" in "U.S. Open" and "British Open" means exactly that: anybody, pro or amateur, with a USGA handicap not higher than 1.4 can attempt to qualify. Not *all* the spots are open, however, since many pros automatically qualify, but there are quite a few. At the 2004 U.S. Open, 76 pros were automatically in, which left 80 spots open to anybody else. More than 7,000 golfers from around the world—including a 13-year-old and an 81-year-old—tried to qualify for those spots. You want in? Show proof of your handicap, pony up the $125 entry fee…and then play some really good golf.

But if you do get in and you play well, you could be set for a long time. The top 10 finishers in the U.S. Open automatically get a full Tour Card for the following year. And if you *win* either the U.S or British Open, you not only get the prize money, you're also fully exempt on the PGA Tour for the next five years.

Some major Open qualifiers who did pretty well:

• Ken Venturi won the U.S. Open as a qualifier in 1964.

• Orville Moody did the same in 1969. At the time, winning a major meant a lifetime Tour Card. (Not anymore—today it's good for a five-year exemption.)

• The last qualifier to win the U.S. Open: Steve Jones in 1996.

Monday Qualifying. Many PGA Tour events have an 18-hole qualifying round played the Monday before the event. A maximum of about 150 nonmember golfers are accepted; the top four get in. This used to be a fairly common way to fill out a field—tournaments accepted a lot more than four in the old days—and there was even a name for golfers who did it regularly: "rabbits" (because they jumped from event to event all over the country, usually living in their cars along the way). But the game, the money, and the number of stars grew, and today there are only four open spots per tournament (and not even for *every* tournament).

To use Monday qualifying to get a Tour Card, you must prove your handicap, pay a $400 entry fee, qualify for enough tournaments—and then do well. As with sponsor or foreign exemptions, you have to win enough money to make the top 125. Or you can enter just one tournament and win it, which gets you a two-year exemption. How often does a rabbit get on the Tour? Almost never:

• In 1986 Kenny Knox made it to the Honda Classic as one of the four Monday qualifiers…and won. Diehard rabbit Knox, who had $2,200 left in his bank account at the time, earned $90,000 for the win and got a Tour Card for the next two years.

• That same year, Fred Wadsworth qualified for the Southern Open and won—the last time a rabbit won a PGA Tour event.

THE NATIONWIDE TOUR

In 1990 the PGA started a new tour, a "minor league" for players who weren't quite good enough to make the PGA Tour. They called it the Ben Hogan Tour. By 1993 it had gotten big enough for sponsors to notice and Nike bought in, renaming it the Nike Tour. In 1999 it became the BUY.COM Tour, then in 2003 it became the Nationwide Tour. Regardless of the changing names, the tour has proven to be a huge financial success and has helped a lot of players get ready for the big leagues.

Could the Nationwide Tour be a possible route for you? If you are one of the top 20 money winners on the Nationwide Tour, or if you win three events in a single year, you automatically get on the PGA Tour for the next year. Some golfers who have used the Nationwide Tour to get into the PGA: Ernie Els, John Daly, David Toms, Jim Furyk, and David Duval.

Q SCHOOL

Since its inception in 1964, the PGA Tour Qualifying Tournament is the most common way to get on the PGA Tour. Every year, 30 new players get their Tour Cards this way. And "new" doesn't always mean rookies, since lots of former pros who lost their cards go to Q School to try to get them back. So, how do you get into Q School?

1) Pay a $4,500 fee for the first stage in October and finish in the top fourth of a 72-hole tournament. If you make the cut, you'll be one of more than 1,300 people trying to get one of those 30 spots.

2) Finish in the top fourth of a second 72-hole tournament. Now the field narrows to 325.

3) The final stage takes place in December. It's one 18-hole competition every day for six days in a row—a total of 108 holes of golf. Finish in the top 30 and you're on the PGA Tour for the coming year. Those who have gone through the process call it the

---

On an episode of *Mr. Ed,* the horse hits an inside-the-park home run off pitcher Sandy Koufax.

most pressure-packed golf they have ever played, harder than any PGA Tour event because there's so little room for error.

Some golfers who made it to the PGA Tour through Q School: Curtis Strange (failed in 1976, then made it in 1977), Rich Beem, Luke Donald, Kirk Triplett, Jason Allred, Ty Tyron (at age 17), and Todd Hamilton, who won his first Tour Card through Q School in 2004 at the age of 39...and won the British Open that year.

Consolation Prize: If you don't make one of the top 30 spots at Q School, take heart. The next 50 automatically qualify for the upcoming Nationwide Tour, where you can try once again to do well enough to make it to the PGA.

Q SCHOOL HEARTBREAKERS

• In 2001 Roland Thatcher was on the final hole of the final stage of Q School and needed only a routine par to get his first PGA Tour card. But inexplicably, he sailed his ball over the green, where it bounced off a cart path and landed on top of the clubhouse. He ended up with a triple-bogey...and no Tour Card.

• In 2000 Jaxon Brigman shot a 65 on the last day to win his card by a single shot. But his partner accidentally wrote down "66." Brigman didn't notice the goof and signed the scorecard. Result: the 66 stood. So even though he had golfed well enough, Brigman missed getting on the Tour. "It was almost like a death in the family," he said later. "For five minutes, I had my PGA Tour card."

*   *   *

RANDOM GOLF FACTS

• When he played on the Stanford golf team, Tiger Woods picked up a new nickname: "Urkel," after the nerd on TV's *Family Matters*.

• In 1996 a company in California introduced "Peace Missile" golf clubs, made from melted-down Soviet nuclear missiles.

• Golfers buy more than 500 million new golf balls every year.

• Results of a 2002 poll: 75% of professional golfers—whether religious or not—admitted to praying on the golf course.

Many golf industry insurance companies offer hole-in-one insurance for tournaments.

AGELESS ATHLETES

Baseball great Satchel Paige once said, "Age is a case of mind over matter. If you don't mind, it doesn't matter." These sportsmen and women would agree with that.

NEVER TOO YOUNG

• **Kirsen Wilhelm** biked across the U.S. in 66 days… at age 9.

• **Thomas Gregory** swam across the English Channel… at 11.

• **Marjorie Gestring,** a diver in the 1936 Olympics, won a gold medal… when she was 13.

• **Joseph-Armand Bombardier** invented the snowmobile… at age 15.

• **Joe Nuxhall** played one game for the Cincinnati Reds in 1944… just shy of his 16th birthday.

• **Bep Guidolin** joined hockey's Boston Bruins in 1942… when he was 16.

• **Pelé** led Brazil to the World Cup of soccer… at the age of 17.

• **Magic Johnson** led the Los Angeles Lakers to an NBA title… at age 20.

NEVER TOO OLD

• **Gordie Howe** played professional hockey from 1946 until 1980… when he was 52 years old.

• **Satchel Paige** pitched for the Kansas City Athletics in 1965… at age 59.

• **Oscar Swahn,** a shooter in the 1912 Olympics, won a gold medal… at age 64. (He also won a silver medal eight years later… at age 72.)

• **Clifford Batt** swam the English Channel in 1987… at 67.

• **Walt Stack** completed the Ironman Triathlon… at 73.

• **Corena Leslie** skydived in Arizona… at age 89.

• **Otto Bucher** scored a hole-in-one on a Spanish golf course… at age 99.

• **Ichijirou Araya** climbed Mount Fuji… at the age of 100.

While attending a 1996 Texas Rangers game, Jimmy Carter caught a foul ball.

BASEBALL
TEAM NAME ORIGINS

Here are the stories of how major league teams got their colorful nicknames (although Uncle John would one day like to see an actual pirate fight an actual bear cub).

PITTSBURGH PIRATES. In 1882 they were known as the Alleghenys, named after the nearby Allegheny River. But in the 1890s, they earned a new nickname—the Pirates—after they lured (or stole) a few players from a rival club.

LOS ANGELES DODGERS. When the team was formed in Brooklyn, New York, in 1890, the city had hundreds of trolley cars zigzagging through its streets, and pedestrians were constantly scurrying out of their way. That's why their team was called the Brooklyn Trolley Dodgers (later shortened to Dodgers).

SEATTLE MARINERS. Seattle is one of the country's most important seaports, so the name of the team reflects the city's association with the maritime industry.

DETROIT TIGERS. Legend says that the Detroit Creams (the cream of the baseball crop) became the Tigers in 1896, when Phil Reid of the *Detroit Free Press* remarked that the team's striped uniforms looked like those of the Princeton Tigers.

CHICAGO CUBS. In 1902 the team was without a name (abandoning tries with the Colts and the Orphans). That's when a sportswriter named them "the Cubs." Why? Because it was short enough to fit into a newspaper headline.

PHILADELPHIA PHILLIES. In case it's not obvious, a "Philly" is someone from the city of Philadelphia.

FLORIDA MARLINS. Named after the minor league team it replaced, the Miami Marlins, which was named after the large fish found in the waters off the coast of Florida.

In 1970, 127 runners ran the New York City Marathon. In 2005, 36,562 did.

SAN FRANCISCO GIANTS. The New York Gothams baseball club was fighting for a National League championship in 1886. After one particularly stunning victory, manager Jim Mutrie proudly addressed them as "my big fellows, my giants." The name stuck. The New York Giants moved to San Francisco in 1958.

KANSAS CITY ROYALS. Kansas City already had a long baseball tradition when the American League expanded in 1969. The Kansas City Monarchs of the Negro National League played there from 1920 until the franchise folded in 1965. The Athletics were there from 1955 until they moved to Oakland in 1968. So the city was a natural choice for a new expansion franchise, which they named after the "American Royal," one of the biggest livestock shows in the United States, held annually in Kansas City.

TORONTO BLUE JAYS. When Toronto was awarded an expansion team in 1976, the new owners, Labatt Breweries, were trying to come up with a name. At a meeting, Labatt board member (and former Ontario premier) John Robarts was talking about his morning routine: "I was shaving, and I saw a blue jay out my window." One of the other members said, "Now, that's an interesting name."

LOS ANGELES ANGELS. *Los Angeles* is Spanish for "the angels." It was also the name of an old minor league team in Los Angeles.

MINNESOTA TWINS. The team represents the Twin Cities of Minneapolis and St. Paul. It's also the first team named for an entire state.

WASHINGTON NATIONALS. The District of Columbia had two major league teams from 1901 until 1971: one known officially as the Senators—then the Nationals, and then the Senators again—that played from 1901 to 1961 (they became the Minnesota Twins); and another team called the Senators that played from 1961 until 1971 (they became the Texas Rangers). When Washington, D.C., got another team in 2005, the choice for a name was between those two, and the Nationals won out. Why? Mayor Anthony Williams wanted to protest the district's lack of representation: He said it would be an outrage to name the team the "Senators"—because D.C. has no senators in congress.

In 1888 a new rule allowed baseball bats to have one flat side. (It was revoked the next year.)

IT'S A WEIRD, WEIRD WORLD OF SPORTS

More proof that truth really is stranger than fiction.

COOLEST CLIMBER

In 2004, 35-year-old Paul McKelvey of England walked 100 miles from Liverpool to the top of Mount Snowden (3,560 feet)…with an 84-pound refrigerator strapped to his back. The ex–Royal Marine completed the trip in four days. And though it may have been a dubious achievement, he did it for a good cause: he raised money for a children's hospice called Zoe's Place.

RIDE 'EM, ROBOT

The most popular spectator sport in the United Arab Emirates is camel racing. The traditional choice for camel jockeys has always been children—they're small and lightweight. Until now. When human rights groups actively started to condemn the practice as a form of slavery, U.A.E. interior minister Sheikh Khalifa bin Zayed al-Nahayan found an alternative: he hired several private high-tech labs to create a generation of *robot* jockeys. The tiny, human-looking robots are smaller and lighter than child jockeys and respond to commands via a remote control system mounted on the camel.

FOOTBALL INJURY

In January 2000, a British professional soccer player named Rio Ferdinand strained a tendon in his leg and had to be put on the team's disabled list. Cause of injury: "He left his leg propped for too long on his coffee table while watching the Super Bowl on TV."

WEATHERING CHANGE

Dexter Manley played defensive end in the NFL for 10 seasons until he failed his fourth drug test in 1991. The following year, he resumed his career by playing for the Ottawa Rough Riders of the Canadian Football League. That appears to be when he got in

---

Half of the members of the Rodeo Cowboys Association have never worked on a ranch.

touch with his "inner Canadian." In 1994 Manley claimed he was visited by the ghost of deceased Canadian prime minister William Lyon Mackenzie King. "We talked about thunder and lighting," Manley said.

WHITE ON!

"A University of Northern Colorado intramural basketball team has been inundated with T-shirt requests since naming itself 'The Fightin' Whites.' The team, made up of Native Americans, Hispanics, and Anglos, chose the name because nearby Easton High refused to change *its* nickname from 'Reds' and drop its American Indian caricature logo. The team plans to donate profits from the shirts to an American Indian organization. The shirts show a 1950s-style caricature of a middle-aged white man with the phrase 'Every thang's gonna be all white!'"

—*USA Today*

BACK ATCHA

In 1995 a woman named Jeannine Pelletier was playing golf with her husband at the Fort Kent Golf Club in Portland, Maine. Pelletier hit a tee shot that, amazingly, bounced off a train track and straight back at her, hitting her in the nose. She and her husband sued the club—she for physical damages, he for "loss of consortium with his wife." The case went all the way to the Maine Supreme Court, who awarded her $40,000. Her husband got zilch.

LOVE FOR SALE

The executor of the estate of the late basketball legend Wilt Chamberlain reports that he is having trouble selling the Big Dipper's Bel Air estate, even after reducing the price from $10 million to $4.3 million and tearing out the "playroom," which featured a waterbed floor covered with black rabbit fur and a wraparound pink velvet couch. (The retractable mirrored roof over the master bed has been preserved; so has the traffic light in the bedroom that signals either a green light to "Love," or a red light for "Don't Love.") Executor Sy Goldberg admits that Chamberlain's boasting that he slept with more than 20,000 women in his lifetime may be part of the problem, but he says that holding that against the house is "ridiculous."

SCIENCE IS SO AWESOME, DUDE!

*What do extreme sports like surfing, skateboarding,
and snowboarding have in common, besides
the board? It's the excellent science!*

ANTI-GRAVITY?
Athletes who excel in board sports—riding powerful
waves, doing flips above the pavement, or spinning high
over a snow-covered half-pipe—seem to break all the rules that
keep most of us on the ground. But are board-sporters really
defying gravity? Not at all. If anything, they're working *with*
gravity—and with other facts of physics like momentum and
rotational motion. Without those forces, there would be no
board sports.

ALL ABOARD

Surfing, the sport that started the board craze, is hundreds of years
old. Ancient Hawaiians surfed on big, heavy wooden boards. In
the 1950s, the sport caught on in Southern California, where new
engineering techniques and materials like fiberglass allowed for
lightweight, smaller boards that still supported the mass of the
surfer on the water. Spectators flocked to the sight of surfers standing on seemingly flimsy boards while cresting the tops of breaking
waves. Most didn't realize that what they were seeing was a lesson
in rotational motion and physics.

Of course, balance is an important part of surfing. But how
does a surfer stay balanced on a board that's cresting a wave?
Along the lengthwise center of the board and slightly toward its
tail, where there's extra mass, lies the center of the board's gravity. This point is the board's axis—like the fulcrum at the center
of a seesaw. Where the surfer stands in relation to the axis controls the board's rotational motion exactly like the up-and-down
rotational motion of a seesaw. If the surfer's weight moves too far
toward the nose of the board, the board tips (or torques) forward
and the nose sinks. Too far backward, and the tail sinks. Either

---

Sport with the largest playing field: polo (300 yards by 200 yards).

way, it's a wipeout. A good surfer straddles the center of gravity with one foot toward the tail and one toward the nose. The two torques cancel each other out, and the surfer stands stationary and balanced.

POWER PLAYERS

But it takes more than an understanding of rotational motion to make a brilliant surfer. The athlete also needs a thorough (if intuitive) understanding of the development of *potential energy* and how that can be turned into *kinetic energy*.

Here's how it works: Let's say you've paddled on your surfboard to the top of a wave just before it breaks. By taking up this position, you've gained potential energy—the potential product of you and your equipment's weight or mass, and the vertical distance you're about to fall. You now convert this potential energy into kinetic energy—the energy of a body that's in motion—when you drop off the crest down toward the flat of the wave. This conversion into kinetic energy gives you the power to propel yourself along, despite the friction of the water currents against the board. Result: You've ridden the wave.

TAKING IT TO THE STREETS

Any surfer also knows that when the wind blows toward the shore, there are no great waves to ride. So during the 1960s, some bored surfers started buying boards that were fitted with wheels on the bottom. When the ocean was glassy and calm, surfers could use their surfing skills on dry land, rolling along the hot Southern California pavement.

The first skateboards were unwieldy, with clay wheels that didn't grip the pavement well. One of the earliest improvements was the kicktail, the turned-up end at the back of the board. Now a skateboarder could lean back a little as he rolled along, taking the weight off the front wheels and making the board more maneuverable. Tough, long-lasting urethane and verethane wheels, which gripped the road better and offered more stability, turned a part-time hobby into a full-blown craze.

GETTING WHEELS

Two more ideas changed skateboarding from a way to get around on pavement into a way to defy gravity and fly through the air. In 1977 a skateboarder named Willi Winkel was riding down a standard quarter-pipe (an elevated ramp that led downhill to help a rider pick up speed). Winkel thought that two quarter-pipes might be better than one, so he put together a U-shaped ramp, or half-pipe. Though he probably didn't know it, Willi would soon be using the rules of acceleration and velocity to overcome gravity. His total mass, that is, his weight, was pulled by gravity down the half-pipe, creating speed, which gave him the momentum to take him vertically up the other side of the U and even soar out over the lip to "catch some big air," a term borrowed from surfing.

BIGGER AIR

In the late 1970s, skateboarder Alan "Ollie" Gelfand worked on a new move that literally took the power of rotational motion to new heights. As he sped up the vertical incline of a half-pipe, he made a crouching jump while shoving down on the kicktail of his board with his back foot, deliberately torquing the back of his board down and causing the front of the board to fly up. If left to itself, the board would simply have flipped over backward and fallen to the ground—and it probably did the first few times that Gelfand tried it. But eventually, while the board was in the air, Gelfand learned to slide his front foot forward several inches, which put torque on the front of the board and leveled it out before gravity pulled rider and board back down to Earth.

The result was something of an optical illusion: the board seemed to hover under his feet during the jump. Spectators were wowed; it looked as if Ollie was strapped to his skateboard, but he wasn't. The next time you see a skateboarder jumping over an obstacle or slide up onto a curb, he or she is doing what boarders now call an "ollie."

THE SCIENCE OF SNOWBOARDING

It was only a matter of time before boards were adapted for snow. By the 1980s, innovators had adapted the skills of skateboarding to ski hills and were "shredding" down mountains on snowboards. Like skateboarders, they rode either regular (with their left foot in front) or "goofy foot" (with their right foot in front). They even adapted the half-pipe, picking up enough momentum in a high, curving trench packed with snow so they could slide up over the top of the lip and catch some big—but cold—air.

Snowboarders also take advantage of the forces of friction, gravity, acceleration, and momentum. A board speeds downhill pulled by gravity, but it also melts the snow as it goes, so that it actually skims along on a film of water.

Like all board riders, snowboarders position their body mass and exploit the board's rotational motion to stay balanced. One side of the board will have more contact with the snow than the other, so the rider keeps his or her center of gravity over whichever edge of the board is in contact with the snow (the riding edge). To end a ride, a snowboarder turns uphill so that the forces of friction and gravity drag on the momentum to slow the board to a stop.

BOARD OF SCIENCE

So next time you take your snowboard to the slopes or see the kids at the local skatepark, think about all the science those little boards are dealing with. Or better yet, just catch some air and have a good time.

*   *   *

SURFING TERMINOLOGY

- **Clucked:** scared of the wave
- **Gnarly:** impressive, intimidating
- **Pucker factor:** the impact of a gnarly wave on your ability to relax
- **Thrashed:** when a gnarly wave does its worst to you
- **Jag:** to slink away after being thrashed
- **Sick:** first-rate, incredibly cool
- **Getting worked:** when a wave introduces you to how a sock feels in the washing machine

The Austrian army trucked in 1.4 million cubic feet of snow for the 1964 Olympics in Innsbruck.

JUMPING FOR JOY

The origin of the trampoline is just the kind of story we love at the BRI: one man's dream and persistence creates something that millions of people have benefited from.

SKIN-SPIRATION

As a typical teenage boy in Cedar Rapids, Iowa, in the 1920s, George Nissen loved the circus. He was most fascinated with the acrobats—the way they would gracefully fall into the large nets from the high wire, sometimes doing amazing tricks and twists as they bounced. Nissen also loved vaudeville acts. One of the gags he liked best was the springboard. A man would be pushed off the stage into the orchestra pit, only to "magically" bounce back up onto the stage. He wanted to do that! When Nissen read in a high-school textbook that Eskimos sometimes stretched walrus skins between stakes in the ground and then bounced up and down on them just for fun, that did it—he decided to make his own "jumping table."

Still in high school, Nissen started his project in 1926. He scavenged materials from the local dump and tinkered away in his garage...for 10 years. In that time he had become a world-class tumbler, winning the national championship three times in a row, from 1935 to 1937. It was around this same time that Nissen was putting the final touches on his new invention. With the assistance of a local gymnastics coach named Larry Griswold, Nissen used rails from a bed, some strips of inner tube, tightly wound rope, and canvas to build his first jumping table. He called it the trampoline, from the Spanish word *trampolín*, which means "springboard." They took it to the local YMCA, where Nissen worked as an instructor to test-market it. The kids loved it—they stood in long lines for a chance to jump on the new contraption.

BOUNCING BACK

The trampoline became so popular in Cedar Rapids that Nissen began mass-producing them in 1938. One problem: no one bought them. Why? Nissen believed that even though the trampoline intrigued them, people saw it as something only for circus per-

---

In trampolining, a front somersault with one and a half twists is called a "Rudolph."

formers. So he strapped a trampoline to the top of his car and took off cross-country, giving exhibitions anywhere a crowd was gathered—schools, fairs, playgrounds, and sporting events.

Taking a lesson from circus legend P.T. Barnum, Nissen taught a kangaroo to jump on a trampoline. He trained it using dried apricots as treats and quickly learned that the best way to avoid getting kicked was to "hold hands" with the kangaroo's front paws. A photograph of man and beast high in the air was printed in newspapers all over the country—exactly the publicity Nissen wanted. It brought the crowds out, and sure enough, sales improved.

Then when World War II started, Nissen convinced the Army that trampolines could train pilots not only to achieve better balance, but also to be less fearful of being upside down. And jumping on a trampoline was great for physical conditioning. The military agreed; thousands of cadets learned to jump on trampolines.

IT'S A FAD!

Still, even after the war, trampolines were mostly found at gymnasiums, primarily used by athletes. Then, in the late 1950s, a new fad emerged: trampoline centers. Here's what *Life* magazine said about it in May 1960:

> All across the nation the jumping business is jumping, and a device called the trampoline, once a tool of tumblers, has overnight become a popular plaything. Matrons trying to reduce, executives trying to relax and kids trying to outdo each other are plunking down 40¢ for a half hour of public bouncing at trampoline centers which are spreading the way miniature golf courses spread several decades ago.

And trampolining wasn't just for the average person. Nissen boasted that "Vice President Richard Nixon, Yul Brynner, the Rockefellers, and King Farouk" were all avid jumpers as well.

But while Nissen must have been happy that his invention was finally catching on, he was very critical of the trampoline centers. Profiteers, he said, were just buying the trampolines and allowing patrons to jump unsupervised. Many of the jumpers were either inept or intoxicated. After a few high-profile injuries (a beauty queen lost her teeth and a high-school football star was paralyzed), the centers started folding. Nissen tried opening his own properly supervised centers, called Jumpin' Jiminy. But it was too late—the injuries had given trampolines a bad name.

IT'S A SPORT!

When Nissen saw the interest in trampolines start to dwindle, he understood why. "You have to have programs," he said. "I bounce too, but if I didn't have something new to do on a trampoline, I would lose interest."

So he set his sights on turning trampolining into a sport. First he tried "Spaceball," a combination of jumping and volleyball, but that turned out to be too dangerous. He also tried combining trampolining and running by putting little bounce pads at either end of a track, but that didn't catch on, either.

Then Nissen met a Swiss economist in California named Kurt Baechler, who also happened to be a gymnast. Together they combined trampolining with gymnastics, creating the sport Nissen was looking for. They organized the Nissen Cup trampoline competition, formed the International Trampoline Federation, and financed the first trampolining World Championships in the Royal Albert Hall in London. As the trampoline center fad gave way to hula hoops and pinball arcades, the sport of trampolining started taking off.

Today, trampolines can be found in backyards worldwide. And the Nissen company is still a major manufacturer of gymnastics equipment and trampolines. George Nissen holds 35 patents on sports and fitness equipment (including the seat cushion that protects your bottom from rock-hard bleacher seats). At 83 years old Nissen won California's Senior Fitness Award. And he finally achieved his goal of having competitive trampolining—the idea he came up with when he was 19 years old—recognized as a real sport. It became an Olympic event in 2000.

TRAMPOLINE FACTS

• Jeff Schwartz of Illinois bounced on a trampoline for 266 hours, 9 minutes in 1981, setting a world record. He was allowed breaks for eating, sleeping, and going to the bathroom.

• Another world record was set on July 24, 1999, when a team of 20 people in West York, United Kingdom, did 29,503 somersaults in exactly five hours using two standard trampolines. That averages out to 1,500 somersaults per person.

• The U.S. Consumer Product Safety Commission reported that there were 83,212 trampoline-related injuries in 1996, up from only 19,000 in 1976.

THE COLOR BARRIER, PART II

Here's the second installment of our look at how pro golf became integrated. (Part I is on page 286.)

GOING PUBLIC

When Joe Louis heard from the president of the PGA that he and Bill Spiller couldn't golf in the 1952 San Diego Open because they were black, he decided he was going anyway. So he called up Walter Winchell, then one of the most popular radio personalities in the country. Winchell raised a stink on his national show, and suddenly the eyes of the country were on San Diego. Louis turned the heat up even further when he gave an interview to the *San Diego Union*. He told them that even if his invitation were withdrawn, he'd be on the course the next morning at 7:00 to qualify for the tournament on his own.

"I want to bring this thing out into the light," he told the newspaper. "I want the people to know what the PGA is. The PGA will have to tell me personally that I can't play." He insisted that Bill Spiller be allowed to play as well.

BACKING DOWN

PGA president Horton Smith had a problem on his hands. Joe Louis was a World War II vet and one of the most popular athletes in the country, admired by blacks and whites alike. And here he was, challenging the PGA to a public fight over its policy of discrimination—a fight that Louis told reporters was the biggest of his life.

Smith tried to diffuse the controversy. When he arrived in San Diego, he met with Louis and told him he'd arrived at a decision: since Louis was playing as an amateur, he was not subject to the PGA's rules. The tournament's sponsors were free to invite him, and he was free to accept. Bill Spiller was another matter—he was a professional golfer. Since he was black, he couldn't become a member of the PGA. And since he wasn't a member of the PGA, he wasn't eligible to play in the tournament, either.

Rules were rules, Smith explained.

DOWN TO THE WIRE

The tournament was about to begin. Horton Smith had offered Louis some of what he wanted, but not all of it, and Louis had to decide whether "some" was enough. He and Smith continued to negotiate right up until tee time. In the end, Louis agreed to play after Smith promised he would work with Louis to find some kind of compromise to accommodate black professional golfers.

For *this* tournament, though, Bill Spiller was out. Spiller was so mad at the PGA—and with Louis for letting him down—that he went and stood on the first tee box and tried to stop the tournament from getting underway. Louis eventually talked him into ending his protest. After that, the tournament went off without another hitch.

Louis and Smith met after the tournament and hashed out a plan by which *some* black professional golfers would be allowed to participate in *some* PGA tournaments: A committee of five black golfers—Louis, Spiller, Teddy Rhodes, Eural Clark, and Howard Wheeler—would come up with a list of "approved" black golfers. The list would have to be approved by the PGA; then, if a tournament's sponsor and the hosting golf club both approved, blacks on the approved list could be invited to play. But black golfers still could not *join* the PGA—its caucasians-only clause stayed on the books. Tournaments and golf clubs that wanted to discriminate against blacks could do so with the PGA's blessing.

The new deal wasn't much, but it was better than nothing, and even Bill Spiller reluctantly agreed to put up with it for the time being. The new rules would be tested at the Phoenix Open, less than one week away.

SOME WELCOME

Seven African Americans made the trip to Phoenix: Louis, his secretary Leonard Reed, Eural Clark, and Joe Roach entered as amateurs; Bill Spiller, Teddy Rhodes, and a third golfer, a UGA champion named Charlie Sifford, entered as pros. Just how little Louis had accomplished in San Diego became apparent when the men arrived at the Phoenix Country Club. The tournament had been opened to blacks, but the clubhouse had not. Louis and the others learned this at the first tee of the first round, when a club official told them to remove their belongings from the locker

---

Tennis star Althea Gibson was the first African American member of the LPGA in 1964.

room and put them in the caddie shack. The showers were off-limits, too, and eating in the dining room (which was staffed by black waiters) was out of the question.

Louis and the others could have made a fuss about the way they were being treated, but they decided to grit their teeth and see the tournament through. Things got worse: They were the first group to tee off at the tournament, and when they got to the first green, they discovered that someone had defecated into the cup just moments earlier. Then, when they came up to the scoreboard, they noticed that one of the radio announcers was wearing a Confederate cap. All of the golfers kept their cool except Spiller. He decided he'd had enough and told the others he was going to the locker room to shower; then he stormed off. Ten minutes later, a tournament official asked Louis to get Spiller out of the showers before someone killed him. Louis went and got him.

The next three rounds of the tournament passed fairly smoothly; then the golfers went on to Tucson and played another event. No other PGA tournaments invited blacks that winter.

STRIKING THE CLAUSE

By the late 1950s, fewer than 15 of the more than 40 tournaments on the PGA Tour had opened themselves to black golfers. Like a lot of his peers, Bill Spiller dreamed of making his living on the pro circuit, but the purses were smaller then and he was shut out of so many tournaments that he couldn't make ends meet. He ended up running a doughnut store with his wife in Los Angeles and caddying at the Hillcrest Country Club on the side.

One day in 1960, Spiller was carrying the bags of a club member named Harry Braverman. When Braverman asked him why he wasn't trying out for the PGA Tour, Spiller told him about the PGA's caucasians-only clause. Braverman repeated the story to his friend, California attorney general Stanley Mosk, and Mosk decided to do something about it. He contacted the PGA and told them that holding segregated tournaments on public golf courses was illegal in California, and he threatened to sue the organization if they continued the whites-only policy. That fall, the PGA's national convention entertained a motion to remove the caucasians-only clause from their constitution. The motion was voted down 67–17; the clause stayed in place.

In 1961 Mosk contacted the PGA again. This time he told them that holding a segregated tournament on a *private* golf course would also be illegal, and he threatened to block the 1962 PGA Championship, which was scheduled to be held at the Brentwood Country Club in Southern California. The PGA responded by moving the tournament to Pennsylvania, but then at the fall 1961 national convention it brought the caucasians-only clause up for another vote. This time the PGA's executive committee recommended that the clause be removed—the resolution passed unanimously and the caucasians-only clause was stricken from the constitution.

The door to the PGA Tour had finally swung open, and the pace of progress gradually began to quicken. In 1962 Charlie Sifford became the first black golfer to play on the PGA Tour full-time. He went on to win the Greater Hartford Open in 1967 and then the Los Angeles Open in 1969. In 1975, after qualifying for the third year in a row, Lee Elder finally received an invitation to Augusta National and became the first black golfer to play in the Masters.

MISSED THE CUT

For Bill Spiller, the change in the PGA's constitution and all the progress that followed came too late. By the time the vote was taken in 1961, he was in his late 40s and well past his prime. But he still played golf whenever he could get away from his doughnut store, and for the next several years he continued to dream of playing on the PGA Tour.

In 1967 he went to the PGA's qualifying school in Florida but failed to score well enough to make the Tour. The following year Spiller tried again. In the end it came down to eight rounds of golf—144 holes. If Spiller scored well enough, he'd qualify for the Tour. If he didn't, he might never get another chance.

Now 55 and suffering from so many ailments that friends nicknamed him the "Medicine Man" for all the pills he took, Spiller had swing problems and had a shaky putting game. Still, he did well in the first seven rounds and had a good chance of making the Tour. But in the eighth round, his luck ran out. On one of the last holes, he shanked three shots and missed qualifying by a single stroke.

A: Fencing. (They're all parts of a fencer's uniform.)

BITTER END

Bill Spiller fought for 25 years to make it into the PGA, but never succeeded and never got over the defeat. When he died in 1988 at the age of 75, his wife sold his golf clubs. His son Bill Jr. remembers that when he called the newspapers to give them his father's obituary, nobody ran it. "I see my father as forgotten, overlooked, and unappreciated, never getting credit for what he actually did."

Spiller *was* underappreciated, but his contribution to the game is undeniable, having paved the way for a generation of minority golf pros to play on the PGA Tour. The same year that Lee Elder became the first black golfer to play in the Masters tournament—1975—was the year that Tiger Woods was born. In 2000 Woods became the first black golfer to win it.

*   *   *

AHEAD OF HIS TIME

In 1896 John Shippen played in the second U.S. Open, held at Shinnecock Hills in New York. What's so special about that? Shippen was black. The 16-year-old Shippen and several other local kids had been taught to play by the club's Scottish pro, Willie Dunn. Dunn recognized that Shippen was a very talented golfer and entered him in the tournament, along with Shippen's friend, Oscar Bunn—a Shinnecock Indian.

The British pros who had come to play complained to USGA president Theodore Havemeyer, telling him he had to get "the black boys" out of the tournament...or *they* wouldn't play. Havemeyer responded that if they didn't want to play in the tournament, they could go home and the event would be played with just the two boys in it—and one of them would be declared champion. At that, the Brits relented, and the second U.S. Open in history was played with an African American golfer and a Native American golfer in the field.

Bunn's score is lost to history, but Shippen finished fifth and won $10, making him one of the first—if not *the* first—American-born golfer to earn money in a pro golf tournament. He would play in five more U.S. Opens, although none as well as his first, the last one being in 1913. But had Havemeyer's example been followed, American golf might have been integrated from its outset.

Minority players make up only 3.3% of America's 26.4 million golfers.

WRESTLING LINGO

Can't get enough pro wrestling? Well, if you want to sound like a "real" pro, you have to know the special lingo. Here's a sample.

Face (noun). A "good guy." (Wrestlers with *pretty faces* are often cast as good guys.)

Heel (noun). A "bad guy." Someone who cheats and breaks the rules to win.

Feud (noun). A grudge match, frequently between a face and a heel.

Turn (noun or verb). When a heel changes his persona and becomes a face, or vice versa.

Potato (verb). To injure a wrestler by hitting him on the head or causing him to hit his head.

Stiff (adjective). A move intended to cause real injury.

Run-in (noun). Intervention in a match by an audience member or other nonparticipant.

Blade (verb). To intentionally cut yourself with a hidden piece of razorblade in order to produce "juice" (see below).

Juice (noun or verb). Blood. Usually caused by blading.

Job (noun). A staged loss.

Post (verb). To run someone into the ring post.

Hardway juice (noun). Blood from an unintentional injury.

Heat (noun). The level of the crowd's enthusiasm for a fight.

Pop (noun or verb). A sudden rise in the heat of the crowd, such as when a popular wrestler makes his entrance.

Bump (noun). A fall or other move that results in the wrestler falling out of the ring.

Jobber (noun). A wrestler who does a job—he's hired to lose to the featured wrestler. Also known as redshirts or PLs, short for "professional losers."

Clean job (noun). A staged loss that doesn't involve illegal wrestling moves.

Screw-job (noun). An ending that isn't clean—someone, usually the heel, wins by cheating.

Shoot (noun). The opposite of a job—one wrestler really is trying to hurt another.

THE BIRTH OF BASEBALL, PART III

*By 1860 the basic rules for baseball had been set (see
page 266). After that, most changes in the game took
place not on the field, but behind closed doors.*

THE WAR YEARS

Even though baseball was growing more popular among
the middle class in the Northeast and Midwest, it wasn't
the foremost thought on most Americans' minds as the 1850s
drew to a close. The United States was in crisis—the Southern
states were threatening to secede, and the Civil War was immi-
nent. But instead of fading away, baseball became even more popular during the war. At prisoner-of-war camps in the North,
Union soldiers taught the game to Confederates, while Yankee
prisoners in the South taught it to their Rebel captors.

This introduced baseball to a whole new class of players. Up
until then, teams were primarily made up of doctors, lawyers, and
shopkeepers who could afford to take afternoons off. During the
war, almost everyone had time to play, regardless of economic status. Even out on the front lines, troops played baseball during long
days of waiting for their next battle. In a letter home to his family,
Union soldier Alpheris B. Parker of the 10th Massachusetts wrote:
"The parade ground has been a busy place for a week or so past,
ball-playing having become a mania in camp. Officer and men forget, for a time, the differences in rank and indulge in the invigor-
ating sport with a schoolboy's ardor."

BA$EBALL

Even before the Civil War ended in 1865, a few players were getting paid—the first may have been A. J. Reach, who played second
base for the Brooklyn Eckfords at the Union Grounds in New Yok
City, the first enclosed ballpark that charged admission. But people
weren't accustomed to the concept of paying athletes to play a
game—amateurism was considered "noble." So those first payments
were made in secret...but not for long. "In the late 1860s, advanc-

ing skills led to heightened appetites for victory," writes John Thorn in his book *The Game for All America*, "which inevitably led to *sub rosa* [secret] payments and, by 1870, rampant professionalism." The first openly salaried team was the 1869 Cincinnati Red Stockings, who went undefeated and made it no secret that their players were paid.

And just as increased skills had led to salaries, the salaries, in turn, resulted in an even *more* competitive game on the field. Batters started hitting the ball harder, base runners started stealing bases, and a few pitchers even started trying to strike hitters out. Off the field, however, baseball was being transformed in smoke-filled rooms by wealthy men, some of whom loved the game, and some of whom just saw dollar signs.

THE ASSOCIATION IN CHAOS

This "rampant professionalism" rendered the National Association of Base Ball Players obsolete—most teams were going pro. So in 1871, a new league was formed, the National Association of *Professional* Baseball Players, and it had problems from the very beginning. Without a central governing body, the individual teams couldn't maintain control over basic necessities of the game such as consistent rules, schedules, and venues. And the teams didn't even have to be that good—they just needed to pay the $10 entrance fee, giving many cities multiple teams of varying quality.

It was a mess…but it wasn't a failure. "It's easy now to criticize the way the N.A. was set up," says sports historian Ralph Hickok. "But it must be remembered that this group of clubs was trying to do something totally new, so it's not surprising that this first attempt was far from perfect. When the National League replaced the N.A. in 1876, it avoided many of the mistakes that the association had made. But it also built on the foundation that the association had laid down." The man who had the biggest part in building upon that foundation was the president of the Chicago White Stockings, William A. Hulbert.

DEAD ENDS

Hulbert was a no-nonsense oil baron who wanted to construct a strong—and profitable—team in Chicago, which was still rebuilding after the great fire of 1871. Yet he met resistance at every turn.

The bumps on a table tennis paddle are called *pimples.*

He was frustrated by Eastern teams that were out of the pennant race deciding at the last minute not to make the trip to Chicago—or, worse, not showing up after Hulbert's team had traveled all the way to *their* towns. As Hulbert's complaints were repeatedly ignored by his Eastern counterparts, he surmised—correctly—that they were conspiring to keep the best players in the N.A.'s four main cities: New York, Philadelphia, Boston, and Hartford. When Hulbert's star shortstop, Davy Force, announced that he was leaving to play for the Philadelphia Athletics, Hulbert demanded that the N.A. put a stop to "contract jumpers"—players who sold their services to the highest bidder. Again, he received no response.

That was the last straw. Hulbert needed more power to fight the system, and to get that, he needed a powerful ball team. So he did some backdoor dealing of his own and stole Cap Anson, the game's first great hitter, from Philadelphia. Hulbert then acquired four players—including pitcher Al Spalding—from the Boston Red Stockings, the reigning dynasty that had monopolized the best talent and won four straight N.A. pennants.

MAJOR LEAGUE BASEBALL

Hulbert had an ulterior motive: He wanted to end the reign of the N.A. and form a new league, one run by a central governing board that would preserve the integrity of the game. In what amounted to a coup d'etat, Hulbert first secured the support of three other Midwestern teams—the Cincinnati Red Stockings, the St. Louis Brown Stockings, and the Louisville Grays—and then called for a meeting with the owners of the New York Mutuals, the Philadelphia Athletics, and the Boston Red Stockings. On February 2, 1876, at the Grand Central Hotel in New York City, the other owners gave in to Hulbert's demands, marking the beginning of the National League of Base Ball Clubs (note the substitution of "Clubs" for "Players").

The N.L. began with four eastern and four western teams, and for the first time their schedules were actually set before the season started. No city with fewer than 75,000 people could join the league, and only one team was allowed per city. Hulbert strove to keep the new league "pure" by turning down invitations to play games against "minor league" teams. He also banned drinking, gambling, and playing on Sundays.

Perhaps most importantly, Hulbert played a major part in creating baseball's first "reserve clause." This was designed to put a limit on salaries—each club's largest expense, and one that made it difficult for them to keep solvent. But the reserve clause also put an end to contract jumping. If a player was named in his team's reserve clause, the only way he could switch teams was to be traded or released. No other team could sign him, ensuring that a club's best talent would remain with that club for years. When it was enacted in 1879, only five players per team were given a reserve clause, but that number soon rose. The players didn't like it (some even compared it to slavery), but without the reserve clause the National League might not have lasted into the new century.

OFF AND RUNNING...

With that, the foundation of Major League Baseball was laid. It was off to a rocky start, as gambling scandals, inconsistent rules, and umpire abuse marred the first 25 years of the National League. But the league was able to weather those storms—as it would when, in 1902, the upstart American League threatened the "Senior Circuit" for baseball supremacy. After a tense season, the first World Series took place in 1903...but few people acknowledged its validity. After two more tense years of threats, boycotts, and lawsuits, the first *actual* World Series took place in 1905. The N.L. New York Giants defeated the A.L. Philadelphia Athletics. And with *that*, Major League Baseball—as we know it today—was born.

That's been the cycle of baseball ever since: Rule changes and subsequent realignments shake things up, but the game keeps going. Scandals come and go, and some even leave a nasty stain, but none has been catastrophic enough to put an end to baseball altogether. It just goes to show that no matter how much the less-savory aspects of baseball threaten to kill the game, it's impossible to stop a bunch of grown men from hitting a little ball with a stick and then chasing it around a field...while thousands of people cheer them on.

*　　*　　*

"Baseball never had no 'fadder'; it jest growed."

—Henry Chadwick

Fastest animal in sports: A racing pigeon can reach speeds of over 100 mph.

TEE TIME

Mark Twain described the game of golf as "a good walk spoiled." But that doesn't matter to these folks.

"When I play my best golf, I feel as if I'm in a fog, standing back watching the Earth in orbit with a club in my hands."
—Mickey Wright

"That's when you know you're weird."
—John Ellis, saying that he enjoyed golf so much, he even requested *Golf Digest* for bedtime stories when he was three years old

"I play in the low 80s. Any hotter than that, I won't play."
—Joe E. Louis

"A hole-in-one is amazing when you think of the different universes this white mass of molecules has to pass through on its way to the hole."
—Mac O'Grady

"You can talk to a fade but a hook won't listen."
—Lee Trevino

"To be truthful, I think golfers are overpaid. It's unreal, and I have trouble dealing with the guilt sometimes."
—Colin Montgomerie

"No matter what happens, never give up a hole…In tossing in your cards after a bad beginning you also undermine your whole game, because to quit between tee and green is more habit-forming than drinking a highball before breakfast."
—Sam Snead

"It took me 17 years to get to 3,000 hits in baseball. I did it in one afternoon on the golf course."
—Hank Aaron

"There's an old saying, 'It's a poor craftsman who blames his tools.' It's usually the player who misses those three-footers, not the putter."
—Kathy Whitworth

"Through years of experience I have found that air offers less resistance than dirt."
—Jack Nicklaus on why he tees his ball high

"If I had cleared the trees and drove the green, it would've been a great shot."
—Sam Snead

The Harlem Globetrotters were originally called the Savoy Five.

PAC-MANHATTAN

*Are you old enough to remember odd but simple college
stunts like swallowing live goldfish or cramming people
into Volkswagen Beetles? Here's a new college fad
that's just as nutty...but a lot more complicated.*

THINKING BIG

In 2004 graduate students at New York University's Interactive Telecommunications Program set out to create a real-life version of the 1980s video game Pac-Man—one that could be played on the streets of Manhattan, with people in costumes assuming the roles of the five characters: Pac-Man and the four ghosts, Inky, Pinky, Blinky, and Clyde. They called their game "Pac-Manhattan." Been a while since you played a game of Pac-Man? Here's a refresher:

• The playing field consists of a maze that's filled with a trail of tiny white dots. Pac-Man must travel around the entire maze and eat all the dots while avoiding Inky, Pinky, Blinky, and Clyde. If they catch him, he dies.

• There are four "power pellets" on the playing field, one in each of the four corners of the maze. When Pac-Man eats one of the pellets, he becomes energized, all the ghosts turn blue, and for a short time he can eat the ghosts—so *they* have to run from *him*.

GET REAL

So if one person can play Pac-Man, how many does it take to play Pac-Manhattan? Ten—five play Pac-Man and the four ghosts, and each of the other five serves as one of the character's "generals." While the characters run around on city streets, the generals remain in a special Pac-Manhattan "control room" and keep their characters updated on the game's progress by cell phone.

• The area of play is a 6 x 4 city-block area surrounding Washington Square Park in New York's Greenwich Village, which simulates the Pac-Man video-game board. The city streets serve as the maze; each time a character moves to a new intersection, they are required to report their position to their general. The information

---

Wilt Chamberlain had a superstition about always wearing a rubber band around his wrist.

is then displayed on a computer screen in the control room that looks just like the screen on the original Pac-Man arcade game.

• There are no white dots on the city streets, but they are displayed on the computer screen. As Pac-Man moves from one intersection to another, the dots disappear from the screen. His general is responsible for keeping him up to date on which streets he still has to cover.

• The intersections at the four corners of the maze serve as power pellets. When Pac-Man reaches the intersection and tags the street sign, he "eats the pellet" and becomes invincible for two minutes. If he can tag any of the ghosts before the two minutes are up, they are "eaten" and have to return to their starting point before they can continue chasing Pac-Man. Of course, after the two minutes, the ghosts can chase and eat Pac-Man again.

• Pac-Man is the only character who knows everything that is happening in the game—his general is allowed to tell him where the ghosts are, but the ghosts' generals are not allowed to tell them where Pac-Man is. Each ghost is allowed to know where the other ghosts are and whether or not Pac-Man has eaten a power pellet and become invincible, but they have to find Pac-Man on their own without help from their generals.

• The game continues until Pac-Man eats all of the dots or is eaten by one of the ghosts. Games can last anywhere from under 10 minutes to over an hour, depending on luck and how well the characters and their controllers work together.

DO TRY THIS AT HOME

Pac-Manhattan is a work in progress; the inventors say they'll open their game to the public once it's perfected. But you don't have to wait until then—if you've got 10 people with 10 cell phones and a map of the streets where you live, you can set up your own game. The rules are posted on www.pacmanhattan.com.

*   *   *

VERY SUPERSTITIOUS

Olympic speed skater Bonnie Blair ate a peanut butter and jelly sandwich before every race. It worked: She won five gold medals.

The phrase "back to square one" comes from soccer—announcers used it to refer to starting positions.

DUSTBIN OF HISTORY: BERNARR MACFADDEN

He was a founder of the fitness movement in America and the most successful publisher of the early 1900s. He even hobnobbed with national politicians and Hollywood stars. Yet hardly anyone today has heard of him.

THE WEAKLING

Bernard McFadden was born into an impoverished family in Mill Spring, Missouri, in 1868. Both his father and mother died by the time he was 11, and after he was orphaned, he was placed with a farmer in Illinois and put to work.

Bernard had been frail and sickly his entire life, but the fresh air, hard work, and wholesome foods on the farm turned him into a strong, healthy boy for the first time. Then when he was 13, he moved to St. Louis and found work in an office, where the sedentary lifestyle and bad eating habits quickly caught up with him, and soon he was as sick as he'd been before he got to the farm. "By the age of 16 I was a physical wreck," he wrote in his memoir. "I had the hacking cough of a consumptive, my muscular system had so wasted that I resembled a skeleton; my digestive organs were in a deplorable condition."

BACK TO BASICS

Even at that early age McFadden didn't trust doctors—he had nearly died in childhood after receiving a "vaccination" from a quack—so he put himself in charge of regaining his health. He began working out with a dumbbell and walking as many as six miles a day. He also became a vegetarian.

McFadden's reformed lifestyle produced quick results. His health returned and he developed a strong physique, which prompted him to take up gymnastics and later wrestling. He excelled at both, and in the process he discovered that he loved performing in front of the public. In 1887 he became what today would be called a personal fitness trainer (McFadden called himself a "kinestherapist" and practitioner of "higher physical culture"); then in 1889 he signed on as an athletic coach at an Illinois military academy.

WHAT'S IN A NAME

Working with the athletes gave McFadden a chance to develop his ideas on nutrition, fitness, and exercise, and over the next few years he formed detailed theories on how to live a healthy life. By 1894 he was ready to share them with a larger audience, so he quit his job, moved to New York City, and converted his two-room apartment into a fitness studio. It was at this time that he also changed the spelling of his name to Bernarr Macfadden—"Bernarr" sounded like the roar of a lion, he thought, and Macfadden seemed a more masculine spelling than McFadden did.

In the mid-1890s, he patented an exercise machine made with ropes and pulleys. It made him a lot of money, but in the end it was the instruction booklet that came with it that became the foundation for his fortune: Included along with the instructions were so many health and diet tips that many customers mistook the booklet for a magazine and asked Macfadden for a subscription.

PAPER PULPIT

Macfadden decided that if his customers wanted a magazine, he would give them one. Working from a desk he rented in a real-estate office, he began work on a magazine he called *Physical Culture*. The first issue hit newsstands in March 1899.

Physical Culture was one of the very first fitness magazines in the United States, and it was completely unlike the ones that had come before it. The magazine was packed with photos of scantily clad, muscular young men and women—which no doubt broadened the magazine's appeal—at a time when other magazines had only a few photographs or none at all. Like the instruction booklet that inspired it, *Physical Culture* was overflowing with Macfadden's maxims on healthy living: Vegetables, fresh air, and exercise were good; white bread (the "staff of death," he called it), alcohol, tobacco, and caffeine were bad. The healthy human body was an object of beauty. Sexual desire was normal and healthy; sex itself was meant to be enjoyable. Doctors were pill-pushing frauds, and most diseases could be cured with fasting and hot baths. *Really* bad diseases like cancer, syphilis, and gout could be cured with an all-milk diet. Macfadden had opinions on everything, and they all ended up in the pages of *Physical Culture*.

By 1903 *Physical Culture* had a circulation of more than 100,000, making it one of the best-selling magazines in the country. And yet as popular as the magazine was, it attracted few advertisers—not many businesses wanted to be associated with Macfadden's risqué photographs and kooky medical advice.

Macfadden managed to turn this to his benefit by filling the magazine's pages with his *own* ads for his books (he wrote 79 in all), health products, and other business ventures. In the years to come, he expanded his empire with Bernarr Macfadden bodybuilding contests, Bernarr Macfadden sanatoriums, Bernarr Macfadden health-food restaurants, and the Bernarr Macfadden Institute, which schooled coaches, trainers, and physical therapists in his theories and methods. The name Bernarr Macfadden was as well known in his day as Martha Stewart and Donald Trump are today.

TAKE IT FROM ME

For all his accomplishments in the fitness and health arena, Macfadden's most lasting contribution (not to mention his fortune) came from the fact that he also helped usher in America's "confessional culture." Over and over again in the pages of *Physical Culture*, he recounted the story of how he'd transformed himself from a scrawny weakling into America's greatest he-man through clean living, vigorous exercise, and sheer force of will. His openness and honesty about his own failings (long since corrected, of course) prompted readers to write in asking for help with their own problems; others wrote in with tales of their triumphs over adversity.

Broken hearts, unrequited love, marital problems, out-of-wedlock pregnancies, things that weren't even discussed *in private*, let alone in the pages of a national magazine—these were the things that Macfadden's readers shared with him. He established such a powerful bond with them that they wrote to him about anything and everything, and with their permission he published it all.

UP, UP, AND AWAY

By 1919 interest in *Physical Culture*'s confessional stories had grown so much that Macfadden spun them off into a magazine of their own called *True Story*. It was a hit from the first issue and soon shot past *Physical Culture* to reach a circulation of two mil-

---

...a patch on their uniforms with a caricature of him.

lion. *True Story's* success prompted Macfadden to launch scads of other magazines, including *True Romances, Dream World, True Detective Stories, True Ghost Stories,* and *Photoplay.* By the mid-1920s, America's biggest fitness guru was also the country's most successful magazine publisher and a multimillionaire.

AND THEN THE FALL...

Even as he was reaching his greatest heights, Macfadden was also laying the groundwork for his eventual demise. In 1924 he took his publishing company public, which gained him access to outside investors but also put him under their thumb. Not that Macfadden saw it that way: He continued to spend company funds as if they were his own until 1940, when the investors sued to get the money back. Macfadden eventually had to settle the case by selling his stock, resigning as president, and repaying his investors $300,000.

And then there were the women. Macfadden was a man who practiced what he preached, and enjoying sex was no exception. He was a notorious philanderer, and that, combined with his iron will and his conviction that he was right all the time, made him difficult to live with. He married and divorced four times, his last marriage ending when his 44-year-old wife caught him in bed with another woman. (He was 82.)

Macfadden learned the hard way that big businesses can lose money as fast as they make it. One by one, his remaining enterprises shut their doors. By the early 1950s, he was so short on cash that he was jailed for nonpayment of alimony. Twice.

...INTO THE DUSTBIN

In the fall of 1955 Macfadden, nearly broke, was living in a run-down hotel in New Jersey. As confident as ever in his own medical theories, when he started having abdominal pains he tried to treat his condition with fasting and hot baths. By the time his landlord found him comatose on the floor of his hotel room, it was too late to save him. He died on October 12, 1955, at the age of 87. Cause of death: "Jaundice, aggravated by fasting." Killed by the same theories that turned him into a household name, he left his nine surviving children an estate valued at $5,000.

As of the summer of 2008, *True Story* magazine is still in print.

The ski flying (extreme ski jumping) world record is currently held by Bjørn Einar Romøren (784').

THE STRANGE TRAIL OF THE STANLEY CUP

*We told you about the origin of the Stanley Cup on
page 47. But that's only the beginning. The
Stanley Cup has an unusual history.*

S TANLEY CUP FACTS
• In 1919 the Spanish flu struck the Montreal Canadiens.
They offered to play the last scheduled game with substitutes, but their opponents, the Seattle Metropolitans, declined, and for the first time in history, nobody won the Cup.

• In 1924 the trustees started putting more than just the team names on the cup. Today it is the only trophy in professional sports that has the names of winning players, coaches, management, and club staff engraved on it.

• In 1927, after decades of being a multileague championship, the Cup came under the exclusive control of the NHL.

• It got bigger: With each winner, a new ring was added to the lower portion of the cup. By the 1940s, it was a long, tubular trophy nearly three feet high. In 1948 it was reworked into a two-piece trophy with a wider base. In 1958 it was reworked again and got the five-ring, barrel-like shape it has today. It now weighs 35 pounds.

• In 1969 the original bowl was retired to the Hockey Hall of Fame in Toronto because of its fragile state. A silversmith in Montreal made an exact replica—down to scratches, dents, and bite marks—which is awarded today.

• There's one name crossed out. Peter Pocklington, the owner of the 1984 champion Edmonton Oilers, put his dad's name on it. The NHL wasn't amused, and covered it with "XXXXXXX."

• At this point, there are well over 2,000 names on the Stanley Cup—including those of seven women.

• The cup is actually out of compliance with Lord Stanley's wishes—he wanted it to be a trophy for amateur athletes only.

An average golf course uses 6,000 gallons of water a day; some desert courses use a million.

ROWDY GAME, ROWDY TROPHY

Since each winning player and even the management gets to take the Stanley Cup home for a day, it has seen its share of wild times. Here are a few of the more notorious escapades:

• After the Ottawa Silver Seven won the Stanley Cup in 1905, one of the partying players boasted he could kick it across the Rideau Canal. The drunken group went home and groggily remembered the incident the next day. Luckily, the canal was frozen over. When they went back, the Cup was sitting on the ice.

• In 1907 the Montreal Wanderers wanted their team picture taken with the Cup. After the photo session, the team left the studio—and forgot the Cup. It stayed there for months until the photographer's housekeeper took it home and grew geraniums in it.

• In 1924 the Cup-winning Montreal Canadiens went to Coach Leo Dandurand's house for a late-night party. The car carrying the Cup got a flat tire, and the players put the Cup on the side of the road while they changed it. Then they drove off...without it. When they got to Dandurand's house, Mrs. Dandurand asked, "Where's the Cup?" They realized what they'd done and went back. Incredibly, the Cup was right where they'd left it.

• Muzz and Lynn Patrick found the Cup in their basement in Victoria, British Columbia, in 1925. (Their father was the coach of the champion Victoria Cougars.) The boys etched their initials onto the Cup with a nail. Fifteen years later, they got their names on it for real—as members of the 1940 champion New York Rangers.

• When the New York Rangers won the Cup in 1940, the players celebrated by urinating in it.

• The Cup was stolen from the Hockey Hall of Fame twice in the late 1960s. One of the thieves threatened to throw it into Lake Ontario unless the charges against him were dropped.

• In 1962 the Montreal Canadiens were playing the defending champions, the Chicago Blackhawks. During one of the games, a Montreal fan went to the Chicago Stadium lobby display case where the Cup was kept, took the Cup out of the case, and walked away. He almost made it to the door when he was stopped by a security guard. Later, he said he "was taking the Cup back to Montreal, where it belongs."

• Chris Nilan of the 1986 champion Montreal Canadiens photographed the Cup with his infant son in it. He said, "His butt fit right in."

• A player on the 1987 champion Edmonton Oilers (purported to be Mark Messier) took it to a strip joint across the street from the rink and let everybody drink out of it. (It happened again in 1994 when the New York Rangers won. Mark Messier was also on that team.)

• In 1991 the Cup turned up at the bottom of Pittsburgh Penguin Mario Lemieux's swimming pool.

• In 1994 Mark Messier and Brian Leetch took the cup on *The Late Show with David Letterman*. There it was used in a sketch called "Stupid Cup Tricks."

• The Cup has been used for baptisms at least twice. In 1996 Sylvain Lefebvre of the Colorado Avalanche had his daughter baptized in it, and in 2008 the honors went to an infant cousin of the Red Wings' Tomas Holmstrom.

• Rangers Brian Noonan and Nick Kypreos brought the Cup on *MTV Prime Time Beach House*, where it was stuffed with raw clams and oysters.

• The Rangers took the Cup to fan Brian Bluver, a 13-year-old patient awaiting a heart transplant at Columbia-Presbyterian Medical Center. According to his father, Brian "smiled for the first time in seven weeks."

*　　*　　*

THE ELUSIVE 20-GAME WINNER

In the modern 162-game baseball season, a starting pitcher plays only in every fifth or sixth game. Between the inevitable losses and no-decisions, reaching 20 wins is very difficult, and increasingly rare: While 96 pitchers won 20 games in a season in the 1970s, only 37 pitchers accomplished the feat in the 1990s. And 2006 was the first full year in Major League Baseball's 130-year history in which there were no 20-game winners.

70% of Fortune 500 CEOs regularly do business on the golf course.

HOW TO RIG A COIN TOSS

A long-held secret of carnies and hucksters.
With a little practice, it really works.

WHAT YOU NEED
A large coin. The bigger and heavier, the better. When you get really good at it, you can use a quarter, but until then, a fifty-cent piece or silver dollar is best. The trick is nearly impossible with a nickel, dime, or penny.

HOW TO DO IT:

1. Place the coin in the middle of your palm with the side you want to win face-down. For example, if you want "heads" to win the toss, put the heads side of the coin face-down in your palm.

2. Hold your arm straight out and clench all the muscles in your arm so it's as stiff as possible.

3. While holding that arm out tight, toss the coin into the air.

4. Here's the tricky part: As you keep your arm clenched and toss the coin up, jerk your hand slightly back. In other words, very subtly pull your hand ever so closer to your body. The move may be somewhat noticeable, but don't worry. Nobody will be watching your hand—all eyes will be on the coin in the air.

5. Catch the coin in your palm. Result: The coin will turn over in the air exactly once. It will land exactly the same as it was before the toss—with the predetermined winning side face-down in your hand.

6. Slap the coin onto your forearm to reverse the coin and reveal the winning side—which is what was face-down in your palm when you started and what you rigged it to be.

It takes some practice to learn when and how hard to jerk back your hand to spin the coin only once. The heavier the coin, the easier it is—a small coin weighs so little that it tends to spin too many times. With a heavier coin, you've got more control. Now get out there and cheat...er, uh...amaze your friends.

BOBBY GOES A-COURTIN'

*In 1973 an aging tennis pro named Bobby Riggs proclaimed himself
the world's biggest "male chauvinist pig" and boasted, "Even an
old man like me with one foot in the grave could beat
any woman player." Here's what happened when
two female champs took him up on his dare.*

TENNIS WAS HIS RACKET

By the time he was 12, Bobby Riggs was both a brilliant tennis player and something of a con man, eager to take a sucker's buck. Wearing street clothes, Bobby, a self-described "runt," would walk awkwardly onto Los Angeles's public tennis courts, challenging older, more powerful opponents to a game. His older brother John would find people to bet against poor little Bobby—and the Riggs brothers would go home richer.

Bobby was discovered by Dr. Esther Bartosh, a women's tennis champ who noticed his quick footwork, perfect balance, and smooth racket control. She took over his coaching, and believed the youngster could make a name for himself in tennis.

Riggs started on the junior circuit in 1934, when tennis was a gentleman's game dominated by the wealthy. Fiercely competitive and money-hungry, he was no gentleman. The powerful men who made the rules in the tennis establishment discouraged Riggs; they told him he'd never make it to the top. But although he had a crass side, he also had a reverence for his sport. The son of a preacher, he practiced long hours until his game was what he called "airtight."

GOING FOR THE GOLD

By 1936, at only 18 years old, Riggs was ranked number four in U.S. tennis. By 1939 he was the best in the world, winning the U.S. National Championship and at Wimbledon. True to form, he also scandalized the aristocratic purists who didn't want gambling polluting the courts of Wimbledon.

Highest paid sports announcer: John Madden made $8 million per year.

On the eve of Wimbledon, Bobby went to a London betting parlor and bet every dime he had that he'd win the singles, doubles, and mixed doubles titles. No one debuting in Wimbledon had ever won a triple title, so the odds were about 200 to one. The bookies smiled when Bobby made his bets; they weren't so happy when he won all three titles and collected the equivalent of $108,000 (more than $1 million today). Though betting was frowned upon by the tennis establishment, it was perfectly legal. So Riggs kept his fortune.

MAN IN A RAINCOAT

Fast-forward to 1973. The women's movement was at its zenith, shaking up the status quo. Riggs, now 55 years old, had had a brilliant amateur and pro career, and had refused to retire. To hustle up interest—and some decent prize money—for his matches, he would do just about anything—even playing tennis while wearing a raincoat and carrying an umbrella, or holding a lion cub on a leash. But playing off the spirit of the times, Riggs thought up his biggest hustle yet: a battle of the sexes.

At the time, many Americans believed that women weren't capable of coping with high-pressure situations. It was a standard excuse for not letting "ladies" venture into the military, the world of business, or professional sports. Capitalizing on American unease about the changing role of women in society, Riggs announced—to any reporter who'd listen—that he could prove women were the less capable sex. Declaring himself an old has-been, he challenged all the reigning female champions of tennis to a match. Australian-born Margaret Court, three-time Wimbledon champion and the number-one female tennis player at the time, took the bait.

BATTLE OF THE SEXES I

On Mother's Day 1973, in Ramona, California, Riggs and Court played a winner-take-all match for $10,000. Three thousand spectators watched as Riggs played his woman-baiting role to the hilt. The usually confident Court was obviously out of her element. Riggs psyched her out again and again, and kept her off balance with tricky shots that he'd perfected over years of play, like drop shots and high lobs. In short, Riggs demolished Court, 6–2, 6–1.

He then declared himself "the greatest female tennis player in the world."

After the "Mother's Day Massacre," Riggs knew he could attract a big audience. He immediately upped the stakes to $100,000 and challenged the top five women in tennis to exhibition matches. Was there anyone out there, he asked, who would fight for the reputation of women tennis players?

A DIRTY JOB, BUT SOMEBODY HAD TO DO IT

Riggs may have been seeing dollar signs after his match with Court, but a 29-year-old tennis pro named Billie Jean King saw something entirely different. Like Riggs, King had worked hard to prove herself in tennis and had also been disdained by the sport's establishment. In King's case, it was because she was fighting to get the same pay and prize money for women as for men—a radical idea at the time. The men who ran the tennis associations in the 1970s didn't think women would ever be taken seriously or pull in big audiences.

King had watched in horror when Riggs trounced Court in the first Battle of the Sexes, seriously worried that he'd destroyed any chance of women achieving equality in tennis—or anywhere else. King didn't know if she could beat Riggs, but she decided to challenge him to a match.

They agreed to play a highly publicized best-of-five-set winner-take-all match. The prize was $100,000. Millions of people who'd never seen tennis before were suddenly fascinated by the fine points of the game. Bookmakers gave the odds to Riggs, and nearly everyone—even other female tennis players—bet against King. While Riggs kept himself busy with commercial endorsements, King focused on her game.

CLEOPATRA VS. THE SUGAR DADDY

On September 20, 1973, before 30,000 spectators at the Houston Astrodome and 50 million television viewers at home, the second Battle of the Sexes took place. Riggs and King had both agreed to play their parts in the hyped-up pageantry. King wore a mint-green sequined tennis dress made by fashion designer Ted Tinling and entered the arena like Cleopatra, resting on an Egyptian litter carried by four University of Houston football players in togas. Bespectacled Riggs rode onto the court in a rickshaw pulled by his "bosom buddies," six curvaceous show-girls. Riggs gave King a gigantic Sugar Daddy sucker, and she handed him a live baby pig.

Finally, the actual match began.

"ROBERTA" GETS SLAMMED

The scene was pandemonium, with fans in the arena screaming, some for King and some for Riggs. King's father, Bill Moffitt, leaped out of his seat hollering "Go, baby go!" at every point his daughter made. So did George Foreman, the heavyweight boxing champion at the time. At one point in the match, King playfully called Riggs "Roberta," and the crowd went wild.

King later admitted she barely heard the fans because she was so focused on her play. And it worked: She tired Riggs out with long rallies, returning his best shots with ease. She dominated the game completely, running an exhausted Riggs from one side of the court to the other. In the end, she beat him in straight sets, 6–4, 6–3, 6–3. When the match was over, Riggs jumped the net to pump Billie Jean's hand and praise her game. She had beaten him with an "airtight" game of her own, and in the end, he was a good sport about it.

MAKING A DIFFERENCE

King's win helped put women's tennis on the map. It also brought her fight for equal pay into the spotlight—a favorable light. And as he pocketed his endorsement cash, even Riggs seemed to realize that he'd been part of something revolutionary.

Riggs was surprisingly gracious about his defeat at the hands of a woman; he and King became close friends. Even though his loss soon sent him back to obscurity, friends say he remained proud that he'd—however inadvertently—boosted women's success in sports as well as in the workplace. It may have been all bravado, but Riggs stuck with that attitude right to the end. In 1995, not long before his death, Riggs said during an interview with King, "We really made a difference, didn't we?" In 2007 the major tennis championships finally agreed to equal pay for men and women.

LIFE'S A GAMBLE

We'll give you 5 to 1 odds that even if you're a regular gambler, you don't know the origins of these games.

BLACKJACK

Description: Players add up the numbers on the cards they are dealt and try to get as close to 21 points without going over. Face cards count as 10; aces count as 11 or 1.

History: Originally called *vingt-et-un,* or "twenty-one," blackjack is believed to have been invented in France in the early 1700s. Today it's one of the most popular casino card games in the world, but it took a while to catch on. A casino in Evansville, Indiana, introduced it to the United States in 1910. The only way gambling houses could get poker players to give the game a try was by awarding bonus payouts for valuable hands. The biggest payout of all, $10 for every $1 bet, went to the player who held the ace of spades and either of the black jacks. The name that resulted—*blackjack*—lasted a lot longer than the bonus payouts did.

KENO

Description: A game similar to bingo, except that players get to pick their own numbers instead of being stuck with the ones printed on their bingo card. After a player picks several numbers, the house randomly picks 20 numbers between 1 and 80; if the house picks most or all of the player's numbers, the player wins a payout. Many state lotteries operate along similar lines.

History: This game was invented in China during the Han dynasty (202 B.C. to A.D. 220), reportedly when a city came under siege and had to raise money for the army to defend it. Why burden people with an extra tax when you can get them to contribute voluntarily? So officials devised a lottery system instead, one in which 20 out of a possible 120 Chinese characters were chosen at random. Players selected 10 characters of their own, and prizes went to anyone who had at least 5 matching characters. The game saved the city and became popular over so large an area that homing pigeons were used to send messages to

---

Your tax dollars at work: The U.S. military operates 234 golf courses.

people telling them whether they'd won or lost. That's how the Chinese version of the game became known as *pok kop piu*, or "white pigeon ticket."

The American version of the game dates back to 1928, when some Chinese men asked a Butte, Montana, bar owner named Joseph Lyden to organize a game of white pigeon ticket for them. Lyden dropped the Chinese characters in favor of numbers and renamed the game keno (from a French game called *quine*, which means "five winning numbers"). He's also the guy who brought the game to Las Vegas after casino gambling was legalized in 1931.

SLOT MACHINES

Description: You don't know what a slot machine is?

History: Mechanical poker machines were popular in taverns as far back as the 1880s: the player put in a nickel and pulled a lever, which caused five rotating reels with playing cards painted on them to spin and "deal" a poker hand. These machines didn't give direct cash payouts—there are too many different winning combinations in poker for the machine to be able to pay them all. Instead, when you got a winning hand you showed it to the bartender. He poured you a free drink, made you a sandwich, or gave you whatever other prize was listed next to the machine.

Then in 1887, a man named Charles Fey built a much simpler machine called the Liberty Bell. It had only three reels and only five symbols: horseshoes, diamonds, spades, hearts, and bells. The simpler design made automated payouts possible: when a player got three bells, they won the highest jackpot of all—ten whole nickels! Mobster Bugsy Siegel was the first in Las Vegas to put slot machines in his casino, the Flamingo Hotel, in 1947. At the time, they were little more than novelty items designed to keep wives and girlfriends busy while the men played poker or blackjack or shot craps. Today they're computerized, and they bring in between 60 and 80 percent of a typical casino's total profits.

VIDEO POKER

Description: Just like it sounds—a video-game version of poker. You put in your money, the machine deals your "cards" onto a video screen, and you play poker as if you were sitting at a poker table.

History: Another descendant of the early mechanical poker machine, video poker was invented after slot machine manufacturer Si Redd saw the Pong video game in the early 1970s. "We just copied it," he told an interviewer in 2001. Redd started out making both blackjack and poker machines, but dropped blackjack after gamblers realized that their money lasted a lot longer in the poker machines.

As with slot machines when they were first introduced, Redd thought video poker was little more than a novelty; he figured people entering the casino would play a few games before getting down to more serious gambling. Wrong again—gamblers too intimidated to play at the poker tables made video poker machines a mainstay.

THE BIG SIX WHEEL/WHEEL OF FORTUNE

Description: If you're familiar with TV's *Wheel of Fortune*, you already know how this game works. The only differences are that in casinos the wheel is mounted vertically, not horizontally the way it is on TV, and the dealer spins it instead of the players. Pegs divide the wheel into 54 different sections that offer different payouts according to how many times they appear on the wheel. Sections that pay $1 for every dollar wagered are scattered all over the wheel, but there may be only one or two sections that pay $20. When the wheel is spun, the pegs rub against an arrow pointer that slows the wheel down; the winning section is the one the arrow is pointing at when the wheel stops spinning.

History: The wheel of fortune is so old that nobody knows for sure how it originated. One story, most likely apocryphal, is that Roman soldiers invented the game as a means of divvying up the battlefield spoils of defeated enemies. Rather than fight over who got what, each soldier inscribed a mark in a section of the wheel of an overturned chariot. A spear was stuck into the ground next to the wheel to serve as a marker, and then the wheel was spun. The booty in question went to the person whose mark was closest to the spear when the wheel stopped spinning. From there the game is said to have spread to harvest festivals and other public gatherings, where the large wheel made it possible for crowds of people to follow the action. Roulette, which means "small wheel" in French, may have started out as a more portable version of the same game.

PITCHING ZINGERS

Pitchers always look so serious on the mound. But off the mound...

"The way to make coaches think you're in shape in the spring is to get a tan."

—Whitey Ford

"I'd always keep it in at least two places, in case the umpire would ask me to wipe off one. I never wanted to be caught out there without anything. It wouldn't be professional."

—Gaylord Perry, on using foreign substances

"I've never seen anyone on the disabled list with pulled fat."

—Rod Beck, on his weight

"I told him I wasn't tired. He told me, 'No, but the outfielders sure are.'"

—Jim Kern, on being removed from a game

"How can a guy win a game if you don't give him any runs?"

—Bo Belinsky, after losing a game 15–0

"When they operated on my arm, I told them to put in a Koufax fastball. They did—but it was Mrs. Koufax's."

—Tommy John

"I'm throwing twice as hard as I ever did. It's just not getting there as fast."

—Lefty Gomez

"Don't tell me I don't know where to play the hitters!"

—Ray Culp, after a hit ricocheted off his head and was caught by the centerfielder

"Scenario games, like, 'Would you rather open-mouth kiss a bum or get into a sleeping bag with your manager?'"

—Brian Fuentes, reliever, on what goes on in the bullpen

"Baseball's a very simple game. All you have to do is sit on your ass, spit tobacco, and nod at the stupid things your manager says."

—Bill "Spaceman" Lee

"I never throwed an illegal pitch—just once in a while I used to toss one that ain't never been seen by this generation."

—Satchel Paige

"I'm working on a new pitch. It's called a strike."

—Jim Kern

PIONEER ON ICE

At the winter Olympics, the Canadian and U.S. women's hockey teams always dominate. One reason may be this little girl.

A DIFFERENT WORLD

Kids' sports in the mid-1950s looked a lot different than they do today. Where nowadays you might see hundreds of girls turn out for a track and field meet or a youth soccer league, back then, their options were much more limited. Girls played on softball teams and a few played golf—but that was about it. But in Canada, where hockey is the national pastime, women's hockey teams had existed since the first half of the century. Teams like the Preston (Ontario) Rivulettes, the Canadian women's champions from 1930 to '40, were local sensations. Still, any hint of competition between young girls and boys was quickly dismissed because boys were thought to be too rough.

LI'L AB

Abigail Hoffman's brothers played hockey near their Toronto home when they were growing up in the '50s. She was as devoted to the game as her brothers, and was known as a skilled and determined player. When she was eight, she decided to register for a boys' team as "Ab Hoffman." With her short tomboy haircut, no one suspected she was a girl. The league signed her up.

Most of the kids on her new team, the Tee Pees, put on their hockey gear at home, only pulling on skates and gloves at the arena. So, with no locker room to contend with, there was no danger that someone might find out she was a girl. With plenty of practice and competitive games, "Ab" soon became one of the best defensive players in the league: a quick, agile skater who had no fear of chasing the puck into the action. At the end of the season, she was named to the league all-star team.

PAPER TRAIL

But in her second season, when her team was entered in the important Timmy Tyke Tournament, one tournament rule stated

---

Bullfights are legal in the United States, but the matador is not allowed to kill the bull.

that each player had to bring a birth certificate to prove their age. When the organizers noticed that hers said "Abigail," her secret was out. And when word spread that a girl was playing boys' hockey, Abigail Hoffman became an instant celebrity. Her story began showing up in newspaper articles and TV and radio shows, and she handled the firestorm of publicity with surprising poise for a nine-year-old. She was invited to attend NHL games in Toronto and Montreal, and she continued to play for the Tee Pees, where she was well liked by her fellow players. One of her teammates insisted that none of them had had any idea of Abby's secret. But they wanted her to stay, he said, because she was "really good."

UP AND RUNNING

At the end of her second season, Abby joined a girls' team, but said that it wasn't much of a challenge. She tried and succeeded in other sports before devoting her athletic energy to track and field. She worked her way up through the tough ranks of middle-distance running and competed in two Olympics, winning a bronze medal in the women's 800 meters event at the 1972 Games in Munich.

LASTING IMPACT

A few years after she retired as an athlete, Hoffman was named director of Sport Canada, a government-backed agency that supervises amateur sports, including the allocation of government funding for Canada's Olympic athletes. And in 1982 she helped organize Canada's first women's hockey championship, now known as the Abby Hoffman Cup.

About her days as a hockey player in a boys' league, she once said, "I was nothing except a girl who loved to play hockey and had done it with her brothers every chance there was from the time she got skates. When my 'secret' was revealed, my teammates just shrugged as if it didn't matter. What difference did it make?" It may not have made a difference to her teammates, but to the millions of North American girls who heard or read about her story, it made a *big* difference. In 1998 women's hockey officially became an Olympic event—and the U.S. and Canadian teams squared off for the gold medal. The U.S. won, 3–1, fueling a sports rivalry that continues to this day.

WHIZ! SPLAT!
IT'S PAINTBALL!

*You've got to love a game that lets you suit up in a Darth
Vader helmet, goggles, and knee pads...and splatter
everyone in sight with globs of paint.*

CAPTURE THE FLAG

Who says you have to grow up? Not the millions of people
who spend their weekends blasting each other with pellets
of salad oil and food coloring. Since its debut in 1981, paintball
has grown to a sport played by 5.5 million people in amateur and
professional leagues around the world. A combination of the children's games "tag" and "capture the flag," a paintball game's chief
virtue is its simplicity: All your team has to do is capture the
opposition's flag and bring it back to your home base—while you
and your opponents try to to knock each other "out" by tagging
each other with splotches of paint. If you're hit, you're out.

Another attraction of paintball is its variety—games can be
played in open fields and forests ("woodsball") or on specially
designed paintball courses ("speedball") with bunkers, barriers,
and other obstacles to be used as cover. Games can last anywhere
from a few minutes to hours at a time, and anyone can play,
though the winners tend to be those with the greatest skills in
stalking and evasion. It also helps if you're able to drop and roll
with ease. Not surprisingly, there's a strong military feel to many of
the competitions. Some of the best players are former soldiers, and
most teams adopt a platoon-like structure during games, with tactics and strategy based on guerrilla-style fighting. The action is
close enough to real battle that the U.S. Army has even used
paintball games to train recruits.

GAME OF SURVIVAL

One day in the late 1970s, three avid hunters from Henniker,
New Hampshire, were having a few drinks when they started dis-
cussing what made certain people better than others at surviving
in the woods. The three friends were stockbroker Hayes Noel,

Kentucky Derby winner Go for Gin ate oats out of hockey's Stanley Cup in 1994.

sporting-goods dealer Bob Gurnsey, and writer Charles Gaines, who later became famous for bodybuilding books like *Pumping Iron*. Could a person, they wondered, who is not specifically trained for outdoor survival but who has been successful in a competitive, cutthroat field like business or finance, be able to compete with someone like a soldier or hunter, if put to the test? They began brainstorming a stalking game that might prove the point for one side or the other. But how could they do it in a way that simulated "real-life" action, without actually hurting anyone? None of the trio had an answer...yet.

HAVE GUN, WILL SPLATTER

The debate continued, on and off, for a couple of years. Then a friend of theirs saw something in a catalog that piqued his curiosity: a marking gun used by loggers to tag trees. These air guns had been around since the 1950s, used by forest surveyors who went into the woods in advance of the logging crew to mark—with bright spray paint—the trees that were to be cut. But trees aren't always easy to get to; sometimes thick underbrush or deep ravines block the way. Enter the Nel-Spot 007 marking gun. Using compressed air, this pistol could fire a pellet full of paint several hundred feet with accuracy comparable to a regular gun. Gaines and his friends immediately recognized that the Nel-Spot 007 could turn their imaginary game into the real thing.

The men picked up some of the airgun markers and tried them out. They shot at trees, stumps, and tin cans...and were impressed. The gelatin pellets filled with water-soluble paint splattered nicely on the targets, which would make it easy to tell who'd been "tagged." One problem: No one had ever tried out the gun on a human subject. A volunteer was recruited (Gaines's teenage son Shelby) and, after being shot once, he said it didn't hurt...much. A game was scheduled and invitations sent out.

WEEKEND WARRIORS

On June 27, 1981, the first game of paintball took place on 80 acres of woods outside Henniker. Twelve players had been invited, each paying $175 to cover the cost of equipment, food, and drinks. They came from varied walks of life: a trauma surgeon, a builder, a film producer, a venture capitalist, a couple of sportswriters, a farmer, a forester, and a Vietnam Special Forces veteran (the pregame favorite). Four stations had been set up around the course, with 12 flags at each one. The object: Each player had to collect a flag from each station before anyone else did. If another player tagged you with paint, you were "killed" and out of the game.

The first to "die" was the venture capitalist, who was marked within seconds of the start. The doctor turned out to be the best shot, bagging five victims before being tagged himself. But the winner was the forester, Ritchie White. As the Vietnam vet, Lionel Atwill, wrote later, "White crept through the woods from station to station, gathering flags as easily as a schoolgirl gathers flowers." Ironically, White won that historic first game without ever firing a shot.

OFF THE GROUND

That first game didn't settle any arguments about who was better equipped to survive in the woods. The debate raged on during the postgame festivities, but all the players agreed on one thing: They'd never had so much fun in their lives. "The weekend bubbled with humor, honor, fun," Atwill wrote, "and obnoxiously friendly, yet intense, competition." There were three writers in that first game: One wrote an article about it for *Sports Illustrated*, the others for *Time* and *Sports Afield*. All raved about the adrenaline rush that went along with the mock hunt. Letters poured in from readers demanding to know how they could get in on this new game. So the three founders—Noel, Gurnsey, and Gaines—put together a starter kit: a Nel-Spot 007, paintballs, goggles, a compass, and a rule book. They called their new sport the National Survival Game, or NSG.

THE BIG TIME

The second game of paintball took place four months later in Alabama and was open to anyone who wanted to play. Encouraged by the impressive turnout, Gurnsey took over marketing the game (with the blessing of Gaines and Noel, who stayed out of the business). In early 1982, he opened the first commercial course in New Hampshire, became the exclusive distributor for Nelson Paint Company paint guns, and was turning a profit within six months. By late 1982, courses were popping up around the U.S., enough to justify the first national championship tournament in 1983. Held in New Hampshire, the competition was won by a team from London, Ontario, who took home a prize of $3,000 and were later featured in *People* magazine.

Today, the sport is still going strong. The paintball World Cup tournament draws 3,000 players to Kissimee, Florida, every October—and offers a top prize of $10,000.

PAINTBALL SLANG

Dead box: A marked area where eliminated players are sent to wait out the rest of the game.

Dead man's walk: A sneaky tactic often outlawed in competition. The player walks toward the dead box, giving the impression that he's been eliminated. When his opponents turn away from him to look for new prey, he peppers them with paint.

Bunker: To sneak up on a player, trap him, and shoot him at point-blank range while he's behind a bunker.

Bunker bunny: One who's been "bunkered" by an opponent and then gets hammered with paint by other competitors who don't realize that he's out.

H2K: A player who's exceptionally skilled, as in "hard to kill."

Blindfire: A player holding his gun around a corner and pulling the trigger without looking.

Hoser: A player who shoots excessive amounts of paint.

Superman: A headfirst dive to get below a line of incoming paintballs.

Renegade: A team's last remaining player holding out against a large number of opposing players.

Bouncer: A paintball that doesn't break when it hits a player. A lucky break for the player, because under most rules you're not "out" unless the paintball leaves a mark.

Wiping: The cardinal sin of paintball: wiping the paint off from a hit to avoid being eliminated from the game.

Bonus ball: To fire at a player who's already been eliminated, usually as payback for wiping.

THE FIRST MODERN OLYMPICS

At the 1896 Olympics—the first "official" Games since ancient Greece—280 athletes competed. By 2008, the number was up to 11,000. A few other things have changed since then, too.

LET THE GAMES BEGIN

Although the 1896 Olympics in Athens are considered the first "modern olympic games," a number of 19th-century athletic festivals billed themselves as "Olympics." One was the Wenlock Olympic Games in Shropshire, England, started in the 1850s by a local doctor named William Penny Brookes to "promote the moral, physical, and intellectual improvement of the inhabitants of the Town and neighbourhood of Wenlock." Olympic enthusiast Baron Pierre de Coubertin visited the Wenlock games and used them as a model for promoting the larger international version—the modern Olympic Games—that he would eventually organize. The Wenlock Games are still held annually.

BUDGET BUSTER

Two years before the first 1896 Olympics were slated to open in Athens, the organizing committee faced a crisis: The cost to put on the Games, they discovered, would be three times what Coubertin had estimated. It was such a shock that the committee offered to resign in disgrace, but Coubertin and other organizers quickly mobilized and came up with a new plan: an appeal to the host country. The Greek public responded with a fundraising drive, and the Greek government issued special postage stamps and persuaded businessmen to donate to the Games. One such contributor, Greek philanthropist George Averoff, paid almost a million drachmas (about $120,000 at the time) to restore Panathinaiko Stadium in Athens, where many of the games were to be held. In appreciation, a statue of Averoff was placed at the stadium and remains there still.

The U.S. Open tennis trophy is made by Tiffany & Co.

WHO LET *HIM* IN?

Unlike today's Olympics, in which most competitors train their whole lives and qualify months in advance for one sport, many athletes at the 1896 Games competed in their own sport—and one or two others while they were at it. For example, that year's winner of the Greco-Roman wrestling tournament was a German gymnast named Carl Schumann, who also won three gymnastics medals. Likewise, American shot-putter Robert Garret decided to sign up for the discus competition the night before the event, even though he'd never thrown a regulation-sized discus before. He ended up shocking the heavily favored Greek discus team—and the rest of the world—by winning.

GOING FOR THE SILVER

There were no gold medalists at the 1896 Olympics—because there were no gold medals. The winner of each competition was given a silver medal and an olive branch. The second-place winner: a bronze medal and a sprig of laurel. The third-place winner got nothing. The current gold-silver-bronze medal set-up was introduced at the 1904 Olympics in St. Louis, Missouri.

SELF-SERVICE

Olympians today get financial backing from national Olympic committees, colleges, and communities, and are provided lodging at the Games in an "Olympic village" maintained by the host country. In 1896 travel and lodging were much more informal—athletes had to find their own way to the games and hunt for a place to sleep. And before they left for the Games, community support wasn't always a sure thing. When Harvard track-and-field star Ellery H. Clark asked permission to take a leave of absence to compete in the Olympics, the college dean only reluctantly agreed, and warned Clark not to cash in on his Harvard association: "The fact that you are a Harvard man is accidental." Another Harvard athlete, James Connolly, withdrew from the school when his request for an absence was denied. Clark didn't embarrass Harvard—he won the high jump and long jump competitions. Connolly won the triple jump (which, as the first event of the Games, made him the very first modern Olympic champion).

VERY MIXED DOUBLES

Fourteen nations competed in the 1896 Olympics, but on the medal tallies there's a 15th slot with the IOC designation "ZZX." What mysterious nation was this? No nation at all, but a designation for "mixed teams"—those that featured athletes from different nations. Mixed teams medaled three times in the 1896 Olympics, all in doubles tennis, where the winning team consisted of Great Britain's John Pius Boland and Germany's Friedrich Traun. The second-place team featured two Greeks but was considered a "mixed" team because one of them, Dionysios Kasdaglis, was also claimed by the country he lived in, Egypt. Mixed teams were no longer allowed after the 1904 Olympics in St. Louis.

MEN'S CLUB

The first modern Olympics shared one feature with the ancient Olympics: It was strictly a mens' event, with no women athletes competing. But the exclusion didn't last long. In the 1900 Olympics in Paris, women competed in golf, croquet, and tennis—and British tennis player Charlotte Cooper became the first female Olympic champion in history.

*　　*　　*

WORDPLAY WITH YOGI BERRA

Interviewer: Alright Yogi, we're going to play "word association."

Yogi: What's that?

Interviewer: I'm going to say a word, and you give me the first word that comes to your mind when I say it. Okay?

Yogi: Sure.

Interviewer: Are you ready?

Yogi: Okay.

Interviewer: Mickey Mantle.

Yogi: What about him?

PARTY GAMES

*Some fun and challenging ways for you
and your friends to pass the time.*

UN-THUMB HEROES

What you need:
1 roll of Scotch tape
1 roll of wrapping paper
1 pair of scissors
1 pair of shoes with laces
A pad of paper and pencils

How to play:
1. Have the players help each other tape one of their fingers to their thumb.
2. Now see if they can accomplish different tasks without using their thumbs: tying shoes, wrapping a gift, writing their names.
3. First to finish wins.

APPLE BEAR

How to play:
1. The first player says a word that begins with A.
2. The next player repeats the A word, then thinks of a word beginning with B...and so on.
3. Each player has to say all of the previous words before thinking up a new one.
4. If someone goofs, start over.
5. If everyone can make it through the entire alphabet, everybody wins!

SNIFF TEST

What you need:
1 four-inch square of tissue paper
2 breath mints (optional)

How to play:
1. Two players stand nose to nose.
2. One keeps the tissue stuck to his nostrils by sniffing in.
3. The other tries to capture the tissue by sniffing it away.
4. After 30 seconds, whoever has the tissue wins.

WRITE WRONG WAY

What you need:
Paper and pencil
4 thumbtacks

How to play:
1. Each player writes his or her name on a piece of paper.
2. Tack a piece of paper to the wall.
3. Take a pen and stand on your right leg facing the paper.
4. Swing your left leg in a circle, clockwise, while writing your name on the paper.
5. The winner is the player with the closest match to his or her original signature.

George W. Bush and Laura Welch's first date was at a miniature golf course.

WEIRD SPORTS MOVIES

*Baseball movies? Football movies? Seen 'em. But have
you seen these films, based on sports that are a little
outside the mainstream…or don't exist at all?*

Movie: *Rollerball* (1975)
Sport: Rollerball, a combination of roller derby, basketball, and rioting, in which two teams skate (some players ride motorcycles) around a banked track and score points by throwing a steel softball into a tiny hole in the wall of the track.

Plot: In a post-apocalyptic future, the world is run by giant, evil corporations, especially the Energy Corporation, which controls housing, communication, and food. The company owns a Houston team in the worldwide rollerball league, an ultra-violent sport that has taken the place of war. But one star player named Jonathan E (James Caan) is becoming too popular—his individuality undermines the company's "state above all" philosophy. So the Energy Corporation revokes all of rollerball's rules—making it even more violent—in hopes of killing him off during a game.

Bonus: The movie was remade in 2002 and set in the futuristic year of…2005. Dropping the global-corporation theme, this version's rollerball is just a brutal televised sporting event in Eastern Europe (and with more motorcycles). The company running rollerball decides they want more violence in the sport, not to kill off the star (Chris Klein)…but to increase TV ratings.

Movie: *The Blood of Heroes* (1989)
Sport: The Game, which is given no other name, though it resembles an extra-violent version of rugby. Each team scores by hanging a dog skull on the other team's goalpost. The skull-carrier runs while his teammates (called "juggers") protect him, battling the other team with clubs and spears.

Plot: In a post-apocalyptic future, the world is so barren that people eat dogs and scrounge in the dirt for food. For entertainment, traveling teams play the Game in front of cheering crowds. One player named Sallow (Rutger Hauer) takes his team to the Nine

---

Legendary football coach Vince Lombardi coined the phrase "game plan."

Cities, an underground enclave of the ruling aristocracy. He challenges the team there to a death match.

Bonus: Real teams of "juggers" have formed leagues in Germany, Australia, and the United States, although they use foam-padded clubs and a foam "ball" instead of a dog skull.

Movie: *BASEketball* (1998)

Sport: A combination of baseball and the basketball game H-O-R-S-E. The rules: A basketball hoop is set in the middle of a baseball diamond. Baskets made from various distances are scored as a single, double, triple, or home run. If the "batter" makes the shot, he take a base. If not, he's out. In lieu of a pitcher, the opposing team gets to send up a player to "psyche out" the batter; techniques include making fun of the batter's dead mother and grossing him out by eating a bag of liposuctioned belly fat.

Plot: Two losers in their twenties (Trey Parker and Matt Stone, the creators of *South Park)* invent BASEketball in their backyard and it becomes a national craze with a professional league. The inventors struggle with fame, sell out, and lose all their money.

Bonus: BASEketball is based on a game that director David Zucker and his friends played in their own driveways. At one point Zucker intended to make a game show based on the sport, but wrote a screenplay instead.

Movie: *Dodgeball: A True Underdog Story (2004)*

Sport: Dodgeball, the same game played in gym class and at recess, in which you throw balls at the other team. You hit a player, he's out. He catches it, you're out.

Plot: Peter (Vince Vaughn), the owner of Average Joes gym, is on the verge of getting pushed out of business by Globo-Gym, owned by the hyper-competitive and evil White Goodman (Ben Stiller). With a team of out-of-shape misfits from the gym, Peter wins the national dodgeball championship over White's team of all-stars and gets the $50,000 he needs to keep his gym open.

Bonus: The movie inspired a brief dodgeball fad. Adult intramural leagues popped up, as did the National Dodgeball League, with teams like the Seattle Blue Dogs, the Los Angeles Chaos, and the Chicago Vendetta.

For professional golfers, the most common injuries involve the hands and wrists.

THE ORIGIN OF BASKETBALL, PART III

*We could "shoot" the breeze all day about basketball, but we have to
"rebound" and move on to other subjects. So this is the last piece
of our basketball history. (Part II starts on page 241.)*

BY ANY OTHER NAME

In 1891, when James Naismith posted the rules to his new game on the YMCA bulletin board, he didn't bother to give it a name. He just called it "A New Game." One of the Incorrigibles suggested calling it "Naismith Ball"…but the phys-ed teacher just laughed.

"I told him that I thought that name would kill any game," Naismith recalled in his memoirs. "Why not call it Basket Ball?" The delighted player spread the word, and it's been basket ball (changed to *basketball* in 1921) ever since.

SCORE!

The Incorrigibles took to the game right away, and by the end of the week their games were drawing a crowd. Teachers and students from a nearby women's school started showing up on their lunch hour; a few weeks later, they began organizing their own teams.

When the Incorrigibles went home for Christmas a few weeks later, they brought copies of the rules—and their enthusiasm for the game—to YMCA chapters all over the country. In January, a copy of the Springfield school paper, complete with an introduction to basketball (including diagrams and a list of rules), was sent to each of the nearly 200 YMCAs in the United States. "We present to our readers a new game of ball," the article read, "which seems to have those elements in which it ought to make it popular among the Associations."

In the months that followed, these chapters introduced basketball to high schools and colleges in their communities; YMCA missionaries to other countries began spreading the game all over the world.

In 1888 Yale football coach Walter Camp fell ill. His wife coached for the entire season.

"It is doubtful whether a gymnastic game has ever spread so rapidly over the continent as has 'basket ball,' " Dr. Gulick wrote proudly in October 1892, before the game was even a year old. "It is played from New York to San Francisco and from Maine to Texas by…teams in associations, athletic clubs, and schools."

But just as soon as the rules for basketball began to spread, people began trying to change them. Sometimes they succeeded—even in the face of opposition from its founders—and sometimes they didn't. Overall, the game proved to be extraordinarily adaptable, a factor that has been instrumental in keeping it popular.

THE INVENTION OF DRIBBLING

One of the first rules to come under attack was the no-running-with-the-ball rule. When he invented the game, Naismith wanted the person with the ball to stand still and throw it to another player…who then had to stop moving and either shoot or pass.

But players quickly found that when they were cornered and couldn't pass, they could escape by either rolling or throwing the ball a few feet, then running to get it themselves. From there it was just a matter of time before they realized that by repeatedly throwing the ball in the air, they could move across the court alone—even though they weren't supposed to be moving at all. "In the early years," Paul Ricatto writes in Basket-Ball, "it was not uncommon to see a player running down the floor, juggling the ball a few inches above his hand. This so closely approximated running with the ball [traveling] that a rule was inserted saying that the ball must be batted higher than the player's head."

DOWN TO EARTH

Players also discovered that it was easy to move with the ball if they repeatedly bounced, or "dribbled," it with both hands. The idea is believed to have been born on the urban playgrounds of Philadelphia; from there it spread to the University of Pennsylvania and beyond. Eventually it became the preferred method of advancing the ball down the court (beating out juggling the ball over one's head).

Dr. Gulick and other basketball powers were not amused. In 1898 they inserted a rule into the official basketball rulebook outlawing two-handed dribbling. "The object of the [new] rule," Dr. Gulick wrote, "is largely to do away with dribbling...The game must remain for what it was originally intended to be—a passing game. Dribbling has introduced all of the objectionable features that are hurting the game."

Gulick assumed that the issue was dead, since one-handed dribbling was obviously too difficult for anyone to try. But players confounded the doctor. In fact, one-handed dribbling proved so effective that it became the standard.

HOW MANY PLAYERS?

Naismith originally recommended using nine players per team, but said the game could be played with almost any number—depending on the size of the court and how many people wanted to play.

Some teams took this advice to extremes: in the early 1890s, Cornell University played a game with 50 people on each side. So many spectators complained about losing sight of the ball at such games that most college teams began scaling back. Then in 1896, the University of Chicago and the University of Iowa played the first collegiate basketball game with only five players on a team. It worked so well that within a year, nearly every college team in the country used five players.

OUT-OF-BOUNDS

In his original list of rules, Naismith wrote that the first player to retrieve a ball after it had gone out-of-bounds got to throw it back into play. But he wasn't sure if the rule worked, since it seemed to encourage dangerous play: "It was not uncommon," Naismith wrote in his memoirs, "to see a player who was anxious to secure the ball make a football dive for it, regardless of whether he went into the apparatus that was stored around the gym or into the spectators in the bleachers."

The rule ended for good one day while Naismith was supervising a game in Springfield. As occasionally happened, the ball ended up in the balcony that circled the gym. Normally, the teams would race up the stairs to get to the ball first. But on this day, while one team scrambled upstairs, the other showed it had been practicing in secret. They used an acrobatic maneuver, boosting one player up onto the shoulders of another until they were high enough to jump over the railing onto the balcony. Naismith immediately changed the rule to what it is today (the last team to touch the ball before it goes out of bounds loses it).

NOTHING BUT NET

The wooden peach baskets broke easily when players threw balls at them, and within a year the YMCA replaced them with sturdier wire mesh trash cans. But these were a problem, too: Every time someone scored, the action had to stop until the referee climbed a ladder and retrieved the ball by hand. (Apparently, nobody thought of removing the bottoms of the baskets.)

Over the next few years, the trash cans were replaced by specially made baskets with trapdoors that opened when the referee pulled a string...and then by bare metal hoops, which let the ball drop to the ground by itself.

But the bare hoops went a little too far. When nobody was standing near the basket, it was difficult to tell whether the ball really had gone in. So the YMCA suspended a rope net under the hoop to catch the ball. Believe it or not, these nets were closed at the bottom—the ball was pushed out with a stick. It wasn't until 1912 that they finally cut off the bottom. From then on, the "swish" made it obvious whether the ball had gone in or not.

THE ORIGIN OF BACKBOARDS

It's hard to imagine shooting a basketball without a backboard. But the backboard wasn't created to help players score—it was created to keep fans out.

In gyms like the one at Springfield, the only place for fans to sit was in the balcony. It became common for them to gather near the basket during the game. From there, Robert Peterson writes,

> It was easy for a fervid spectator to reach over the rail and guide the shots of his favorites into the basket or deflect those of his opponents. So for 1895–96, the rules called for a 4-by-6-foot wire or wood screen behind the basket to keep fans from interfering. Wire screens were soon dented by repeated rebounds, giving the home team an advantage because the players knew...

John McEnroe once retied his shoelaces seven times during a match at Wimbledon.

their own backboard. So wood gradually supplanted the wire mesh boards.

ON THE MAP

From Dr. Gulick's point of view, basketball was an unqualified success. It had helped encourage interest in sports and physical fitness, increased attendance at YMCA chapters all over the country, and raised the profile of the YMCA in the communities it served. "One of the best solutions to the difficulty of maintaining the interest of the members has been the judicious introduction of the play element into the work," the journal *Physical Fitness* reported in the summer of 1894, "and in this line nothing has been so peculiarly and generally satisfactory as Basket Ball." Thanks in large part to the success of the new sport, Dr. Gulick's critics were silenced and the YMCA became synonymous with sports and physical fitness.

WAR GAME

For all its successes, basketball was still just a game and might never have become a national pastime if it hadn't been for some bad publicity the U.S. Army generated for itself.

In 1916 General John J. Pershing led the "Punitive Expedition" into Mexico in an unsuccessful attempt to capture Pancho Villa. "The newspapers had made much of the drinking and prostitution that had served to entertain an army with time on its hands," Elliott J. Gorn and Warren Goldstein write in *A Brief History of American Sports*, and when the U.S. entered World War I in 1917, it was determined that such embarrassing publicity would not be generated again.

"For the first time in American history," Gorn and Goldstein write, "sports were formally linked to military preparedness...As American troops were deployed overseas in 1917, they were accompanied everywhere by 12,000 YMCA workers who brought sports along with them"—including basketball. More than a million U.S. troops fought in World War I, and tens of thousands of them learned to play basketball while they were in Europe. By the time the war was over, basketball had become an inextricable part of American life.

---

15 runners started the first-ever Boston Marathon in 1897. Only 10 of them finished it.

GOLF FLUBS

Uncle John was always embarrassed by his golf game...until he read these stories of big-time blunders made by big-time golfers.

Golfer: Bobby Cruickshank
Flub: Cruickshank was leading by two strokes in the final round of the 1934 U.S. Open. At the 11th hole, he looked on in dismay as his drive plopped into a creek. But to his surprise, the ball bounced off a submerged rock and rolled onto the green less than 10 feet from the hole. Cruickshank was so happy he tossed his club in the air and shouted thanks to God. The club came down and hit him on the head, knocking him flat on the ground. He got up after a few moments, but never quite recovered. He finished third.

Golfer: Gary Player
Flub: Player was in the lead at Huddersfield, England, in 1955, but on the final hole, he needed a par four to win. His second shot landed near the green, a few inches from a stone wall. Because there was no room for a backswing and he didn't want to waste a stroke knocking the ball clear of the wall, Player decided to ricochet the ball off the wall. It didn't work out exactly the way he planned. The ball bounced back and hit him in the face. Player was knocked for a loop and was penalized two strokes for "impeding the flight of the ball." He lost the tournament.

Golfer: Elaine Johnson
Flub: Johnson once drove a ball that hit a tree, bounced back, and landed in her bra. "I'll take the two-stroke penalty," she said, "but I'll be damned if I'm going to play the ball where it lies."

Golfer: Andy Bean
Flub: Bean was playing in the 1983 Canadian Open when his ball came to rest a mere two inches from the cup on the 15th green. Just to be cute, he tapped the ball into the cup using the grip of his putter instead of the head. Oops. He had forgotten about Rule 19, which states that "the ball shall be fairly struck at with the head of the club and must not be pushed, scraped or spooned." Bean was assessed a two-stroke penalty, which came back to haunt him when he lost the match...by two strokes.

The First Church of Tiger Woods explores the notion that Tiger Woods may actually be God.

ONE PAIR, TWO PAIR...

Bet you didn't know that poker is a relatively new invention. Think we're bluffing? Read on. (By the way, can you guess Uncle John's favorite poker hand? That's right—the royal flush.)

PLACE YOUR BETS
If anyone tells you they know the true origin of poker, they're not playing with a full deck. People have been betting on cards for more than 1,000 years, about as long as cards have been around—and that makes it hard to trace poker back to any one particular game. For that matter, poker may have descended from several different games that were mixed and matched over the centuries to create the game played today. Some likely candidates:

• **Domino Cards,** a game played in China as early as A.D. 900. As the name suggests, these playing cards were marked like dominoes, with each card representing the scores thrown by a pair of dice—a one and a six, for example.

• **Tali,** a dice game played in the Roman Empire. In Tali throws of the dice are ranked in much the same way as poker: Three of a kind beat a pair, and high numbers are worth more than low ones.

• **As Nas,** a four-player Persian game that used a deck of 20 cards divided into four different suits. (According to some sources, there was also a five-player, 25-card version.) There were five types of cards in the deck: lions, kings, ladies, soldiers, and dancing girls; when played with a modern deck of cards, aces, kings, queens, jacks, and tens are used instead. Each player is dealt five cards, one at a time, per hand.

• **Primero,** an Italian card game played from the 16th century on. Thanks to the Napoleonic Wars (when soldiers weren't fighting, they liked to sit around and play cards) in the early 19th century, Primero spread across much of Europe and evolved into a number of different regional versions: *brag* in England, *pochen* in Germany, and *poque* in France.

Survey results: The average Nevadan gambles $846 annually in casinos ($2.31 per day).

BORN ON THE BAYOU

Modern poker is all-American—it evolved from card games that were played in New Orleans in the early 19th century. Exactly how it developed isn't entirely clear, but it's possible that poker came about when the French colonists, already familiar with poque, learned to play As Nas from Persian sailors visiting the port city. In poque the only hands that counted were pairs, three of a kind, and four of a kind; but As Nas recognized two pairs and the full house. At some point, card historians speculate, players dumped many of poque's rules and replaced them with those from As Nas to make the game more interesting.

The name "poque" may have been combined with As (from As Nas) to get *poqas*, which when spoken with a Southern accent sounded like "pokah." Steamboats took pokah up the Mississippi and Ohio rivers to the north, where people pronounced it "poker." From there, poker spread by wagon train and railroad across the continent.

DECKED OUT

Have you ever taken notes during a poker game? Hardly anyone ever does—that's one reason why the history of poker is so difficult to trace. Luckily, in 1829 an English actor named Joseph Crowell saw poker being played on a steamboat bound for New Orleans and recorded what he saw, providing a rare glimpse of what poker was like in its earliest form.

Like today, each player was dealt five cards and then placed bets; whoever had the best cards won all the money that was bet. But at that time, the deck still had only 20 cards (four suits of aces, kings, queens, jacks, and tens)—it wasn't until the 1840s that the full 52-card deck came into use.

Why were so many cards added? There were two main reasons:
• When the concept of the *draw*—replacing some of the cards in your hand with new cards taken from the deck—was introduced in the 1840s, a 20-card deck wasn't big enough anymore.
• People who'd been cheated by card sharks playing a crooked game called three-card monte thought a game with 52 cards instead of just three would be a lot harder to rig.

The 52-card version of poker (and other games) became so popular that the 20-card deck eventually died out altogether.

WAR GAME

The Civil War was a period of great innovation in poker, thanks to the fact that millions of soldiers learned the game during the war and played it whenever they had a chance. Draw poker became very popular, and a newer variation, stud-horse poker (stud poker for short), in which some cards in a hand are dealt face-up, and others dealt face-down, also became widespread. The straight (five cards of sequential rank, such as 3, 4, 5, 6, and 7) also became a recognized poker hand during the war.

PLAY CONTINUED

When the Civil War ended and the soldiers went home, they brought poker with them, and the innovations continued:

• The wild card was introduced in about 1875.

• Low ball (the *worst* hand, not the best, wins the pot) followed in about 1900.

• Why settle for playing only one type of poker per game? "Dealer's choice" games—in which the dealer gets to pick any version of poker they want for that hand—also became popular at the turn of the century.

YOUR GOVERNMENT AT WORK

Were it not for this period of innovation, poker might have faded into obscurity or disappeared altogether. All forms of gambling fell out of favor in many parts of the country at the turn of the 20th century, and many states passed antigambling laws. These laws naturally applied to poker, too... or did they?

In 1911 California's attorney general had to decide whether poker was a form of gambling and thus should be outlawed. His conclusion: standard poker and stud poker, in which you had to play the cards you were dealt, were purely games of chance. That made them a form of gambling, he reasoned, and that made them illegal. Draw poker was another story. Drawing new cards from the deck—or deciding not to—made it a game of skill, and games of skill were not illegal under California law. So draw poker not only survived, it thrived—and today hundreds of different variations of draw poker are played all over the world.

...Women's water polo debuted at the Olympics in 2000.

I'LL SEE YOU AND RAISE YOU
Here's a look at some of the most popular forms of poker. How many have you played?

• **Seven-Card Stud.** Two down cards (face-down) and one up card (face-up) are dealt to each player. They bet, and then four more cards are dealt one at a time—three up and the last one down—and bets are placed after each of these cards is dealt.

• **Razz.** Like seven-card stud, except that the lowest hand wins, not the highest.

• **Texas Hold 'em.** Each player gets two down cards, then they place their bets. Three *common* cards are dealt face-up to the center of the table, then the players place their bets again. Two more common cards are dealt, with bets being placed after each one. The best combination of five cards you can make from your two cards and the five on the board constitutes your hand; the highest hand is the winner.

• **Omaha High.** Each player gets *four* down cards; then bets are placed as in Texas Hold 'Em. Players use two of their cards and three from the board to make a hand.

• **Omaha High-Low.** The same as Omaha high, except that the high hand and the low hand split the pot (the winnings).

• **Five-Card Stud.** Each player is dealt one down card and one up card, then bets are placed. Each player is dealt a second up card, and bets are placed again. A third and then a fourth up card are dealt to each player, each one followed by a round of betting.

• **Five-Card Draw.** Each player is dealt five cards down. Bets are placed, then each player may discard one or more cards and replace them with new cards from the deck, and then bets are placed again.

• **Lowball.** The same as five-card draw, except that the lowest hand, not the highest, wins.

• **Indian Poker.** Each player is dealt one card only, which they are not allowed to see. They hold it up against their forehead—supposedly like an Indian feather—so that everyone else can see it, then bets are placed. High card wins. The idea is that this game is the opposite of all the others—you know what everyone else's cards are, but you don't know your own.

WHY MUST THEY BOO?

Irate fans are a part of baseball. Some players handle them better than others.

"I don't understand why the fans were booing at me. They showed me today they just care about themselves. That's no fair. Because when you're struggling, you want to feel the support of the fans."

—Carlos Zambrano, Cubs

"They have the right to boo people because they've been waiting for 99 years (for a World Series) and sometimes we don't do a good job and they get frustrated, too."

—Carlos Zambrano, one day after the previous quote

"There's not a lot of teams that I've seen in a fight for the division, in control of a ballgame the whole time, never lose the lead, and still get booed. It's certainly a boost for us to play in front of a full ballpark. If they decided to root for us, that would be even better."

—Scott Linebrink, Brewers

"Philadelphia fans would boo funerals, an Easter egg hunt, a parade of armless war vets, and the Liberty Bell."

—Bo Belinsky

"I think the only sport where they don't boo is golf."

—Lou Piniella

"You're trying your damnedest, you strike out and they boo you. I act like it doesn't bother me, like I don't hear anything the fans say, but the truth is I hear every word of it and it kills me."

—Mike Schmidt

"Those boos really motivate me to go out and make something happen."

—Barry Bonds

"I kind of appreciated the fact that I was booed by the Yankees' fans. I was kind of like, 'Okay, I'm a major league player now.' I'll try not to get booed at Tropicana Field."

—Akinori Iwamura, Devil Rays, after hitting a home run in New York

"It's like going to a Broadway show, you pay for your tickets and expect to be entertained. When you're not, you have a right to complain."

—Sparky Anderson

Like baseballs, early basketballs had laces on the outside.

"I actually welcome boos as part of the game. I love to see that from my opponents' fans. Last night I think those fans didn't boo hard enough."

—Ichiro Suzuki, Mariners

"There are always about 20,000 Red Sox fans here when we play them. Maybe it was only Sox fans who were booing."

—Mariano Rivera, Yankees, after blowing a save against the Red Sox

"I've been treated there just like everywhere else: everyone boos me. I take that as a compliment."

—Albert Belle, on playing in Baltimore

"The Expos fans discovered 'boo' is pronounced the same in French as it is in English."

—Harry Caray

"The fans here are too stupid. You have to play perfect every game. You can't make an error. You can't go 0-for-4. Are we like machines?"

—Rey Ordóñez, Mets, after getting booed for going 0-for-4 and making an error

"F*** those f***ing fans who come out here and say they're Cub fans that are supposed to be behind you, ripping every f***ing thing you do. I'll tell you one f***ing thing, I hope we get f***ing hotter than s***, just to stuff it up them 3,000 f***ing people that show up every f***ing day, because if they're the real Chicago f***ing fans, they can kiss my f***ing a** right downtown and PRINT IT!"

—Lee Elia, Cubs manager

"Fans don't boo nobodies."

—Reggie Jackson

*   *   *

UNCLE JOHN'S STALL OF SHAME

The Soap and Detergent Association's 2007 study of people's hand-washing habits at "major public attractions" in four major cities revealed some alarming results: Men wash their hands only 67% of the time (compared to women's 88%). Even more alarming, the research team found that the lowest occurrence of hand-washing by men happened at baseball stadiums, with only 57%.

Horse jockeys are the only U.S. athletes legally allowed to bet on themselves.

MORE OLYMPIC CHEATERS

Here are a few more Olympians who were accused of playing by their own rules. (Part I is on page 83).

HAMMOU BOUTAYEB AND KHALID SKAH, members of the Moroccan track team
Year: 1992
Place: Barcelona, Spain
What happened: Boutayeb fell so far behind in the 10,000-meter event that the two front-runners, Khalid Skah and Kenya's Richard Chelimo, were about to lap him. Rather than let them pass, Boutayeb blocked Chelimo for an entire lap before officials finally dragged him from the track and disqualified him. But by then it was too late—he'd allowed his teammate, Skah, to sprint past Chelimo into first place and win the race.
Reaction: Skah's excitement was short-lived. Spectators booed loudly and pelted him with garbage as he made his victory lap; 30 minutes later, Olympic officials disqualified him and took away his gold medal, figuring that he and Boutayeb had been in cahoots. Skah appealed the decision...and won: the next day the appeals committee took the gold medal back from Chelimo and returned it to Skah.

STELLA WALSH, Polish 100-meter runner
Years: 1932 and 1936
Places: Los Angeles and Berlin
What happened: Walsh won the gold medal in the 100-meter race in Los Angeles and a silver medal in Berlin. But she aroused suspicions. "She ran like a man," says Roxanne Andersen, a women's track coach in the 1930s, who also noted that at the 1936 Olympics, Walsh appeared to have a "five o'clock shadow."

Walsh's victories went unchallenged until 1980, when she was gunned down by a man robbing a Cleveland, Ohio, discount store. An autopsy revealed that she had a genetic condition known as *mosaicism*, which gave her "traces of male and female genitalia," as well as male and female chromosomes. Walsh had kept her condi-

---

Tug-of-war was an Olympic event from 1900 to 1920.

tion secret her entire life and would probably have taken it to the grave had she not been murdered. If people had known about her condition in the 1930s, she would almost certainly have been barred from competing as a woman. "Maybe that's why she refused to room with anybody else," Andersen remarked to reporters.

Reaction: In 1991 the U.S. Women's Track and Field Committee decided not to strip Walsh of her titles, concluding that her gender identity was more complex than it seemed, and that "allegations Walsh either masqueraded as a woman or was definitely a man were unfair." (Gender testing of female athletes has been standard since 1966.)

BORIS ONISCHENKO, member of the USSR pentathlon team
Year: 1976
Place: Montreal
What happened: The defending silver medalist was in the middle of the fencing competition when the British team noticed that he scored points even when his sword didn't touch his opponent's body. Olympic officials examined his sword...and discovered it had been rigged with a "hidden push-button circuit-breaker" that enabled him to score a hit every time he pushed the button.

Reaction: Soviet officials initially protested, but later "admitted" Onischenko's guilt and apologized. "He lost many of his privileges and his career was left in ruins," says Carl Schwende, fencing director for the Montreal Games. "I heard he was working as the manager of an aquatic center in Kiev...Then I learned he was found dead at the pool. Drowning, suicide, accident? My Soviet colleagues won't talk about it."

Onischenko denied any knowledge of the rigging for the rest of his life, and no one knows if he really *was* responsible. The sword may not even have been his: "The Russians had about 20 identical-looking weapons lined up for their use," Schwende says. "A fencer is handed his mask and weapons by a coach only when his name is called....It's possible someone else rigged the weapon, but we had no proof. If we had, we would have disqualified the entire Soviet team." One theory: Onischenko was sacrificed by the Soviets to save the rest of the team. But no one will ever know.

THE AGONY (AND VICTORY) OF DE FEET

Looking for a way to be a better athlete? Just look down.

FEET OF ENGINEERING

Most of us don't think much about our feet. We use them every day—we walk on them, run on them, and even use them to grab the remote off the coffee table. But when you study them closely, the feet are nothing short of a miracle. Mobile, complex machines made up of 26 bones, 33 joints, and 112 ligaments, not to mention countless nerves, blood vessels, and tendons, our feet are our personal transportation network. They balance, support, and propel us through sports. Whether we're rock climbing, bowling, boxing, or playing softball, soccer, or basketball, our feet have a lot riding on them.

On a mile run, your feet endure about 1,500 heel strikes at a force of more than twice the body's weight. For a climber, they're grippers and levers. For a skater, they're accelerators, steering mechanisms, brakes, and shock absorbers. For a high jumper, they're levers and launching pads. But for all their versatility, our feet may never have been intended to hit the ground at all.

Recent fossil discoveries in Latvia and Estonia indicate that one of our earliest ancestors crept out of the sea on four stubby fins (not feet). And the fossil remains of our likely hominid ancestors show that their feet were suited for grasping and climbing African trees. The feet, scientists theorize, were a sort of evolutionary afterthought.

ARC D'TRIUMPH

Watching Tiger Woods swing a golf club, you may not notice how well balanced he is on the balls of his feet. When LeBron James leaps to make a basket, few people comment on how his carefully placed feet launch him into the required dynamics. Similarly, when Serena Williams smashes a tennis ball over the net, you're probably not concentrating on the way her feet pivot as she moves

---

In the NFL, the host team must have 26 footballs inflated and ready.

her body weight into the stroke. But in golf, basketball, and tennis, as in most other sports, feet are the foundation of an athlete's performance.

HOW THEY WORK

Your feet are comprised of three bony arches: a tall one along the inner edge of the foot, a smaller one on the outer edge, and the crossways curve that runs across the foot from the ball to the heel. Together they form an arched vault that not only distributes your weight but is also flexible enough to help you move.

The ligaments that bind the bones of your arch are elastic so they can flatten out, then spring back to shape. When you take a step, your foot rolls outward and your arch flattens and stiffens into a lever to push your foot off the ground. Then your arch springs back to a curve with an added bounce that propels you along. When you set your foot down, your arch rolls outward and becomes flexible to absorb impact.

With every step your foot propels you, stabilizes you, and absorbs shock—all while supporting your weight. How difficult is this? The footwear industry has spent millions researching shoes stiff enough to stabilize your foot and cushioned enough to absorb shock. They're still searching for the perfect combination.

IF THE FOOT FITS

Every foot is unique. A key to athletic success is hooking up the right athlete to the right sport, and even small structural differences in our feet can determine whether we can be a star at the 100-meter hurdles or a powerhouse on the tennis court.

Talent scouts who are searching for speedy quarterbacks, sprinters, or base-stealing ballplayers might do well to examine a candidate's big toe. For most of us, the big toe isn't as long as the next toe. But some people have big toes that protrude out beyond the second toe. These fortunate few have an advantage over the rest of us when they need speed. They can lean their weight onto their big toe to push off and get a fast start. The second toe is not as strong and can only exert about half as much force.

Other lucky athletes might not have an extra-long big toe, but they have a unique advantage in the first metatarsal bone, which is attached to the big toe. If the first metatarsal bone hangs lower than the other metatarsals (the bones to the other toes), then the big toe will also hang lower than their other toes. Athletes with a low first metatarsal can also put weight on their big toe, pushing off for a fast start.

THE FEET SMELL OF SUCCESS

If your big toes are just average, don't fret. There are other ways to take advantage of the sports equipment attached to your ankles.

If your feet tend to roll outward and your arches are stiff and rigid, you might want to try out for track or volleyball. Rigid feet are good levers that make running and jumping easier.

If your feet tend to roll inward and your arches are extremely flexible, it could give you an advantage at tennis or aerobic dancing. Flexible feet are better at handling constant changes in direction with quick, short pivots.

People who've been told they have flat feet are often wary of participating in sports. But most flat feet are just feet with lower arches—and they have their own advantages. They usually fall in the category of flexible feet with good range of motion. Even just plain big feet can be an advantage in swimming (think flippers).

DELICATE PARTS

Both rigid and flexible feet have their downsides. Rigid feet don't absorb shock well, which can lead to bruised and even broken bones. Flexible feet can lack stability, which puts added strain on feet, ankles, and legs; this can cause sprains, charley horses, and shin splints.

Close to 600,000 people a year in the U.S. make a trip to a hospital emergency room because of basketball-related injuries. Most often, the injured parties are playing on an uneven surface and their foot lands awkwardly, which in turn twists (and sometimes breaks) their ankle.

WHEN FEET GET NAKED

Nowhere is the miracle of the foot more obvious than when running—especially if the runner is barefoot. In 1960, at the Rome Olympics, Abebe Bikila of Ethiopia shocked the world when he

---

JFK helped popularize football. He and his staff played the game on the White House lawn.

won the marathon and set a new world record—in bare feet. Zola Budd of South Africa, another barefoot runner, once held the women's world record for the 5,000 meters.

Sports scientists have studied the performance and health of barefoot runners. Research shows that the bare foot—which has sensitive sensory mechanisms for judging impact and absorbing shock—can do a better job of avoiding impact injury than cushioned running shoes.

Since there are so few barefoot joggers, there haven't been any controlled studies of whether bare feet are really better than shoes. But over 50 years ago, a study from the *Journal of Chiropodists* (foot doctors) reported that rickshaw coolies, who spent long days running barefoot while pulling passengers on hard roads in Asia, had healthier feet than shoe-wearing, sedentary Westerners.

NO FEET DOESN'T MEAN DEFEAT

Despite everything we've said about the importance of feet, there's one superathlete who has no feet at all.

In 1998 Tony Volpentest's 100-meter world record of 11.36 seconds was less than 2 seconds behind Donovan Bailey's world record of 9.84 seconds for the same distance. The difference was that Volpentest, who was born without hands or feet, ran in the Paralympics (for people with disabilities) on carbon-graphite feet bolted to carbon-composite sockets that encased his legs. These prosthetics were designed to give Volpentest's artificial feet stiffness and springiness while absorbing the shocks of impact.

Pretty much like nature designed our feet.

*   *   *

WALK THE WORLD

According to the American Podiatric Medical Association, the average person takes 8,000 to 10,000 steps a day, which they estimate add up to 115,000 miles in a lifetime—four times the circumference of the globe.

A runner consumes about seven quarts of oxygen while running a 100-yard dash.

ANCIENT ORIGINS OF GOLF, PART III

Did golf come from paganica, colf, daiku, pukku-mikku, gambuca, or some other game? Here are a few more theories. (Part II of the story begins on page 167.)

CHOLE: THE FLEMISH THEORY

Some historians say golf's most direct recent ancestor was a game played by the Flemish peoples of northern France, parts of which are now Belgium. One theory, put forward by the prominent golf historian Robert Browning in his book *A History of Golf*, revolves around the Hundred Years' War, a long period of nearly constant warfare between England and France in the 14th and 15th centuries.

During the latter half of this bloody era, the embattled French leaders enlisted, and received, the help of another archenemy of the English—the Scots. Thousands of Scottish soldiers fought side-by-side with French soldiers well into the 1400s. There, says Browning, the Scots were introduced to a Flemish game called *chole*, which records show was already a popular sport in northern France as far back as the 1300s. The game: a rock or ball was hit by a curved stick toward a goal, such as a pole, a rock, or a gate, but could be miles away. According to Browning, the Scots took the game home, changed the goal to a hole, and—voilà—golf was born! (Chole is still played in Belgium and northern France today.)

JEU DE MAIL: THE FRENCH THEORY

Jeu de mail (game of mail) was played in France since at least the 1500s. In *The Story of Golf*, author George Per says of the game:

> Originally developed in Italy, it was a curious blend of billiards, croquet, and golf, played with long-handled mallets and large wooden balls within a well-defined area. The object was to hit the ball through one or more iron hoops, using the fewest possible strokes.

According to Anthoine Ravez, president of the French Croquet Federation, jeu de mail has an even farther-reaching influence. "Borrowed by the British around 1300," claims Ravez, "jeu de mail was modified over the centuries: the Scots made golf out of it, the Irish turned it into croquet. Louis XIV, suffering from being unable to play jeu de mail during the winter, miniaturized it on an indoor table and laid the basis of billiards."

What is known is that jeu de mail spread to England, where it was played as the game *pall-mall*. That game became so popular that the London street that runs between Buckingham Palace and Piccadilly Circus is still called Pall Mall.

CHUIWAN: THE CHINESE THEORY

Yes, you read correctly: golf was invented in China. At least that's what some experts, like Professor Ling Hongling in Lanxhou, China, say. Ling believes that games involving the hitting of a ball into a pit or hole were played in China as far back as 300 B.C. The earliest verified records date to A.D. 943, when *chuiwan*—literally, "whack ball"—is mentioned in Chinese literature.

Further proof: Ling claims that in the Palace Museum in Beijing is a Ming dynasty painting called *Xuanzong at Play*. It is a painting of Emperor Xuanzong playing chuiwan. He says it shows the emperor with many different types of clubs to choose from, "caddies" (probably court eunuchs) waiting on him, and even sticks marking the holes with flags on them. Chuiwan was introduced to Europe by the Mongol armies of the khans in the 1300s. It found its way to Scotland, he says, where it was stolen and claimed as Scotland's invention.

TO SCOTLAND

Which theory is accurate? The answer is unknown. But whatever its ancient origin, few dispute that golf is Scotland's game, which gave rise to the British Open, the most prestigious tournament in the world. (For that story, hook on over to page 441.)

*   *   *

CADDIE-LAC

At the Talamore Golf Course in Southern Pines, North Carolina, golfers have the option of renting an old-fashioned golf cart for $20...or a llama caddie for about $100 (free llama T-shirt and hat included).

JACK JOHNSON vs. THE GREAT WHITE HOPE

Nobody gives much thought nowadays to the idea of African American athletes competing against caucasian athletes—it's an everyday occurrence. But back in the early 1900s, it was unthinkable.

THE GALVESTON GIANT

In 1908 Jack Johnson became the first black heavyweight boxing champion of the world. He never considered himself an ambassador of his race and never tailored his public behavior to suit the racist social notions of the day. Instead, Johnson played on white America's fears and prejudices, creating a public persona designed to provoke. He flaunted his wealth with fancy clothes and fast cars and, perhaps most distasteful to the bigoted newspaper sportswriters and editors of that era, he traveled and appeared regularly with white mistresses—two of whom he eventually married.

FIGHT CLUB

John Arthur Johnson was born in Galveston, Texas, in 1878. At the age of 13 he began participating in the notorious Battles Royale—contests between three to five fighters, usually black, with the last man standing taking the purse. By the time he turned 16, Johnson had become a full-time professional boxer.

Pugilism at the dawn of the 20th century was a rougher sport than it is today. Boxing gloves, which had been used to reduce injuries during training for over 100 years, were only just replacing bare knuckles in sanctioned professional bouts. There were no set limits for the number of rounds in a fight—bouts went on until one of the contestants could no longer continue. Professional boxers often fought once a week or more for relatively small purses and in unforgiving circumstances.

Black fighters weren't offered opportunities to fight for world titles—particularly not in the glamorous heavyweight division. The best black boxers traveled the country fighting white contenders in non-title contests, or fighting one another. Two of the

---

In the United States, Frisbees outsell baseballs, basketballs, and footballs combined.

best black heavyweights of Johnson's era, Sam Langford and Joe Jeanette, fought each other 15 times. Johnson fought Jeanette 10 times before winning the title but then never offered Jeanette a title match. They would only fight again in 1945 at the respective ages of 67 and 66 for a war bonds promotion in New York.

IN THIS CORNER...

It was in this harsh and undeniably racist atmosphere that Johnson, after nearly 100 fights and four years as "Black Heavyweight Champion of the World," got his world heavyweight title shot against reigning champ Tommy Burns. On the eve of the fight, held in Australia, a Sydney newspaper wrote that "citizens who never prayed before are supplicating Providence to give the white man a strong right arm with which to belt the coon into oblivion."

Burns was paid a record $30,000 for the fight; Johnson, $5,000. Johnson beat Burns decisively; police had to stop the fight in the 14th round for Burns's safety. American author Jack London, writing in the *New York Herald*, observed that "the battle was between a colossus and a pygmy. Burns was a toy in Johnson's hands." London then called upon former champion Jim Jeffries, who'd retired undefeated to a Nevada farm, to avenge the white race. "Emerge from your alfalfa fields," he wrote, "and remove the golden smile from Johnson's face. Jeff, it's up to you. The White Man must be rescued."

The search for the Great White Hope was on.

DEFENDING THE TITLE

Boxing promoters quickly arranged for middleweight champ Stanley Ketchel to be the first of the Great White Hopes. For 11 rounds Johnson toyed with the smaller Ketchel, taunting him with insults and landing blow after blow. In the 12th round, the battered and bleeding Ketchel caught Johnson with a lucky shot that sent him to the canvas. The champion picked himself up and ended the fight with one last punch, knocking Ketchel's teeth out.

Several other white fighters followed, trying to dethrone Johnson. They all failed. Eventually, the undefeated Jim Jeffries was coaxed into taking up the challenge. White America was convinced that Jeffries was their last, best hope for a white champ. The stage was set for one of the most socially explosive bouts in boxing history.

BEFORE THE FIGHT

James J. Jeffries was the only heavyweight champion ever to have retired undefeated. He'd been contentedly raising crops on his farm for six years when London and others convinced him to return to the ring. His fight with Johnson, scheduled for July 4, 1910, in Reno, Nevada, was one of the most anticipated sporting events of the age.

Promoter Tex Rickard sold a record 40,000 tickets to the contest. Eastern newspapers arranged to keep tabs on the fight via telegraph. Rickard spread rumors of celebrity referees, including H. G. Wells and Sir Arthur Conan Doyle, and hired former (white) champ James J. Corbett to make inflammatory publicity statements like, "Take it from me, the black boy has a yellow streak and Jeff will bring it out when he gets him into that ring."

The pre-fight hysteria over Jeffries's hope of "avenging his race" even affected the bookmakers—they made the aging, overweight Jeffries a 10 to 6 betting favorite, prompting Johnson to wire his brother Claude in Chicago to "bet your last copper on me." The fighters were to receive among the largest purses ever awarded in a prizefight at the time: $60,000 plus a $10,000 advance for Johnson, $40,400 to Jeffries, with an additional $50,000 apiece for the sale of film rights.

Leading up to the fight, Johnson continued to taunt his detractors. At his training camp two miles out of town (which was open to the press), he had two white women with him. The atmosphere surrounding the fight was summed up by playwright Howard Sackler in his 1967 play *The Great White Hope*:

> The fight was going to decide in the eyes of the world not just who was the better man, but who was the better race. The fear that underlay this was a nightmare fear, of this smiling black man, the strongest black man in the world, who made no bones about wanting and being able to have white women. That touched something very deep in the American consciousness.

AND THE WINNER...

The once-great Jeffries was humiliated in a 15-round knockout, Johnson making it clear that he was only toying with the ex-champ and that he could have ended the fight at any time. The news of Johnson's victory went out over the telegraph lines and

---

...exactly 24 years after his father's first major league hit was a double.

within hours race riots broke out in every Southern state, as well as in Pennsylvania, Colorado, Missouri, Ohio, New York, Illinois, and the District of Columbia. Former president Theodore Roosevelt called for a ban on prizefighting, and Congress hastily passed laws prohibiting the interstate transportation of motion pictures, to prevent films of the fight being shown around the country. Before the dust settled, at least 14 black men had been lynched in the fallout over the fight.

THE WHITE SLAVE ACT

After the Jeffries debacle, Johnson continued to plow through his opponents and infuriate his enemies. Black journalists and social critics pressured him to tone down his antagonistic act and become a more acceptable black role model for the white press. But Johnson refused to yield.

Unable to find a match for him in the ring, white authorities arrested Johnson in 1912. The charge: violation of the Mann Act, which prohibited the transport of women across state lines "for immoral purposes." Known as the "White Slave Act," the law had been created to stop interstate prostitution rings. The white woman Johnson was convicted of crossing state lines with was Lucille Cameron, his fiancée. The judge who convicted him was Kenesaw Mountain Landis, who, as commissioner of baseball, would later work tirelessly to keep black players out of the major leagues.

Rather than face prison, Johnson fled to Europe, where he continued to box, fighting exhibition bouts all across the continent. After three years, he began to tire of the strain and agreed to defend his title against the new Great White Hope, the 6'7" Jess Willard. Some writers believe the promoter convinced Johnson that a pardon could be arranged if he took the fight. Whether this is true remains uncertain. What is certain, however, is that no real pardon was ever offered.

ON THE ROPES

The fight was held close to home, but not quite on American shores—in Havana, Cuba, on April 5, 1915. It was a grueling bout, scheduled to last 45 rounds in 100-degree heat. But in the 26th round, Willard knocked out the 37-year-old Johnson.

In later years, Johnson claimed to have thrown the fight. As

Deion Sanders is the only man to play in the World Series and the Super Bowl.

evidence, he pointed to films that show him lying on his back using his arms to shade his eyes from the sun as the referee counts him out. Was Johnson really knocked out, or was he faking? It didn't matter: he lost the fight, and white America felt redeemed.

FINAL ROUND

Johnson returned to the United States in 1920 and spent a year and a day in Leavenworth Prison, where he served as athletic director. On his release, he returned to the ring, where he earned decent money fighting exhibitions and non-title fights. He also continued his extravagant lifestyle, complete with white wives and fast cars. It was in such a fast car that Jack Johnson met his end in 1946. On his way to New York to watch the second black heavyweight champion, Joe Louis, defend his title against young Billy Conn (who also bore the Great White Hope burden), Johnson crashed his car in North Carolina and died at the age of 68. He is buried in a family plot in Chicago next to his two wives, in an unmarked grave to prevent vandalism.

RANDOM FACTS

• On April 18, 1922, Jack Johnson received U.S. Patent #1,413,121 for a type of wrench he invented.

• When Howard Sackler's play *The Great White Hope* opened in 1967, the actress playing Johnson's wife received hate mail and death threats over a scene depicting the interracial couple in bed. (James Earl Jones played Jack Johnson.)

• During World War I, a heavy artillery shell was referred to as a "Jack Johnson."

• "The possession of muscular strength and the courage to use it in contests with other men for physical supremacy," said Johnson, "does not necessarily imply a lack of appreciation for the finer and better things in life." Johnson *was* a man of refined tastes: he wrote two memoirs, played the cello, acted in plays and in vaudeville, and was romantically linked to exotic figures such as Mae West and German spy Mata Hari.

• Other celebrities arrested for violating the Mann Act: Charlie Chaplin in 1944 and Chuck Berry in 1962. Chaplin was acquitted. Berry served two years in prison. The act was repealed in 1986.

"One man practicing sportsmanship is better than a hundred teaching it." —Knute Rockne

THE GAME OF UNO

Have you ever played the game of Uno? It's consistently been one of America's best-selling toys. Here's where it came from.

INVENTED BY: Merle Roberts, a barber from Cincinnati, Ohio

ORIGIN: In the 1960s, Roberts created a simplified version of the card game Crazy Eights, and sold it out of the trunk of his car and at Kiwanis conventions. That might well have been all there is to write about it…if a neighbor hadn't played the game with an acquaintance named Bill Apple. Apple, in turn, showed the game to his brothers-in-law Bob Tezak and Ed Ackeman on Thanksgiving Day in 1971.

"It was miserable weather that weekend so we just played game after game," Tezak recalls. He and Ackeman enjoyed it so much that they talked Apple into buying it. "We paid Roberts in the neighborhood of $100,000 for all rights to the game, which in 1972 was a considerable amount of money," Tezak says. "I got a lot of strange looks, but I did it. At the time I didn't know any better."

SELLING IT: Tezak was a florist and funeral home director. The trio set up shop in the back room of his family's funeral parlor while Ackeman took a two years' leave of absence from his job as a bank teller to develop and sell Uno. In their first year of business, they sold 5,000 games and made $54 in profits—which they split three ways.

Their big break came in 1977 when Tezak made a sales presentation at the Wal-Mart headquarters in Bentonville, Arkansas. "I can see this guy isn't about to place an order," Tezak remembers, "but I'm still making my pitch when Wal-Mart's founder Sam Walton walks in and says, 'How ya' doin', son?' So I told him about Uno. When I got done, he was quiet for awhile. Then he said, 'Buy a couple gross from the boy.' That made us. What Wal-Mart buys, everybody buys."

Since then, Uno has sold more than 100 million decks, making it the number-one card game in the world (after playing cards).

THE PINBALL STORY

If you like pinball (and who doesn't?), here's the next best thing to actually having a machine in the bathroom. Hmm…interesting idea. Imagine what it would sound like to people waiting to use the toilet. "What are you doing in there? What's that noise? Hey, are you playing pinball?!!?"

ROLLING STONE
Have you ever heard of a game called *Bagatelle*? No one plays it anymore, but for centuries it was one of the most popular pastimes of the European upper classes. Originally, it was played outside. People threw stones up a hill and hoped that, as the stones rolled down, they'd fall into holes that had been dug in the hillside.

By the middle of the 17th century, the game was played indoors. Players pushed small balls up an inclined felt board with a stick, then let the balls go. Again, the object was to get the balls to drop into holes. But now each hole was surrounded by small pins (actually brass nails) to make it harder. The more points a hole was worth, the more pins were nailed around it. That, of course, is how *pinball* got its name.

THE NEXT STEP

Bagatelle remained popular in various forms for centuries. But modern pinball didn't evolve until 1931, when game manufacturer David Gottlieb created a version called Baffle Ball. He made two important changes to Bagatelle:

1. He incorporated a spring-loaded mechanism (virtually indistinguishable from modern-day pinball shooters), so balls were launched rather than pushed or dropped.

2. He made it a coin-operated machine, designed to sit on retailers' countertops.

There weren't any lights, bells, mechanical bumpers, or even flippers. Players shook and jostled the machine (technically, they weren't even supposed to do *that*) to get the ball into one of the high-scoring holes. But it was a cheap, appealing diversion during the Great Depression, and was very popular.

According to the California Medical Association, 87% of professional boxers have brain damage.

As Russell Roberts wrote in the *Chicago Tribune*:

> To an American public haunted by economic disaster, facing day
> upon dreary day of hanging around street corners with nothing to
> do and no hope in sight, the new games were a welcome respite.
> For either a penny or a nickel (for which you got 7 or 10 balls,
> respectively), you could forget, for a few minutes anyway, the world
> and all its troubles. Soon every drugstore, bar and candy store had
> at least one.

Baffle Ball was also a source of employment. The games sold
for only $16. Anyone who had the money could buy one, put it in
a store, and split the profits with the store owner. "Pinball route-
men," explains Candice Ford Tolbert in *Tilt: The Pinball Book*,
"were anyone and everyone who could come up with a little cash
and who had the time to service and collect from machines out on
locations."

THE BIG THREE

Demand for Baffle Ball was so great that Gottlieb couldn't fill all
his orders. So some of his distributors started to build their own
games. In 1932, Gottlieb's biggest distributor, Ray Moloney,
invented a game called Ballyhoo. It was so successful that he
formed the Bally company and began designing games full-time.

Another distributor—an aspiring Disney cartoonist named
Barry Williams—came up with so many innovations that Gottlieb
offered him a royalty for his designs. (Later, Williams formed his
own company.) Their first joint venture was a game called
Advance. Roger Sharpe writes in *Popular Mechanics*:

> One of the breakthrough attractions of Advance was its delicately
> counterbalanced gates, which were vulnerable to jabs and nudges
> from players. One day, in 1932, Williams went to a drugstore and
> saw a player hit the bottom of Advance to score points without
> having to aim. This so enraged Williams that he took the game
> off location and hammered five nails through the bottom of the
> machine. In Williams' words, "Anybody who tried to affect the
> play of the game by slapping the flat of his hand against the
> game's undersurface, would now think twice before trying it
> again."
>
> However, Williams knew this was a cruel and temporary solu-
> tion. So, he developed a simple, effective device that stopped play

---

The seventh-inning stretch makes baseball the only sport where *spectators* do calisthenics.

if the machine was handled roughly. The device consisted of a small ball balanced on a pedestal. If the game was shaken or pounded, the ball fell from the pedestal and struck a metal ring that immediately stopped play.

Williams called the device a "stool pigeon"…but not for long. "I never quite liked the name 'stool pigeon,'" he recalled years later, "but I just couldn't come up with anything else." So he set one of the games up in a nearby drugstore and waited to watch the response. Sure enough, a player came along and handled the game too roughly, setting off the stool pigeon. "Damn, I tilted it!" he exclaimed. From then on, the mechanism was known as the *tilt*.

THERE HAS TO BE A TWIST

There were four other important steps in creating the pinball machine as we know it:

1. Themes. In 1933, David Rockola (later a jukebox tycoon) came up with Jigsaw. Players could put a puzzle together by hitting certain targets and holes. Its popularity showed that the public wanted variety and novelty in their pinball games.

2. Electricity. Williams introduced Contact, the first pinball game to use electricity, also in 1933. It had an electrified "kick-out hole" that returned a ball to play after awarding points, and a bell that rang every time a player scored. Features like automatic scoring and "lighted back glass" quickly appeared on new machines.

3. Bumpers. Bally introduced Bumper in 1937. It used the first "electrically operated wire and spring bumpers."

4. Flippers. The first flippers appeared in a Bally game called Humpty Dumpty, in 1947. Before this breakthrough—created by accident when a technician touched two loose wires together—pinball machines were almost entirely games of chance. In Humpty Dumpty, the balls jumped around at the player's command. This feature quickly became indispensable on the machines…and turned pinball into a worldwide phenomenon. "In most of Europe, in fact, they're called flipper games and flipper machines," Roger Sharpe writes in *Pinball!* "Today, we have ramps, drop holes, underground networks, multiball games, drop targets and spinners, but they all don't necessarily have to be on every game. A flipper does."

Golf courses cover about as much of the U.S. as Delaware and Rhode Island combined.

PINBALL AND THE LAW

In 1933 pinball manufacturers made a mistake that would haunt them for decades. They decided to compete directly against slot machines, electronic bingo, and other gambling machines by building "payout" pinball machines, which rewarded successful players either with cash or tokens that could be redeemed for cash.

To many people, the move made pinball machines synonymous with gambling. And when communities outlawed other types of gambling machines—before and after World War II—they often got rid of all types of pinball machines as well.

Pinball manufacturers countered by introducing "free play," machines that rewarded players with extended games instead of cash. But even these were controversial. Free games are objects of value, and therefore a kind of gambling payoff. Tamer "add-a-ball" features were condemned, too. In fact, it wasn't until America was exposed to the excesses of the 1960s that pinball finally regained acceptance as the lesser of many evils.

Believe it or not, however, many cities and states still have anti-pinball laws on the books, although they're seldom enforced anymore. Ironically, Chicago—home of Gottlieb, Bally, and Williams, the big three manufacturers of pinball machines—is one of the cities that had a long-term ban on the game. It wasn't until 1976 that pinball was finally legalized in its own hometown.

PINBALL FACTS

• David Gottlieb may have invented pinball, but he didn't have much faith in it. His second game was called Five Star Final, supposedly named after his favorite newspaper, the *Chicago Tribune*'s end-of-the-day edition. Actually, though, Gottlieb figured the pinball "fad" was over and this was his "final" game. A few decades later, in the golden age of pinball, new machines were being designed and shipped every three weeks.

• It takes a team of six designers about nine months to invent and perfect a pinball game.

• Pinball designers work toward these ideals: the game should be easy enough to keep novices from getting discouraged, yet challenging enough to keep "wizards" interested; the average game should last from 2 ½ to 3 minutes, or roughly 47 seconds a ball; and the player should get one free game for every four played.

There are 32 leather panels and 642 stitches on a regulation soccer ball.

DUMB JOCKS?

Sports stars say the darnedest things. Are they trying to be funny... or are they just not all there? You be the judge.

"My wife doesn't care what I do when I'm away as long as I don't have a good time."
—Lee Trevino

"Be sure to put some of them neutrons on it."
—Mike Smith, baseball player, instructing a waitress on how to prepare his salad

"This taught me a lesson, but I'm not sure what it is."
—John McEnroe

"I want all the kids to do what I do, to look up to me. I want all the kids to copulate me."
—Andre Dawson, Chicago Cubs outfielder

"They shouldn't throw at me. I'm the father of five or six kids."
—Tito Fuentes, baseball player, after getting hit by a pitch

"That's so when I forget how to spell my name, I can still find my clothes."
—Stu Grimson, hockey player, on why he has a photo of himself above his locker

"I've won on every level, except college and pro."
—Shaquille O'Neal

"I could have been a Rhodes Scholar, except for my grades."
—Duffy Daugherty, Michigan State football coach

"People think we make $3 million and $4 million a year. They don't realize that most of us only make $500,000."
—Pete Incaviglia, baseball player

"If history repeats itself, I think we can expect the same thing again."
—Terry Venables, professional skier

"After a day like this, I've got the three Cs: I'm comfortable, I'm confident, and I'm seeing the ball well."
—Jay Buhner, outfielder, after a perfect 5-for-5 day

"Just remember the words of Patrick Henry—'Kill me or let me live.'"
—coach Bill Peterson, giving a halftime pep talk

Which sport has *first slips*, *silly points*, and *fine legs*? Cricket—they're all fielding positions.

SIX GREAT THINGS ABOUT DAVE WINFIELD

Baseball player Dave Winfield played for 22 seasons, was a 12-time All-Star, and was named by ESPN as the third-greatest athlete in history (behind only Jim Brown and Jim Thorpe). Here are a few more facts, from Uncle John's Bathroom Reader Plunges into Minnesota.

1. HE WAS DRAFTED BY FOUR TEAMS IN THREE DIFFERENT SPORTS.

Winfield's prowess on the diamond has been well documented, but the 6'6" sensation was also a phenomenal basketball player who played power forward at the University of Minnesota. That versatility created some intriguing possibilities. Following his university career, Winfield was drafted in 1973 by baseball's San Diego Padres, the NBA's Atlanta Hawks, the Utah Stars of the American Basketball Association, and the NFL's Minnesota Vikings. What makes the Vikings selection all the more extraordinary is that Winfield never actually played college football. The pick itself was something of a novelty for the Vikings, who chose Winfield with their final pick in the 17th round, hoping they could convince him to use his size and skilled hands on a football field rather than a baseball diamond.

2. HE NEVER PLAYED IN THE MINORS.

The Padres considered Winfield such a sure-fire prospect that he became one of the few players to jump directly from the amateur ranks to the major leagues. Despite his lack of time on "the farm," Winfield flourished and hit .277 during his rookie year.

3. HE COULD HAVE BEEN AN PITCHER.

In 1969 Winfield decided to go to the University of Minnesota on a baseball scholarship. While in college, Winfield was a starting pitcher before he suffered a shoulder injury. The setback did have an upside, though; it forced him to focus on his hitting. That change helped him hit .385 and slug eight home runs and 33 RBIs during his senior season. Along the way, he also helped lead the

---

A matador's cape, called a *muleta*, has a red side and a yellow side.

Golden Gophers to the semifinals of the College World Series, where he was named MVP.

4. HIS BIRTHDAY HAS HISTORICAL SIGNIFICANCE.

Mention October 3, 1951, to baseball fans, and they'll think of the "shot heard 'round the world." Winfield was born the same day that New York Giants outfielder Bobby Thomson connected with a pennant-winning hit. Winfield had a similar moment himself in 1992 when his 11th-inning, two-out double allowed the Toronto Blue Jays to win their first world championship. It was also the first World Series title won by a team outside the United States.

5. HE GOT GEORGE STEINBRENNER BOOTED OUT OF BASEBALL.

Winfield repeatedly knocked heads with Yankees owner George Steinbrenner during his nine years with the club. For the most part, Winfield could stand the public chiding, but when Steinbrenner refused to pay the Winfield Foundation the $300,000 guaranteed in Winfield's contract, the ballplayer decided to take the matter to court. Incensed, the Yankees boss tried to ruin Winfield's reputation by paying a gambler named Howie Spira $40,000 to uncover dirt on his star player. It didn't take long for Steinbrenner's scheme to become public, and Major League Baseball commissioner Fay Vincent suspended him from running the Yankees for two years beginning on July 20, 1990. In the end, neither Spira nor Steinbrenner was able to tarnish Winfield's reputation.

6. HE WAS THE FIRST HALL OF FAMER TO ENTER COOPERSTOWN AS A PADRE.

One of baseball's traditions is that players entering the Hall of Fame get to choose which team's hat they wear on their official plaque. When it came time for Winfield to decide where his allegiances lay, the decision was an easy one. Despite spending his most productive years as a Yankee, Winnie decided to reward the franchise that gave him his start by entering Cooperstown as a Padre. The decision so angered George Steinbrenner that he tried (and failed) to have it reversed.

Olympic gold medals are made of mostly silver.

ROLLER DERBY

What sport was popular in the 1940s and the 1960s, helped make TV popular, and helped set the rules for televised sports? No, it's not badminton. Here's the story of a strange sport that will not go away.

RACE ACROSS AMERICA

Along with other bizarre fads such as flagpole sitting and goldfish swallowing, "marathon" entertainments were popular in the 1920s. Depression-era audiences seemed to enjoy watching other people suffer as they danced for 20 hours, bicycled for six days, or walked around a track until they dropped. But by 1935 the fad was pretty much over, and a dance-marathon promoter from Portland, Oregon, named Leo Seltzer had to find another way to make a living. He'd read in a magazine that 97% of Americans had roller-skated at some point in their lives, and that gave him the idea to switch from dance marathons to roller-skating marathons.

He held the first one on August 13, 1935, in the Chicago Coliseum. A large, flat oval track was constructed in the center of the arena; 18 laps equaled a mile. The rules were simple: Teams of one man and one woman raced to skate 57,000 laps—about 4,000 miles. They would skate 11 hours a day every day for a month. The skaters earned $25 a week, good money at a time when jobs, if they could be found, paid about $12 a week.

THE RACE IS ON

The event drew 20,000 people. It was so successful that Seltzer decided to select the best 20 skaters and take the show on the road, calling it the Transcontinental Roller Derby Association. He added a few flourishes, such as a giant map of the 4,000-mile New York–to–Los Angeles trip with lights along Route 66 indicating the skaters' "progress." He also created "sprints," special periods in which skaters could earn bonus points for lapping other skaters. Fast-paced and competitive, sprints were a crowd favorite. But despite the urge to push other skaters out of the way, physical contact and fighting were strictly forbidden.

Seltzer continued to tweak the contest format, ultimately turning the marathon into a game. In the middle of the national tour, he changed the troupe of 20 skaters from 10 pairs of players to two 10-person teams of five men and five women each. That change increased the instances of what the audience loved most: lapping. The Route 66 map was eliminated in favor of a pass-for-points system. They got a point every time they lapped an opponent.

RACING TO VIOLENCE

Two events would permanently alter the tone of the game:

• At a race in Louisville, Kentucky, in 1936, skater Joe Laurey passed two opponents and purposely smashed into them. As they lost their balance, he threw them over the railing. Laurey was immediately kicked out of the game, and as he stormed out of the arena and threw his skates on the track, the crowd went wild.

• In Miami in 1937, some of the faster—and skinnier—skaters tried to break through a pack of slower, more muscular opponents and steal laps. The larger skaters pushed back, elbowing and shoving. But when the referees moved in to break up the tussle, the audience booed. They loved the violence.

Seltzer decided to lift the ban on physical contact. Not only did he make it part of the game, it soon became a vital part of the scoring process. Sprints became "jams" (the crush of skaters resembled a traffic jam), and that became the final element of the roller derby: A skater could earn one point for his or her team by passing another skater, even if it involved beating them up to do it.

GOING IN CIRCLES

Roller derby grew steadily in popularity as it toured from town to town around the United States. By 1940 the league had expanded from two squads to eight traveling teams, the same year roller derby events attracted four million people. It looked like the sport would continue to grow, but when America entered World War II in 1941, most of the male skaters were drafted into military service, reducing the league back to two teams. The squads kept playing the circuit, cheering up wartime crowds the way early skating marathons had entertained Depression-era audiences. But with only two teams touring, there were fewer derby events, and by the

...racehorse Secretariat, in 1973.

late 1940s, the sport's popularity dwindled. With more pressing world issues going on, the sport seemed silly and old fashioned.

But Leo Seltzer wasn't about to give up. He had invested his life—and his life savings—in roller derby. And, fortunately, there was a new tool at his disposal: television. Seltzer theorized that if the derby could be beamed all over the country, it would draw paying customers to the live events. CBS agreed to run derby matches once a week for 13 weeks in 1947. (The same two teams, the New York Chiefs and Brooklyn Red Devils, played each other every time.) The idea paid off: After five weeks of TV exposure, the derby was a top-10 show and the 69th Regiment Armory in New York City sold out all 5,300 of its seats for the event.

The broadcasts were so successful that after the initial 13-week run, a bidding war ensued. Seltzer ultimately signed with ABC. ABC was a brand-new network and needed to fill a lot of airtime cheaply, so it aired roller derby three nights a week and on Saturday afternoons. To meet the demand, Seltzer expanded for the first time in nearly a decade, creating a six-team organization he called the National Roller Derby League, consisting of the two New York teams plus the Jersey Jolters, the Chicago Westerners, the Philadelphia Panthers, and the Washington Jets. It was ABC's most profitable broadcast. But Seltzer was unhappy: He envisioned the roller derby as a legitimate sport. He wanted to air derby matches for 40 weeks a year with an end-of-season championship game. ABC didn't see it that way. To them it wasn't a sport, it was a TV show, and they wanted to air it 52 weeks a year…and ABC got their way.

BE CAREFUL WHAT YOU WISH FOR

Although 82,000 people packed New York's Madison Square Garden for the 1951 championship game, in 1952 the league didn't have enough money to pay its skaters. Why? ABC's 52-week schedule had overexposed the roller derby. The ratings dropped, and by 1952 it was off TV and could barely scrape by without the broadcast and advertising revenue. And like movies and other live entertainment, roller derby saw its attendance diminish as TV became more popular in the early 1950s. Seltzer realized that for the derby to survive, it would have to get back on TV, so he moved the league headquarters from New York to Los Angeles to court the TV industry. But none of the networks were interested.

Q: What sport would you enjoy if you were a *toxopholist?* A: Archery.

By 1958 Leo Seltzer was tired of struggling to keep the derby going and turned over management duties to his son, Jerry Seltzer, who promptly moved league headquarters to San Francisco. Smart move: The city was in the midst of a professional sports boom. The New York Giants baseball team had just moved to San Francisco, and the 49ers football team had enjoyed their first winning season in 1957. The roller derby team based in the area, the Bay Bombers, became a local hit. Once again, the derby was about to be pulled out of a financial hole...by television.

REEL CHANGE

But this time games wouldn't be broadcast live. They were recorded on a new format: videotape. The harsh, fast-moving look of videotape made the games appear, ironically, *more live*. What's more, there was very little videotaped product in 1959, so this set the derby apart. Local TV stations around the country were looking for inexpensive content to plug the holes in their schedules and by 1963, 120 stations were airing Bay Bombers games. The games were taped according to Jerry Seltzer's careful specifications. He told cameramen to *not* film all the fights and punches. The crowd would go wild, but the TV audience would hear it, not see it, which Seltzer thought would draw crowds to the live matches. He even made the crowd louder on the broadcasts to increase the air of excitement. Seltzer's ideas worked. The Bombers went on a national tour in 1962 and sold out everywhere they appeared.

Roller derby was the most popular sport in northern California, too. The Bombers outdrew professional basketball, professional wrestling, professional soccer, hockey (and the Oakland A's) in the Bay Area from 1962 to 1972. It did well elsewhere, too:

• In 1970, two million tickets were sold for derby races in 100 cities. Eight million people watched weekly on television.

• Fifty thousand people attended a 1972 event in Chicago's Comiskey Park.

• The sports pages of several major newspapers began printing roller derby results in 1972.

• Raquel Welch starred in *Kansas City Bomber*, based on the life of star skater Joan Weston.

The ropes of a boxing ring must be at least one inch in diameter.

• Until the WNBA started in 1997, the roller derby was the only national professional team sport that featured female players.

ROLLING AWAY

For a number of reasons, the derby was in financial trouble again in 1972. The sport's popularity was waning and attendance was inconsistent. Skaters wanted more money (stars made $50,000 a year, but rookies made $5,000) and went on strike in 1972. The expense of setting up the large skating track, for both home games and road tours, ate into profits. The 1973 oil crisis made travel more expensive. The higher costs forced Seltzer to cancel entire tours. He thought that a massive four-team championship series in May 1973 at New York's Shea Stadium might put the derby back in the black. Instead, it was a disaster: Because of a computer glitch, only a fraction of the tickets were sold.

In December 1973, Jerry Seltzer announced to his players that the roller derby was folding. The last game was played on December 8, 1973, in Long Island. The game ended not with players punching, shoving, and throwing each other over the railings, but with them joining hands and crying.

RACING BACK?

Since then, several attempts have been made to revive roller derby.

• From 1989 to 1991, a syndicated TV series called *RollerGames* aired. It was more violent than previous derby incarnations and even featured an alligator pit in the middle of the track.

• In 1999 the Nashville Network played down the violence and campiness with a more athletic roller derby called *RollerJam*. But the show's creators had failed to see that the violence and campiness were what made the roller derby attractive to fans, and *RollerJam* also bombed.

• What set the derby apart from other sports in its heyday was that women competed. Today, more than 80 small women-only leagues are reviving roller derby. One is the Texas Rollergirls Rock N' Roller Derby, a Texas-based league that's heavy on the theatrics and violence. It began play in 2003, with teams that include the Honky Tonk Heartbreakers, Hotrod Honeys, and the Hell Marys.

THE BIRTH OF THE NFL, PART II

Professional football was in trouble...until George Preston Marshall rode into town. (Part I begins on page 331.)

ACTION ATTRACTION
Let's face it: Americans prefer watching sports that have the potential for a lot of scoring. That's why professional football was still on the fringe in the 1930s. Most games featured one, maybe two touchdowns, and field goals were rarely attempted because the goalposts were at the back of the end zone. Result: many games ended in ties. College football fared better because the intense rivalries added drama, and the players were younger, faster, and played "for the love of the game." With the exception of a few standouts, pro players, on the other hand, were seen as washed-up wannabes at best, or cheating thugs at worst. But was it the players' fault—or the rules and business practices of the NFL?

THE MARSHALL PLAN

George Preston Marshall, a wealthy football fan, blamed it on the inherent faults of the game. Pro football needed excitement, and he made it his mission to add some—no matter what the purists thought. In 1932, using the small fortune he made from a laundromat chain, Marshall bought part ownership of the tottering Boston Braves. With him he brought a list of changes and set to work lobbying the other NFL owners to approve them.

• Marshall liked to watch the players throw the ball, which rarely happened because of so many restrictions on the forward pass. In 1933 he helped persuade the other teams to remove them.

• He thought the ball would be easier to throw if it was smaller and pointier, so the following year he got the NFL to reduce the size of a regulation ball by about 1 ½" at the fattest part.

• At Marshall's insistence, the NFL moved the goalposts from the rear of the end zone to the goal line. That made field goals and extra-point kicks more likely to succeed, which increased scoring and reduced tie games.

• Another innovation Marshall pushed through was moving the ball 10 yards in from the sideline whenever play went out of bounds. That sped up the pace of the game; teams no longer had to waste an entire down (or two) getting it back to the center of the field.

• Marshall was also the driving force behind splitting the league into eastern and western divisions. That added drama to the season by creating two races for divisional titles, followed by a championship game to decide the league's best team.

• In 1936 Marshall helped implement the NFL's first college draft system, which evened out league play by giving the worst teams in the league the first shot at the best new players.

IT'S A HIT

Marshall's changes worked. Pro football became more fun to watch, which put more paying customers in the stands, making the sport more commercially viable. The average attendance at an NFL game—about 5,000 people in the early 1930s—rose to nearly 20,000 by 1939.

But the NFL still lacked the national attention it craved. That came thanks to a championship game in 1940. Marshall was once again in the middle of it all—but this time he lived to regret it.

The Chicago Bears were up against the Washington Redskins, who Marshall had relocated from Boston after he bought the team. Two weeks earlier, the Redskins had finished the regular season by beating the Bears 7–3 after a Bears receiver dropped a pass in the fourth quarter. Chicago wanted an interference call; the refs didn't make it, so the Bears went home losers. However, they knew that revenge was waiting for them in the upcoming championship game against those same Redskins.

It didn't help matters when Marshall, who had a reputation as a loudmouth (and a bigot—he was one of the last NFL owners to integrate his team), attacked the Bears after the game. "They can't take defeat," he told reporters. "They are a first-half club. They are quitters—the world's greatest crybabies."

Marshall's attack got the public interested in the rematch, which, by coincidence, would also be the first pro football game

First pro football team to have emblems on their helmets: the L.A. Rams.

ever broadcast nationally over network radio. For millions of people living in cities with no pro football franchise, the broadcast would serve as their introduction to the NFL. (It was also the last NFL game in which a player—Bears end Dick Plasman—would play without a helmet.) If the game proved to be interesting to the folks listening at home, they'd probably tune in again during the 1941 season. The future of the entire league, not just the Bears and the Redskins, was riding on the game.

The Bears heard Marshall's "crybaby" taunts and came out fighting. Under the leadership of their coach and owner, George Halas, the Bears slaughtered the Redskins 73–0, still the most lopsided defeat in the history of the NFL. More than 36,000 people witnessed the carnage at Washington's Griffith Stadium, including a record 150 sportswriters from all over the country.

George Preston Marshall, the man credited with saving the league in the 1930s by reinventing the game, would also be remembered for the worst loss ever.

ON THE AIR

Thanks to that one championship game, pro football was more popular then ever in 1941, but it still wasn't the draw that baseball—or even college football—was. Radio helped to spread its appeal, but it was television that solidified it.

TV was a brand-new medium in the late 1940s and NFL owners didn't care about it—few people owned televisions. By 1950, however, there were an estimated four million TV sets in the United States, reaching some 30 million viewers. At first the NFL was against broadcasting its games, afraid that people would stay home and watch TV for free instead of paying to come to the stadium. What happened in California that year proved them right. The Los Angeles Rams decided to televise their entire season. Result: attendance at Rams games dropped by nearly half from 205,000 in 1949 to 110,000 in 1950. The Rams got the message. The following year they televised only away games, and attendance at home games shot up to 234,000. By the end of 1951, most teams were broadcasting their away games, but *only* away games. If fans wanted to see a home game, they had to watch it in person.

Football and television seemed made for each other. Advancing the ball 10 yards to gain a first down gave the game a lot of

Britain's annual Scorton Arrow archery contest has been held every year since 1637.

drama between touchdowns, and the short breaks between plays left plenty of time for analysis and commentary by experts. Even people who were new to football could learn about the game by listening to the announcers.

Pro football's fan base began to soar, and spending Sunday afternoon watching football quickly became an American institution. By 1954 an estimated 34 percent of the Sunday afternoon viewing audience was tuned to the NFL. Thanks to television, pro football was finally beginning to eclipse college football as the most watched, most important form of the sport. The National Football League—which for so long had been on the brink of failing—was now truly a "national" league. And it was here to stay.

* * *

...ONE MORE THING: THE AFL

In 1959 Lamar Hunt, son of Texas oilman H. L. Hunt, applied to the NFL for an expansion franchise...and was turned down. So Hunt and several other spurned suitors formed the American Football League, which was the eighth league by that name (all the others had collapsed). The NFL responded to this challenge the same way it had all the others—it ignored the AFL and waited for it to die on its own.

Seven years later the AFL was still in business in spite of the fact that CBS, which broadcast NFL games, refused to give AFL scores in its news broadcasts and *Sports Illustrated* printed only black-and-white photos instead of the color shots it used with the NFL. So in 1966 the two leagues agreed that their champion teams would meet in the first AFL-NFL World Championship Game on January 15, 1967. In 1970 the two leagues merged.

"AFL-NFL World Championship Game" was a pretty clunky name, and Lamar Hunt wanted something better. One day he saw his daughter bouncing a rubber ball and asked her what it was. "A Super Ball," she told him. "Super Bowl" started out as a nickname, but by the third interleague championship game, played on January 12, 1969, the name was official. Today the Super Bowl is one of the biggest events of the television year, with 40 percent of U.S. homes tuning in to watch the game.

Chance that a pro football player will be injured at least once in his career: 100 percent.

THE STORY OF LITTLE LEAGUE

If you're into baseball, chances are you've had something
to do with Little League. It's an American tradition
now, but it started out as one man's obsession.

ACCIDENT OF FATE

One afternoon in 1938 a man named Carl Stotz went out into his Williamsport, Pennsylvania, yard to play catch with his two nephews. They would have preferred to play baseball, but the yard was too small to use a bat. So they just had a catch.

On one throw, a nephew tossed the ball so far that Stotz "had to move to the neighbors' side of the yard," he recalled years later. "As I stretched to catch the ball, I stepped into the cut-off stems of a lilac bush that were projecting several inches above the ground. A sharp stub tore through my sock and scraped my ankle. The pain was intense."

THE GOOD OLD DAYS

As Stotz sat nursing his ankle, he was suddenly reminded that he had played on the same kind of rough turf when he was a kid…and he remembered a promise he'd made to himself when he was a young boy. Back then, equipment was scarce—he and his friends hit balls with sticks when they didn't have any bats, and used baseballs until the threads unraveled and the skins came off. Then they patched them up with tape and used them until there wasn't anything left to tape back together. Some of his friends had even played barefoot because they didn't have any shoes.

"I remembered thinking to myself, 'When I grow up, I'm gonna have a baseball team for boys, complete with uniforms and equipment. They'll play on a real field like the big guys, with cheering crowds at every game.'"

DOWNSIZING

Stotz didn't have any sons of his own, but he decided to fulfill his

---

In rowing team races, if one rower falls out, the boat must continue on to the finish line.

promise by organizing his nephews and the other neighborhood boys into baseball teams. That way, they could experience the thrill of playing real games on real fields, wearing real uniforms—not just play stickball in open fields and abandoned lots.

He spent the next few months organizing teams and rounding up sponsors to pay for the equipment. At the same time, he set about "shrinking" the game of baseball so the kids could really play. "When I was nine, nothing was geared to children," Stotz explained in his book A *Promise Kept*. Take bats, for example:

> We'd step up to the plate with a bat that was both too heavy and too long. Choking up on the bat merely changed the problem. The handle would then bang us in the stomach when we lunged at the ball. We didn't have the strength or leverage for a smooth, controlled swing.

TRIAL AND ERROR

Stotz finally found child-sized bats and equipment for his teams, and at every team practice he adjusted the distances between the bases and between the pitcher's mound and home plate, trying to find the ideal size for a field.

"I was trying to find out what distance would enable the boys to throw a runner out from third base or shortstop while still giving the batter a fair chance to beat it out, depending on where he hit the ball," he later wrote. "When I finally had what I thought was the ideal distance, I stepped it off and used a yardstick at home to measure my strides. The distance was so close to sixty feet that I set that as the distance we would use thereafter."

About the only thing Stotz didn't change was the size of the baseball itself. He figured it would enable kids to practice with any baseball they already had on hand. "Remember, this was 1938 when I was making these decisions, and the Great Depression was still with many families," he wrote. "I was afraid the expense of buying special-size balls would be too much for some families and might keep boys from becoming Little Leaguers."

SPONSORS

Shrinking the game turned out to be a lot easier than finding sponsors willing to pay for uniforms and equipment for the three teams in the league. "Ten prospects turned me down," Stotz wrote.

Abraham Lincoln often delayed presidential business to play rounders (an early form of baseball).

"Then 20...40...50." Finally, two and a half months after he'd started, Stotz made his 57th sales pitch at the Lycoming Dairy Farms. He landed his first sponsor; they chipped in $30.

A LITTLE PROBLEM

Stotz used the money to buy uniforms at Kresge's 25¢-to-$1 Store, and set the date of the league's first game for June 6, 1939. He paid a visit to the offices of *Grit*, Williamsport's Sunday paper, and asked them to mention the league's first game in the paper.

Bill Kenoe, *Grit's* sports editor, asked Stotz what the league was called, but Stotz didn't know yet. "I'd been thinking of calling it Junior League Baseball," he explained, "until I remembered there's a woman's organization named 'Junior League.'" Because he'd modeled his kids' league after the "big leagues," he'd considered calling it either the Little Boys' League or the Little League. But he couldn't decide between them. He didn't like the sound of "Little Boys' League," but was worried that people would think the "Little League" meant the size of the league, not the size of the boys. In the end, he let Kehoe choose between the two names... and Kehoe picked Little League.

OUT OF THE PARK

Little League grew slowly over the next several years. As late as 1946, there were only 12 local leagues in the entire United States—all in Pennsylvania.

The turning point came in 1947, two years after the end of World War II. America's fighting men were back home, settled into their new lives, and they finally had time to participate with their sons in Little League. In 1947 Little League, now up to 17 independent leagues, held its first "World Series"—an event that was covered by the Associated Press and other wire services. Stories and photographs appeared in hundreds of news-papers...and soon Little League headquarters was deluged with letters from all over the country, asking how to set up their own leagues.

MAKING NOISE

As Little League grew, it began to experience a problem: adults were taking the competition more seriously than the children did.

Michael Jordan always wore his North Carolina basketball shorts under his Bulls uniform.

In 1947 parents and other spectators began routinely booing players and officials during games.

"Some of them seemed unable to see the games as simply little boys having fun in a structured…athletic program," Little League's founder Carl Stotz wrote in *A Promise Kept*. "After all, many of the 8-to-12-year-old boys had played baseball less than a year. There was certainly no valid excuse for such adult criticism. And it was becoming quite discouraging to some of the boys."

Stotz and other Little League officials complained, and newspaper editorials condemned the conduct. "Fortunately," he wrote, "the booing fad of 1947 faded out." It was one of Little League's first brushes with controversy…but certainly not its last.

LITTLE LEAGUE, INC.

By the beginning of 1950, Little League had grown to more than 300 local leagues all over the United States; by the end of the year it had more than doubled in size to 776 leagues. There was even one in British Columbia, the first outside the U.S. The organization had grown so much that it could no longer be managed effectively by part-time volunteers. So in 1950 Little League voted to incorporate itself and began hiring a paid, full-time staff. Carl Stotz was appointed president and commissioner of the league. He didn't realize it, but his Little League days were numbered.

AND NOW A WORD FROM OUR SPONSOR

A year earlier, in 1949, the U.S. Rubber Corporation had become Little League's first national sponsor. In return, they wanted to help determine the direction of the organization—so executives of the company approached Stotz to discuss it. "Essentially," Stotz wrote, U.S. Rubber "proposed a national body that would have total control of the leagues that evolved from it. That body would own every Little League playing field and every Little Leaguer would be a paying member."

U.S. Rubber's plan was exactly the opposite of Stotz's vision; he favored completely autonomous local leagues, joined together in a national organization that would be run by representatives elected from the ranks of the local leagues.

The discussions broke off without any change in the direction of Little League...yet. "Our discussion ended amicably," Stotz later wrote. "In retrospect, though, I can see that it was the beginning of a deep philosophical conflict."

THE LITTLE SCHISM

By the early 1950s, Little League was doubling in size every couple of years. It was an enormous success, but Stotz wasn't satisfied; he was concerned about the increasing commercialism that accompanied Little League's rise to national prominence.

Another concern was the prominence placed on the Little League World Series, which was played every year in Williamsport, Pennsylvania. U.S. Rubber and the Little League board of directors wanted to maximize the importance and the publicity value of the event; but Stotz wanted to de-emphasize the series. He feared that teams trying to "win their way to Williamsport" would encourage cheating at the expense of good sportsmanship and fair play. The lure of the national spotlight, he worried, would encourage teams to recruit players who were ineligible either because they were too old or lived outside their league's territorial boundaries.

Yet another controversy erupted when Stotz tried to invite legendary pitcher Cy Young, then in his 80s, to come to the 1951 Little League World Series. "Two members of the board sought to veto Carl's suggestion," Kenneth Loss writes in *A Promise Kept*. One director "said Cy Young was an old man who probably couldn't control his bladder, and would embarrass Little League." Stotz invited Young anyway (nothing happened), but his differences with Little League Inc. continued to fester.

YOU'RE OUT!

In 1952 Stotz stepped down as the president of Little League, but remained as commissioner of the league. He was replaced as president by a U.S. Rubber executive named Peter McGovern.

Stotz still retained a great deal of power...but not for long. In 1954 the board of directors adopted a new set of bylaws that effectively stripped the office of commissioner of much of its power and gave it to McGovern. Then, in 1955, McGovern fired Stotz's secretary while Stotz was out of town promoting Little League, and replaced her with one of his own aides.

That was it—a few months later Stotz resigned as commissioner and filed suit against McGovern, alleging that he was ignoring Little League volunteers. When Stotz lost the suit, he cut all ties to Little League forever. A few teams left with him to form the unaffiliated Original Little League, which played their games in a field not far from where Stotz had founded Little League in 1939. Stotz boycotted every Little League Inc. World Series game until 1990, when, at age 79, he attended a game to honor the 50th anniversary of the founding of Little League. He died two years later.

* * *

ACTUALLY, IT'S A CURVEBALL

In 1985 *Sports Illustrated* ran a 14-page cover article on a young baseball phenomenon, pitcher Sidd Finch. Orphaned as a child, the article said, Finch grew up in Tibet, where he learned the rudiments of baseball by throwing rocks. Photos showed the youngster's odd, straight-armed windup that resulted in a jaw-dropping 168-mph fastball—60 mph faster than any ever recorded. He'd recently arrived in the United States carrying his only possessions—a French horn, a rug, and a food bowl—and was immediately drafted by the New York Mets. Finch, it was claimed, was on the verge of revolutionizing baseball. Excited fans wanted to know more; reporters clamored to interview him. Baseball commissioner Peter Ueberroth fielded phone calls from major-league managers who were concerned that Finch's blistering fastball might injure batters.

But alert readers smelled something fishy when they saw the issue's cover date: April 1. And if they looked carefully, the first letters of every word in the article's first paragraph spelled out "Happy April Fools' Day." Two weeks later, *Sports Illustrated* admitted that the story was a hoax dreamed up by writer George Plimpton and a handful of editors, who'd hired an Illinois middle-school teacher to pose as Finch. *SI* received 7,000 letters from readers—some angry, some applauding Plimpton for the elaborate practical joke. Seven readers were so disgusted that they cancelled their subscriptions—all, reportedly, Mets fans.

First king to play golf: King James IV of Scotland, in 1504.

THE BRITISH OPEN

The British Open—properly known as the Open Championship—is one of golf's four major tournaments. To many fans, it's the most prestigious of the four, largely because it's the granddaddy of them all—the oldest professional golf tournament in the world.

OLD-TIMER

In 1860 two wealthy members of Prestwick Golf Club in Ayrshire in eastern Scotland suggested to fellow members that they all donate money for a golfing trophy. More and more "professionals" were playing all over Scotland, they argued, and it was time to decide a national champion. It was a novel idea—there were no official golf tournaments then and no prize money; pros made their living through caddying, teaching, making equipment, and gambling.

The members agreed and commissioned the Championship Challenge Belt: a wide, lavishly adorned red leather belt with a big silver buckle. Theirs would be the first tournament to determine the "champion golfer of the world." The basics:

• Only professional golfers would be invited to play.

• They would play three rounds at Prestwick's 12-hole course.

• The winner would get to keep the belt for a year and then turn it over to the next champion.

OPENING UP

On October 17, 1860, now-legendary golfer and golf course designer Willie Park won the tournament. The next year they announced that the tournament would be "open to the world," professional and amateur alike (12 golfers entered). It's been the "Open Championship" ever since.

"Old" Tom Morris won the Challenge Belt in 1861. He won again in 1864 (his third time) and took home the tournament's first prize money: £6. From 1868 to 1870, Morris's son, "Young" Tom Morris, won the event three times in a row. According to the rules, that meant he got to *keep* the Challenge Belt—which meant the club would need a new trophy. To be able to afford a more lavish prize, Prestwick joined up with two other clubs: the Royal and

Ancient Golf Club of St. Andrews and the Honourable Company of Edinburgh Golfers in Musselburgh. No tournament was held in 1871, and when Young Tom Morris won again in 1872—a still-unsurpassed four times in a row—they didn't have a new prize ready, so they awarded him a medal instead.

INTRODUCING CLARET

In 1873 Mackay Cunningham & Company of Edinburgh was commissioned to create a large cup, officially named the "Championship Cup," but commonly known as the "Claret Jug." Claret is a red wine from the Bordeaux region of France that had been popular in Scotland for centuries. It was one of the favorite drinks of the wealthy golfers in Prestwick's clubhouse. They even used it as currency, by the bottle or by the case, when they gambled on rounds of golf. In honor of the tradition, the Championship Cup was made to resemble the silver jugs from which the Prestwick golfers sipped claret.

That was also the first year that the Open was held not at Prestwick but at St. Andrews. The first winner of the Claret Jug: Tom Kidd, a St. Andrews caddie. For the next 18 years, the Open would rotate between Prestwick, St. Andrews, and Musselburgh. Since then the list of host clubs has expanded, but not by much. Only 14 clubs have hosted the event—seven in Scotland, six in England, and one in Northern Ireland.

Today, more than 2,000 golfers from all over the world attempt to qualify for the event every year, hoping to be crowned Open Champion and win the immense first-prize money (Todd Hamilton won in 2004 and got $1.4 million).

BRITISH OPEN HIGHLIGHTS

• **1868:** Young Tom Morris scores the Open's first hole in one.

• **1890:** John Ball Jr. becomes the first Englishman, the first non-Scot, and the first amateur to win the Claret Jug.

• **1892:** The tournament is expanded to 72 holes played over two days to accommodate the growing number of entrants.

• **1894:** The Open is played outside of Scotland for the first time, at Royal St. George's in Sandwich, England.

• **1896:** Harry Vardon wins. He will go on to win six times over the next 20 years, a record that still stands today.

• **1898:** From eight golfers in the first Open in 1860, the number has grown to 101. To keep the numbers down, the cut is introduced, eliminating the lowest scoring half of players after 36 holes.

• **1900:** J. H. Taylor, Harry Vardon, and James Braid finish 1-2-3. They become known as the "Great Triumvirate" and will win 16 British Opens in a 21-year span.

• **1907:** Frenchman Arnaud Massy becomes the first player not from the British Isles (and still the only Frenchman) to win.

• **1915–19:** The Open is suspended due to World War I.

• **1920:** The Royal and Ancient Golf Club of St. Andrews takes over the running of the British Open, although it will still rotate among different venues.

• **1921:** Jock Hutchison becomes the first American to win (though he was born in Scotland and moved to the United States as a teen).

• **1922:** Walter Hagen becomes the first American-born golfer to win. Americans will win 10 of the next 11 Opens.

• **1927:** A 36-hole qualifying round is added to further limit the growing number of golfers entering.

• **1930:** American amateur Bobby Jones wins for the third time. He also wins the U.S. Open, U.S. Amateur, and British Amateur titles. It is the first "Grand Slam," meaning a player has won all four majors in one year. (Those were the four majors at the time.)

• **1940–45:** The Open is suspended due to World War II.

• **1951:** The Open is played in Northern Ireland at Royal Portrush Golf Club. Max Faulkner wins and is the last Brit to do so for nearly two decades.

• **1953:** Ben Hogan plays in his only British Open—at Carnoustie Links—and wins.

• **1955:** The BBC first airs the event on television. Australian Peter Thomson successfully defends his title at St. Andrews. He will win the next one, too, and become the only modern golfer to win

Harpo Marx and George Burns enjoyed golfing together in their underwear.

three British Opens in a row.

• **1962:** Arnold Palmer wins his second British Open title and sets a scoring record at Royal Troon with a 276 total. His participation helps revive the popularity of the event in the United States, which had fallen in recent years.

• **1963:** New Zealander Bob Charles becomes the first left-handed golfer to win.

• **1977:** Jack Nicklaus and Tom Watson compete in the Open's most epic battle, at Turnberry in Scotland. They play the last two days paired together and, battling each other shot for shot, leave the rest of the field behind. On the final hole, Nicklaus sinks a 35-footer for a birdie to tie Watson. Watson then sinks a two-foot birdie putt to win by one stroke, with a record-setting total of 268. (The legendary matchup is memorialized in Michael Corcoran's book *Duel in the Sun*.)

• **1993:** Greg Norman wins his second British Open with a record score of 267.

• **2000:** Tiger Woods wins his first British Open by an eight-stroke margin, the largest in 87 years.

• **2003:** American Ben Curtis, a 26-year-old PGA rookie with only 14 PGA tournaments under his belt, none of which included a top-10 finish, and at the time ranked 396th in the world, shocks the golf world by winning the British Open. Playing against such golfers as Ernie Els, Vijay Singh, Davis Love III, and Tiger Woods, Curtis's win has been called one of the biggest upsets in the history of sports.

*　　*　　*

SURVEY SAYS...

Two thousand U.S. golfers who play more than 25 rounds a year were surveyed by *Golf* magazine. Results:

• 8% have had sex on the course (the figure rises to 18% for low handicappers).

• 16% have broken a club in anger; 43% have thrown a club.

• 59% have improved their lie when fellow players weren't looking.

• 37% said if they could ban one thing from the golf course, it would be slow players.

The trophy for the King Hassan Golf Tournament is a jewel-encrusted dagger.

CARD SHARKS, PART II

Part II of our story about card counting and how some kids from MIT won millions at gambling casinos with a system that was unbeatable…almost. (Part I is on page 121.)

THE HOUSE RULES

The casinos in Nevada had developed ways to uncover and thwart card counting…but they had no idea that the greatest threat to their control of blackjack gaming was being quietly developed 2,500 miles away.

The Massachusetts Institute of Technology has some of the smartest minds in the world among its student body. What's less known is that MIT students are notorious for their maverick attitude: They love to crack seemingly unsolvable problems just for the fun of it. Sometimes the problems can involve quantum mechanics and string theory. In this case, the question was: "How do we beat the casinos?" The answer was elegantly simple—and, for the casinos, very expensive.

DREAM TEAM

In 1992 a group of MIT students formed an underground club innocently named "Strategic Investments." Their real intent was to apply Edward Thorp's card-counting system in a radical new way. Previous card counters were all lone wolves. They worked solo, using a technique called *bet spreading*—betting low when the deck is against you, betting high the minute it turns in your favor. And that made them easy targets for casino security.

The MIT card counters played as a team. One person was the "spotter." His job wasn't to play but to observe the game and count cards, watching for the crucial moment when a deck went positive. Next was the "controller," a decoy who bet small while verifying the spotter's count and, most importantly, calculating when to make the big bet. The controller wouldn't make the bet, though. That was the role of the aptly named "big player." He'd wait for the controller's signal, then sweep up to a table and wipe it out with one massive bet. To all appearances—and to casino security—he was just another high roller who happened to get lucky one time.

The MIT team trained for months before trying out their system. Then they went to Las Vegas…and proceeded to win millions. At their peak they had 125 people working the tables. For months the casinos couldn't figure out what was going on, but they knew that, whatever it was, they had to stop it quickly or they'd be out of business. It was that serious.

RAISING THE ANTE

To make matters worse for the casinos, in 1993 three of the best MIT players split from Strategic Investments to form their own group. Semyon Dukach (big player), Katie Lilienkamp (controller), and Andy Bloch (spotter) were one of the most successful SI teams in the field. But they were tired of sharing their winnings. Why was this a bad development for the casinos? Because the new team (they called themselves the Amphibians) was convinced they could come up with a system that was even better.

Counting cards is difficult for most blackjack players, but it had never been an issue for the nimble brains of these young math wizards. The Amphibians decided that if they were going to raise their game, they had to focus on the betting side of the equation. They started by writing a complex computer program that could run simulations of every type of hand they had encountered. Their analysis brought them to a level of hand recognition that was simply awesome, and the new combination—perfect card counting and flawless betting strategy—was devastatingly effective. The Amphibians went on a winning rampage. But the casinos were about to respond with a powerful counterpunch—a woman named Beverly Griffin.

A FACE IN THE CROWD

Griffin ran a private-investigation company specializing in casino operations. In the summer of 1993, she was hired by a consortium of desperate casino owners. Their instructions: find a way to stop the card counters for good. Griffin started by creating a database of suspected card counters based on information supplied by the casinos. Then she started looking for connections. Names weren't very helpful, as many gamblers (including the Amphibians) routinely used aliases when they played. Addresses—required by the casinos before they can pay out—were another matter, and that's where Griffin made her breakthrough.

Official national sport of Bulgaria: weightlifting.

She noticed an unusual concentration of winners from the Boston area. More telling was that most of them appeared to play only on weekends and were in their early 20s—college age. Acting on a hunch, Griffin got hold of some MIT yearbooks. She opened one up and, as she said later, "Lo and behold, there they were. Looking all scholarly and serious, and not at all like card counters."

Working with the casinos and using the MIT yearbooks to build a new database, Griffin and her team helped develop some of the first facial-recognition software. Using images taken from the hundreds of security cameras on the casino floor, a suspected card counter's face could be compared against the computer database and picked up before he or she reached the blackjack tables. Once the Amphibians learned of the casinos' "secret weapon," they knew their card-counting days in America were over. So they decided to take their show on the road. They went to Europe.

THE LAST STAND

For three weeks the Amphibians—Dukach, Lilienkamp, and Bloch—played and won in London, Paris, and other major gambling locales. Finally they arrived at the mecca of gambling—the Grand Casino in Monte Carlo. The evening started well. All three played the same table, and they were winning. Then Katie Lilienkamp decided to take a potty break. On her way back to the table she was stopped by four security guards and ushered into a side room.

Semyon Dukach and Andy Bloch were already there. A picture of the three of them was scanned and uploaded to the Griffin Investigations office in Las Vegas. The Internet had made the Las Vegas database a global one, so when the identification came back positive (since they were all known Las Vegas card counters), they were unceremoniously shown the door. As Bloch recalled, "The guy said if we ever set foot in the country again, we were going to be really hurt."

Wisely, the Amphibians chose that moment to disband their club and retire.

ENDGAME

The war between the casinos and the best card counters in the world was over. As for the Amphibians, they went on with their

---

In 1969 a soccer match caused a three-day war between Honduras and El Salvador.

lives. Although they had won lots of money, the whole operation had been mostly a lark, an intriguing hobby that paid out as much in adrenaline as it did cash. (None of the MIT groups will say how much cash they won.) "I love playing," Semyon Dukach said later. "I love beating the casinos, knowing that my team was ahead of them, and tricking this huge $50 billion industry." Remember, what they did was not illegal (only Taft's personal computer fell into that category). Katie Lilienkamp went back to MIT and became an engineer. Andy Bloch became a professional poker player. Dukach teaches blackjack for a living.

And what about Edward Thorp, the genius who started it all? He took his mastery of probability theory to the biggest gambling table of all: Wall Street. He founded hedge funds and made untold fortunes managing them using techniques based on his understanding of the odds—and his willingness to place well-calculated bets.

*   *   *

GAMBLING TRIVIA

• The expression "rolling the bones" means to roll dice. And it used to be literal. Dice were made from animal bones—the Romans used sheep's knuckles—for thousands of years.

• The oldest known dice with regular sides were found in northern Iraq. They're made of baked clay and date to about 3000 B.C.

• President Richard Nixon won $6,000 playing poker in his first two months in the U.S. Navy during World War II. He used it to help fund his first campaign for Congress. (He won that, too.)

• More than 50 million decks of cards are sold in the United States every year.

• Do you know the book *According to Hoyle*? It's considered the seminal book on the rules of poker (and many other games of chance). It refers to Edmond Hoyle, who wrote the book *A Short Treatise on the Game of Whist* in 1742 (whist was a popular card game at the time). Hoyle died 150 years before poker was invented.

TALKIN' NASCAR

Gentlemen, start your mouths...

"Driving a NASCAR is like dancing with a chainsaw."
—Cale Yarborough

"I feel like I got a pile of cattle chasing my ass, and I'm pedaling as hard as I can to stay in front of 'em."
—Rusty Wallace

"There's no bigger surprise than to be tooling along at 200 mph and suddenly get hit from the rear."
—Darrell Waltrip

"Why did I take up racing? I was too lazy to work and too chicken to steal."
—Kyle Petty

"It was more thrilling to win a race because I was competing against people who were equal to me."
—Junior Johnson, on his pre-NASCAR bootlegging days running from cops

"If you're solidly in the top 10 but settling for second, well, you might as well kiss your aunt with a hairy mustache."
—Tony Stewart

"Second place is just the first loser."
—Dale Earnhardt

"They must have been confused—they were signaling to me that I was number one, but I was still in second place."
—Kyle Busch, on his fans

"I think if the fans are throwing things at you, you've just done something really cool."
—Jeff Gordon

"I pity the fool who don't think NASCAR is a sport!"
—Mr. T

"I taught you everything you know, but I didn't teach you everything *I* know."
—Dale Earnhardt, to his son Dale Jr.

Pit crew member Jeff Clark: How do the gauges look?
Dale Earnhardt Jr.: Nice. They're silver and they all have nice little red needles.

"Well, you still having fun?"
—Lynda Petty, to husband Richard as he woke up in the hospital after a wreck

More people die playing golf than any other sport. Leading causes: heart attacks and strokes.

LOVE OF THE GAME, MICHIGAN STYLE

Why are so many sports movies set in Michigan?
Uncle John's not sure, but he likes them.

PAPER LION (1968)
Could writer George Plimpton hack it as a football player with the Detroit Lions? He tried it once, for a story he was writing. This film is based on his experience at the Lions' training camp, with a pre-M*A*S*H Alan Alda playing Plimpton. For realism, the film uses a number of real-life football players of the time, including Alex Karras and Frank Gifford, and also features a cameo performance by Vince Lombardi.

THE LIFE AND TIMES OF HANK GREENBERG (1998)
One of the nation's first Jewish sports stars, Hank Greenberg helped the Detroit Tigers win four pennants and two World Series titles in the 1930s, all while maintaining his faith. This engrossing documentary blends archival interviews with Greenberg and contemporary footage of notable admirers, ranging from Alan Dershowitz to Walter Matthau.

HARMON OF MICHIGAN (1941)
Michigan Wolverine football legend and Heisman Trophy winner Tom Harmon plays a fictional version of himself in this film, in which he goes from recent college grad to head football coach during the course of a season (or so it seems; the film's timeline is a little fuzzy). It was designed to appeal to fans who couldn't get enough of "Ole 98." Harmon went on to establish himself as a top-flight sports announcer for many years before his death in 1990.

FOR LOVE OF THE GAME (1999)
Kevin Costner plays a Tigers pitcher at the end of his career who reminisces on the last five years of his life, contemplates the wreck of a relationship he's having with costar Kelly Preston, and tries to pitch a perfect game.

The sport of *skijoring* involves a skier being pulled by a horse.

THE LEGEND OF GORGEOUS GEORGE

On page 320 we told the story of professional wrestling's earliest days. Since then, the big stars have been Hulk Hogan, The Iron Sheik, The Rock...and this man, who became TV's first "big-time" wrestling villain. TV made him a star, and in many ways, he made television.

IN THIS RING, I THEE WED

In 1939 a 24-year-old professional wrestler named George Wagner fell in love with a movie theater cashier named Betty Hanson and married her in a wrestling ring in Eugene, Oregon. The wedding was so popular with wrestling fans that George and Betty reenacted it in similar venues all over the country.

With the sole exception of the wedding stunt, Wagner's wrestling career didn't seem to be going anywhere. After 10 years in the ring, he was still an unknown, and that was a big problem: nobodies had a hard time getting booked for fights.

THE ROBE OF A LIFETIME

Wagner might well have had to find something else to do for a living had his wife not happened to make him a robe to wear from the locker room to the ring before a fight, just like a prizefighter. Wagner was proud of the robe, and that night when he took it off at the start of his fight, he took such care to fold it properly that the audience booed him for taking so long. That made Betty mad, so she jumped into the crowd and slapped one of the hecklers in the face. That made George mad, so he jumped out of the ring and hit the guy himself. Then the whole place went nuts.

"The booing was tremendous," wrestling promoter Don Owen remembered:

And the next week there was a real big crowd and everyone booed George. So he just took more time to fold his robe. He did everything to antagonize the fans. And from that point he became the best drawing card we ever had. In wrestling they either come to like you or to hate you. And they hated George.

The U.S. Grand Prix car race was originally held in Las Vegas, in a giant parking lot.

PRETTY BOY

Out of this hatred, George discovered the shtick he was looking for—and over the next several years gradually changed his look. Where other wrestling villains had always been dirty and ugly, "Gorgeous George," as he began to call himself, set out to become the prettiest, daintiest pro wrestler the sport had ever seen. He grew his hair long, curled it, and bleached it platinum blond. And before each fight, he secured it in place with golden bobby pins and a golden hair net. He amassed a collection of more than 100 frilly purple robes, made of satin and silk and trimmed with sequins, lace, and fur. He made sure to wear one to every match, and before he would enter the ring, he insisted that his tuxedoed "valet" be allowed to spray the mat, the referee, and his opponent with perfume.

Then, as the lights were dimmed and "Pomp and Circumstance" played over the loudspeaker, George would enter the hall under a spotlight and slowly traipse his way to the ring. He made such a show of climbing into the ring and removing (with the assistance of his valet) his robe, his hair net, and his golden bobby pins, that his entrances sometimes took longer than his fights, giving wrestling's blue-collar fans one more reason to hate him.

FIGHTING DIRTY

Appearances aside, Gorgeous George was no sissy—not out of the ring and certainly not in it. He fought hard and he *always* cheated—gouging eyes, biting ears, butting heads, punching kidneys, kicking crotches, and pulling every other dirty stunt he could think of. He gloated when he was winning, squealed and begged for mercy when he was losing, and bawled like a baby when his opponents mussed his hair, which they did every fight. All of this was fake, of course, but the crowds either didn't know or didn't care. They ate it up, fight after fight.

Gorgeous George's antics may not sound like much compared to the wrestling of today, but at the time, they were mind-boggling. He became famous in the late 1940s, not long after the end of World War II. Many wrestling fans were veterans, and the ex-soldiers who landed at Omaha Beach on D-Day or battled their way across the Pacific had some pretty rigid ideas about what it

There are about 10,000,000,000,000 ways to play the first 10 moves in a game of chess.

meant to be a man. And bobby pins, frilly bathrobes, and platinum blond hair were definitely *not* considered manly. Gorgeous George broke all the rules, and these guys hated him for it. They *loved* to hate him for it. People got in their cars and drove for hours to see him fight, just so they could hate him in person. Gorgeous George made 32 appearances at the Los Angeles Olympic Auditorium in 1949; he sold it out 27 times.

A BOOB FOR THE BOOB TUBE

But what was most remarkable about Gorgeous George was the impact he had on TV sales. In Los Angeles, wrestling matches—many featuring Gorgeous George—were broadcast on TV as early as 1945, and they proved so popular that by the late 1940s, many TV stations around the country were broadcasting live pro wrestling every night of the week. It was the perfect sport for television—the ring was small and easy to film and the action was larger than life, so viewers had no problem following the fights at home on their tiny black-and-white screens. Baseball and football players looked like ants by comparison.

TV turned Gorgeous George into a national star, even for people who didn't watch wrestling. And in the process, he helped make television the centerpiece of the American living room. Appliance dealers put TVs in their store windows and pasted pictures of Gorgeous George onto their screens. People who'd never owned a TV before came in and bought TVs…just so they could watch Gorgeous George. As Steve Slagle writes in *The Ring Chronicle*,

> In a very real sense, Gorgeous George single-handedly established the unproven new technology of television as a viable entertainment medium that could reach literally millions of homes all across the country. Pro wrestling was TV's first real "hit"…and Gorgeous George was directly responsible for all of the commotion. He was probably responsible for selling more television sets in the early days of TV than any other factor.

A CATCHY ACT

As we told you on page 90, a young pro boxer named Cassius Clay, soon to change his name to Muhammad Ali, reinvented his public persona after he happened to meet Gorgeous George on a radio show in Las Vegas in 1961. Ali wasn't the only one—Gor-

In 1968 the LPGA officially sanctioned miniskirts for tournament play.

geous George is credited with inspiring Little Richard...and even Liberace. "He's imitating me," George groused to a reporter in 1955.

THE FINAL BELL

There was, however, a limit to how long American TV viewers could stand to watch live pro wrestling every single night of the week, and by the mid-1950s, the craze had died down. George continued to wrestle until 1962, when a liver ailment—brought on by heavy drinking—forced him into retirement. Nearly broke from two expensive divorces, George had a heart attack on Christmas Eve 1963 and died two days later. He was 48.

Ironically, the fame that made Gorgeous George a national celebrity may have also contributed to his death. Believe it or not, he was a shy person, and for years he had used alcohol to stiffen his spine and give him the courage to be Gorgeous George.

"He really didn't have the nerve to do all those things," his second wife, Cherie, remembered. "That's why he drank. When he was sober, he was shy."

*   *   *

SIGNATURE WRESTLING MOVES

Lord Blears: The Oxford Leg Strangle

The Leduc Brothers: The Lumberjack Bearhug

Baron Michele Scicluna: The Maltese Hangman

Leo "the Lion" Newman: The Diamond-Drill Neck Twist

Hard-Boiled Haggerty: The Shillelagh Swing

Johnny Valentine: The Atomic Skullcrusher

Cowboy Bob Ellis: The Bulldog Headlock

Danny Dusek: The Filipino Guerrilla Hold

Lord Athol Layton: The English Octopus

The Sheik: The Camel Clutch

Studies show: Cyclists have the largest hearts of any group of athletes.

CURIOUS RULES

Loony laws even make it into the world of golf.
Here are some official—but odd—rules of the game.

• Other than glasses or contact lenses, you're not allowed to enhance your vision or estimate distance from the hole through the use of binoculars, a range finder, sextant, or global positioning system.

• The dress code of the PGA Tour dictates players wear long pants. In 1992 Mark Wiebe showed up at the Anheuser-Busch Classic in shorts—to deal with the 102-degree temperature—and was fined $500.

• If an opponent asks how many strokes you've taken on a hole, you must tell the truth.

• When you hit a ball out of play, you must take a "drop" by holding a ball out at arm's length, shoulder high, and letting it go. You must then play it from that spot. At one time, however, the rule was that you dropped the ball over your shoulder. Result: the ball would often bounce off the player's body and roll away, so the rule was changed.

• If a ball comes to rest near a bird's nest, the player may take a drop without penalty, provided that playing through would damage the nest.

• A free drop is also permitted for directly dangerous situations, such as if the ball lands near, on top of, or inside an alligator, rattlesnake, or bees' nest.

• Drops are not allowed in plant-related dangerous situations. If the ball falls into a patch of poison ivy or poison oak, for example, golfers must play it where it lies.

• The PGA assesses a two-stroke penalty for accidentally hitting your partner with a ball…but no penalty for hitting anybody else.

• In years past, golfers couldn't legally replace balls on the green with markers because maneuvering around other players' balls

---

Rule at Yellowknife Golf Club, Canada: "No penalty assessed when ball carried off by raven."

while putting was considered part of the game. The rules were changed in the 1950s after several pro tournaments were decided by players intentionally hitting their opponents' balls to move them farther from the hole.

• It's possible to become an amateur again after going pro, but you have to do it within five years of becoming a pro.

• In PGA tournaments, once a player gets to the ball, he is penalized a stroke for taking longer than 45 seconds to hit it.

• It's against the rules to ask for advice from anyone but your caddie or partner. You also can't give advice, solicited or not.

• Straddling the ball and putting it croquet-style was banned in 1968. The USGA banned the use of pool cues for putting in 1895.

• If a ball is hit off the course, onto the parking lot, and comes to rest underneath a parked car, the ball must remain in place. The car should immediately be moved and the ball played where it lies.

• Ant hills are considered "movable obstructions" and may be moved if they get in the way of playing a ball.

• A golfer may move another player's ball, but only under one of two conditions: 1) an opponent's ball may be lifted and replaced with a marker if it is physically in the way of one's shot; 2) an opponent's ball may be moved if the golfer feels the other person's ball is mentally interfering with his play.

*   *   *

WHATEVER IT TAKES TO WIN

Jack Nicklaus and Lee Trevino were tied for the lead at the end of the 1971 U.S. Open, forcing a playoff. Shortly before the first playoff hole, Trevino pulled a rubber snake out of his bag and tossed it to Nicklaus. Nicklaus had seen the snake earlier and had a pretty good idea that it was meant for him. He caught it and playfully threw it back to Trevino...but the tactic worked: Nicklaus hit his balls into bunkers on the second and third holes. Trevino won the tournament by three strokes, becoming the only player to ever beat Jack Nicklaus in a major playoff.

Bob Feller pitched the only opening day no-hitter in major league baseball history (1940).

THE BIRTH OF BASEBALL CARDS, PART II

The origin of baseball cards (see page 188) is tied in with the history of cigarettes in America. The rest of the story is about kids...and money.

KIDS' STUFF
In the years following tobacco's exit from the baseball card business, cards were marketed directly to kids. They were used as promotions for candy, chewing gum, and cookies—but none were especially successful until 1928, when the Fleer Corporation introduced bubblegum. As one sports historian writes, "Baseball cards had found a marketing partner to replace tobacco."

The Goudey Company was the first to combine bubblegum and cards, and they became the most popular distributor of cards in the 1930s. Other companies joined in, adding gimmicks to make cards appealing to kids. They issued sets with players' heads superimposed on cartoon bodies, included coupons for fan clubs, offered chances to win baseball gear, and so on. By the end of the 1930s, card collecting was beginning to take off as a hobby. Then World War II broke out, and resources were diverted to the war effort. Baseball cards all but disappeared.

CUTTHROAT COMPETITION

The business of baseball cards began in earnest after the war. The Bowman Company came out with the first annual sets of cards in 1948, and secured their investment by signing baseball players to contracts that gave Bowman exclusive rights to sell cards with bubblegum.

But with the introduction of color cards in 1950, baseball card collecting became the fastest growing hobby among boys in America—and competitors began lining up. The most influential of them was Sy Berger, an executive at Topps (the company that made Bazooka bubblegum), who genuinely liked baseball.

Berger convinced his bosses that they should start manufacturing and selling cards. He started hanging around the clubhouses of the three New York teams, signing players to Topps contracts. To avoid infringing on Bowman's right to package cards with gum, Topps offered its cards with a piece of taffy. Bowman filed suit—but the court ruled that Bowman couldn't stop Topps from signing players to card contracts.

By 1955 Topps had outhustled its rival for player contracts. In 1956 Bowman conceded defeat and sold out to Topps. From the '50s through the '70s, Topps had a virtual stranglehold on the business. When the Fleer Corporation tried issuing cards with a cookie, Topps took them to court and won.

MONEY, MONEY, MONEY
Topps was selling 250 million cards per year, raking in millions of dollars in profits. But what did the players get? A whopping $125 for a *five-year contract*—plus a $5 "steak money" bonus. The amazing thing is, they were glad to get it; the average player salary in the 1960s was only $19,000.

Two things changed that: 1) a baseball players' union was formed and got involved in contract negotiations with Topps, and 2) in 1980, Fleer won an anti-trust suit against Topps. The judge ruled that any company was free to negotiate a card deal.

A year later, there were three companies willing to sign players to card contracts. And by 1988 there were at least a half-dozen more. Cards got fancier and more expensive...and baseball cards turned into big business.

• By 1985 baseball cards had passed stamps and coins as the most popular collecting hobby in the country.

• By 1988 card companies were selling *five billion* cards per year.

• By 1992 sports cards were nearly a $1 billion-a-year business. The industry leader, Upper Deck, was selling $250 million worth of cards and sports memorabilia annually. They paid former superstar Mickey Mantle—who made $100,000 a year at the peak of his career—$2.5 million to make 26 promotional appearances at memorabilia conventions.

PARADISE LOST
A baseball card glut, combined with the bad press that the 1995 baseball strike generated, slowed down the card business—and it may never hit those highs again. But there's no going back to the

innocence of earlier decades. An adult attitude has settled over the hobby. As one critic puts it, "Once kids stuck the cards of their favorite players to the spokes of their bicycles. Now adults store their collections in safe-deposit boxes and fret over how much to insure their 1952 Mickey Mantles for."

THE MODERN BASEBALL CARD

Bill Hemrich owned the Upper Deck sports card and memorabilia shop, located just a short walk from the stadium where the California Angels played their home games. Around 1987, he shelled out $4,000 for a stack of Don Mattingly rookie cards—which turned out to be fakes. Paul Sumner, a printing company executive, heard the story and contacted Hemrich. He sketched out an idea for a baseball card using hologram technology. The hologram design would be impossible to counterfeit, Sumner explained. Plus, it would set the cards apart from all the rest with a hip, high-tech look.

Together they formed Upper Deck Cards, got rich, and changed sports cards forever.

CARD MISCELLANY

• The first cards to list player stats on the back were put out by Mecca Cigarettes in 1918.

• In 1969 Topps goofed on Angels third baseman Aurelio Rodriguez's card. They photographed the Angels' batboy, thinking he was Rodriguez, and put the *batboy's* picture on the card.

• In 1989 a card of Baltimore Oriole Billy Ripken (brother of Cal) made headlines when it slipped past Fleer proofreaders. The card shows Ripken holding a bat over his right shoulder in a posed stance. At the bottom of the bat knob, written in black felt pen, is a profanity. "Sometimes players play practical jokes on the photographers," said a Fleer spokesman. "We try to catch them before they go to press, but this one must have made it through."

*   *   *

"I believe everyone should carry some type of religious artifact on his or her person at all times."

—Bob Costas, explaining why he carried a Mickey Mantle card in his wallet

HORSE VS. HORSE

*Match races—one-on-one contests between two champion racehorses—
were once an American obsession. The spectacles drew millions
of fans…until 1975, when one tragic race ended them all.*

GENTLEMEN, START YOUR HORSES

Ever since humans have been riding horses, they've been racing the fastest ones against each other. But in medieval Europe, wealthy landowners made a science out of it, breeding horses for speed and stamina and staging private races between pairs of them. These two-horse contests became known as "match races," and an elaborate system of wagering grew up around them. Modern horseracing, with carefully bred horses and betting spectators, has its roots in those aristocratic match races.

In 1823 America's first "national" sporting event was a match race pitting American Eclipse, the North's fastest horse, against Sir Henry, regarded as the best horse from the South. Tensions between the northern and southern states were already on the rise, and on race day, 60,000 fans—including 20,000 Southerners who'd made the trip north—packed New York's Union Course track. The race consisted of three four-mile heats and carried a prize of $20,000—an enormous sum at the time.

The Southern horse won the first heat, but the Northerner came back to win the final two—and the prize. The repercussions went far beyond the racetrack: When Wall Street brokerage houses heard of Eclipse's loss in the first heat, the stock market crashed as Northerners sold off shares, fearing they'd lose their wagers. Later, after American Eclipse won the third heat, many Southerners found they'd lost their entire plantations—slaves and all—on their own bets. Facing ruin, several committed suicide.

THE PRINCE AND THE PAUPER

American match races reached their pinnacle during the Great Depression. In 1938 War Admiral and Seabiscuit both ruled racing in the U.S., but they were very different horses. "The Admiral" was sleek and elegant, with a fiery disposition. He'd made a reputation for blazing past his competition from the beginning of

---

January 1st is the official "birthday" for all racehorses born in North America.

the race to the end, and was well known for his hatred of starting gates—he'd held up the 1937 Kentucky Derby for eight minutes by balking at the gate, then won the race and went on to win the Triple Crown. Undefeated, War Admiral was named 1937's Horse of the Year. But out west in California, there was a horse that had earned more money than War Admiral—and was being promoted as his only real competition.

Seabiscuit, like War Admiral, had excellent breeding, but he'd earned his glory the hard way. A small horse with crooked legs and an ungainly stride, he'd been undertrained and over-raced early in his career, with lackluster results. He was considered a has-been until a new owner and trainer began to turn things around for him. Then Seabiscuit started to win—big. By 1937 he'd become "The People's Horse" as millions of Americans suffering through the Great Depression took hope from his rags-to-riches story. Seabiscuit and War Admiral had never faced each other, so a match race was proposed to settle the question of which was the better horse.

NATIONAL SENSATION

Forty-thousand people showed up at Maryland's Pimlico racetrack on November 1, 1938, to see "the race of the century." An estimated 40 million more—including President Franklin Roosevelt—tuned in via radio. Most fans rooted publicly for Seabiscuit...but quietly bet on War Admiral, since every journalist and handicapper in the country felt sure he couldn't be beaten.

Those same experts predicted that War Admiral would lead from the start. So the crowd gasped when Seabiscuit shot from the starting line, leaving War Admiral behind for the first quarter of the race. Then War Admiral closed the gap, the horses running neck-and-neck, until War Admiral edged slightly ahead. It seemed as if the experts had been right. But what the crowd didn't know was that Seabiscuit's jockey had been instructed to hold him back slightly until he could see his rival in front of him—in the past, the sight of another horse moving past him always made Seabiscuit put on a burst of speed. Despite the already blistering pace, Seabiscuit surged and again pulled ahead of War Admiral—this time for good. In front of a screaming crowd, Seabiscuit won by four lengths and set a new track record. Seabiscuit still remains one of the best-loved American racehorses of all time.

THE QUEEN AND THE COLT

After three different colts won each of the Triple Crown races in 1975, the New York Racing Association began making plans to host a Race of Champions between the three. But racing journalists protested. There could be no contest of champions, they said, without Ruffian, one of the most exciting horses the nation had ever seen…but who'd never even run in a Triple Crown race.

Born at Clairborne Farms in Kentucky, Ruffian was a nearly black filly, exceptionally tall and elegant. Spectators flocked to see her miles-eating gallop, and not just because of her speed—her rocking stride was also beautiful to watch. Racing appeared to be a romp for the undefeated horse, who'd broken a track record in her very first outing and had led at every point in every one of her races—10 in all. Nicknamed "Queen of the Fillies," she'd won the 1975 Filly Triple Crown Championship.

Foolish Pleasure was the only horse whose record could compare to Ruffian's. Undefeated as a two-year-old, the colt had easily won the Kentucky Derby and came in second in the Preakness (where it was claimed that he was fouled) and in the Belmont. In an era that had already seen a "Battle of the Sexes" between tennis stars Billie Jean King and Bobby Riggs, race officials decided to set up a similar "battle" between the popular colt and filly.

AND…THEY'RE OFF

Media hype had swirled around the race for weeks, and on July 6, 1975, the grandstands at Belmont Park overflowed, while some 18 million viewers watched on television. Ruffian's jockey, Jacinto Vasquez, rode Foolish Pleasure to his Derby victory two months earlier, but turned down the chance to ride the great colt in the match race, believing Ruffian would win.

At the start of the race, Ruffian slammed her shoulder against the starting gate, and the jolt visibly slowed her down. True to form, though, she soon caught up with Foolish Pleasure, and by the first quarter of the race she was slightly ahead. As they ran on, Ruffian slowly began pulling away. She'd opened up a half-length lead over Foolish Pleasure when the jockeys heard something: a sharp sound like a dry twig snapping. Ruffian stumbled.

The sound had been a tiny sesamoid bone breaking in the filly's front right ankle. Vasquez immediately knew something was wrong and tried to pull her to a stop, but the big filly fought him and kept running. By the time he was able to stop her, Ruffian's leg hung useless, bones exposed. The silent crowd watched as Foolish Pleasure crossed the finish line alone. A team of workers rushed onto the track to treat Ruffian where she'd stopped, then loaded her into an ambulance.

It took a team of vets 12 hours to reconstruct Ruffian's shattered ankle. But then there was more trouble: When she came out of anesthesia, the disoriented horse began thrashing violently on the ground, breaking her cast and irreparably damaging the rest of her leg. Knowing she was unlikely to survive even more extensive surgery, the medical team had to euthanize her. Ruffian was buried in Belmont Park.

AFTERMATH

Since Ruffian's breakdown, there has never been another major thoroughbred match race. One reason was simply the bad publicity. Another is that many trainers believe that match races are unusually hazardous: A one-on-one race, they say, amplifies the horses' competitive nature and is more likely to cause stress or injury than racing in a group, a more comfortable setting for the herd animals.

Ruffian's high-profile tragedy did have one positive effect: It changed the way injured racehorses are treated. In particular, it brought about the introduction of a "recovery pool"—a vat of warm water that horses are immersed in as they come out of anesthesia so they won't harm themselves as they begin to move their legs.

Ruffian's final race also added more fuel to an ongoing debate over whether horseracing as a sport is inhumane. Critics argue that thoroughbreds like Ruffian are bred for speed rather than strength or stamina and are too susceptible to breaking down. They also question whether horses are raced too early, since many begin racing at two years old, placing extreme stress on their still-growing bones.

Now, more than 30 years later, the tragedy of America's last match race comes back to haunt the industry every time a great horse breaks down, like Barbaro in the 2006 Preakness or Eight Belles in the 2008 Kentucky Derby. Trainers, owners, and officials are making strides to stop fatalities, but the debate continues in racing stables and living rooms all across the country.

LOU HOLTZ

After coaching professional and college football for 35 years (most notably at Notre Dame), Lou Holtz has since moved on to become a college football analyst and motivational speaker. Here's why.

"It's not the load that breaks you down, it's the way you carry it."

"Ability is what you're capable of doing. Motivation determines what you do. Attitude determines how well you do it."

"You'll never get ahead of anyone as long as you try to get even with him."

"If you burn your neighbor's house down, it doesn't make your house look any better."

"It is a fine thing to have ability, but the ability to discover ability in others is the true test."

"A bird doesn't sing because it has an answer; it sings because it has a song."

"You're never as good as everyone tells you when you win, and you're never as bad as they say when you lose."

"You might not be able to outthink, outmarket, or outspend your competition, but you can outwork them."

"No one has ever drowned in sweat."

"There's nothing is this world more instinctively abhorrent to me than finding myself in agreement with my fellow humans."

"If you try to fight the course, it will beat you."

"I can't believe that God put us on this earth to be ordinary."

"In the successful organization, no detail is too small to escape close attention."

"I think everyone should experience defeat at least once during their career. You learn a lot from it."

"When all is said and done, more is said than done."

OLYMPIC MYTHS

Every two years, we're treated to another round of Olympics. Whether you watch them or not, it's impossible to avoid all the hype—which, it turns out, isn't all true. Next time someone refers to "Olympic tradition," read them this.

THE MYTH: Athletes who competed in the ancient Greek Olympics were amateurs.

THE TRUTH: Technically, maybe. But in fact, they were handsomely rewarded for their victories. "Contrary to popular belief," says David Wallechinsky in his *Complete Book of the Olympics*, "the Ancient Greek athletes were not amateurs. Not only were they fully supported throughout their training, but even though the winner received only an olive wreath at the Games, at home he was amply rewarded and could become quite rich." Eventually, top athletes demanded cash and appearance fees—just like today.

THE MYTH: In ancient Greece, the Olympics were so important that everything stopped for them—even wars.

THE TRUTH: No war *ever* stopped because of the Olympics. But wars didn't interfere with the games because: 1) participants were given nighttime safe-conduct passes that allowed them to cross battlefields after a day's fighting was done, and 2) the Olympics were part of a religious ceremony, so the four Olympic sites—including Delphi and Olympia—were off-limits to fighting.

THE MYTH: To honor ancient tradition and discourage com- mercialism, organizers of the modern Olympics decided that only amateur athletes could compete.

THE TRUTH: Not even close. It was "amateurs only" strictly to keep out the riff-raff. Baron Coubertin, the man responsible for bringing back the Olympics in 1896, was a French aristocrat who wanted to limit competitors to others of his social class. "He saw the Olympics as a way to reinforce class distinctions rather than overcome them," writes one historian. Since only the rich could afford to spend their time training for the games without outside support, the best way to keep lower classes out was to restrict them to amateurs.

THE MYTH: The torch-lighting ceremony that opens the games originated with the ancient Greeks.

THE TRUTH: It has no ancient precedent—it was invented by the Nazis. The 1936 Olympics took place in Berlin, Germany, under Hitler's watchful eye. Carl Diem, who organized the event for the Führer, created the first lighting of the Olympic flame to give the proceedings "an ancient aura." Since then, the ceremony has become part of Olympic tradition...and people just assume it's much older than it really is.

THE MYTH: The 5-ring Olympic symbol is from ancient Greece.

THE TRUTH: The Nazis are responsible for that myth, too. According to David Young's book, *The Modern Olympics*, it was spread in a Nazi propaganda film about the Berlin Games.

THE MYTH: Adolf Hitler snubbed U.S. runner Jesse Owens at the 1936 Olympics in Berlin.

THE TRUTH: This is one of the enduring American Olympic myths. Hitler, the story goes, was frustrated in his attempt to prove Aryan superiority when Owens—an African American—took the gold. The furious Führer supposedly refused to acknowledge Owens's victories. But according to Owens himself, it never happened. Hitler didn't congratulate anyone that day because the International Olympic Committee had warned him he had to congratulate "all winners or no winners." He chose to stay mum.

THE MYTH: Drugs have always been taboo in the Olympics.

THE TRUTH: Drugs weren't outlawed until the 1968 Games. In fact, according to the *Complete Book of the Olympics*, drugs were already in use by the third modern Olympic Games: "The winner of the 1904 marathon, Thomas Hicks, was administered multiple doses of strychnine and brandy *during* the race."

*   *   *

"Coaches are like ducks: calm on top, but paddling underneath. Believe me, there's a lot of leg movement."

—NHL coach Ken Hitchcock

First known rearview mirror: Ray Harroun mounted one on his car at the Indianapolis 500 (1911).

AY, THERE'S THE RUBE

One of baseball's early stars, Rube Waddell had pitching abilities that were matched only by the great Cy Young. Yet today Waddell is mostly forgotten. Here's the story of one of baseball's best athletes—and strangest characters.

POSTER BOY

The 1902 Philadelphia A's drew twice as many fans as the previous year's team. One of the biggest attractions was the team's newest acquisition—a hard-throwing, unpredictable pitcher named Rube Waddell. A few days before he was scheduled to start, posters went up all over town advertising his odd exploits, enticing fans to go out to the park just to see what "the Rube" would do next. Maybe he'd run through the stands begging for candy and picking fights with fans. Or maybe he'd be found on the sidewalk outside the ball park playing marbles with a group of kids. Or perhaps he'd perform cartwheels on his way back to the dugout after striking out the side.

No one quite knew what to make of George Edward Waddell. Born in Bradford, Pennsylvania, in 1876, he's been described by historians over the years as "autistic," "mentally retarded," "Peter Pan," and even "a drunk Forrest Gump." Or as A's manager Connie Mack put it: "The Rube had a two-million dollar body and a two-cent head." And connected to that two-million dollar body was one of the best left arms in the history of the game.

A LOOSE CANNON

During the dead ball era, most pitchers were just throwers, tasked with getting the ball over the plate so the batters could slap it into play. Not Waddell. At 6'1" and 200 pounds, he frightened hitters. He'd yell animal noises and then blast the ball right by them. In Waddell's minor league days, he once told his defensive team to stay on the bench, then went out alone...and struck out the side. He tried it again at an exhibition game in the majors, but because the rules dictated that nine players must be on the field, Waddell told his teammates to sit down in the grass...while he struck out the side.

Waddell's impressive arsenal included a blistering fastball, a screwball, and a sharp-breaking curve that was way ahead of its time. He used what Mack described as "the most perfect overhand delivery I have ever seen on a lefthander" to rack up a career 2,316 strikeouts, a 2.16 ERA, and 50 shutouts. He led his league in strikeouts for six consecutive years. To this day, Waddell holds the A.L. single-season strikeout record for a lefty, with 349. The only pitcher in either league who equalled him in strikeout power was Cy Young (when Young threw his perfect game in 1904, Waddell was the opposing pitcher and lost 3–0).

So if the Rube was so dominating, how come it's called the Cy Young Award and not the Rube Waddell Award? And how could a pitcher who specialized in strikeouts lose so many games? (His career record was 193–143.) The problem was that, between his childlike qualities and legendary thirst for alcohol, Waddell was nearly impossible to manage. Only one man, Connie Mack, was (somewhat) able to keep the Rube under control.

RUBE AND MACK

Mack first managed Waddell briefly in Milwaukee in 1900, but just as with the Rube's previous coaches, Mack had trouble putting up with his quirks. Two years later, though, Mack was so desperate for good pitching in Philadelphia that he sent two Pinkerton detectives to find Waddell (who had walked out on the Chicago Orphans to play baseball with a group of traveling barnstormers) and bring him to Philadelphia. The agents found Waddell in California, pitching for the Los Angeles Loo Loos, and put him on a train to Philadelphia.

Under Mack's watchful eye, Waddell helped the Athletics win the 1902 American League pennant by striking out 210 batters on his way to a 24–7 record in only 33 starts. Waddell had his best years in Philadelphia, becoming a fan favorite and adding the spark to a pitching rotation that also included future Hall of Fame pitchers Eddie Plank and Chief Bender. But Mack had his hands full keeping Waddell focused on pitching.

• Waddell loved fishing. After he'd pitched (and won) a 17-inning game, the first game of a doubleheader, Mack convinced him to pitch in the second game (a shortened five-inning game) by promising an all-expenses-paid, three-day fishing trip. Result: Waddell went out and pitched a one-hit shutout.

Number of NFL players who weighed over 300 pounds in 1990: 39. In 2004: 339.

• Mack could deal with the Rube's fishing mania; it was the alligator wrestling that scared him. Waddell discovered the "sport" during spring training in Florida...and was reportedly very good at it. But instead of trying to bribe him into giving it up, Mack simply threatened to fire Waddell if he didn't quit. (He quit.)

• Dealing with Waddell was often less like managing and more like keeping tabs on a toddler. For example, the only safe way to keep Waddell close to the team was to pay his salary in small installments. When Ossie Schreckengost, Waddell's catcher and roommate, threatened to quit unless Waddell stopped eating Animal Crackers in bed (teams saved money by making players share a bed on the road), Mack added an "Animal Crackers clause" to Waddell's contract, forbidding the pitcher to eat cookies in bed.

• Another constant concern for Mack: Waddell's desire to be a hero—which was fine, except that he often had no regard for his own safety. In the space of three days in 1905, Waddell stopped a fire in a crowded department store by picking up a flaming oil stove and carrying it outside, assaulted his father-in-law with an iron, saved the life of an injured teammate by carrying him all the way to the hospital, and was arrested for bigamy (he "forgot" to divorce his first wife before marrying his second).

A HERO'S DEMISE
But it wasn't an alligator or a collapsing building that led to the end of Waddell's career; it was a playful wrestling match for a teammate's straw hat in 1905. Waddell fell on his throwing arm and it immediately stiffened up. The timing couldn't have been worse—the A's were about to play in the World Series, which Waddell was forced to sit out. After the New York Giants trounced the A's, rumors began circulating that Waddell had faked the injury after accepting a $17,000 bribe from a gambling ring. Mack vehemently denied this for the rest of his life: "Money meant nothing, glory everything, to him."

Waddell's shoulder never fully healed and his pitching career steadily dwindled. Reluctantly, Mack released him in 1908. (The team's home attendance dropped 30%.)

Waddell's youthful spark briefly returned in 1911 when the 34-year-old pitcher joined the minor league Minneapolis Millers and won 20 games. Still too erratic to find a job on a major league

---

Statistically, a Major League home run is most likely to be hit in the 4th inning, on a Sunday.

team, Waddell was living on his manager's farm in Hickman, Kentucky, in January 1913 when a dike holding back the Mississippi River broke and released floodwaters into the small town. Waddell stood in nearly freezing water for 13 hours, stacking sandbags in an effort to rebuild the dike. He helped save the town but contracted a severe cold, which led to pneumonia, and then to tuberculosis. Waddell never fully recovered. He tried to keep on pitching, but by this point was only a shadow of his former self. On April Fool's Day 1914, Waddell, down to 130 pounds and living in a tuberculosis sanitarium, died at the age of 37.

A decade later, Waddell's impact on the game was put into perspective by the *Sporting News*: "No player that ever lived, not even Babe Ruth, has so captured the affections of the fans of his day as did Rube Waddell." He was inducted into the Baseball Hall of Fame in 1946.

*   *   *

A FEW MORE OF RUBE WADDELL'S ANTICS

• One time during spring training in Jacksonville, Florida, the Rube went missing on his pitching day. He was found a few hours later leading a minstrel parade down Main Street.

• Opposing teams would sometimes bring toys—such as those little drumming monkeys—and play with them in the dugout while Waddell was on the mound, trying to distract him and take his focus off the game. (The tactic often worked.)

• After being fined $100 on a road trip, Waddell demanded to know why. He was told it was for that "disgraceful hotel episode in Detroit." To which Waddell responded, "You're a liar! There ain't no Hotel Episode in Detroit!"

• After besting Cy Young in a 20-inning game in 1905, Waddell traded the "game ball" for free beers at a local bar. A few weeks later he traded another "game ball"—from the same game—for free beers. Legend has it that there are more than 50 scuffed-up baseballs out there, all claiming to be the genuine Cy Young vs. Rube Waddell game ball.

First official female umpire in men's baseball: Amanda Clement (1905–11).

LET'S WATCH KUNG FU!

Were you a fan of the TV series Kung Fu? You aren't alone—it was one of the most popular shows of its day. Along with the films of Bruce Lee, it helped launch the martial arts craze of the 1970s.

EAST SIDE STORY

In the late 1960s, a man named Ed Spielman was studying radio and television production at Brooklyn College in New York City. He was also a martial arts buff and a big fan of Japanese movies. One day a martial arts instructor he knew happened to tell him in passing that his wife, who was trained in the Chinese martial art of kung fu, could knock him to the ground using only one or two fingers. Intrigued, Spielman began reading up on kung fu.

Spielman earned money writing comedy with his friend Howard Friedlander, who was also fascinated by the Far East. Whenever Spielman read anything interesting about kung fu, he shared it with Friedlander.

Friedlander had a favorite tale about a man who travels through China and meets up with a warrior-monk from the Shaolin temple, where kung fu has been practiced for more than 6,000 years. One afternoon the two men were walking down Broadway toward Times Square when Friedlander stopped suddenly, turned to Spielman, and said, "Ed, why don't we write an *Eastern* Western? We can take the monk from the temple and place him in the West."

RAISING CAINE

The pair set to work writing a film screenplay, and in early 1970 they finished a story about a half-Caucasian, half-Chinese Shaolin monk named Kwai Chang Caine who flees to the American West after he accidentally kills the nephew of the emperor of China. When Caine gets to the United States, he learns that he has a half-brother, Danny Caine, and for much of the rest of the screenplay Caine searches for his brother.

Meanwhile, the Warner Bros. studio was looking for ways to use its Old West film sets now that Westerns were declining in popularity. Spielman and Friedlander's script seemed to fit this

---

At his first appearance at the Masters in 1979, golfer Larry Nelson forgot his clubs.

need, so the studio bought it in late 1970 and made plans for a
feature film...only to shelve the idea indefinitely in 1971. Reason:
According to studio spokesmen, *Kung Fu* was too violent, not to
mention too expensive to film. Besides, they said, the Eastern
themes were too "esoteric" for American audiences.

A few months later, Harvey Frand, the Warner Bros. liaison
between the studio's feature film and television departments, happened to read the *Kung Fu* script and was impressed. He pitched it
to the ABC network as an original movie of the week, and they
bought the idea and turned it into a 90-minute film.

SPLIT PERSONALITY

Since Caine was half-Caucasian and half-Chinese, casting either a
white actor or an Asian actor in the part would have worked. Two
actors were considered: Bruce Lee, then best known for the role of
Kato in the *Green Hornet* TV series, and David Carradine, son of
screen legend John Carradine. Carradine was the calmer, more
serene of the two actors, and the creators thought he would make
a better Caine than the tense, energetic Lee. (Besides, studio
executives worried that American audiences would not be interested in a series with an Asian male lead.) Carradine got the part.

When the film aired on February 22, 1972, 33% of the American viewing audience tuned in to see it. In those days, people had
only the big three networks to choose from, along with an independent channel or two. Still, getting one in three viewers to tune
in to a brand-new show was impressive. *Kung Fu* had something
for everyone: peaceniks liked the fact that Caine lived his life
according to an Eastern philosophy of nonviolence, and action
fans loved how the bad guys got a beating at least once in every
show. ABC ordered four more episodes, and when these pulled in
large audiences, the network ordered 15 more.

IT'S A FAD!

Kung Fu's timing couldn't have been better—Americans were
beginning to take an interest in martial arts, thanks in large part to
the guy who *didn't* get the part of Caine, Bruce Lee. By the time
Lee got the news that he'd lost the part to Carradine, he was
already in Hong Kong filming the first of the "chop-socky" martial
arts films that would make him an international star. That caused

---

The coxswain (navigator) in a rowing competition must weigh over 110 pounds...

Hollywood to take a second look, and in 1973 Bruce Lee made *Enter the Dragon* for Warner Bros. Then, just weeks before *Enter the Dragon* was scheduled to premiere, Lee died suddenly from cerebral edema, or swelling of the brain. He was 32.

By then *Kung Fu* had been on the air for several months, and the combination of the TV show and Lee's movies—made all the more popular by his untimely death—helped launch the martial arts craze of the 1970s. People watched *Kung Fu* on TV, went to see chop-socky movies, and signed up for martial arts classes in greater numbers than ever before (or since). Elvis got a black belt. Kids wore *Kung Fu* T-shirts and read *Kung Fu* comic books and pulp novels while eating sandwiches out of *Kung Fu* lunchboxes. In 1974, when a singer named Carl Douglas spent 10 minutes recording what was supposed to be a B-side song called "Kung Fu Fighting," it went all the way to #1 on the *Billboard* pop chart. The song got it right—everybody *was* kung fu fighting.

KEEPING IT REAL

• The creators of *Kung Fu* were sticklers for authenticity, so they inserted real-life traditions from kung fu and other martial arts wherever they could. Walking across rice paper is a part of traditional ninja training in Japan, and snatching a pebble from the master's hand was inspired by a similar practice at the Shaolin monastery.

• Another scene taken from real life: the one where Caine, in his final act before leaving the temple, walks down a long corridor and lifts a red-hot urn filled with coals with his wrists, branding a tiger and a dragon into his skin. Monks at the Shaolin temple ran a similar gauntlet: as they walked down a long corridor, they dodged acid dropped from the ceiling and spears thrust through holes in the walls and floors. If they made it to the end of the corridor, they branded themselves by lifting the urn with their arms or, if they needed to, with their stomach. "There's more to a disciple's leaving the temple than branding his arms," Carradine says. "We left the rest out because we doubted whether anyone would believe it."

KEEPING TRACK

Even when *Kung Fu* episodes are shown out of sequence, there are visual cues that viewers can use to place each episode in its proper chronological place in the series' three-year run:

• Carradine shaved his head at the start of the series and didn't cut his hair again until the final episodes. The longer Carradine's hair, the later the episode appears in the series.

• When Bruce Lee died in 1973, Carradine changed the color of the shirt he wore from brown to orange-yellow.

• The original martial arts advisor for the show was not a genuine Shaolin master, but he was eventually replaced with someone who was, which helped make the kung fu action sequences more authentic. Carradine marked the change by having Caine lose his signature fedora hat. "If you see me without a hat, it's genuine kung fu," he says.

BEHIND THE SCENES

• Spielman based the character of the blind, sympathetic Master Po on his grandfather, a Russian immigrant. "He was a moral and spiritual man. When he died," Spielman says. "I was only a teenager, too immature to thank him or tell him how much I loved him. The relationship between Master Po and young Caine was my way of doing that."

• Actor Keye Luke wore special opaque contact lenses to make him appear blind. He could see out of a tiny hole drilled into each lens, but other than that, he really was almost blind when he had them on, and he tended to leave them on all day—even when he wasn't filming a scene—to help him "get into character."

NOT AS THEY SEEMED

• One of the most famous scenes in the series is when Caine arrives as a young orphan boy (played by Radames Perá) at the Shaolin temple and is accepted as a student. Master Kan, who runs the temple, points to a pebble in his open palm and tells Caine, "As quickly as you can... snatch the pebble from my hand." Caine tries and fails, and Master Kan says to him, "When you can take the pebble from my hand, it will be time for you to leave." Filming the scene was tougher than you might think—actor Philip Ahn's reflexes were so slow that he couldn't stop Perá from grabbing the pebble. Finally, after about 15 takes, director Jerry Thorpe told Perá to signal with his left hand before grabbing with his right.

• In another important scene, young Caine is taught to tread lightly—symbolically and literally—by walking across fragile rice paper without breaking it. "When you can walk the rice paper without disturbing it," Master Kan explains, "then your steps will not be heard." But the prop department couldn't find any rice paper, so they used regular butcher paper instead, which is much stronger. Perá couldn't rip it no matter how hard he tried, even when the crew glued sandpaper to the bottom of his feet. They finally shot the scene by having Perá walk over paper that was already torn, but didn't show the paper until he'd already walked over it.

THE PRICE OF FAME

• Eleven-year-old Radames Perá, who played the young Caine, had his own problems. Child labor laws limited the number of hours he could be on the set each day, which meant that there was no time for makeup artists to apply a bald cap to his head—so they shaved him bald for much of the show's three-year run. He was a big TV star, but the bullies at his school picked on him anyway, slapping his bald head and calling him "eightball." Perá drew strength from the show's scripts. "As I was dealing with my personal struggles," he says, "young Caine was dealing with his. Asian philosophy helped us both."

• Like George Reeves (TV's Superman) before him, David Carradine had to worry about overly enthusiastic fans who really did believe he was an indestructible warrior monk. "People were throwing themselves at his car in the street," Harvey Frand says. It eventually got so bad that Carradine spent most of his free time on the set hiding in his dressing room.

SO LONG, GRASSHOPPER

Kung Fu might have continued for season after season save for one thing: David Carradine. Apparently worried that he would be typecast in the part, he was determined from the beginning not to play Caine for longer than three years. Just as he'd promised, he left the show. The last original episode aired on April 19, 1975.

Three attempts to revisit *Kung Fu* were made; two succeeded. *Kung Fu: The Movie* was a 1986 made-for-TV movie that starred Carradine as Caine and Bruce Lee's son Brandon as his son, Chung

Wang. That did well enough to inspire a 1987 pilot for a show set in the 1980s. Brandon Lee signed on to play Caine's great-grandson... but Carradine thought the script was stupid—he called it "*Kung Fu* car crashes"—and passed. The pilot aired in February 1986 but died without Carradine's support. He did, however, agree to star in *Kung Fu: The Legend Continues*, which ran from 1993 to 1997. In this series, set in the 1990s, Carradine plays the original Caine's grandson (also a kung fu master named Kwai Chang Caine), and Chris Potter plays Caine's son Peter, a big-city police officer.

LASTING INFLUENCE

The original *Kung Fu* left an indelible mark on film and television. One huge fan was Quentin Tarantino, who lists the show as one of his earliest inspirations. He even wrote the part of Bill in his revenge flick *Kill Bill* with Carradine in mind (who got the role after Warren Beatty dropped out). Carradine's Bill is sort of "an evil Kwai Chang Caine, offering deep-sounding Chinese parables with psychopathic twists, in between the soothing tunes of Caine's trademark wooden flute," writes Chris Pepus, one of the many critics who praised the film.

And *Kill Bill* is just the latest role in a long career for David Carradine, who's appeared in more than 100 film and television projects. Yet nearly every biography about Carradine echoes these same words: "...best known for his role as Caine on the 1970s series *Kung Fu*."

*　　*　　*

PASS 'N' PLUG

In TV ads, football players end up selling the strangest things.

• Former Chicago Bears linebacker Dick Butkus made TV ads for the Kwik-Cook, a portable grill that burned newspapers for fuel.

• Bassett Furniture carries a line of furniture designed by former Denver Broncos quarterback John Elway.

• Joe Namath plugged Beautymist Panty Hose, which he claimed to have worn under his football uniform.

The blanket of flowers awarded to the Kentucky Derby winner contains 554 red roses.

KUNG FU WISDOM

Serious philosophy or TV gobbledygook? You be the judge. These quotes are from the only Buddhist Western in television history, Kung Fu.

"Man, like the animals, is meant to live in groups. But the meaning of belonging to a group is found in the comfort of silence and solitude."
—**Master Kan**

Master Po: Close your eyes. What do you hear?
Caine: I hear the water, I hear the birds.
Master Po: Do you hear the grasshopper that is at your feet?
Caine: Old man, how is it that you hear these things?
Master Po: Young man, how is it that you do not?

"No man can see through another's eyes or hear through his ears, or feel through his fingers."
—**Caine**

"Does not tomorrow begin now?"
—**Caine**

Caine: Do evil demons exist?
Master Kan: Do wars, famine, disease, and death exist? Do lust, greed, and hate exist? They are man's creations, brought into being by the dark side of his nature.

"Superstition is like a magnet. It pulls you in the direction of your belief."
—**Master Po**

"A man feels grief. One who does not fails in his capacity to be a man."
—**Caine**

"Learn first how to live. Learn second how not to kill. Learn third how to live with death. Learn fourth how to die."
—**Master Po**

Caine: Our bodies are prey to many needs. Hunger, thirst, the need for love. Shall we then seek to satisfy those needs?
Master Kan: Only acknowledge them, and satisfaction will follow. To suppress a truth is to give it force beyond endurance.

"Perfect wisdom is unplanned. Perfect living offers no guarantee of a peaceful death."
—**Master Po**

Caine: What is the greatest obligation that we have?
Master Po: To live, Grasshopper. To live!

THE BIRTH OF BIG-TIME SPORTING EVENTS

Ever wonder how they come up with all those tournament championship events that fill the weekend TV schedule? Well, like everything else, they all had a beginning. Here are a few of the biggest.

THE MASTERS

In the 1920s, the world of golf was dominated by a lawyer from Georgia named Bobby Jones. Jones retired from the golf circuit in 1930 at the age of 28, having hit the peak of his career when he won not only the U.S. and British Opens but also the U.S. and British Amateurs all in the same year—a feat known as a Grand Slam.

Throughout his career, Jones maintained amateur status—he never earned a penny playing golf. Then he retired from the game to spend more time with his family and build his law practice. He went on to write golf books and articles, design better clubs, and make instructional movies. But more than anything else, he wanted to design the world's finest golf course near his hometown of Atlanta—a private course where he could play without being mobbed by fans.

Of Course

Jones teamed up with New York banker Clifford Roberts and began to look for property. They wanted land that had a stream, contours, and beauty. As soon as they laid eyes on Fruitlands Nursery, they knew they had found what they were looking for.

Fruitlands was the first commercial nursery in the South, started by a horticulturist named P. J. Berckman. It was a 365-acre farm with trees, flowers, and shrubs imported from all over the world. When Berckman's son, Prosper, died in 1910, the business closed and his heirs began to look for a buyer. The purchase price—at the outset of the Depression—was $70,000. Jones and Roberts bought it.

Work on the golf course began in 1931 and progressed slowly. Each of the holes was named after one of the shrubs or trees that

---

Oldest American college sport still in existence: rowing.

grew there: Pink Dogwood, Juniper, Firethorn, and so on. Jones hit thousands of test shots as the course was being made. He wanted three approaches to each hole: the safe route, the hard route, and the crazy route. It was finally finished in 1933.

The course was so beautiful that the United States Golf Association approached Jones with the idea of holding a tournament there, but he declined, feeling that if there were to be a tournament on his course, he should host it. So that's what he did. He held his first tournament in 1934, calling it the Augusta National Invitation Tournament. People came from 38 states to watch golfers compete for a $1,500 purse, and every hotel room in the town of Augusta, population 60,000, was full.

Call Me Master
Roberts wanted to call it "the Masters," but Jones thought that sounded presumptuous. But everyone called it the Masters anyway, so in 1939, Jones relented and the title was officially changed. The Masters remains the only major golf tournament to return to the same site every year.

Bobby Jones played in the first 12 tournaments, but never won. His best finish was a tie for 13th place, which was at the very first tournament. He never even broke par, but continued to participate because his name was a big draw. He died in 1971 at the age of 69.

THE AMERICA'S CUP
Most people think the America's Cup is American. But it isn't... or at least it didn't start out that way. In 1851 Prince Albert hosted the Great London Exhibition in order to pay tribute to the technological advances of the day. In conjunction with the event, Queen Victoria invited all nations of the world to participate in a 53-mile yacht race around the Isle of Wight. The prize was a trophy made of 134 ounces of pure silver.

Over a dozen British vessels entered the race...and one American boat, called the *America*. Owner John Cox Stevens was certain he was going to win. And he did—by a wide margin.

The trophy, then called the One Hundred Guinea Cup, was awarded to Stevens and his crew. He considered having it melted down and cast into medals, but instead donated it to the New York Yacht Club in 1857, with the stipulation that it be awarded to win-

---

The Australian national soccer team is nicknamed the Socceroos.

ners of an international boat race. The trophy and the race were named after the boat, and the America's Cup was born.

The Streak

The race is held approximately once every three years. Americans sailing under the New York Yacht Club flag won the trophy 25 times in a row over 126 years—the longest winning streak in sports. It wasn't until 1983 that an Australian entry took the trophy away from the United States.

The *America* sailed in 51 subsequent races under various owners, but only entered one America's Cup event, where it placed 4th out of 15. In 1921 it was sold to the U.S. Navy and placed in storage in Annapolis, where it suffered years of neglect and decay. In 1942 the roof of the storage shed collapsed under heavy snow, crushing the famous boat. Some of the original wood was salvaged from the ship and used to create a replica, which is now on display at the Naval Academy museum.

THE KENTUCKY DERBY

Edward Smith Stanley, 12th Earl of Derby, was good friends with Sir Charles Bunbury. Both enjoyed breeding horses. Together they founded a new horse race in 1780, a one-mile test of three-year-old thoroughbreds near Derby's country estate in Epsom, England. But before the first race could be held, it had to be named. Which founder should the race be named after—Bunbury or Derby? They flipped a coin…and that's how the word *derby* came to mean a horse race.

In Kentucky, horses flourished on bluegrass pastures that grew from Russian seed brought by immigrants. Because of this, the state became one of the most important thoroughbred breeding centers in the United States, and horse racing became a popular pastime. In 1832 the town fathers of Louisville, Kentucky, bought land from a local family, the Churchills, and built a racetrack.

But the track was too far from town to attract crowds and had to compete against other area tracks that were much more popular. Racing floundered there until the arrival of Meriwether Lewis Clark Jr. "Lutie" Clark was the grandson of explorer William Clark and a member of the same Churchill family on whose property Louisville's racetrack was located.

After a trip to Europe in 1873, where he studied the layout of the Epsom Downs Derby, Lutie was full of ideas of how to improve racing in Louisville and how to eliminate bookmaking by using the French *pari-mutuel* wagering machines. (Pari-mutuel betting is a system where the winners divide the total amount bet, in proportion to the amount they wagered individually. The odds change according to what people wager, and there is less chance of manipulation than with other systems.)

And...They're Off!

With financial backing from his family, Clark leased 80 acres from his Churchill uncles, oversaw construction of a new grandstand and track, sold stock in the venture, and organized the betting. The track—dubbed the Louisville Jockey Club Course—opened on May 17, 1875. Although there were far more important races being run in Kentucky that day, the success of the new track was assured when a horse named Aristides set a new world record for the mile-and-a-half run. The crowd went wild. The Kentucky Derby was born.

In spite of his success, Lutie Clark's quick temper and irascible nature made him quite unpopular. His wife and children left him, and the Churchill family cut him out of the will, leaving him only a few acres of property and a job as overseer of the racetrack. People stopped calling it the Louisville Jockey Club and started calling it Churchill Downs as an insult, to remind Clark who held the purse strings. He committed suicide in 1899.

Back from the Brink

By 1902 the Kentucky Derby was on the verge of bankruptcy. Then Matt Winn became the manager. Winn had a gift for publicity and promotion, which he used to rebuild the legacy. He hired John Philip Sousa's band to entertain. He had two airplanes shipped in for races—and they made the first recorded flights in the state of Kentucky. During World War I, he pledged 10% of track profits to the Red Cross. During the potato shortage of 1918, he turned the entire infield into a huge potato patch. During World War II, he invited the U.S. Army to use the infield for public demonstrations of the new Sherman tanks. He even invited the state fair to hold the event in the grounds.

Winn improved the grandstand seating and built a clubhouse. He courted the press. He courted radio broadcasters. He courted movie stars. Business increased, public opinion changed, and revenues skyrocketed. Because of Matt Winn, the Kentucky Derby became an international event. He ran it until his death in 1949.

Today, the Kentucky Derby is one of the world's best-known races. It's been run every May since 1875. Over 100,000 people come to view the race, and millions more watch it on TV.

THE INDIANAPOLIS 500

Around the turn of the 20th century, automobiles were a new and wondrous invention. And Detroit was emerging as the car capital of the world.

Carl Fisher was a businessman in Indianapolis. He made a fortune selling Prest-O-Lite acetylene-powered headlights. In 1909 he sold his business to Union Carbide for millions…just before the invention of car batteries made Prest-O-Lites obsolete.

Fisher wanted to build something with his money, and he decided that what Indianapolis needed was a racetrack for automobiles. In those days, roads were little more than trails and it was difficult to find a place where a driver could really "open 'er up." A racetrack would also give car manufacturers a place to test their new models and pit them against each other. It would put Indianapolis on the map.

Full Speed Ahead

Fisher set up a consortium, elected himself president, and bought 328 acres of countryside for $72,000. He hired an army of 400 workers who moved, on average, 1,500 square yards of dirt every 10 hours to build the two-and-a-half-mile track.

The track itself was made of crushed stone covered by 300,000 gallons of asphalt oil. Turns were banked to handle speeds up to 70 mph. The track was lighted, naturally, with Prest-O-Lite gas so spectators could watch an entire race from start to finish. Fisher called it the Indianapolis Motor Speedway.

The first races on the new track were held on August 19 to 21, 1909. Ten thousand people showed up. On the first day, there was a crash when a tire flew off due to loose lug nuts. The two men in the car were killed. On the second day, everything went well, but on the third day, in the final race, a tire blew out and the car spun out of control and crashed into the crowd. A mechanic and two spectators were killed. The race continued, but then another car

Hockey great Wayne Gretzky paid $125,000 to play a game of tennis against Andre Agassi.

skidded out of control because the road surface was crumbling under the onslaught. The car slammed into a bridge, injuring the driver. Officials stepped in and stopped the race.

Papers Blast Fisher's Folly

Editorial headlines across the nation blared "Slaughter as a Spectacle" and "Commercial Murder." Protests were mounted. Petitions were circulated. Prohibitions were called for. The Indianapolis Motor Speedway became known as "Fisher's Folly."

But Fisher was not a man to give up easily. First he installed guardrails. Then he decided that the gravel-and-asphalt surface was to blame. He replaced it with bricks—3.2 million of them—and the Indianapolis Motor Speedway became known as the Brickyard. Still, with other racetracks being built in cities like Chicago and Atlanta, business began to fall off. To promote his Speedway, Fisher announced that in 1911, the best American cars would go up against the best European cars for a purse of $25,000. The race would be 500 miles long and was called the Indianapolis Motor Speedway 500-Mile International Sweepstakes. The Indy 500 was born.

What Comes Around Goes Around

The Indy 500 has been run almost every year since 1911, suspended only during the two World Wars. It's now the oldest auto race in the world, and the Speedway is the largest spectator-sport facility in the world, with over 250,000 permanent seats. The purse is now around $9 million. In 2000, the Indy 500 placed first among televised motorsports events and generated over $100 million in sponsorship exposure. Besides the Indianapolis 500, the Speedway also hosts the Brickyard 400 and the United States Grand Prix.

Carl Fisher died in Miami in 1939 at the age of 65.

* * *

KNOW YOUR 19th-CENTURY BASEBALL TERMS

Aces: Runs
The behind: The catcher
The club nine: The team
Cranks: Fans
Dew drop: Slow pitch

Foul tick: Foul ball
The hurler: The pitcher
A match: A game
A muff: An error
The striker: The batter

In 1923 French sports reporter Pierre Labric rode his bicycle down the 347 stairs...

"HE SLUD INTO THIRD"

More verbal gems actually uttered on the air by sports announcers.

"If only faces could talk."
—**Pat Summerall,
NFL announcer**

"Hector Torres, how can you communicate with Enzo Hernandez when he speaks Spanish and you speak Mexican?"
—**Jerry Coleman,
San Diego Padres announcer**

"A lot of good ballgames on tomorrow, but we're going to be right here with the Cubs and the Mets."
—**Thom Brennaman,
Chicago Cubs announcer**

"Lance Armstrong is about to join a list which includes only himself."
—**Mark Brown,
ESPN sports analyst**

"I don't think anywhere is there a symbiotic relationship between caddie and player like there is in golf."
—**Johnny Miller,
golf analyst**

"Referee Richie Powers called the loose bowel foul on Johnson."
—**Frank Herzog, Washington
Bullets basketball announcer**

"It's a great advantage to be able to hurdle with both legs."
—**David Coleman,
British sports announcer**

"The Minutemen are not tall in terms of height."
—**Dan Bonner,
college basketball analyst**

"Jose Canseco leads off the 3rd inning with a grand slam."
—**John Gordon,
Minnesota Twins announcer**

"The offensive linemen are the biggest guys on the field, they're bigger than everybody else, and that's what makes them the biggest guys on the field."
—**John Madden,
NFL announcer**

"Watch the expression on his mask."
—**Harry Neale,
hockey analyst**

"The game's in the refrigerator, folks. The door's closed, the light's out, the eggs are cooling, the butter's gettin' hard, and the Jell-O's a-jigglin'."
—**Chick Hearn,
L.A. Lakers announcer**

Also available
from *Uncle John's
Bathroom Reader!*

THE LAST PAGE

FELLOW BATHROOM READERS:
The fight for good bathroom reading should never be taken loosely—we must do our duty and sit firmly for what we believe in, even while the rest of the world is taking potshots at us.

We'll be brief. Now that we've proven we're not simply a flush-in-the-pan, we invite you to take the plunge: Sit Down and Be Counted! Become a member of the Bathroom Readers' Institute. Log on to *www.bathroomreader.com*, or send a self-addressed, stamped, business-sized envelope to: BRI, PO Box 1117, Ashland, Oregon 97520. You'll receive your free membership card, get discounts when ordering directly through the BRI, and earn a permanent spot on the BRI honor roll!

If you like reading our books...
VISIT THE BRI'S WEB SITE!
www.bathroomreader.com

- Visit "The Throne Room"—a great place to read!
- Receive our irregular newsletters via e-mail
- Order additional *Bathroom Readers*
- Become a BRI member

Go with the Flow...

Well, we're out of space, and when you've gotta go, you've gotta go. Tanks for all your support. Hope to hear from you soon. Meanwhile, remember...

Keep on flushin'!